A VOICE FOR OUR TIME

Radio Liberty Talks

Volume I

A Voice
for
Our Time

Radio Liberty Talks

VOLUME 1

ALEXANDER SCHMEMANN

Foreword by ROD DREHER

Introduction by SERGE SCHMEMANN

Translated by Alexis Vinogradov and Nathan Williams

ST VLADIMIR'S SEMINARY PRESS
YONKERS, NEW YORK
2021

*The publication of this book was made possible by generous donations from
a friend of St Vladimir's Orthodox Theological Seminary, and from
Dr Donald Tamulonis to honor his past and present spiritual fathers:
Very Rev. William Olenick, Very Rev. John Psinka, Very Rev. Daniel Rohan,
Archimandrite Joseph Morris, Very Rev. John Steffaro, and Very Rev. Andrew Nelko.*

Library of Congress Control Number: 2020951943

Translated with permission from the Russian edition:
Беседы на Радио «Свобода» (Москва: Православный
Свято-Тихоновский гуманитарный университет, 2009).

ISBN 978–088141–679–4 (print)
ISBN 978–088141–680–0 (electronic)

Dedication

To all past and present members of the
Alexander Schmemann Legacy Society

Members of the Alexander Schmemann Legacy Society
support and sustain the valuable work
of St Vladimir's Orthodox Theological Seminary
with a bequest in their wills and estate planning.

For a list of Legacy members and information
go to www.svots.edu/support/legacy-society
or call (914) 961-8313 ext. 329.

Contents

PART III
Sources of Christianity

Foreword

An unusual thing happened when I was reading Father Alexander Schmemann's radio talks. I expected to encounter relics of the Cold War, transcripts of one man's attempt to pierce the hideous night of Soviet totalitarianism with the light of the Gospel, and in so doing, be a beacon of hope to the oppressed Russian people. And relics they certainly are. These brief epistles, each line radiating Father Schmemann's keen pastoral intelligence, testify to the tireless efforts of Russian émigrés and their allies in the free world to keep alive the souls of those trapped in the wintry ice of atheist tyranny. At the risk of damning with faint praise, this volume is an invaluable part of the historical record.

Father Schmemann, who began delivering these talks the very month that Stalin died, addressed a people who had been brutalized by over three decades of state-ordered godlessness, the closing of churches, and the mass murder of clergy. In Moscow not long ago, a Russian scholar, now deceased, told me it is impossible to overstate how thoroughly the Bolsheviks cleansed the public's cultural memory of the Russia that existed before the Revolution. This was Father Schmemann's audience: people who had fading memories of Christianity, and people who had never been taught it, except in caricature as a punching bag for atheist propaganda.

And so, Schmemann spoke plainly, assuming nothing about his listeners. At first you may be taken aback by the simplicity of these talks, but then you grasp the pastoral care with which he constructed them. These are not the mini-lectures of a brilliant theologian (though he was) demonstrating his intellectual prowess and rhetorical chops; these are the words of an apostle who wants to communicate the liberating power of the Gospel that sets captives free.

He also spoke to his listeners at a higher level. Schmemann told the Russian audience about how the light of the same Christ who saves them also shines through the novels of Dostoevsky, the poetry of Auden, and the literary testimony of Solzhenistyn. And the priest explained to a people who had been forced to forget the great feasts of the Church, which governed the year of their ancestors for nearly a thousand years, how and why they made time sacred.

For thirty years he committed these words to paper then spoke them into a microphone, not knowing the size of his congregation. In his posthumously published *Journals*, Schmemann recalled a March 6, 1975 visit to the Radio Liberty offices by a priest who had just returned from a visit to Russia, and told him (Schmemann) that he is one of the most popular foreigners in Russia. "Nice to hear that my work does reach someone there," notes Schmemann. As he wrote this in his personal diary, we can be confident that his modesty was genuine. Think of it, though: by then, Schmemann had been giving these radio commentaries for over two decades, and still could not be sure if they were making a difference. He had faith.

As I said, these talks are an important part of the history of the struggle against Communism and the Church's witness to the remnant gathered around the radio throughout Soviet Russia. If that were all they were, their publication would still be a milestone.

But at some point as I read them, it hit me: *He is talking to us too.*

We are approaching the thirtieth anniversary of the day the Soviet standard was lowered over the Kremlin for the last time, and the USSR ceased to exist. Western liberal democracy was triumphant. Yet now, social scientists see that 1991 was the year that Christianity began its long, slow decline in the United States—a decline that has accelerated with the generations coming of age after the Cold War. Studies show that those born in 1999 or later— Generation Z, we call them—are the first truly post-Christian generation in American history.

They, like the Millennial generation that precedes them, will have been raised in a materialistic culture focused on the everlasting now; if they think of the past at all, they condemn it as a cruel age of unremitting darkness. According to the Victims of Communism Memorial Foundation, shocking numbers of young Americans express favorable views of communism and socialism. After hearing a 26-year-old Californian—who, during college, had discarded the faith in which she was raised—speak rapturously about communism, I asked her, "What about the gulags?" She had no idea what I was talking about.

It is hard to blame these young people. The culture that has educated them, informed them, and shaped their worldview, is not neutral about Christianity and its legacy. Churches, Christian schools, and families are conspicuously failing to pass on the faith. In 1966, the cultural critic Philip Rieff wrote that when a civilization fails to pass on its core beliefs to the young, it begins to die. By that standard, we are in grave trouble. Christianity in Soviet Russia nearly died by murder at the hands of the Bolsheviks. If Christianity dies in America, history will judge it a suicide.

Into this materialistic, culturally illiterate, increasingly godless world, crippled by cultural amnesia and an elite class that has made a religion of neo-Marxist ideology, comes the voice of Father Alexander Schmemann. In the autumn of 2020, I published a bestselling book about the lessons that Western Christians grappling with the hostility of the times can learn by listening to believers who kept the faith in the twilight struggle against Soviet totalitarianism. What a joyful surprise to learn subsequently that one of the most compelling voices of them all is that of an émigré priest from the Russian diaspora: Alexander Schmemann, who became one of us.

He spoke our language in more ways than one, Father Schmemann did. For those with ears to hear, in these broadcast talks, he still does. Today, with people who escaped to the West from the Soviet bloc warning that something eerily like what they left behind is beginning to manifest here, it might be that we Americans will need this prophet and pastor as much as the Russians once did.

If so, here, in these pages, are the messages in a bottle Father Schmemann threw into the Cold War's tempestuous airwaves. They have come
to us across the sea of time, washing ashore against the tide of the times,
on a beach made desolate by what the poet calls the "melancholy, long,
withdrawing roar" of faith.

Read on; the news is very good indeed.

Rod Dreher

Introduction

One of my bright memories of my father, Father Alexander Schmemann, was accompanying him as a boy to the studios of Radio Liberty. The station was then called "Radio Liberation," and it was the short-wave voice of an organization called the American Committee for the Liberation of the Peoples of Russia. My father and other Russians in New York called it simply "*komitet*." The weekly visit to the *komitet* became a fixture of my father's life, and with time it became far more than a duty or a chore—it became a weekly visit to other dimensions of his life. For me, accompanying him was an adventure.

Our family moved from Paris to New York in June 1951, when my father, then only twenty-nine, was invited to teach at St Vladimir's Orthodox Seminary. The seminary was then a few modest apartments "uptown," on 121st Street and Broadway, nestled around far larger academic institutions—Columbia University, Union Theological Seminary, Jewish Theological Seminary, the Julliard School of Music. The great Gothic tower of the Riverside Church—the tallest in the United States—was visible from our windows, and on Sundays its famous bells echoed through the neighborhood. Our seminary was barely noticeable in this collection of great institutions—it had only about fifteen students, of whom two or three lived with us in our apartment. The "*komitet*" was also a modest operation, but in a far different neighborhood: its New York studios were in the heart of Manhattan, at 45th Street and Broadway, in the diamond district run by Hasidic Jews. Father Alexander began taping his weekly broadcasts almost from the time the station was founded, shortly after Stalin's death, and he continued them for the rest of his life, more than thirty years.

The adventure began as we emerged from the subway and plunged into the awesome canyons of Manhattan with their bustling sidewalks, stalled traffic, ardent street debates, and steaming hot dog stands, so distant from our academic oasis uptown, so "New York." My father always wore the white collar and black shirt that are the uniform of the clergy in America, which earned him special respect in a country that was then, and remains to this day, a country of believers. "Hello, Father!" "Good morning, Father!" "How are you, Father!" the most unexpected people would say, and Father Alexander loved it: He loved the city as much as he loved the northern Quebec wilderness where we spent our summers, where the skyscrapers were replaced by stands of birch and pine, and the crowded rivers of New York by the clear waters of our Lac Labelle.

The dingy and crowded studios of Radio Liberty were an altogether different universe—the languages of the Soviet empire mingled with the thick cigarette smoke that wafted over a clutter of papers, telephones, recording tapes and overflowing ashtrays. "*Zdrastvuite, Otets Aleksandr!*"—the greetings continued, now in Russian. Soon he was in a sound-proof studio behind a huge mike, and I would hear his rich Russian voice over the loudspeaker in the control room, very different from his English voice, but far more familiar to me. His tone was a mix of sermon, lecture, and conversation, and he was speaking to people he knew intimately, even though at that time we had no idea who was listening, or whether anyone was listening.

Russians, Russia, existed for us then as projections of our own émigré world. We prayed for "our long-suffering country of Russia," we hated Stalin and the godless Communists, we imagined people living in fear and deprivation. But in the dark 50s we had no contacts with Russia, so when the first signs of life began to emerge from behind the iron curtain in the 1960s, we hungrily clutched at them.

When I finally came to live and work in Russia in 1980 as a correspondent for *The New York Times,* I found, of course, a very different world from the one in which I was raised. But I was also struck by how much was familiar—how many children's stories I also knew from my childhood, how many songs, intonations, expressions we shared.

My father was not born in Russia, and he never visited it. But he lived long enough to learn that the Russia with which he conversed all his life had been there all along, and had heard him. His broadcasts were always based on faith, and in the end it was affirmed. When I began working in Moscow, I remember Russians telling me how important it had been to receive confirmation through the *Voskresnye Besedy*, the Sunday Conversations, that Russia's great spiritual legacy was being sustained in the West. And I remember, too, my father's joy at discovering in the literature of the "thaw," and especially in Solzhenitsyn's "One Day in the Life of Ivan Denisovich," that Russia's great culture and faith had not been destroyed in the flames of the Gulag and the war.

I believe the broadcasts were as much an integral part of his sacred mission as his work in the New World. Yes, he dedicated the major part of his life and ministry to Orthodoxy in America, in the West, and he ardently loved America and everything it stood for. But this mission was never in conflict with his faith in Russia, with being Russian. He had been raised in the golden age of the Russian emigration of Paris, and had studied under the great Russian theologians—A. V. Kartashev, Archimandrite Cyprian Kern, V. V. Zenkovsky, Father Nicholas Afanassieff—and even from New York he remained deeply involved with the Russian Christian Student Movement and the *Vestnik* edited by his lifelong friend Nikita Struve. In New York, too, he was always close to the Russian intelligentsia, and especially to *Novyi Zhurnal*, published in those days by M. Karpovich and Roman Goul.

His broadcasts were never propaganda; they could not be. They were, literally, "*besedy*," conversations, in which he spoke as a Russian to Russians, sharing truths and knowledge that he knew, instinctively, they hungered for. The Russians in the Soviet Union were not Cold War enemies; they were his own people who had become tragically separated from their own history, culture, and faith. Father Alexander never saw Russia. He intended to visit me once I began working there, but he fell ill with cancer and died before he could make the trip. But Russia was always in him. He continued his broadcasts almost to his last day. He returned to his first language, Russian, for his great last work, *The Eucharist*. In the introduction, which he wrote in the month before he died, he said of the work: "I wrote this thinking of Russia, with pain and at the same time with joy. We who live out here in freedom can discuss and think. Russia lives by confession and suffering. And this suffering, this faithfulness, is a gift of God, a source of divine help.

"And if even a portion of what I want to say reaches Russia, and if it proves in any way useful, I will consider, with thanks to God, that my work is done."

Serge Schmemann

From the Editors of the Russian Edition

Our publication presents to the reader a printed version of more than five hundred radio broadcasts of Protopresbyter Alexander Schmemann (1921–1983), which he delivered over the years on Radio Liberty. All the texts collected here are the result of transcription and subsequent editorial processing of the tape recordings stored in the archives of Radio Liberty and transmitted to us in the form of audio files. In terms of composition, the proposed publication is identical to the earlier published collection of audio discs, which contain digitized and restored originals of conversations in MP3 format (with a total playing time of more than 80 hours).

The editors express their deep gratitude to the leadership of Radio Free Europe/Radio Liberty (RFE/RL) for their kind permission to publish these conversations and for their assistance in receiving them. In particular, we are grateful to Jeffrey Trimble, who, as Executive Director of the Broadcasting Council, is in charge of all foreign broadcasting in the United States, Ross Johnson, a specialist historian of RFE/RL, John Lindburg, corporate legal adviser to RFE/RL, and also Gene Sosin, the long-time leader of the New York City Radio Liberty division and author of *Sparks of Liberty: An Insider's Memoir of Radio Liberty* (Pennsylvania State University Press, 1999). I would also like to thank Georgy Nakhichevan from the law firm Kilpatrick Stockton for his help.

We consider it a special duty to offer most cordial thanks to Sergey Mikhailovich Ossorguine (SergeAudio Studio, New York), who spent many months finding and digitizing all the recordings of the conversations. One cannot but express deep gratitude to the specialists of the Moscow Vimbo studio (in particular, Alexander Valentinovich Vlasov), because of the high professionalism with which the records, in the original of very uneven quality, were restored and prepared for publication.

Since the majority of available audio recordings are not dated, their distribution by chronological order was deliberately abandoned. And although, relying on numerous "clues" in the conversations themselves, nonetheless we tried to respect an approximate chronology (see numerous notes about the author's contemporaries, as well as about contemporary events, publications, etc.), it was decided to arrange the material on an essentially thematic basis. Vividly revealing the diversity of topics that were the focus of Father Alexander as a missionary and preacher, this principle of classification also determined the structure of this publication, where the texts are grouped into thematic sections (the names of the latter, as well as the conversations themselves, were determined by the editors).

Some of the audio recordings that were handed to us consisted of variants of the same conversations, which seemed to be related to different times (for example, conversations on church holidays were often repeated by Father Alexander several times with more or less significant variations). When arranging audio discs, preference in such situations was given to the most developed options, while others were eliminated. However, for the print version it was decided, taking the best option as the basis of the text, in some cases to combine it with the most successful fragments of the screened ones.

Because spoken and written language is not interpreted in the same way, we publish the texts of radio conversations with editorial revision. The latter suggested, first of all, the elimination of stylistic errors through inversion, the replacement of words, phrases, and, much less often, whole phrases. In other cases, the correction was dictated by the desire to clarify or specify the author's thought and was carried out while taking into account his other texts. Some passages were abridged, primarily when describing the content of previous conversations, and also when vast fragments of Scripture were quoted in two or more consecutive conversations. All these corrections, as well as the correction of accidental omissions, are not specifically noted by us. Most of the corrections in the quotations from the Holy Scriptures, which slightly differ from the Synodal or Church Slavonic texts [in the original Russian], are not specified.

A Note on the English Translation

This is not the first English publication to emerge from the enormous corpus of Fr Alexander Schmemann's Radio Liberty broadcasts. A number of translators participated over the years. In the earliest publication, some years ago, Fr John Jillions translated portions that dealt with the subjects of Belief, the Church Feasts, and the Mother of God, published as three separate volumes in the Celebration of Faith series: *I Believe*, *The Church Year*, and *The Virgin Mary*. Several broadcasts on death and the Lord's Prayer appeared in three later books: *O Death, Where is Thy Sting?*, *The Liturgy of Death*, and *Our Father*—all translated by Fr Alexis Vinogradov.

Fr Alexis Vinogradov also prepared the present translation (with the assistance of others in a few texts), and Fr Nathan Williams performed the final review and editing of the text. This collection does not include material found in the books mentioned above. In commenting on the translation of his seminal work, *The Eucharist*, Fr Alexander Schmemann said that he might have written it slightly differently if he had started out in English, but that overall he felt it carried his message well. We can hope that he would be similarly pleased with how we rendered his message to keep it faithful to his spirit and intent. Naturally, the present audience has the benefit of historical hindsight not available to the oppressed Soviet man at the time these talks were originally delivered and heard.

PART I

FAITH AND UNBELIEF

"I believe in God..."

A Fundamentally Personal Faith

Several years ago, a certain French publication approached a number of well-known people—writers, philosophers, various artists—with a request to write their thoughts on the theme: "What I believe." The majority of these people were believers, and furthermore members of the same church—the Catholic Church, which permits less so-called "freedom of interpretation" than others, for the most part demanding conformity. And yet despite this, the answers of those polled revealed considerable differences, and make for fascinating reading. A single faith, seen through the prism of personal experiences, struggles, and interpretations, becomes new and personal. Yet at the same time it does not cease to be one common faith.

I am speaking about this because in this day and age people often talk about faith, about religion, about Christianity on an "objective," dogmatic level. Not only the enemies of religion, but believers themselves have begun to debate what Christianity teaches, and what exactly is asserted by authoritative theologians. At the same time, in its very nature and essence faith is something deeply personal, and can only truly exist in a given person and his personal experience. Only when a specific teaching of the Church—a "dogma" as we call it, the affirmation of a certain truth—when this becomes my faith, my experience, and consequently, the very substance of my own life, only then is this faith alive.

And if we begin to consider and observe how faith is transmitted from one person to another, it becomes clear that only personal experience is able to truly convince, inspire, and convert. Within Christianity this is particularly important, because the Christian faith, at its heart, is a personal encounter with Christ, the acceptance not of this or that "dogma" concerning Christ, but ultimately the acceptance of Christ himself. In other words, Christianity is fundamentally personal. But this does not at all imply that it is individualistic, for those who encounter him come to know and to love one and the same Christ. But this also means that Christ himself is inclined towards each person whose faith, though rooted in the common faith, is at the same time unique.

It is important to be reminded of this, because in our time the enemies of religion try to reduce every conversation about faith to an "academic" debate, to break down the faithful by "scientific" arguments, as if the conversation is about some kind of objective, demonstrable element of nature, even though this science—or rather pseudoscience—is wholly incapable of proving all that Christians affirm. Christians, however, do not demand this kind of proof, because their faith is the substance of their experience. The reality of their experience is evident to them in the same way that any person recognizes the reality of love and elation, pity and compassion.

What is my true "self"?

I believe in God."
Pronouncing these words, I realize, of course, their incommensurability with everything else that I pronounce. I know that when I say them, I am transported, so to speak, "into another dimension."

And yet, in pronouncing them, ninety-nine times out of a hundred, I do not ponder their meaning—they are spoken simply as though they were part of everyday life with all its little cares. I am used to them—I am used to the fact that I believe in God, as well as to the fact that there are people around me who do not believe in God. And it is precisely this habit that does not allow me to break through to the uniqueness, particularity, and unprecedented nature of that which I affirm as a thing self-evident. Therefore, the process of delving anew into the meaning of these words, rediscovering their meaning, for me at least, can only begin with a sense of wonder—a special reaction to them, as though I were hearing them for the first time.

Such, incidentally, is the secret law of all genuine knowledge: it always begins with the purification and renewal of the sight, the hearing, and all the senses. Only by discovering in oneself a renewed sense of wonder can one begin to penetrate the largely obscured meaning of everything that makes up our lives. And to wonder also means to free oneself from the sense of familiarity, which seems to blanket our perception with a kind of gray dust. And then, thanks to this sense of wonder, the words "I believe in God" begin to sound extraordinary. I turn my inner gaze and ear to them, trying as much as possible more truly, more honestly, more profoundly to answer for myself the question of what they mean.

And the first thing that now becomes obvious to me is that each of these words is shrouded in some mystery, which intensifies as I delve into them.

Who, first of all, is this "I" who affirms his faith in God? Of course, the "I" is I myself; and yet within me I am conscious of a multitude of different "selves." And which of them, and how, and when, is turned toward God?

He that eateth me, even he shall live by me (Jn 6.57), says Christ. But how many hours each day—or rather, how many minutes—does my "self" really live in God? And is it not immersed the rest of the time in concerns and interests that have nothing to do with my faith? And do I then have within me faith, the memory of God, the experience of his presence, or even the need for that presence?

And so it turns out that faith and God come to my mind only when they are strongly needed, and disappear from my life the rest of the time when something else proves more important. But then this is really no longer faith, but superstition, born of fear, ignorance, an instinctive need for protection, etc.

I say all this in the deep conviction that soon our world will have no place for this kind of occasional faith. The Greek sage of old asserted that the world has always been full of gods,[1] but this by no means implies that it has

---

[1] The idea that "everything is full of gods" was expressed by the ancient Greek philosopher Sophocles (*c.* 640–*c.* 547 BC).

always been full of faith. People needed these gods (and here anti-religious propaganda is quite right) for protection, for assistance in everyday affairs, or for comfort—in a word, as a source of stability in this mysterious and extremely dangerous world.

But is this the faith, and are these the gods, of which the Gospel speaks? Let's face it: the whole Gospel is aimed at destroying faith as superstition, as an egoistic expectation of something "beneficial." *If any man serve me, let him follow me* (Jn 12.26), Christ says. And to those who follow him, he promises nothing in this life beyond what constituted his own life—that is, nothing but the cross, nothing but a painful struggle with the evil of this world, nothing but infinitely difficult obedience to the will of God and to God's great plan for the world.

All this means that in relation to the "I" that is me, the words "I believe in God" require a profound and painful test. And this test must show me that my "I," in daring to declare my faith in God, is not only the deepest, most central core of my true "I," but also unites all the rest by its responsibility for them.

To say "I believe in God" means that I freely and responsibly choose what will now be the most important thing in my life and the judge of everything else in it, so that my whole life, including my other "I's," will be wholly relegated to my faith and evaluated in its light. Thus, one who asserts "I believe in God" has already crossed a certain line—the most important, significant line, which henceforth defines his whole life. For faith is not something that immediately gives me something, but that which first gives up my own self, making my whole life something infinitely important, after which it is no longer possible to live as though I had not uttered these words, "I believe in God." From now on, in my life there cannot and must not be anything neutral or insignificant. In the light of my decision and my choice, everything takes on a special meaning: everything becomes either loyalty to or a betrayal of my faith. And all this is because the faith that I accept with this irrevocable statement is a kind of light that illuminates my whole life as a new and holistic understanding of it.

In our next conversation we will examine this faith, attested by the second word of the statement, "I believe in God."

What Does "I Believe" Mean?

I believe in God." But what is faith?

Is it not strange to ask the same question again and again, first and foremost of oneself? And have we not heard innumerable answers from all peoples throughout the ages?

And yet in my last talk I said that if you ponder this statement more intently, it ceases to seem familiar. Above all, it turns out that faith is not the same as knowledge—in any case, not in the common, everyday sense of the word.

To state "I believe in God" means, "I know that God exists." We by no means equate this knowledge to my knowledge that there is a table in my room, or that it is raining outside. Knowledge of the latter kind, which we call "objective," does not depend on me; it enters my consciousness regardless of my will, regardless of any free choice. This knowledge is in fact "objective," and I, that is, the subject, the personality within me, can only accept it and make it my own.

The affirmation "I believe in God," however, implies a choice, a decision: that is to say, it implies a highly personal participation of my entire being. And as soon as this personal participation disappears, my faith becomes dead and virtually nonexistent. I spoke about this in my last conversation, stating that by no means do we always truly believe, because faith cannot be turned into an "objective," self-evident part of my convictions, my worldview.

Many turn to God in fear, unhappiness, or suffering. But the difficult times pass, and they return to a life that has nothing to do with faith. They continue to live as if there were no God.

There are even more people who believe not so much in God, but, oddly enough, in "religion." They simply feel good, comfortable, and calm in church. Since childhood, many of them have become accustomed to this "sacredness" of the temple and its rituals, where everything is so beautiful and deeply mysterious—a relief from the drab ugliness of everyday life. And they hold on to this "sacredness" without really giving thought to anything. Of course, this kind of "religion" sometimes provides bright, exalted sensations that help one get through life, but nevertheless it stands on its own, apart from that life itself.

There are also those who consider religion useful and necessary for the nation, for society, for the family, for the sick and the dying, for promoting morality—in other words, they reduce it to being something "beneficial." I remember how, when I was still a young priest, mothers would come to me requesting that I use confession to help them eradicate evil inclinations in their children: "Tell my child that God sees everything! That will frighten him and he'll stop doing those things."

Religion for help and comfort, religion as a certain pleasure derived from the sacred and exalted, religion as something beneficial . . . It is worth noting that there is a grain of truth in this understanding of religion. And yet, reduced *solely* to this, religion has nothing whatsoever in common with the faith about which, at the dawn of Christianity, the apostle Paul said, *Faith is the assurance of things hoped for, the conviction of things not seen* (Heb 11.1 RSV). Let us consider these strange words: the assurance of things hoped for, the conviction of things not seen. Strange, because they seem to contain a contradiction. For if I hope for something, it is precisely because it has not yet come to pass; otherwise there would be no reason to hope for it. And how can the invisible—that is, what cannot be verified and attested to—become a conviction within me, a reality, something that I possess?

And yet, the apostle Paul defines faith by just such apparent paradoxes. First of all, we note that in this definition the word *God* is absent. This word appears further on in the subsequent verses of his message. But here he speaks of faith as a particular inherent state of a person, as a kind of gift that he possesses. What then is this gift?

This question can be answered as follows: it is a pull toward or craving for what is most desired, a premonition of something completely different from what is already there, an expectation of the only thing worth living for. Oddly, the atheist philosopher Sartre defines man in almost the same way. "Man," he says, "is a useless passion."[2] Useless, because its object is

---

[2]Jean-Paul Sartre (1905–1980): French existentialist philosopher. In adulthood he was close to the Communists, and subsequently adopted extremely leftist views. The formula "Man is a useless passion" ("L'homme est une passion inutile") is found in his book *Being and Nothingness* (*L'être et néant*), 1943.

illusory, and there is in fact nothing for a person to strive for, nothing to hope for, nothing to crave. But it is important that Sartre himself observes in man this expectation and this thirst.

Thus, faith, according to the apostle Paul, is a thirst, an expectation, and at the same time the desire for something a person already knows from profound experience. If what man longed for did not exist, he would not experience this expectation and longing, and without this longing there would be no encounter—no encounter in which the invisible becomes a certainty, something that is real and can be grasped.

All this means that faith in Christian experience is not the result of reasoning and scrutiny, not a fleeting emotional experience, but rather it is the encounter of man's most profound expectation with its fulfillment, which is sometimes unknown to the person himself.

Regarding this encounter, this fulfillment of things hoped for and conviction of things unseen, Blessed Augustine expressed it best: "You have created us for yourself, Lord, and our heart will not rest until it finds its rest in you."[3]

In Which God?

No man has seen God, nor could he (cf. 1 Tim 6.16). This was said not by an atheist, nor by an agnostic, not by a doubter in search of faith, nor by a layman with no time for the sublime. Rather, this was said by the apostle Paul, whose fiery faith sears anyone who reads his epistle two thousand years later.

What then does eternal faith mean? To what or to whom is it directed? What significance does a person ascribe to that most mysterious, most inexplicable of all words, *God*?

Thus far we have spoken about the first two words of the statement "I believe in God"—about the "I" with which it begins, and about the faith that this "I" professes. We have said about faith that it is, first of all,

---

[3] St Augustine, *Confessions* 1.1.

a kind of giving of oneself that can occur only when a person has recognized that to which he is able to give himself, just as love ignites in our souls when our beloved appears. But in this example we see the beloved, and in seeing we recognize, and in recognizing we love. Yet no man has seen God.

Does this mean that we feel him? Here our words are shown to be impoverished and helpless to express what is most important, which consequently remains inexpressible. For it is quite obvious that the word *feel* can mean so many different states and moods that it alone cannot express our perception of God. Yes, we undoubtedly feel God, but this feeling is profoundly different from all other feelings, and quite alien to them in nature. For feelings are in many ways similar to tastes, and taste is not customarily debated. One person likes one thing, another person likes another; one feels one way, another feels otherwise. If faith is one of these fleeting feelings, if it depends on our transient emotions, then it really is not up for debate.

And yet those who oppose faith reduce it to just such a subjective feeling, a fleeting emotion. "Some," they say, "believe in the number 13 is unlucky, others believe in incantations, others in holy water, and others in something else altogether!" And so it turns out that faith is backed neither by firm knowledge (because no one has seen God), nor even a universal feeling (because feelings depend on human temperament). Therefore, we repeat: the word *feeling* is not enough, or else it must be clarified, cleansed of everything that is not related to faith itself.

What then constitutes the uniqueness, the absolute singularity of the state that we call faith? The fact that faith is an answer. And this answer not only presumes the presence of the One answered, but also confirms his presence. This could also be expressed somewhat differently: faith is a reciprocal movement. The movement is not of one's soul alone, but of the whole person, his whole being, which has suddenly recognized something and given itself over to what it has recognized. In the language of Christianity, this can be expressed as follows: faith comes from God, in answer to his summons. Faith is always an answer to him—it is man's giving of himself to him who gave himself. Pascal expressed this wonderfully: "God tells us: you would not seek me unless you had already found me"[4]

And precisely because faith is an answer, a reciprocal movement, in it there always remains a search, a thirst, and an aspiration. I seek in myself, in my experience, the answer to the question: "Why do I believe?"—and I do not find it. What is God for me? The key to understanding the world and the meaning of life? No, because for me it is obvious, first, that it is not through this explanation that I believe in him, and second, that my faith in him does not in fact explain all the secrets and mysteries of the world. More than once I have had to stand at the bed of a child dying in terrible torment. And could I "explain" anything to those around me, "religiously justify," as they sometimes say, this torment, this death? Never! I could only say one thing: "God is here, God exists!" I could only confess the incommensurability of his presence with our sorrowful earthly questions.

No, of course faith is not born of our need for explanations. But then where does it come from? From a fear of the afterlife? From my inherent passionate and ultimately egoistic desire not to utterly disappear? No, for the most clever philosophical discourse about the afterlife, about eternity, etc., seems but useless babble to me. What do I know about all this? And what can I say to others? And I do not believe in God because I desire the afterlife and eternity, but rather I believe in eternal life because I believe in God.

But then to the question of all questions, "Why do I believe?" only one answer can be made: because God gave me this faith and gives it to me all the time. He gave it as a gift, and I am convinced of its reality by the unique joy that does not depend on anything in the world, the peace that does not depend on anything external, which I experience in myself in those rare moments when the word *God* ceases to be just a word, becoming a boundless waterfall of light, love, beauty, and true life that washes over me. *Peace and joy in the Holy Spirit* (Rom 14.17)—this is what Paul said about this, and there are no other words. For when you believe and live by faith, words are not necessary; indeed, they are impossible.

---

[4]Blaise Pascal (1623–1662): French mathematician, physicist, and religious thinker. Cf. "Console thyself, thou wouldst not seek me, if thou hadst not found me." *Pensées (Thoughts)*, § 553. Translation in *Pensées*, trans. W. F. Trotter (New York: The Collier Press, 1910), 181.

But people will ask: "Why is not this gift of faith given to all? Why do some believe and others do not? Why are some chosen and others not?" Indeed, when you look around you are amazed at the depth of unbelief and godlessness that has permeated the world. And doubt creeps into the soul: "God is all-good, but is he really all-powerful?"

We will move on to these issues, which are organically related to the nature and essence of faith, in our next talk.

The Destiny of Mankind

Faith, according to Christianity, is a gift from God. *No man,* Christ says, *can come to me, except the Father which hath sent me draw him* (Jn 6.44).

But why then is this gift not given to everyone? Why does God appear to choose some and draw them to him, while remaining inaccessible to others? This question is indeed an agonizing one, and the defenders and interpreters of Christian doctrine have often tripped up on it one way or another. For example, Calvin, one of the founders of Protestantism, put the doctrine of predestination at the forefront of his understanding of Christianity, according to which some have been chosen and destined by God for salvation, and others for perdition. Naturally, our Christian conscience cannot accept this terrible doctrine. We are told by the apostle of love that *God is love* (1 Jn 4.16), and it is also said that *God sent not his Son into the world to condemn the world, but that the world through him might be saved* (Jn 3.17).

That is why the question with which our talk began is so painfully difficult. And to it there is naturally only one answer. Yes, faith is a gift from God and this gift is given to everyone, as we hear in the wondrous prayer of the Church concerning "the light of Christ that illumines every person that comes into the world."[5]

The whole Gospel is permeated with a unique arithmetic, according to which the good Shepherd leaves ninety-nine sheep to save one that was lost. The whole Gospel exudes love for the sinner, for the fallen, for the

[5]Prayer of the First Hour, and at the Liturgy of the Presanctified Gifts (alluding to Jn 1.9).

perishing. Consequently, the question is not to whom the gift of this faith is given or not given (for this gift is given to all), but why everyone does not accept it, why believers always comprise a *little flock* in the world (Lk 12.32), why Christ himself asks bitterly, *When the Son of man cometh, shall he find faith on the earth?* (Lk 18.8)

And so, in searching for an answer it is best, perhaps, to begin with Dostoevsky's profound words: "Each of us is responsible for everything and to every human being."[6] We might add to this that we are responsible first and foremost for our concealment or even outright denial of the divine gift, thereby making millions hopelessly blind and deaf to faith. It is no accident that the Gospel speaks so often of children. It is said of them: *Whosoever shall not receive the kingdom of God as a little child shall in no wise enter therein* (Lk 18.17). What does this mean? It means that it is typical for a child to perceive life itself as a kind of paradise, that in his perception everything is whole and joyful, everything is faith in the deepest sense of the word, only not yet separated from life, not in opposition to it. It manifests itself as wholehearted trust, everywhere expecting only love. And we all know how as childhood fades this integrity is destroyed, and how the experience of evil, separation, and suffering enters one's life.

And here, somewhere near this crucial moment in a person's life, a terrible battle for the soul begins, the outcome of which is the preservation or loss of this initial experience as a gift from above. It is here that at some point everything hangs in the balance, and one word, or the lack thereof, may prove decisive. And yet, terrible as this may be, again and again we see that the experience of evil, or rather evil itself, always comes to a person from other people. We determine the lives of those around us—for good or for evil—by our own words and deeds, by our whole life. As faith arises in one person from another's faith, so also unbelief grows from another's hypocrisy and lies, from the surrounding triumph of evil and sin.

[6]Fyodor Dostoyevsky, *Brothers Karamzov*. This is a leitmotif of the novel, perhaps most fully articulated by Elder Zosima in his final exhortation on his deathbed: "There is only one means of salvation, then take yourself and make yourself responsible for all men's sins, that is the truth, you know, friends, for as soon as you sincerely make yourself responsible for everything and for all men, you will see at once that it is really so, and that you are to blame for every one and for all things" (Book 6, Chapter 3). Translation in Fyodor Dostoevsky, *The Brothers Karamazov*, trans. Constance Garnett (New York: The Macmillan Company, 1922), 340–41.

The whole world lieth in wickedness (1 Jn 5.19). But who plunged it into this evil? If the gift of faith often is not alive in believers themselves (or rather they themselves do not live by it), if while speaking of love and righteousness they continue to hate, and while calling on the highest they are completely immersed in the earthly, then how infinitely difficult it is for those who observe them to find faith! Then soul-eroding doubts begin to arise. Then comes the terrible experience of a loveless, joyless life. Then the dark fire of denial, of hatred of what is higher, and an almost unconscious thirst to destroy one's inner shrine ignites in the heart.

I quoted the words of the apostle Paul: "No one has ever seen God, nor can see him" (cf. 1 Tim 6.16). But now he appears to us in men, who are his image. We have seen him and we know him in Christ, but we can see him in every person, just as in every person we can be visited by demonic rejection of God and all the darkness of satanic hatred for God's world.

"I don't believe in God," says the unbeliever, "because I see too much evil, suffering, and nonsense around me. If God existed, he would not allow this." "I believe in God," says the believer, "because in the midst of evil, suffering, and nonsense I experience the strength, joy, and truth of faith." The same world, the same knowledge of it—and two completely different experiences! No, God does not deprive anyone of his gift, his love, and his calling, but too often they are hidden by a veil of evil that hangs over the world and darkens a man.

But then the question inevitably arises: where does this evil come from? And why does it so often triumph, rather than the all-powerful, all-good, all-loving God? Why is it that, in its struggle against evil, good most often relies on evil's methods, and itself gradually transforms into evil? This will be the subject of our next talk.

Is the Experience of Faith Actually My Own?

Today let us summarize our musings on the most important and most mysterious of all human statements: "I believe in God."

In stating this we recognize and affirm, however imperfectly, by a sort of intuition of our soul, a certain gift from above. I do not so much consciously, deductively, and rationally come to faith in God as I find it in myself, and I find it with surprise, joy, and gratitude. I find it in myself as a presence—the mysterious but clearly palpable presence of him who is entirely peace and joy, silence and light. This presence cannot come from anything in me, for neither in me nor in the surrounding world is there such joy, such light, such silence. Where then is it from?

And so I pronounce the word by which all this is expressed and named and which, isolated from this experience, from the authenticity of this presence, makes no sense. I pronounce the word *God,* which I could not have spoken if I had not had this experience. However, in pronouncing it, I free this experience, this feeling of presence, from its subjectivity, its fleeting nature, its vagueness. I affirm the substance of this experience and thereby accept it as a gift, and respond to this gift with a reciprocal movement of my whole being. "I believe in God!" And it turns out that the faith that I discovered at the very depths of my soul is not only my own personal and indescribable experience, but also that which connects me anew to other people, to life and the world, becoming a liberation from the loneliness to which all men are doomed to one degree or another.

For if it is a joy to acquire faith in one's own soul, it is no less joyful to discover the same faith, the same experience in others. And not only in the people around me now, but also in those separated from my time by many centuries. Here I open a book written more than a thousand years before Christ, in a world that so little resembles today's world, and I read:

O Lord, thou hast searched me, and known me.
Thou hast known my down-sitting and mine uprising; thou
    understandest my thoughts from afar.
Thou hast traced my path and my lot, and hast foreseen all my ways.

For there is no deceit in my tongue; lo, O Lord, thou hast known all
     things,
the last and the first; thou hast fashioned me, and laid thy hand upon
     me.
Thy knowledge is too wonderful for me; it is mighty, I cannot attain
     unto it.
Whither shall I go from thy Spirit? And whither shall I flee from thy
     presence?
If I go up to heaven, thou art there; if I go down to hell, thou art
     present.
If I take up my wings at dawn, and dwell in the uttermost parts of the
     sea,
even there shall thy hand guide me, and thy right hand shall hold me.
And I said, "Surely the darkness shall cover me"; even the night shall
     be light to my delight.
For the darkness shall not be dark to thee, and the night shines like
     the day; its darkness and its light are both alike to thee.
For thou hast possessed my reins, O Lord; thou hast helped me from
     my mother's womb.
I will praise thee, for thou art fearfully wondrous; wondrous are thy
     works . . .
How precious also are thy friends unto me, O God!
How their rule has been strengthened!
I shall count them, and they shall be multiplied more than the sand; I
     awake, and I am still with thee. . . .
Search me, O God, and know my heart; try me, and know my paths;
and see if there be any wicked way in me, and lead me in the way
     everlasting.

                                        (Ps 138.1–14, 17–18, 23–24).

   This is Psalm 138, written, I repeat, three thousand years ago. And yet
I read and am amazed and rejoice: Lord, all this is exactly what I feel and
experience! This is what I have known; it is talking about me, as though
the words were my own! And even this childish, tongue-tied attempt to

express what is above words is also mine. Thus, this faith has lived and continues to live throughout the ages, meaning that millions of people have felt the same way.

And my heart is filled with joy as these amazing words surface in an abundance of faith: *For the darkness shall not be dark to thee, and the night shines like the day; its darkness and its light are both alike to thee.* And in this light I see a new world. Despite all its darkness, it has been illuminated for me by the primordial light. Truly, wondrous are your works, and my soul recognizes this!

I echo the Psalmist: I glorify you because I am marvelously made—and I see myself anew, sinful, weak, and enslaved though I am, for I have been given the secret organ of internal knowledge to comprehend that which is exalted, marvelous, and glorious, to desire higher knowledge and a higher way of life, to distinguish between the path of corruption and the path eternal.

And this faith reveals something else to me, as well—that everything in the world manifests God and radiates with him: the morning dawn, but also the nocturnal twilight; happiness, but also suffering; joy, but also sadness. And if so many do not see this, if they do not feel the night of life to be as bright as day, it is only because I and others like me are very weak witnesses of faith, because from early childhood we encompass people with lies, urging them not to seek a life of depth, but their own little earthly happiness, tethering them to vain and transient pursuits. In such persons the craving for light and love dies away, and their world becomes filled with a cloying darkness of skepticism and unbelief, of bitterness and hatred.

But in this darkness, and in this terrible fall, God did not leave us. And my helpless words about faith would be empty if, in conclusion, I did not confess faith not simply in God, but in that one Man in whom God came into the world, and in the world to every man, to rescue and restore them to life.

I believe in God, but in the fullness of the joy of possession God is revealed in Christ. *No man hath seen God at any time*, says the apostle John the Theologian, and then adds: *the only-begotten Son, which is in the bosom of the Father, he hath declared him* (Jn 1.18). And he likewise affirms to us that his words are a testimony that *we have seen with our eyes . . . we have looked upon, and our hands have handled . . . the Word of life* (1 Jn 1.1). Concerning him, the Word of life, we shall speak in our next conversation.

The Only Name

At the conclusion of our reflections on faith, we have come to a name that, for us Christians, constitutes both the content of this faith and its source. We have come to the name of Christ.

We have only to speak it, and each time our heart is filled with renewed amazement. And perhaps it is with this astonishment that it all begins.

Nearly two millennia separate us from the events described in the Gospel. During this time, so many tremendous changes have taken place in the world, so many heroes have succeeded each other, leaving a panorama of memories good and bad, that it would seem that the image of Christ, recorded in one of the shortest of books, ought to have darkened and faded away to nothing. It is an image of One of whom we know immeasurably less than of Napoleon, Lenin, or Einstein, whose biographies are detailed in thousands of books, and whose every word is carefully analyzed. Yet this image has not faded at all, because for those who believe in Christ he is alive, and love for him, communion with him, comprises the meaning and substance of their lives.

We read the Gospel and repeat the words of those whom the Pharisees sent to Christ in order to find at least some accusation against Him: *Never has a man spoken like this man* (Jn 7.46). And to this day we sense the truth, the absolute truth, of these words. Indeed, no man has ever spoken like this Man. No one in the world uttered words filled with such truth and at the same time such love, such humility. And by listening to them, we begin by believing Christ, for we cannot but believe, we cannot but accept with all our heart all that he says. And in believing him we come to faith in him.

The path from believing him to faith in him can be described as follows. At first we feel—and again with the whole depth of our being—that this Man could not lie. If his words are a lie, then everything in the world is a lie, all is darkness and pointlessness. And when he says that he was sent to save man, that one who believes in him will find joy that no one can take away, in accepting these words we believe in Christ. And this faith is confirmed by the indwelling in us of such joy and such peace that no other evidence is needed. *I will not leave you comfortless: I will come to you* (Jn 14.18); *I am with you always, even unto the end of the world* (Mt 28.20). And our heart is struck by this presence, and the same thing happens to each of us as to the unbelieving Thomas, who wanted proof, but ended up exclaiming, *My Lord and my God!* (Jn 20.28).

No, our faith is not in the abstract deity whom the atheists deny; its substance lies not in this, but in the God whom Christ has revealed to us. And it is neither by miracles nor by force and power that he draws us, but by the love, kindness, and beauty that pour forth from his image. Truly never has a man spoken like this Man!

Everything in the world changes and is forgotten, everything passes. But Christ remains as he was—the object of such love, such faith and fidelity, that millions of people prefer death and suffering to renouncing him. Moreover, in their very sufferings they see an opportunity to share the suffering of Christ, and in death they see the surety of being with him. And what on earth can compare with this love, with this faith and fidelity?

> Your breadth and span, O motherland,
> In visage of a lowly slave,
> Traversed the King of Heaven, blessing.[7]

These lines by Tyutchev are about Russia. But they can be equally ascribed to the whole earth, and to every age. For this traversal, this presence of Christ among us, is still just as apparent as two thousand years ago in Galilee.

Our conversations about faith can therefore be summed up as follows: in saying "I believe in God," I see before me the face of Christ. He appears to be looking at me alone. I know with my mind that he is for everyone, but I sense in him a call addressed specifically to me, a love directed towards

[7]From the poem by F. I. Tyutchev, "These poor villages . . ." (1855).

me, and I seem to hear the words: "I have come to you, and for your sake I wholly give myself up! I love you and desire eternal communion with you!"

And in the moments when this experience is not drowned out in me by the bustle of life, I give myself back to him with reciprocal love, and I need neither evidence nor reasoning. I know with all my being that in this same way he knocks at everyone's heart. And I want to say, "Look at him, listen to his words, for never has a man spoken like this Man. And you will experience that unique encounter whose depth and joy are not comparable to anything in the world. A new life will begin, and a new light will shine forth. And no matter how often we fall, no matter how often we may prove unfaithful to his words on the path of life, no one will take this joy away from us!" (cf. Jn 16.22).

Here, in essence, is the substance of our faith, but also its source. This faith begins with Christ, arising from an encounter with him, and in Christ it culminates. It often seems to die in us, and we forget about it, plunging into the hustle and bustle of everyday life; but then we take up the that little book once more—and again the same image appears before our inner gaze, and Someone again stands at the door of our heart and knocks (Rev 3.20).

And how important it is, how infinitely important amid the clamor of life, to hear and recognize this knocking!

An Endless Debate

Time to Assess

In the world, only one debate seems to never end: "There is a God!" "There is no God!" And so man, human thought, and human culture continually oscillate between these two assertions.

And it is ridiculous to think, as many people do today, that this dispute may end, resolved by something outward—science, philosophy, flights into outer space, etc. It is ridiculous to read that in our time science has supposedly proven that there is no God—after all, in the thirteenth century the same science proved that God exists, and it seemed to medieval philosophers that the subject was closed to debate. No matter how far we go down the ages, everywhere we see sacrifices to God and we hear the words of the Psalmist: *The fool has said in his heart, "There is no God"* (Ps 52.1). One thing, it would seem, should be obvious to everyone: this dispute has never been resolved, nor can it be resolved by any proofs!

But does it follow that this dispute is irrelevant and that it should simply be abandoned? Of course not. For this question is the most pressing, the most relevant of all human concerns. Without it, man would not be man, for this above all else is his own debate with himself, and this endless debate takes place in the deepest recesses of his consciousness.

The world is not divided into believers and unbelievers, but into believers who are constantly tested by unbelief, and unbelievers who are constantly tested by faith. No proofs have made the believer believe—by no means! This is why he seeks evidence of his faith: because it is constantly being eroded by unbelief. *Lord, I believe; help thou mine unbelief* (Mk 9.24) the man tearfully exclaims in the Gospel, revealing the persistent, inescapable fragility of faith, which always seems to be suspended over unbelief. But even a desperate unbeliever, when he passionately and even fanatically claims that there is no God, cannot help but sometimes feel or realize that there is already something strange about this passionate denial itself. For why deny so vehemently that which does not exist?

Yes, as soon as you plumb the depths of this perennial dispute, you immediately understand its complexity and paradox, and you understand that this is a dispute of a person with himself. And it is not resolved externally—not in philosophy, not in science, not in calculations and evidence—but always and only in the human soul, and each time in a new way. There are no two identical beliefs, just as there are no two identical unbeliefs. But if a man cannot "prove" what he believes, is he perhaps still able to speak about it, to disclose it to others? After all, all religion is essentially neither more nor less than a story about faith, a manifestation of faith. But both anti-religion and atheism are also a kind of story of unbelief, a manifestation of its essence. This is stated in the Gospel: *Ye shall know them by their fruits* (Mt 7.16). And these fruits of both religion and anti-religion can be studied objectively and even scientifically.

And then for everyone who approaches faith and unbelief objectively, that is, as phenomena to be studied, and not as a priori affirmations or denials, the question will certainly arise: why does anti-religion need to lie about religion in order to succeed, while religion has no need to lie about anti-religion?

Indeed, all anti-religious propaganda is built solely on falsification of facts. It never says, "Yes, the teaching of Christianity is beautiful and sublime, it furnished us with examples of a life of infinite beauty and purity, it has inspired art and culture like no other phenomenon in world history. But, sadly, the teaching is false for the simple reason that there is no God." No, this propaganda is obliged to vilify Christianity, to deny the self-evident, pervert the positive, and above all, to hide the true essence of religion from those whose faith it is determined to destroy.

This fact is truly surprising, and merits investigation. For one could just as objectively prove that on this point at least religion behaves differently—according to the principle proclaimed in the New Testament: Seek, and ye shall find (Mt 7.7); *Prove all things; hold fast that which is good* (1 Thess 5.21). In other words, here searching, verifying, testing, and debating within one's heart of hearts is not only allowed, but recognized as profitable, and faith that has not passed through the crucible of doubt is not considered firm and authentic faith.

Therefore, what appears on the surface as a dispute about God is, in essence, a dispute about the fruits of faith and unbelief. And these fruits are how the world and man are understood. The question, in essence, is simple: in what light do they appear to the believer and the unbeliever?

Is it time, perhaps, to simply compare these two worldviews? Perhaps by themselves they will prove nothing. But in a world that is bewildered, uncertain, filled with fear and hatred, this comparison, this debate about the fruits of these divergent worldviews, may perhaps reveal and clarify something. And only this path is worthy of man, for all propaganda is always mere deception and violence.

Inexplicable Unbelief

If we aim beyond superficial reasoning, and delve deeper, then we really ought to be surprised not by faith, but by unbelief. What does it mean to not believe? It means to deny not only the existence of God, but also the reality of spirit, the whole spiritual life of man.

This is exactly how a consistent or, as he calls himself, a "scientific" materialist behaves: "Only matter is real," he says; "only the struggle for food is real." Hence the primacy of economic or "production relations" phenomena in the world. And not only the primacy, for everything else—everything in any way related to the spiritual sphere—is declared to be "superstructure" superimposed on this matter, wholly and completely determined by by it.

In theory this all seems to come together quite nicely. But the moment one returns to reality, these words and theories prove to be a monstrous absurdity. For immediately the old but never obsolete question arises: how does one get from matter, from the struggle for existence, and, so to speak, "from the belly," to Beethoven's Ninth Symphony, to Rublev's "Trinity," to Lermontov's "An Angel Flew Across the Midnight Sky"?[1] How did we manage to get from "production relations" to the wondrous teaching at the center of which we hear the words, *Greater love hath no man than this, that a man lay down his life for his friends* (Jn 15.13)? And this question has not grown obsolete, for not one consistent and confirmed materialist has ever answered it. For now the question remains unanswered, and cannot be discounted.

Indeed, how did the concepts of beauty, goodness, moral perfection, and holiness arise in man out of the "struggle for existence," out of "class struggle" and the "dialectic of economic development"? Nothing can be resolved here by contemptuous, dismissive remarks about "bourgeois morality," "bourgeois aesthetics," etc. St Seraphim of Sarov, for example, was not "bourgeois" by any standard. What kind of "bourgeoisie," what "surplus value" could create a person who called everyone who came to him "my joy"?

And certainly nothing is decisively explained by the notorious materialistic doctrine concerning the origin of religion. Religion, according to the teachings of Feuerbach, and later of Marx, was produced entirely by exploitation. But it still remains quite unclear who created it—the exploiters or the exploited? According to Feuerbach, it was the exploited. "The poor man," he says, "believes in a rich God"; that is, he creates for himself an idealized image of what he lacks on earth. He is ill on earth, but will be well in heaven; the bourgeois exploiting him is evil, but God is good; and so on. Conversely, others contend that religion was invented by deliberate deceivers, who then promptly began to believe in it themselves. For it is difficult to suppose that all priests, theologians, and saints were always conscious deceivers.

Thus, materialism does not answer any of the serious questions put to it, and knowing this, upon coming to power it acts by gross coercion instead of offering an answer. Meanwhile, all these questions indicate the inexplicability and inconsistency not of faith, but rather of unbelief.

---

[1]From the poem by M. Yu. Lermontov, "The Angel" (1831).

In their explanations of faith, believers may debate about God, about how he should be understood, but they begin from an obvious and irrefutable fact—the existence of a reality that cannot be reduced to matter and material processes; the reality within man of the experience of beauty, goodness, perfection, holiness, and, finally, of faith—not as abstract ideas, but as living communion with a realm of higher being. I repeat, here the starting point is clear: there is matter with its own laws and there is spiritual reality with its own dynamics. This corresponds to the perennial experience of man.

But then the materialist comes along and says, "There is no spiritual reality; there is only matter." But how did he arrive at this and, if this is the case, how is it that a person has spiritual needs and questions? But the materialist, deaf to objections, continues to babble: "Everything in the world is determined by the law of cause and effect; everything has its own cause." He is timidly asked: "But then, shouldn't matter also have its own cause, its own beginning? Where did it come from?" "No," he states firmly and stubbornly; "matter is eternal and has no beginning."

In what a strange and inexplicable world our unbelieving materialist dwells! The invisible reality, so obvious to many, he simply rejects outright: "It is not there; it is a phantom. It's all fiction: beauty, goodness, perfection, 'An Angel Flew Across the Midnight Sky'—all this is mere superstructure!" Regarding visible reality, he claims to know its laws. But where, for example, did Marx's understanding of history come from? For understanding is also superstructure. How then did the material process and the dialectic of production relations create Marx, who spent his whole life engrossed in books, and never participated in any production whatsoever?

And there comes a point when you say to yourself: my God, how far-fetched, stupid, and unconvincing this all is! And how can millions of people see in this not only truth, but even "liberation"? How much more intelligent, deeper, closer to life and reality is faith—that experience of the reality of the spirit and the spiritual world by which people have lived in every time and place! How much higher, purer, and, finally, more believable! How natural and human it is to believe in the Source and Purpose of life, to believe in the spiritualization of matter, to discover in life and in oneself the bright and eternal law of truth, goodness, and beauty! And how miserable and simplistic the materialist's worldview appears in comparison!

Right indeed was the ancient poet and Psalmist who exclaimed, *The fool has said in his heart, "There is no God"* (Ps 52.1).

At The Final Depth

Recently, while re-reading an article by the famous Russian philosopher Frank, "Materialism as a Worldview," I was struck by the following phrase. "If we take materialism as . . . a scientific and philosophical theory," Frank writes, "then it is one of the few philosophical constructions about which one can say with full certainty that its falsity and inconsistency . . . have been irrefutably proven. They have been proven with the reliability and distinctness that are inherent, for example, to mathematical truths."[2] I was struck by this phrase, because upon reading it the following thought immediately comes to mind: if this is so reliable and self-evident, then why do so many people fail to see and accept this reliability and self-evidence? Why, on the contrary, do they see materialism, the reduction of everything to matter, as equally reliable and obvious?

And this, in turn, raises doubts about what we call proof. "It's been proven!"—how many times this solemn and, so to speak, "final" word has been declared in this world! For example, it is impossible to find a book in which the first page does not contain something like, "As Karl Marx (or Engels or Lenin) proved . . ." But then in the opposite camp they also say, "It has been proven!" And so we continue to live in a world where, on the one hand, everything has supposedly been proven, and on the other, these proofs are ineffectual, or rather they affect only those who have no real need of them, because they believe what is proven to be the truth, without any evidence whatsoever.

[2]S. L. Frank, "Materialism as a Worldview" (1928), in *Christianity, Atheism and Modernity,* 2nd ed. (Paris: YMCA Press, 1969), 145 (Russian). Sergey Ludwigovich Frank (1877–1950): Russian philosopher and religious thinker. In 1922 he was exiled from the country by the Bolshevik government.

What does all this mean? Here, from somewhere deep down, come these words of Christ: *Men loved darkness rather than light* (Jn 3.19). "Loved"! No, no proofs, no mathematical calculations led them to what they subsequently began to attempt to prove. They were led to this by love, meaning a certain profound, all-embracing choice, which is not made in the mind, but arises from somewhere in the recesses of the human soul.

It seems to us—no, we are certain—that everything we love, everything on which our love is focused, is light and good. But Christ says that darkness can be loved more than light. What frightening words! Yet how suddenly they explain, with what inexorability they highlight what seemed incomprehensible and inexplicable! How clear it suddenly becomes that the worldview couched within the abstract scientific term "materialism" is in fact man's terrible and mysterious love of darkness.

For materialism is not a creed at all, but a passionately intense denial. Materialism, first of all, does not *want*. It does not want for there to be spirit, a spiritual reality, that lies beyond matter, transcending it and within it. It does not want mysterious things such as beauty, goodness, and truth to be anything but "superstructure" to the fundamental, impersonal, and base—that is, to the material. And wherever materialism comes up against spirit, it denies and denounces it. What kind of proofs are these? They are nothing but unbridled hatred!

But hatred is always the flip side of love: I hate one thing because I love another, and because what I hate hinders the object of my love. Thus, the materialist hates religion, but not because it is evil, deceitful, and a fraud, as he claims, but because it is simply incompatible with his own faith and his own love—with faith in darkness, with love for darkness. The question remains: why then did people love darkness more than light? Why do they continue to choose darkness and serve it, infusing this service with such passionate faith?

And it is here that we approach the final depth of human tragedy and the real secret of human freedom. "Secretly the heart wants death,"[3] the poet once said. Why? Because in his heart of hearts a person subconsciously refuses that high, truly divine calling that he finds in himself, that he cannot

[3]From a poem by A. A. Bloc, "The Damned" (1907).

help but find. Oh, the delight of those men who finally rid themselves of Christ, who gave him over to death! How he had interfered, how he had troubled them, reducing everything on earth to what is central and ultimate: *Seek ye first the kingdom of God* (Mt 6.33); *Be ye therefore perfect* (Mt 5.48); *Blessed are they which do hunger and thirst after righteousness* (Mt 5.6)! And how their malice and hatred towards him intensified!

But such is man's eternal misfortune: seeing light, he chooses darkness. For darkness is simpler, more understandable; it does not require inner freedom of a person; on the contrary, it seems to say, "Give up your useless freedom, replace it with an objectively reliable life without a soul and ultimate light! Become a nameless member of the herd, a number in the column, a mere stage in the process! After all, you did not exist before, and will not exist hereafter; therefore serve the impersonal and the common!" Ah, how much more relaxing this is than the unbearable light that erupts into the world, than the call to eternal and divine freedom!

This is why no proofs really mean anything: everything is decided at that depth where a person makes his final choice.

The Original Substance

One of the classic, oft repeated accusations against religion is that it shackles a person's freedom, imprisons him in the iron cage of dogma, and thus stifles progress—movement forward, the discovery of new truths, the development of knowledge, science, etc. Conversely, according to this theory, atheism frees a person, making him the master of his own destiny. Is this really the case?

This accusation is repeated so habitually that even believers themselves often give up and even seem to agree with it: of course, my faith constrains freedom, but since it contains the truth, I can manage without freedom . . . It is therefore absolutely necessary to show that this accusation is in fact monstrously false, and that nowhere is the old concept of "passing the buck" more applicable than here. In fact, it is high time to recognize that it is not faith that denies freedom outright, but the very atheism that is proclaimed and imposed as a necessary component of a "comprehensive ideology," and has long since revealed its truly anti-progressive nature. But let's begin with faith.

Perhaps believers themselves will be surprised by the extent to which the Christian concept of faith, that is, the faith of which the Gospel speaks, is inseparable from freedom. The key to this faith is in the words of Christ: *Seek, and ye shall find* (Mt 7.7). But Christ never says that finding stops the search, or that, having found what he sought, a person can relax and stop searching. According to the Gospel, this seeking, that is, the constant, unceasing forward movement of a person, is an integral part of human nature itself. *Blessed are they which do hunger and thirst after righteousness* (Mt 5.6)—that is, blessed are those who strive for ever greater truth. This is the Gospel image of man, and all complacency, all self-satisfaction, all stony rigidity are alien to it. "The spirit breathes wherever it wills" (cf. Jn 3.8), says Christ, and he calls on his disciples to seek this spirit, inspiration, and movement. And this is how Christ's disciples and followers understood his teaching. *Prove all things; hold fast that which is good* (1 Thess 5.21), the apostle Paul wrote; and in another place, *Stand fast therefore in the liberty with which Christ hath made us free* (Gal 5.1). He compares the believer with an athlete who is never satisfied with his achievements, but always strives to do better: "Forgetting everything behind me, I strive forward" (cf. Phil 3.13).

All this clearly shows that the Christian concept of faith and religion is not static, but dynamic. *I am come that they might have life, and that they might have it more abundantly* (Jn 10.10), says Christ. And it is this abundant life, this eternal hunger and thirst, this movement, effort, and seeking, that comprise the original substance of religion. Christ denounces nothing with such force as the quality of being a self-righteous Pharisee and a know-it-all—all that quenches the spirit and reduces the life of man to formal precepts. Conversely, atheism is the epitome of a static understanding of man and his essence, and therefore it is atheism that truly enslaves him. Atheism says to a person: "Do not look for what you are searching for—it does not exist, and this has been proven as surely as two and two make four. Everything has already been said, all is defined, all the whys and hows answered. All your searching is a delirium of the imagination: in reality life is flat and ultimately has no meaning." For how can they really believe that the meaning of life is the material well being of some "future generations"? When these future generations finally achieve "heaven on earth," what will they do then? What will be their purpose in life? Atheism is a denial of personal search because the dogma has been found, but this is the purest expression of slavery. According to Christian doctrine, seeking, thirst, flight, and ascent constitute the essence of man and, consequently, imply freedom as a necessary condition. According to atheism, all this simply does not exist, nor should it. Read Marx and you will know everything, and when you do, you will be content. Instead of freedom, there is absolute predetermination.

It is no coincidence that those who defend and propagate official atheism simultaneously stifle human art and creative freedom. For art is akin to religion: it too lives and is driven by seeking, it too is based on the principle of the spirit breathing wherever it wills. If, however, it is known in advance how and where the spirit breathes, if art has already been defined as "socialist realism," "service to industrialization," or something else, the creative search is killed and genuine art is impossible. Say what we will, but it remains an absolutely indisputable fact that great art is always, one way or another, connected with religion, and even atheists are forced ultimately to show people cathedrals and icons, have them listen to Bach—in short, point to the spirit as the source of creativity.

According to Christian teaching, faith is liberation from all false absolutism, or, in religious terms, from idols. *Little children*, writes the apostle John, *keep yourselves from idols* (1 Jn 5.21). An idol is a false absolute, but it is precisely this false absolutism on which atheism thrives. By denying God as the source of life, freedom, and spirit, it involuntarily and inevitably invents and promotes a great many false gods. "Class," "matter," "laws of history," "dialectical materialism"—these are actual idols that need to be constantly protected and extolled, and from this they are even more clearly seen to be idols—that is, false absolutes.

But idols can be protected only by violence, and therefore atheism lives exclusively by violence. And so it denounces the Gospel as a "naïve and useless mythology," but God forbid that this same Gospel be put into the hands of the reader! One would think that if everything in this book is so stupid and unscientific, that reading it would be the best means of exposing it—but no: they fear the Gospel like fire. The constitution provides for "freedom of worship" and "freedom of anti-religious propaganda," although it is perfectly clear that these concepts are heterogeneous, and true freedom would also mean freedom of religious propaganda.

Thus, it is time to ask: where is freedom, and where slavery? Where are men called to search, to inspiration, and where to blindly accept dead dogma? Where do we see man open to his highest vocation, and where is the same man degraded to the category of natural phenomena, of absolutely defined "matter"? In the end, all of this will come to light—and this is why the official ideology hates religion, for religious faith affirms the eternal words: "The Spirit breathes where it wills!" (cf. Jn 3.8).

The Highest Intelligence

Thy Nativity, O Christ our God, has shone to the world the light of knowledge . . ." So begins the troparion of the feast of the Nativity of Christ—asserting that, when Christ entered the world, with him there entered not only the image of the perfect man, perfect Good, perfect Holiness, Beauty, and Love, but also the highest, all-encompassing revelation of Meaning.

"The light of knowledge . . ." It is here, on the plane of reason, that a primordial battle is waged against Christianity and against Christ himself. And these words spark rebellion in all those who think that they possess all reason, that in the name of reason and rationality one can and must crush everything connected with the two thousand-year-old Kingdom of the Child born in the cave of Bethlehem. Yes, this debate has continued for nearly two thousand years. Here the Apostle Paul comes to Athens and goes up to the Areopagus, where all the luminaries of science and philosophy of that time are seated. There, in the very intellectual heart of the ancient world, he preaches Christ, crucified and risen. *And when they heard of the resurrection of the dead* these learned sages *mocked* (Acts 17.32). And all the culture and wisdom of the ancient world—and the whole organization of the great Roman Empire that united it—followed them, and Christians were outlawed, like exiles and pariahs. For more than two hundred years Christians were persecuted and killed; they were subjected to slander, their teachings and rites in every way mocked. But through the era of darkness and persecution, the words of the same Apostle Paul did not cease to resound: We are treated *as deceivers, and yet true; as unknown, and yet well known; as dying, and, behold, we live; as chastened, and not killed; as sorrowful, yet always rejoicing; as poor, yet making many rich; as having nothing, and yet possessing all things* (2 Cor 6.8–10).

Time passes, and these same sages and men of learning begin to think about this doctrine, which at first seemed to them so unreasonable. Consider one philosopher by the name of Justin, who lived in the middle of the second century A D.[4] He spent his whole life searching for the truth, studied all the sciences available at that time, and finally arrived at Christianity. What led him to this persecuted faith? In his surviving works he attributes his journey to the light of reason, the highest intelligence, the all-encompassing wisdom of Christianity. Only Christianity, says Justin, is able to answer all questions, to fully satisfy the inquisitiveness of our mind and the thirst of our heart. And does not the Gospel of John say that Christ is the *Logos* (which in Greek means meaning and reason), the Logos of all things? *In the beginning was the Word* [*Logos*] (Jn 1.1)—that is how this Gospel begins. A few more decades pass, and before us stands another representative of the same scholarly and philosophical Olympus of the ancient world—Clement of Alexandria.[5] He likewise states that Christianity revealed itself to the world as the pinnacle of reason, the crown and fulfillment of all human aspirations and quests. And how many others were there like Justin and Clement? But finally the empire itself bows its proud head to the crucified Master, whom it had persecuted and despised for so long. The Christian era of human history begins.

[4] St Justin Martyr the Philosopher was a Christian apologist who suffered for the faith in A D 166.

[5] Clement of Alexandria (second half of the 2nd and early 3rd centuries)—church writer and teacher of the Church of Alexandria.

Is it really possible to forget the roots that put forth everything by which we live and breathe? Christianity pervades the flesh and blood of our lives: without it one can understand nothing of great art, of philosophy, or of science itself, which is engaged in the search for meaning and attuned to the intellect. But once again the pride of man's tiny mind has risen up against this treasury of goodness, reason, and beauty. Observe this rebellion. How is it sustained? Only by brute force. Talking about Christ is forbidden, the Gospel cannot be printed, Christian churches are forcibly closed. Is this the civility of debate and persuasion? The enemies of Christianity ultimately have no other argument than shameless lies, stultifying propaganda, and police coercion. Some "truth" this is, that is defended against Christianity by such methods! Does this "truth" even believe in itself?

No, it is too soon to discount Christianity and consider it dead. With the same force, with the same joyful conviction as so many centuries ago, a triumphant hymn is heard from the churches: "Thy Nativity, O Christ our God, has shone to the world the light of knowledge." We continue to firmly confess that this honest quest, this thirst for truth and this love for it, sooner or later leads to Christ; for, in the words of the evangelist John, *in him was life; and the life was the light of men. And the light shineth in darkness; and the darkness comprehended it not* (Jn 1.4–5). This affirmation holds for us the most important meaning of the feast of Christ's birth. The light of reason, which once entered the world with Christ and illumined it—this light did not leave us, nor did it go out. No matter how far we progress in studying the world, the finest minds of humanity see in it as before a reflection of divine glory, the light of the divine Mind. The star that led the wise men from the East to the cave in Bethlehem no longer seems a fairy tale, and we again sense the eternal truth of the words of the psalm: *The heavens declare the glory of God, and the firmament proclaims his handiwork* (Ps 18.1).

The world strives for unity. But where is it to be found? In the economy? In saber rattling? In the political rivalry of global superpowers? With increasing clarity a longing grows for that which alone is able to be the heart of all life and its all-illumining light. For humanity has no other heart than Christ: there is no other purpose than the kingdom of God proclaimed by him, and there is no other path to this kingdom than the commandment of love given by him and the perfection manifested in his own person.

It is this cosmic love, this universal light, with which the Nativity of Christ burns and shines upon us. With our spiritual ears we still hear the same triumphant words of praise: *Glory to God in the highest, and on earth peace, good will toward men* (Lk 2.14). With our spiritual sight we still see the same light of knowledge that shone forth in the world, and we respond to this message with grateful praise: "Christ is born—glorify him; Christ is on earth—exalt him; Christ comes from heaven—receive him."[6]

Opening the Shutters

One modern Russian writer describes an elderly person dying after a serious illness. He lies in a room with the shutters closed and painfully seeks to resolve the question: is there anything after death, or not? Finally, exhausted by these doubts, he decides with a sigh: of course, there is nothing; it is as clear as the fact that it is raining outside. "And yet," the writer continues, "a bright spring sun was playing outside the window; while on the floor above a woman was watering the flowers on her windowsill, and the water was falling in noisy drops onto the sidewalk."[7]

This description is surprisingly reminiscent of all the evidence, all the arguments of anti-religious propaganda. To the dying man it was clear that it was raining: he could hear the sound of water. He had no reason to suppose that outside the window it was a jubilant spring day. This symbolizes a certain type of evidence, which is considered scientific and is therefore employed today to solve the most important, profound, and conclusive of questions.

[6]The first hymn from the Matins canon for the Nativity (which paraphrases St Gregory the Theologian, *Oration* 38.1).

[7]Vladimir Nabokov, *The Gift*: "'. . . Of course, then there is nothing.' He sighed, listened to the splashing and gurgling outside the window and repeated unusually distinctly: 'There is nothing. It is as clear as the rain.' Meanwhile, the spring sun was playing on the roof shingles outside the window, the sky was clear and cloudless, and the upper tenant was watering flowers along the edge of her balcony, and the water was gurgling down."

And many people, even believers, swallow this bait of logic and "science." How often, seeing the suffering, chaos, and rampant evil on earth, they ask: "If there were a God, would he really allow all this?" Or: "If there is a God, why then does he not at least in some small but indisputable way reveal himself to us, confirming and proving his existence?" They expect God to answer all these denials, all this propaganda against him. In other words, they want him to stoop to the level of this insignificant dispute.

This is why believers so frequently cite miracles as a decisive argument. A miracle is a violation of the laws of nature, a breach of the supernatural into our lives, and it seems to them to be the "proof," the end-all argument, that will at last overturn all the evidence of the enemies of religion. But it is time we understood that miracles, even if they did once stand at the center of religious consciousness, do not constitute evidence in favor of Christianity. Moreover, Christianity rejects miracles as an argument, as a way of leading people to faith, as the basis of religion. *Let him now come down from the cross, and we will believe him* (Mt 27.42)—thus mocked those who crucified Christ. But he did not come down. If we believe, as Christians have believed for two thousand years, that it was the Son of God who hung upon the cross, would not such a descent from the cross have proven this once and for all? *He trusted in God; let him deliver him now* (Mt 27.43). Yet God did not help him . . .

I am not sure whether Christians themselves are sensitive to or aware of what a fundamental change the Gospel brought about in the very approach to religion as such, in the very depths of religious consciousness. Concerning Christ, for example, the Gospel says that, because of the people's unbelief, *he did not many mighty works there* (Mt 13.58). This means that for Christ himself, miracles—for he did work miracles of love, compassion, and help—were never a self-sufficient phenomenon, a way to prove something or draw someone to himself. That is why for modern detractors of religion, for all those whose evidence is that "it's perfectly clear that . . . ," and "it has been proven that . . . ," etc., not only is it useless to put forward one's own evidence, one's own propaganda, but to do so would mean perverting something most important in Christianity itself.

By hearing ye shall hear, and shall not understand; and seeing ye shall see, and shall not perceive. For this people's heart is waxed gross (Mt 13.14–15) This is the real root and source of unbelief: man himself has become petrified, has closed his heart, and is no longer able to see and to hear, or else sees and hears wrongly. For if he had not grown dull and closed his heart, he would no doubt have called life itself and the world itself a miracle, and held miraculous the blessed ability to see, hear, and breathe, and to sense so clearly in all that exists in the world the presence of infinite love, a call to luminous good, a testament to eternity.

It bears consideration that there are people living among us who, just like us, get up in the morning, dress, and go to work, but whose job, whose daily bread, is to prove that there is no God, and that after death there is nothing, and therefore this whole life is a momentary flash of meaningless being, and that this perception of reality actually "liberates" a person. One is filled with a sense, not even of rancor or anger, but of a kind of sorrowful amazement and genuine pity: how can people live like this? And then we clearly see and physically perceive this hardening of hearts, which cannot be softened, changed by "reverse propaganda," or broken by one's own stones.

And [in Nabokov's story] perhaps the whole point is that in the room of the dying man we discussed, at the moment of his terrible, hopeless conclusion, there was no one to go over to the window and silently open the shutters to reveal the jubilant spring day. And therefore the conclusion to which he came in his dark room seemed to him undeniable and conclusive, when in actuality it was a mistake.

And so it is for millions of people, who do not need proofs and propaganda from us believers, nor tangible evidence, but rather they need light, they need love, and they need goodness. It is essential that in us believers they see not our ideas, our arguments, and proofs, but that new life which provides an encounter with divine reality, with divine life. Only then will the testimony of Christians, the witness of believers in this dark world, where all the shutters are closed, become victorious once again.

A Fruitless Interpretation

R ecently, on the pages of *Literary Russia*, there was an exchange of open letters between Ilya Selvinsky and Lev Ozerov.[8] The subject of this exchange was Selvinsky's new theory of individual immortality, which he had presented in verse and poetry, especially in the poem "The Arctic." Through the words of one of his personages Selvinsky offers a hypothesis based on electron physics:

> Why not
> suppose
> that the recipe for the interaction of electrons
> that gave rise to my breath,
> after tens of millions of years,
> might not by some mistake
> occur again?

Selvinsky seized on this hypothesis and proffers it as a ray of hope. In his warm and even affectionate reply, Lev Ozerov expresses his skepticism: the hypothesis seems unprovable to him, and therefore useless. This is basically the essence of their correspondence. But much in it deserves attention—first and foremost, of course, its subject.

In the fiftieth year since the triumph of the "most scientific" and "all-embracing" ideology, which allegedly liberates man from all deceptions of the past, from all foolish and "unnecessary" questions, two writers admit that they are both infinitely afraid and do not want to die, and that this thought of death turns life into a dark and meaningless abyss. One of them, Ozerov, can think of nothing better and more intelligent than to see the fear of death as a useful incentive for creativity. "The thought of death," he writes, "of its imminent possibility, of its inevitability, is a formidable reminder: *memento mori*, hurry up, do not forget! Without these silent reminders, we would not have the great art of Shakespeare, Dante, Byron,

---

[8] Ilya Lvovich Selvinsky (1899–1968): Russian poet and dramatist. Further quoted in his novel poem "The Arctic," published in 1956. Lev Adolfovich Ozerov (1914–1996): Russian poet, translator and literary scholar. Both letters were printed in *Literary Russia* [Literaturnaya Rossia] 33 (1966): 39.

and Pushkin." That's all. And of course, Selvinsky cannot be reconciled to this—for him, death, as he says, is something "nauseatingly loathsome," and man must not and cannot reconcile himself with it, because it is unnatural for man to deny himself.

And so, I repeat, that this topic even arises is worthy of wonder and special attention, and still more so the powerlessness with which it is treated, as if there were no centuries-old philosophical musings on death, as if there were no final (but far more substantive and convincing) answers to this eternal agonizing question. On the one hand, an incentive to creativity is cited; on the other, a highly improbable accident, which is naturally incapable of offering any real hope. How terribly depressing is this level of philosophy and culture that allows for such an exchange of views—an exchange whose participants are sincerely convinced that they are saying something very brilliant and very new! And this after Plato, after Fedorov with his "Philosophy of the Common Good,"[9] after Bulgakov's theology of death,[10] after John of the Cross,[11] and simply after all of world culture.

But even more telling is the attitude of both thinkers towards religion, which, as though patting it on the shoulder, they simply discount. "The indomitable onslaught of science, the victory of materialism in the world-view of man, decisively overturn naïve tales of a bearded God, of angels and archangels, of paradise and hell," writes Selvinsky, while Ozerov responds in much the same way. I would like to take Selvinsky by the shoulders, look him in the eye, and ask: "Why are you writing this? And first of all, what is this 'indomitable onslaught of science,' what is this 'victory of materialism in man's worldview,' when you express your own worldview with the plaintive cry, 'I adore life and I abhor death,' if your whole worthless

[9]Nikolay Fedorovich Fedorov (1828–1903)—Russian religious thinker and philosopher-cosmologist who taught that overcoming death was the "common duty" of all mankind. "Philosophy of the Common Good" is the name of the collection in which Fedorov's students published a number of his articles and drafts (Vol. 1, 1903; Vol. 2, 1913).

[10]Sergey Nikolaevich Bulgakov (1873–1944) was a Russian philosopher who journeyed from Marxism to a Christian worldview, an economist, theologian, church leader, and Orthodox priest. In 1922 he was exiled from the country by the Bolshevik government. The theme of death is explored, in particular, in his work *Life Beyond the Tomb* (published in Russian in 1955) and *The Sophiology of Death* (published in Russian in 1978–1979).

[11]John of the Cross (1542–1591): Catholic monk, writer. Canonized by the Roman Catholic Church as a "doctor (teacher)" of the Church.

theory is thoroughly saturated with fear? Where is the victory? But still more important is this: you are a poet, you cannot but know, feel, and remember that religion is not 'naïve tales of a bearded God, of angels and archangels,' but something completely different. 'O Life, how dost thou die?'—haven't you heard this staggering beginning of the most beautiful of all church services, the Matins of Holy Saturday, when in the darkness and silence of the night of Pascha we ask the ultimate question and we receive the luminous answer: 'Thou hast destroyed the kingdom of death'?[12] Have you not heard the joyful cry of the Apostle Paul: *The last enemy that shall be destroyed is death* (1 Cor 15.26), and have you not understood that this is not about some 'afterlife,' but about the victory of man over death—a victory won by the whole power of life, love, and faith? You and Ozerov have just now revealed that the 'indomitable onslaught of science' and the 'victory of the materialistic worldview' have actually 'devastated the soul'—these are your words, not mine! Having deprived a person of all hope of an afterlife, science has given him nothing in return. And again I want to ask: what kind of science is this, what kind of worldview, when everything nevertheless turns out to be meaningless and unnecessary, and you, like a drowning man clutching at a straw, seize upon an incredible chance occurrence—the possibility that your 'combination of electrons' may be repeated in ten million years?" What sadness, what vacuous emptiness emanates from this hope and from this entire exchange! It must be frankly admitted: any religious answer is deeper, more intelligent, and philosophically more substantiated.

But in the end, the question of death and immortality is not decided by evidence. Both Ozerov and Selvinsky agree: it is a matter of faith. Selvinsky believes in his unprovable theory, while Ozerov does not, and this is their right. But then we must recognize the right of those who believe not in a "bearded God," but in man's genuine immortality, which depends not on the random coupling of electrons, but on the divinity of the human spirit. We likewise recognize the right of those who with all their souls, with all their hearts, with all their minds know the truth of the Paschal joy—the joy of victory over death. "Christ is risen from the dead, trampling down death

---

[12]"O Life, how canst thou die? How canst thou dwell in a tomb? Yet by thy death thou hast destroyed the reign of death." Verses at the Lamentations (or Praises), Holy Saturday Matins.

by death, and upon those in the tombs bestowing life"[13]—in human terms, this "hypothesis" is no worse than yours, and in any case, it has produced millions of saints and filled millions of hearts with joy. *For to me*, says St Paul, *to live is Christ, and to die is gain* (Phil 1.21)—no, this is not "consolation," as you call it, but faith and joy, which show that this is not a hypothesis, but fact, impervious to all the waves of the materialistic worldview. Here nothing can be "proven," but how very much we might have wished to hear the poet offer not outdated witticisms at religion's expense, but the truth! How we might wish for this argument, which itself proves the indestructibility of the concept of immortality in human consciousness, to arrive at the point where the Christian faith begins!

The exchange of views on the pages of *Literary Russia* between Ilya Selvinsky and Lev Ozerov is a highly symptomatic phenomenon. It proves the very emptiness of the soul of which they both write; it shows that those eternal questions of religion derided by both retain all their significance even for a person committed to the notorious "scientific worldview." It is impossible to simply remove or resolve them without delving deeper into the religious origins of immortality.

Known by Its Fruits

If there is one topic that both believers and unbelievers could discuss especially fruitfully (providing of course that it were an uninhibited, heart-to-heart conversation, without the pressure of communist or other ideologies), it would be the topic of morality.

Morality answers, or perhaps only wishes to answer, the question of how to live, how to properly arrange one's life. Every person, whether a believer or unbeliever, feels within himself this desire to live well, that is, rightly, in accordance with some positive ideal of life. One way or another, everyone is drawn to goodness, to what is good. But what does this positive ideal of life consist of, where does it come from, how can I apply it in my life? These

[13]The troparion of Pascha.

are the questions that man eternally asks himself, to which he never tires of seeking answers. Every philosophical doctrine, every religion sooner or later offers him its own morality, its own ethical system. And perhaps it would be fair to ask each of these systems the question: "Tell me what you want from a man, and I will tell you what you are."

We often hear talk about "communist morality," about the humanism of the communists. Clearly, this system has come up against the same eternal problem, the same relentless question: how should one live? Here we must add that the war on religion is also waged, as a rule, in the name of morality. Christianity, or rather, Christian morality, is accused of amorality, of actually preaching egoism, self-sufficiency, indifference to the human condition, to the suffering of others, to social injustice, to exploitation, etc. Christianity, for its part, makes a series of accusations, also moral in nature, against materialistic ideologies: of inciting hatred, of reducing everything human to "material values," of lack of love, etc. Sometimes these recriminations seem to be a dialogue between the deaf and the dumb. Each has his own clearly defined position, his own understanding of his opponent's position, and refuses to hear anything else. Very often there are unbelievers who say: "Take your monasticism, for example. Is that a moral thing to do? A person abandons everything in order to tend exclusively to his soul. Is this not egotistical, a desertion from the battlefield, indifference to the fate of suffering people? And yet your Church presents monasticism as the highest ideal of life, and thus reinforces religious egoism. And how do you reconcile this with the commandment that you so often cite—Christ's words that there is no greater love than to give your life for your neighbor?"

We must immediately admit that to give a clear, simple, and concise answer to this question is no simple task. The unbeliever appears to be right. But perhaps he only appears so, and his understanding of monasticism is missing the most important thing of all? If so, we should not argue with him, but rather attempt to explain. And for this we need a willingness to listen, a willingness to revise those hackneyed definitions that have proliferated in the world in such abundance, those simplified arguments that make it impossible to understand reality in all its complexity and depth.

"Atheism inevitably leads to a denial of morality, to immorality and crime. If there is no God, then everything is permitted." Such is the conviction of the vast majority of believers. But let us take the French writer Albert Camus, who recently died tragically.[14] He was an unbeliever, yet all his writings comprise a passionate search for an answer to the question: how should one live? One of the heroes of Camus' wonderful novel *The Plague* asks: "How can one be holy without God?" This is the question of the author himself, and it must be admitted that over the past decades in our dark, divided, hate-filled world there have been few such bright and luminous people as the unbelieving Albert Camus.

But one can go even further. Critics of religion often say, "All your good, all your morality is inextricably linked with the doctrine of rewards. Even if you do good, you do so out of a desire to receive a reward and out of fear of being punished, of going to hell. But is such mercenary good truly good? Is this fear of punishment worthy of man?" Once again, merely brushing off this accusation is not so easy. All this means one thing: talking about morality is a conversation worth having. If it is impossible to prove the existence of God as well as his nonexistence, then we can honestly, freely, and openly discuss those ideals of human life that every doctrine offers at its heights and depths—in other words, we can simply try to understand each doctrine's morality. And then we will become convinced that the moral doctrine developed by a particular religion or particular philosophy is, as a rule, very different from how it is variously viewed. We will be further convinced that the basis of all genuine morality is not just a set of rules and regulations, but a holistic and deep-set intuition that encompasses both each individual human life and the life of all mankind. Finally, we will be convinced that morality, that is, this intuition, should be judged not only by texts, but by how it is embodied in the lives of people who adhered to it earnestly and to the end. For here the words of the Gospel are truly applicable: *Ye shall know them by their fruits* (Mt 7.16). Indeed, everything in the world is ultimately known by its fruits—by the reality that results from its ideas and ideologies.

[14]Albert Camus (1913–1960): French writer, whose approach resembled that of the existentialists. The novel *The Plague*, referred to here, was published in 1947.

I repeat: a debate or simply a conversation about morality is an important and long-overdue affair. And it is with this debate and nothing else that one must begin a conversation about religion. Indeed, when we speak about monasticism as an abstract theory, we see one picture; but when we replace this abstraction with reality—St Sergius of Radonezh or St Seraphim of Sarov—the picture is completely different. The fact of the matter is that morality, unlike various theories, does not make much sense on paper. Morality stands or falls, justifies or convicts itself as truth or untruth only in life.

Perhaps, skipping ahead, we ought to say: the whole essence of Christianity is not in its teaching, but only in the fact that this teaching was revealed in the image of a real person, in real life—in Christ. But we will talk more about this later. For now, let us agree that a deep and free discussion of the eternally relevant, eternally agonizing problem, "How should one live and what constitutes a good life?"—is possible and necessary.

The New "Religious War"

"Religion" vs. Religion

A theism is a kind of faith; it is a religion in its own right. It is high time this was understood and admitted by those who without any serious reflection blindly accept the claims of anti-religious propaganda that it wars against religion in the name of an "objective," "scientific" worldview.

In fact, this war is a religious one, and it is waged to ensure the triumph of one religion over another. An atheist is a person who *believes* that there is no God. He believes this in precisely the same way that a religious person believes that God exists. Ultimately, both the one and the other do not act based on evidence and reasoning, but from the deepest aspiration of their whole being, from an internal impulse, from the affirmation of a certain value as universal, primary, and ultimate. In terms of so-called evidence, the atheist can no more prove that God does not exist than the believer can prove he does.

Not a single scientist who even nominally deserves the name, nor a single person who has even a cursory acquaintance with genuine science and its objective methods, will willingly consent for science to be twisted into any kind of propaganda, especially anti-religious. For propaganda and science are mutually exclusive concepts. Therefore, when comparing atheism and religion, it is necessary to compare not evidence, but the experience from which this evidence follows, and, most importantly, those ultimate values, the vision of man and of life, by which this experience is determined, both in the faith of the believer and in the faith of the atheist.

In one of my previous conversations, I quoted the words of the Gospel: "By their fruits you will know them" (Mt 7.16). Yes, only by its fruits—

spiritual, material, cultural—can we evaluate this or that phenomenon and determine its true value.

And so we ask ourselves: what constitutes the ultimate, all-embracing love of the believer, the vision about which one can say in Pushkin's words, "He had only one vision, beyond the mind's grasping"?[1] Naturally, this is a vision of perfection—one in which wisdom, beauty, good, creativity, and freedom merge. This is the reason for Christ's call: *Seek ye first the kingdom of God* (Mt 6.33); that is, desire, love, and strive for that which is truly worthy of desire, love, and striving—that which is the end and fulfillment of all desires. *Be ye therefore perfect, even as your Father which is in heaven is perfect* (Mt 5.48); *For, brethren, ye have been called unto liberty* (Gal 5.13); *A new commandment I give unto you, that ye love one another* (Jn 13.34)—this is the holy of holies, this is the heart of religion! And that this is so, and not otherwise, is witnessed by those who have adopted Christianity earnestly and to the end, making it their life. Such is the testimony of Seraphim of Sarov and his bright Paschal joy; such is the testimony of thousands and thousands of people who have become almost physically permeated with this perfection, this love, this light.

And now we need to ask: how does atheism contrast with all this? What is its "vision"? What is its light? What is its love? This alone is the relevant question, and this alone needs to be asked.

Two Faiths

Whatever people may discuss in earnest, focused debates, ultimately they are seeking the answer to the question: "What is the meaning of life, what are we living for?"

This question ultimately constitutes the theme of culture—that sphere of human activity that is understood as the totality of spiritual quests, creative efforts, and reflection on oneself, in contrast to the philistine life, which is reduced to seeking means of oblivion. Whether we recognize it

[1] From the poem "There Lived a Poor Knight in the World" (1829).

or not, the central fact of human experience is the knowledge that we are all mortal. "I will die" is the only irrefutable statement that I am able to make. Everything else in my life, including what will happen to me in five minutes, is shrouded in obscurity. There is therefore a grain of truth in the assertion by anti-religious propaganda that religion is sustained by the fear of death, by man's inability to bear the fact of his incomprehensible but inevitable end.

We must add to this, however, that not only religion, but in a sense all of culture and all the values it embodies, are also permeated with an awareness of death's inevitability. We might say that a person's childhood ends at the moment when he realizes his mortality. The child is completely unaware of this, and so he dwells amid the most complete, most unalloyed happiness—a happiness that knows nothing of its transient nature. The worldview of an adult (and this applies to all eras and cultures) is determined by the awareness that he is mortal, which is why for him the question of decisive importance is, "What is the meaning of this life, which will inevitably end?" Therefore, everything he does is ultimately an attempt to somehow overcome the pointlessness and horror of his own doom. What Pushkin said—"No, I will not wholly die"[2]—is what everyone would like to say. Therefore, any study of man, of human society, of human culture that does not take into account this tragic depth, this tragic dimension, is an incomplete and ultimately false study. For, I repeat, it is not only religion that speaks of death, it is not alone in trying to explain it, to reconcile people with it. Any ideology does the same, if its purpose and objective are to reveal to man the goal of his life and his work. That is why ideology seeks the same end—to reconcile man with his mortal destiny and to find justification for his brief existence.

We are told that the harm of religion lies in the fact that, by transferring the center of gravity elsewhere, to the afterlife, it tears a person from cares for this present world and makes him indifferent to this life. But the very same thing can be said, for example, about Marxist ideology, in which the goal of human life is defined as working to attain an ideal "society of the future." Indeed, this ideal future is also a different world, a sort of "afterlife,"

[2]From the poem "I have erected a monument to myself, not made by hands . . ." (1836).

because those who are now building it and dying for it do not experience it themselves and do not participate in it. Does religion call men to renounce much in the present for the sake of the future? All ideologies focused on ideal values in the future likewise require the same. The French writer Marcel Proust, an unbeliever, literally drove himself to death by the inhuman efforts he made to complete his famous novel, *In Search of Lost Time*,[3] because for him this novel meant overcoming his own death, by finding immortality in creativity.

Therefore, the dispute, the eternal debate is not about the afterlife, not about whether it exists or not, but about what a person sees as his ultimate purpose, or, more simply, how he overcomes the absurdity of death. The debate is about the reality and the substance of the ideal by which a person lives and for which he is ready to give his life. Man is essentially religious. And if he refuses the religion of the transcendent, that is, of a God who rules creation, it is then necessary to accept the religion of an immanent god, which can be socialism, history, culture—anything. And in both instances we have the projection of human life into some kind of ideal, into an ideal future, not provided to us by everyday experience. In other words, in both cases we see that faith, and thus only faith, whatever may be its object, according to the Gospel, moves mountains (cf. Mt 21.21). It is high time to understand that materialism is also faith, because to say that it is possible to build an "ideal society" on its basis means to make an a priori religious judgment.

The objects of faith may be different, but faith as a movement of human consciousness is the same. Therefore, this dispute in the world is not between faith and unbelief, but between different faiths. Those who do not believe in anything are mere opportunists, dodgers, and philistines, who ultimately fall out of the sphere of human morality.

The peculiar feature of our era is not that it is less religious than other eras, because that is not true, but that in contrast to them our era does not have a common object of faith, a common system of religious values, unconditionally accepted by all. Oddly enough, our era is an era of

---

[3]The series of novels *In Search of Lost Time* (*À la recherche du temps perdu*) is the main work of Marcel Proust (1876–1922), who repeatedly reworked the last parts of the series.

a new religious war, because in it different religious ideals clash, different understandings of the meaning of human life. Previous religious wars were decided by fire and the sword, and we know that this approach failed—in our time, in any case, it is impossible. For if anything can be considered proven, it is the complete impossibility of destroying or silencing ideas. The superiority of ideas over force is, in fact, one of the amazing discoveries of this new era. Therefore, if in the final analysis different theories about the meaning and purpose of human life collide, the only useful battleground between them is free and open debate. For in this battle the only answer that will win is the one which is able to embrace the whole infinite depth of human longing and thirst. And this is precisely what the Gospel calls for: *Seek, and ye shall find; knock, and it shall be opened unto you* (Mt 7.7).

The Debate About God and Gods

Between the assertions 'There is a God' and 'There is no God,' Chekhov once wrote in his notebook, "there lies a huge gap, and it may be crossed only with great difficulty and effort. And so only foolish people think that this is easy."[4]

I quote from memory, but that is the gist of it. Both superficial faith and superficial atheism are equally unconvincing. Many people say, "I believe in God," but they actually live as if there were no God, and this means that their faith is essentially no faith at all, but a habitual nod to a tradition that does not really concern them. Likewise, many so-called unbelievers are quite satisfied with elementary arguments such as this: "Science has proven that there is no God." Nobody knows what this means, nor do they care how science can solve this problem, which is quite outside its sphere. But someone invented the phrase, another repeated it, and this meaningless phrase is presented as a substantiated statement and gets enshrined in textbooks.

[4]Cf. "Between 'there is God' and 'there is no God' lies an enormous field, which the true sage crosses with great difficulty. The Russian man knows one of these two extremes, but the middle ground between them does not interest him; and therefore he usually does not know anything or very little" (A. P. Chekhov, *Notebooks*, Book One).

Meanwhile, as I already said in a previous conversation, the question of faith can in some sense be methodologically separated from the question of the object or content of this faith. And we must start with the indisputable fact that all people believe in something, or, in any case, those who do not believe in anything at all are considered by most people to be defective and helpless beings. One would think that from the standpoint of atheism, which claims to be "scientific" (that is, built entirely on logic and experience), a statement such as "this man does not believe in anything" would be high praise: "Here is a man who is finally freed himself from the foolishness of all beliefs and has come to a truly scientific understanding of the world!" But we have only to open the biography of any revolutionary leader, and we will read on every page that he "deeply believed" in the triumph of ideals, in the triumph of his class, etc. Concerning Chekhov, whom we just mentioned, in the boring preface to the complete collection of his works, we read that he "believed in a brighter future."

So tell me, why is faith in an unknown "bright future" not only allowed, but even extolled, while faith in God and the future life is considered a stupid and harmful superstition? This is simply a hypocritical double standard: you have the right to believe, but only in what you are ordered to believe. Yet after all, the basis of the scientific worldview, the basis of genuine atheism should be, it would seem, a denial of faith—of faith as such, of faith as belief in anything that does not stem from direct experience and knowledge. From the point of view of direct experience and knowledge, ideals and goals such as "freedom," "equality," and "brotherhood" are just as utopian and unprovable as the Kingdom of God. Why then, one might ask, are the books of self-proclaimed inveterate atheists filled with references to faith and exhortations to believe? Why are the biographies of their heroes and leaders, like their party platforms, saturated with essentially religious terminology? The answer is clear: without faith, a person not only will not hear all this, but also will not understand it.

A man who believes in nothing is an animal, one that subjects everything to the lowest and grossest instincts of his body. A man without faith is a nihilist who denies that there is any meaning in life and lives for the moment. This clearly and irrefutably demonstrates that everything that somehow elevates a person above this animalistic, egotistic, nihilistic emptiness is faith. It is therefore necessary to recognize faith to be just as much an inalienable property of man as the desire for knowledge, the ability to love, etc., yet at the same time a property that is entirely different from all others, since it does not arise from the data of direct experience, from a direct perception of reality as such. From a logical point of view, faith is an irrational concept, but it expresses what really exists and without which a person simply forfeits his humanity.

Only by acknowledging this assertion can we go further and inquire into the content and direction of faith. Only now can we ask a person the only correct question, the only one that is worthy of him: "What do you believe in?" Observe: not with the question, "Do you believe or not?"—to which official anti-religious propaganda wants to reduce the whole matter—but, I repeat, with the question: "What do you believe in?" For there is no doubt that he believes in something, and only the question of what he believes in is productive and can elicit any real answer.

Now suppose for a moment that we refer to the object of faith—of any faith—as God. Now, the word *God* is ambiguous and can mean many different objects of faith. Any faith, as we have seen, is directed toward a certain absolute, toward something perfect. To say, "I believe in the triumph of freedom," or justice, or equality, or a classless society, means to acknowledge and profess that all these values are recognized by me as supreme and absolute. And if for the sake of simplicity we refer to any higher and absolute value—since it does not follow from experience and knowledge, but from faith—as "God," then the question we are addressing to another person can be clarified: "Which God do you believe in? What or who is your God?" And the argument between believers then turns into a debate about gods. Does that which you call "God" deserve this name as a truly supreme and absolute value? Is it worthy of faith?

When Christianity was born, its preaching was addressed not to atheists, but to people who believed in something, and in their own way quite deeply. But this is precisely why Christianity addressed them with these words: "What you believe in is not God, but an idol, a false god, and that means you are victims of deception." And now, having declared that the modern world, in the words of the ancient Greek poet, is "full of gods," it must be acknowledged that most of these gods are idols. It is therefore high time to ask: to what does each of us give our heart? For on this basis, and on it alone, a real debate about religion can begin. Indeed, there can be no doubt that all people have some kind of faith, some kind of religion, in one way or another. In our time, the question is one of true religion—of what in our life deserves worship, what deserves the name of God.

The Origin of All Things

The Main Theme

The essence of all religion lies in God alone. Here is what needs to be understood by everyone involved in the long-running debate about religion. Everything else in it is secondary. In a certain sense, one might even agree with the famous formula of Marx: "Religion is the opium of the people,"[1] while on the other hand, if desired, one can easily prove the social and political benefits of religion, and both these arguments will be based on facts. And yet, in actuality, religion begins where a person ceases to think about profit and loss, moves beyond himself, so to speak, and rises above his own limited sphere, his own inevitably limited "I."

"God" is a word all humans employ. It is written, spoken, translated into different languages, analyzed from a philological point of view. But this word has evolved in human language to denote what lies behind all other words, that which does not fully fit into words, which explodes from within their narrow literal or social meaning, leading a person out of the captivity of earthly categories.

The falsehood of the foes of religion, as well as the error of its defenders, is that both the former and the latter often talk about it without any reference to that which alone constitutes its essence. And its essence lies precisely in this experience, in the experience of God and the divine, in this breakthrough to what lies above and beyond. Without this, all talk of religion is meaningless, like the study of musical notes without any concept

---

[1] "Religion is the opium of the people"—the formula of Karl Marx, usually quoted out of context. Compare: "Religious decline is at the same time an expression of real decline and a protest against this real decline. Religion is the sigh of an oppressed creature, the heart of a heartless world, just as it is the spirit of soulless traditions. Religion is the opium of the people."

of the sounds that they represent. But no matter what is said, no matter how people argue about religion in societal or even scientific and philosophical terms, one thing is clear: there has never been an era or a culture in which man did not feel and experience the mysterious presence of the One who in human language is called God. No discoveries, no flights into space can either abolish or debunk this mysterious experience, just as they do not abolish or debunk, say, the experience of love. Science can reveal much about love, but it will never say anything about its very essence, about the miracle of our own transformation when we love. And no science can ever say anything about the miracle of faith. For what is meant by the statements, "There is a God" or "There is no God"? After all, God is not one of the things that can be said either to exist or not. God is an experience of that transcendence that gives a new depth, a new transformative meaning to all our words and ideas, yet does not fit into them.

Even ancient Christian thinkers spoke of "apophatic" or negative theology—that is, about theological doctrine in which experience is what is most reliable, and the presence of God is expressed in negations: "God is not this and not that, but we know that he exists." We also know that throughout world history souls have been ignited with such joy and such light that words were inadequate to express their experience. We know that in sounds, colors, and words man has always tried to express this joy and this light, and that no forces in the world have ever succeeded in destroying this experience.

In this, and only in this, lies the main theme of religion.

Universal Knowledge

*A*nd this is life eternal, that they might know thee the only true God, and Jesus Christ, whom thou hast sent (Jn 17.3).

These words of Christ, recorded in the Gospel of John, give perhaps the most accurate, most complete, most profound definition of the very essence of the Christian faith. In the preceding conversation I spoke about the need to distinguish faith as knowledge from that knowledge, or rather that part of knowledge, that is now called "scientific" knowledge. I said that the chief and truly tragic mistake of many of our contemporaries is their constant reduction of all knowledge available to man to the discursive and empirical method of the natural sciences alone. Only by recognizing the limitations of this type of knowledge as only one area, albeit a very important one, of empirical experience—experience accessible to measurement, laboratory reproduction, and mathematical analysis—only by recognizing this limitation can one turn to other types and fields of knowledge and, above all, faith. For faith, of course, is knowledge, and, as Christianity claims, it is the highest knowledge. More than this, it is a knowledge that gives eternal life. But this knowledge is inaccessible to empirical analysis, calculation, and even description in so-called scientific categories.

What then does this knowledge consist of? Since this knowledge is not rational, how can it be transmitted from one person to another? Finally, how can one prove that such knowledge exists at all? I think that it is necessary first of all to try to answer this last question, because in the confusion of words and concepts in which we live and which is promoted by primitive anti-religious propaganda, this question usually raises the most doubts and objections. In its simplest form, this question is familiar to every person: does God exist or not? This is the famous problem of the so-called evidence of God's existence. I say, "There is a God," while you say, "There is no God." But what do this statement and rebuttal actually mean? Both of them presume, obviously, some kind of knowledge, which in one case can be expressed by the formula, "I know that God exists," and in the other, "I know that there is no God." But what is this knowledge? Its negative formula is proven, as I have already said, by reducing knowledge to "scientific knowledge." In expanded form, it goes like this: "Knowledge is always scientific knowledge, that is, knowledge of something that can be measured, studied, and connected with other existing objects; further, no science, no experiment, no measurement could ever detect the object we call God; ergo, no such object exists. If neither physics, nor chemistry, nor biology, nor economics, nor any other science can even imagine a thing called God, and furthermore have no need of him, we have sufficient grounds to say that there is no God and that we know this for a fact." This, in short, is the essence of the proof that there is no God. And from this point of view, it is quite logical for a cosmonaut to declare that he was in the heavens and saw no God there; for the heavens have always been thought of as the abode of God (consider even the Lord's prayer: "Our Father, who art in the heavens . . .").

But if I am right in denying the legitimacy of simply equating knowledge with this kind of "scientific knowledge," and if I am right in asserting that not only God, but many other things connected with man and the world around him are beyond the sphere of the natural sciences, then all this proof collapses, loses all value, and turns out to be illusory. In this case, the statement "I know that God exists" must likewise be attributed to another plane of knowledge and another plane of experience. I say "experience," for indeed there is no knowledge, nor could there be, without experience, without "self-contained" knowledge, so to speak. Knowledge is always the relation of the subject to the object, and the relation caused by the effect of the object on the subject. I can say, "I see." But in order for me to see, there must be something to see; and for me to hear, one way or another, what I hear must make a sound.

And so the first and most important argument in favor of faith as knowledge is, of course, the universality of religious experience. We say universality not only in the sense that at all times and in every place there have been people who believe in God, but also in the sense of the most profound unity of this experience. Indeed, even from the most secular scientfic standpoint, if the same phenomenon is repeated and is present under a variety of conditions, irrespective of time and space, then it can legitimately be argued that this phenomenon has a common cause. If so many people of different origins, at vastly different stages of cultural, economic, and political development, believed and continue to believe in God; if, further, their experience coincides in its chief aspects and can be reduced to several fundamental statements; and if, finally, no changes in external conditions have ever led to a radical cessation of this experience as a universal phenomenon; then this experience cannot possibly be without cause. Likewise, this basis cannot possibly be other than that which all those who have this experience acknowledge it to be and by which they live.

Here, again, in concise form, is the rationale for the formula "I know that God exists," or an explanation of faith as knowledge. True, several significant objections remain, particularly the following: "You speak of the universality and unity of the experience of God, and yet there are a great many religions that reject each other." That is true. But one can offer this analogy: "In the world there are an infinite number of languages, and for most people the majority of languages are completely incomprehensible. But language as a phenomenon is universal, and a comparative study of languages reveals the unity of their structures." In other words, differences do not negate or exclude unity, since all differences are differences within some primordial unity.

So it is with religions. Differences between them exist within their basic unity. And it is about this unity, expressed in the formula "I know that God exists," that we have been speaking.

We come, therefore, to some very important conclusions. Religion, or faith, is knowledge that is as much based on experience as knowledge in the natural sciences. Further, this experience is not isolated, but like the experience of nature it is universal. Finally, this experience always and everywhere leads to the same statement: "I know that God exists." Only now can we go further and attempt to look inside this experience.

Proof from Light

In the old days, so-called proofs of the existence of God were recorded in textbooks of theology and philosophy. Later, not only unbelievers, but even believers themselves rejected them, acknowledging these proofs as inadequate, or rather ill-suited to their purpose. If one believes in God, this is precisely why one does not "prove" him, because by its very nature faith needs no proof. There is no need to believe in the table of multiplication, precisely because it is entirely built on evidence. Thus, faith can be defined as knowledge that does not need rational evidence, or as knowledge that cannot be proven. I repeat, both believers and unbelievers agree with this.

And only on the basis of this agreement can the main question be posed, whose answer separates believers and enemies of faith. I am talking specifically about faith's enemies, because outside the faith there are many who doubt, vacillate, or do not believe simply because they lack faith, but have no desire to eradicate the faith of others. Active enemies of the faith, however, claim that there is no God and that this can be proven. And this invites the question: how can one prove the absence or nonexistence of something or someone whose existence cannot be proven, when the concept of "God" by its very nature excludes the possibility of proof or disproof?

Believers say, "Our only evidence here is our faith." And if the enemies of faith were to say, "But for us our proof is our unbelief," that would be honest and simple. But no; they argue that the absence of God can be proved "scientifically," and that it has already been proven. But how is it proven? If they cite to the fact that "no one has ever seen God," the Apostle John the Evangelist, an ardent believer, stated the same thing (Jn 1.18). If they reduce God to the category of objects subject to scientific scrutiny, this contradicts the concept of God as being outside and beyond all matter. In other words, if it is impossible to scientifically prove the existence of God, it is equally impossible to scientifically prove his nonexistence. It is therefore high time for so-called scientific atheistic propaganda to stop disgracing itself with ridiculous arguments, because in this question it lags a hundred years behind religion, which does not pretend to prove what cannot be proven.

But does this mean that every possibility for dispute or dialogue between faith and unbelief ends here? On the contrary, only when faith and unbelief are convinced of the impossibility of imposing themselves by force or by the irrelevant appeal to the authority of science, only then does it become possible to really talk about faith. For the object of such a conversation will, of course, be not God himself, but faith in God. But the existence of faith and, moreover, its universality, in all eras of human history and in all cultures, is not difficult to prove. That religion is a universal phenomenon is impossible to dispute.

What is faith? Here again, atheistic propaganda resorts to fraud. It almost never talks about the content of faith, about the experience of faith, about what distinguishes a believer from an unbeliever, but always either about what atheism claims to be the cause of religion, or about the moral short-comings of believers. We immediately discard the second argument, for no one talks about their shortcomings and sins more than believers themselves. We are currently in the season of Lent, and in the churches we hear words of heart-wrenching lamentation, crying out in repentance: "We have sinned, we have transgressed, we have done evil in thy sight. We have not observed or kept thy commandments."[2]

No, there is no point in talking about the shortcomings of believers, for everything has been said about them even in the Gospel itself—for example, in Christ's bitter lament: *When the Son of man cometh, shall he find faith on the earth?* (Lk 18.8)

But equally unconvincing and essentially false is the conversation about the causes of religion. Any complex phenomenon in the world has not one, but thousands of causes. And the old argument that religion is born of ignorance, fear, and exploitation does not stand up to criticism today. "Ignorance"—but ideological censorship has to hide the fact that professors and scientists believe in God. "Fear"—but people have always been ready to die for their faith. "Exploitation"—but the so-called classless society[3] is now in its fiftieth year, and yet religion lives, and if it were not for police brutality and open persecution it would thrive even more. All these expla-nations are worthless, and, of course, we should spend time not on them, but on the content, or rather the experience, of faith.

And here we come to the what is most important. For if we judge this experience by its best representatives, once again there can be no doubt that this experience is positive, bright, and joyful. I cannot and do not want to say that this experience "proves" the existence of God. But I can and will say that humanity has produced nothing higher, purer, brighter, and better than these righteous ones—the true witnesses of faith. And, of course, it is no coincidence that anti-religious propaganda never talks about this. It spends considerable energy trying to prove that there was no Christ, but it

---

[2]Great Canon of St Andrew of Crete, Irmos of the seventh ode. The Church appoints the reading of this canon in the first and fifth weeks of Lent.

[3]This dates Schmemann's broadcast to the mid 1960s.

will never explain what attracts millions of people to him. It will never say that if he had existed, he would be the best human being of all time; it will never quote his words: *Greater love hath no man than this, that a man lay down his life for his friends* (Jn 15.13). And if he was invented, the very existence of such an image among us nevertheless remains a fact that is beyond all comparison.

And so, in every generation throughout the earth, we see people who live with such joy, such love, such power of faith, that for a time the world is illumined by them. Here we see the radiant elder Seraphim of Sarov coming out of his forest cell, and all around him is joy and light. Proof? No, the facts. And only these facts are worth discussing, worth debating, because faith is not a proof, not a theory, but a living example of a person who suddenly feels in himself an indescribable light, indescribable joy, and speaks words that no propaganda can counter: "Great art thou, O Lord, and marvelous are thy works, and there is no word that suffices to praise thy wonders!"[4]

Evidence from Fullness

Perhaps nothing so reveals to us the very essence of faith, its experience and joy, as does the feast of the Transfiguration. We are told: "Faith arises out of fear, out of slavery, out of dissatisfaction; religion comes from a lack of one thing or another. Hence, when prosperity and peace ensue, faith must fade away as a thing irrelevant."

No, friends, you are mistaken, and you deliberately or unconsciously deceive those who still believe you. In fact, faith arises not from want, but from excess, from a fullness of joy. Here on a sunny summer morning a boy runs out into the garden. And everything around him is so beautiful—the sun and the sky, the morning light and the flowers—that he skips, laughs, and shouts, "How good it all is!" This is only a faint image of faith, but the analogy is accurate. And the Gospel relates how Christ took three disciples

---

[4] From the rite of the Great Blessing of Water (prayer of the priest).

with him and climbed a mountain. And there, on the mountain, his face was transformed, and his clothes shone with light. And Peter, one of the disciples, said, *Lord, it is good for us to be here* (Mt 17.4) But then the little boy said the same thing in the garden that morning, and each of us repeats the same thing on the happiest and brightest days of our own lives.

We are constantly pressed to lay out the content of our faith in "strictly scientific" terms. But can science determine the joy of the morning and the sun, of love, and indeed of life itself? No, and no one expects this from it, because science has its own tasks, its own purpose. The Gospel narrative is conveyed in a mysterious language of a distinctly different order. On that mountain top, in the purity and pristine beauty of the world, the state that mankind has been called to was shown—pure joy, light, and fullness. It is a fullness where nothing else is needed, and it remains only to say: "Lord! it is good for us to be here!"

This is the experience of faith. And whoever has experienced this at least once in his life cannot be convinced otherwise: he was on that mountain; he saw, felt, and remembers that light.

Believers can be destroyed, but not belief. You can isolate children from Church and worship, you can forbid reading or even printing the Gospel, you can push the Church to the sidelines, you can print "exposés" about drunken priests and mercenary bishops, you can deploy the state apparatus, the army, the police—all this can be done. But no force in the world can kill faith, just as it is impossible to kill the eternal, undying light of love. Faith will remain and will destroy all barriers. In this world of violence and cruelty, always and everywhere there will be people who can say: "Lord! It is good for us to be here!"—people who can discern in all things that light that shone on earth on the day of the Transfiguration, a gleam of which remains on the earth to this day.

One thing alone can be said about the war on religion: it is waged in vain.

The Possibility of the Impossible

W hen reciting the Creed, which is a summary of what they believe,
Christians always mention Pontius Pilate.

Pontius Pilate was the Roman governor of Palestine when Jesus Christ
was preaching. His name and term of service in Palestine are duly recorded
in the annals of Roman history, and thus there can be no doubt of his historical existence.

I begin by mentioning Pilate because his inclusion in the Creed—which
states that Christ was crucified "under Pontius Pilate"—directly links the
faith of Christians with history and geography. Indeed, the belief that at a
certain point in history, in a certain place on the globe, an event occurred
that was not merely important, but exceptional, and incomparable to any
other—the coming into the world, the birth in the form of an infant, of
God himself—this belief comprises a paradoxical feature of Christianity.

Of course, other religions can also be connected with history to a greater
or lesser degree. For example, Muslims believe in the calling and special
role of the prophet Muhammad, the Jews consider their history to be the
history of God's chosen people, and even Buddhists link themselves to the
quasi-historical person of the Buddha. But only Christianity for almost
two thousand years has claimed as the very core, the holy of holies of its
faith, that the man Jesus, born in Bethlehem of Judea under King Herod,
who suffered and died a shameful death thirty years later under Pontius
Pilate—that this Jesus is God incarnate, who became man to forever unite
the human race with him, to save humanity from sin and death, and to
draw it into eternal life and eternal joy. This faith does not cease to amaze
skeptics. There has never been a time when people who lived by so-called
common sense, by a scientific worldview, etc., have not asked with sincere
perplexity how one can believe all this. One should not think, therefore,
that this question arose only in our days, that only "modern science" (as
the atheistic propaganda in particular asserts) has argued that all this was
fiction, superstition, and legend. The book of the Acts of the Apostles, one
of the earliest texts of Christianity, says that when the Apostle Paul came to

Athens and began to tell the philosophers there about Christ, *some mocked, and others said, "We will hear thee again of this matter"* (Acts 17.32). And so it has always been: there have always been people who considered Christian teaching to be beyond all credibility, and therefore false, always rejecting it in the name of "common sense" and of their sciences.

On the other hand, there have always been people who not only accepted this doctrine, but even considered it the apex of wisdom, the ultimate answer to all human questions, the pinnacle of all philosophy, all knowledge, and all science. There were people like this in the first century of our era, and there are a great many such people today. And no one can prove that the the progressive and the educated always sided with unbelief, while only ignoramuses and simpletons sided with belief. We need not look far: we need only take our own history. We know that Pushkin, Gogol, and Dostoevsky believed that Christ was God, who came into the world; the academician Pavlov believed; the former luminaries of Marxism Bulgakov, Berdyaev,[5] Struve,[6] and many, many others believed. And so in answer to the question, "How can anyone believe that?" some have answered: "It's impossible," while others have answered: "There is nothing more sublime, more beautiful, and more wise than this faith; everything leads to it, and it answers all questions."

One cannot even say that the number of believers is declining. There was a time when it seemed that the intelligentsia believed less, and so-called common people more. But now it's the other way around: the intelligentsia is increasingly returning to faith, while less educated people still repeat the ridiculous statement: "Science has proven that there is no God," as though there were a science whose purpose was to prove something in this area. Whereas in former times education often led people away from faith, now on the contrary it is increasingly leading them to God. Therefore, the question: "How can anyone believe this?" is ultimately a pointless question: if people believe, apparently it is possible.

[5] Nikolai Alexandrovich Berdyaev (1874–1948): Russian philosopher, religious thinker, and publicist. In 1922 he was exiled from the country by the Bolshevik government.

[6] Peter Bernhardovich Struve (1870–1944): Russian philosopher, economist, writer, publicist, social and political activist, member of the White movement. Exiled in 1920.

What is far more important is to find out *what* exactly these people believe—why they not only consider their faith compatible with scientific knowledge, common sense, and modernity, but even see in it the crown of all knowledge, the highest meaning of everything, and the thing most necessary for modern man. And in answering this question, we need to start not with the question of what is possible or not. For if medieval people had been told that man would one day fly across the ocean in a matter of hours, they would also have objected that this was impossible. Yet it proved possible after all. The unbeliever says, "There is no God, and therefore the assertion that God became a man is nonsense." From his point of view, he is of course right—if there is no God, then by the same token everything that is said about him is, to various degrees, nonsense.

But suppose that God exists, that there actually is an Origin of all principles; that there is a Higher Intelligence, the source of all reason; that there is a Higher Good, the measure of all good; that there is a Higher Life, the source of all life. And if God exists, if he is the Source, the Origin, and the Measure of all knowledge, goodness, beauty, and love, then why is it impossible that he should have revealed himself to people in earthly history, in human form, as an image of love, perfection, and suffering? Moreover, if God exists, then not only is all this not impossible, but on the contrary it corresponds to the basic human intuition that God is perfect Good, perfect Beauty, perfect Love, and therefore to reveal himself to people in love, beauty, and goodness is natural for him.

Christ's teaching and his very image cannot be deduced from any materialism or from any science. Impossible—yet this teaching and this image are present in the world. And yet it is this possibility of the impossible, the reality of the unimaginable, the fulfillment of the unbelievable, which we celebrate at Christmas. Again and again we affirm that this is the core and depth of human self-understanding, that this is the beginning of the divine vocation of man.

Historical Figure, Lord, and Teacher

Why does atheist propaganda, which claims to represent science, persist in claiming that Christ is a mythical figure, that he never existed? After all, not a single self-respecting historian shares this theory, and these words are repeated only by those who are ordered to repeat them without employing any authentic scientific method. This is to say nothing of the fact that if Christ had not existed, the existence of Christianity should be acknowledged an unheard-of miracle—far greater than the miracles described in the Gospel.

Christianity appears in history suddenly, spreading for some thirty years. A network of Christian communities soon encompasses all the major cities of the Roman Empire. At the end of the first century, the Roman historian Tacitus (not a Christian, but an enemy of Christianity) already relates what is reported in the Gospel: that Christ lived in Palestine and suffered under Pilate. But Pilate is not a myth: many in Tacitus' day still remembered him. And all the names of people and cities in the Gospel are clearly historical, which does not happen in myths and myth making.

But suppose we set aside historical evidence, despite its irrefutability. Let us consider this need to prove at all costs that Christ never existed. After all, it would have been much simpler to say, "Christ existed, but we do not believe in his teaching, for it is false, it is evil." But no; this is precisely what they do *not* say, and they do not say it because no one has ever made bold to say such a thing directly about Christ's teaching. This would mean calling the doctrine of love, forgiveness and compassion, human brotherhood and solidarity, evil. After all, the Gospel is replete with precisely this doctrine, and Christ did not teach anything else. It is enough to read this book once to be convinced that everything in it is about love for others, everything is permeated with and inspired by this love. A bruised child shoves the chair he has bumped into and angrily shouts, "Go away, I don't want you!" But the chair still stands. In the same way, in the recesses of their souls people who do not want love, who fear it like fire and preach hatred, swat at this little book and shout, "You don't exist!"

But the book remains, and countless souls have been reading it for two thousand years, and despite everything they draw strength from it to live and believe that true happiness is only in love, that love is not a deception, but strength, victory, and joy. At all times, some believed that Christ was God, and some did not. But both believed him—that is, they believed that his teaching is the measure of humanity.

Suppose for a moment that Christ never existed. But then we must admit that there was someone else who said everything that Christ said, who brought people an amazing teaching about sin and forgiveness, about new life, freedom, and love, who invented this death on the cross, and the soldiers who mocked the crucified one, and his Mother who stood by the cross. And the one who invented this must therefore be acknowledged as a unique and irreplaceable teacher. And again we arrive at the same conundrum.

But Christ did exist. And for people who have heard his teachings and try to live by them at least a little, he still remains their teacher and Lord, appealing to that one thing that is worthy of man.

Renewing Faith in the Invincibility of Goodness

Believer," "unbeliever"—what essentially abstract words these are! We say them as if the believer always believes, all the time, and as if the unbeliever lives all the time by his unbelief. In the Gospel, the father of a sick child rushes to Christ with the words, *Lord, I believe; help thou mine unbelief* (Mk 9.24), and in these words there is more truth about man, about profound, genuine truth, than in all abstract debates about faith and unbelief. Here in the courtyard of the high priest the Apostle Peter renounced Christ three times, and Christ looked at him, and Peter remembered how he had promised Christ to die with him, and it is said of him that *he went out and wept bitterly* (Mt 26.75). And finally, Christ himself in his death throes turns to God with these terrible words: *My God, my God! Why hast thou forsaken me?* (Mt 27.46).

What is all our "evidence" worth in comparison with these examples? The believer demonstrates his faith as a thing self-evident, while the unbeliever demonstrates the truth of his unbelief with equal precision. But the believer, if only he is truthful with himself, knows that too often he lives as though there were no God; too often in the bustle and noise of life at times he loses and squanders his faith. And in some unbelievers there is more godly sorrow, more longing for light and truth, than in some self-satisfied Pharisees among believers.

This is why all disputes about faith and unbelief are so empty, so pointless in the final analysis. For faith has never yet been produced in anyone by evidence and arguments. It has not even been produced by miracles. The Gospel is full of stories about the miracles of Christ, but why did everyone ultimately end up abandoning and betraying him? Yet when there was no miracle, when, abandoned by all, he died on the cross, the centurion who had crucified him exclaimed, *Truly this was the Son of God* (Mt 27.54).

I recall another biblical story—about the prophet Elijah, who was told that he would see God. And at first there was a great strong wind, but God was not in the wind; and then there was a fire, and God was not in the fire; and finally, as the Bible wondrously relates, *a still small voice* (1 Kg 19.12), and God was in that still small voice. There was, in other words, a quiet voice, a breath, a touch of something or Someone at the door of the human soul; there was a mysterious encounter.

And all of Christianity speaks of this kind of faith, and its essence lies precisely in this. It is not about thunder, nor about wind, nor about fire. And it often reaches only that person who can, as the Gospel again says, "receive it," that is, who can accept the mysterious words: "The wind blows where it wills . . . but you do not know where it comes from and where it goes" (cf. Jn 3.8), who is able to hear the unprecedented news of the servile guise of the King of Heaven, the incredible Gospel of a humble God.

These thoughts come to mind when you read and listen to debates about religion, when boasting over victories and triumphs abounds on both sides. Strength versus strength, propaganda versus propaganda, hatred versus hatred, and—all too often—evil versus evil. But all of Christianity claims that evil cannot destroy evil, it cannot defeat hatred: all this is what the Gospel calls "this world," about which it has long been said that it *lieth in wickedness* (1 Jn 5.19). And is it not time for us who call ourselves believers to recall this core paradox of Christianity—that only the cross triumphs, by its invincible and unstoppable strength, its unique beauty, and its breathtaking depth? Christ did not come to save us either by force or by external victory, but rather he commanded us to know of what spirit we are, to have the power of the cross within us. And it is astounding that even now, wherever religion is attacked, only those who confront power with the truth, hatred only with love and sacrifice, and the cacophony of propaganda with that same "still, small voice"—only these know the peace and light of genuine faith. And only their voice is heard above the noise, only their light shines in the darkness, and this light really cannot be overcome by the darkness (cf. Jn 1.5).

Vladimir Soloviev once wrote a book with the paradoxical title *The Justification of the Good.*[7] In it he clearly showed that the weakness of Christians is almost always that they themselves do not believe in the good that they preach, and when the time comes to fight evil, they confront it with the same evil, the same hatred. The time has come therefore to justify the good, and this means to once more believe in its power, in its inner and divine invincibility. It is time to counter the world that lies in evil not with miracles, not with power, and not with bread, as in Dostoevsky's legend of the Grand Inquisitor,[8] but with that exultant image of goodness, love, hope, and faith—from the absence of these mankind is perishing. And only by internally justifying the good and believing in it can we begin to triumph once again.

In these post-Paschal days the churches still resound with the hymn, "Christ is risen from the dead, trampling down death by death and upon those in the tombs bestowing life." Death by death, for even before his own resurrection he fills this worst of all evils—death and destruction—with goodness, love, sacrifice, and selflessness. He fills death itself with Life. And when he destroys death, then and only then comes the luminous morning

[7]Vladimir Sergeyevich Soloviev (1853–1900): Russian religious philosopher, poet, and literary critic. His work *The Justification of the Good* was published in 1897 (English in 1918).

[8]"The Grand Inquisitor"— a "poem" by Ivan Karamazov (in Dostoevsky's *The Brothers Karamazov*, Part 2, Book 5, Chapter 5).

of the Resurrection. Then, and only then, to those who have given him all their earthly love and who come, bereft of all hope, to anoint his body in the grave, he says: "Rejoice!" Then Christianity begins.

In these days of rampant hatred, fear, and meanness, one's thoughts turn to this, and one yearns for it.

Why is Christmas Suppressed?

Toward the end of November the approaching feast of Christ's Nativity makes itself tangibly felt. It is as if something is pervading the air itself, in these shorter days of waning light, in the piercing cold of early winter, in the stars ignited in the frosty sky. Christmas is approaching—a holiday whose meaning is being increasingly forgotten in our land.

It is no coincidence, of course, that for so many years attempts have been made to simply destroy it, to erase it from human memory, to replace it with some kind of neutral "Santa Claus." It is no coincidence that some would like people to forget once and for all the strangest and most mysterious story of all—the story of a Child, homeless and helpless, born long ago in a forgotten outpost of the world, and the unspeakable joy that was sparked by his birth.

It is no coincidence, I say. But why? After all, other legends and tales are not forbidden or suppressed. So what is so harmful and so dangerous in this particular story? *Glory to God in the highest and on earth peace, goodwill toward men* (Lk 2.14). *I bring you good tidings of great joy* (Lk 2.10). There is so little peace and goodwill in the world, so little joy, that one would think that everything that heralds them should be valued and protected. But instead we hear a visceral reaction: "dangerous obscurantism," "despotic clergy," "unscientific," "harmful," etc. This Child must be dangerous indeed, if he provokes such enmity and such fear two thousand years after his birth into the world! Why is Christmas hushed up, why don't people speak about it, when thousands of lights sparkle on trees and the joy of children burns brightly around them?

I think that the answers to these questions are very important, that indeed something that is most important in our life depends on them. And the first answer is that the story that occasioned the feast of Christmas—the story of the Child and the joy he brought—contradicts all the ideas about religion, about its content and place in our lives, that people try to impose on us. We are told that religion arose out of fear and slavery, out of exploitation and deception. God, they say, was invented by those who wanted to intimidate other people with some kind of "mysterious forces." But at the very outset of Christianity, nothing of this kind is to be seen—no fear, no threats. On the contrary, it begins with a Child and joy, with words of peace and goodwill, with stars and shepherds. Everything else depends on the beginning, and if at the beginning the Christian faith was based on joy, then who are the real victims of deception? Is it not those who want so desperately for religion to have always arisen out of fear?

Further, the enemies of religion speak of God as something absurd and "unscientific": science has proven that God does not exist, etc. But the Christian religion does not begin with "scientific" discussions about whether God exists, what he is and where he lives, but with an account of how he acts, how he appears to people, what he means in their lives. And—paradox of all paradoxes!—this story is not about thunder and lightning, not about miracles and omnipotence, but again about a Child. Much more clearly and simply than all "anti-religious propaganda" combined, Christian teaching states: *No man hath seen God at any time* (Jn 1.18). But here events occur that seem so simple and uncomplicated, and through them we seem to touch something completely different, something sublime, deep, and pure, and the heart begins to burn with strange joy, and a light shines, and we say, "God." We don't say, "There is a God" or, "There is no God"—we say "God," and this means that something has happened to us, something has been revealed and has entered into us, and this unique, incomparable experience is the experience of God .

And one who has has experienced this no longer doubts, and the arguments of various academicians alleging that science has "proven" something in this regard seem to him ridiculous and stupid. What can science "prove" to me when I have known joy, love, and light, when I have experienced a happiness unlike anything else on earth? We listen again and again to the story of Christmas and pronounce the word "God," and the same word resounds in the hymns of the Church: "Understand, all nations, and submit yourselves, for God is with us."[9] How do we explain this? Perhaps only in hints, hints admittedly incomplete and insufficient, we might say something like this: only God could appear to people in the form of a weak, defenseless Child, for God does not need to "prove himself," God does not need to defend himself, God does not need the uproar of earthly political leaders with their wretched, boring propaganda. After all, a child is only joy, only love, and only happiness. He is no danger to anyone, and he needs only love, selfless love, and nothing more. The child completely surrenders to us, and we also surrender wholly to him. He does not seem to give us anything, but there is no gift like the gift of a child. And those who would hurt a child—need this be proven?—are bad people and servants of evil.

Thus, God's first manifestation to us is not as a harsh ruler, not as wise man sitting on a cloud, but as a Child. He gives himself to us and waits for us to give ourselves to him also—nothing more. And here, in essence, what is most important concerning religion and faith has already been revealed and spoken: "the eternal God was born as a little child."[10] Where does faith begin? It begins with a reciprocal and selfless love—not a love seeking to gain something, but a love that cannot help but love, for its object can only be loved and everything else proceeds from this love. And so, once again the time of this eternal and beloved Child comes to us, the God of love comes to us and comes seeking love. And everything lights up with joy, light, and celebration. It is approaching, it is drawing near . . . Look up at the sky, wait, look for the signs and the call of this single, all-embracing love. In this love lies the meaning of the Nativity of Christ, its strength, eternal beauty, and truth.

---

[9]"God is with us, understand all peoples, and submit yourselves, for God is with us!"—the beginning and final verses of the hymn at Great Compline, composed of selected verses from Isaiah 8.
[10]The Kontakion of the feast of the Nativity.

Blessed are Those Who Do Not See, Yet Believe

The Gospel of John relates how after his resurrection Christ appeared to his disciples, but one of them, Thomas, was not there at the time. And when they said they had seen Christ, Thomas declared, *Except I shall see in his hands the print of the nails, and put my finger into the print of the nails, and thrust my hand into his side, I will not believe* (Jn 20.25).

And so, when Christ appeared a week later and this time Thomas saw him, the Lord said, *Reach hither thy hand, and thrust it into my side, and be not faithless, but believing.* And Thomas exclaimed, *My Lord and my God!* Then Christ said, *Because thou hast seen me, thou hast believed: blessed are they that have not seen, and yet have believed* (cf. Jn 20.27–29).

This story can be applied to the whole complex problem of faith and unbelief, which the state's anti-religious propaganda attempts to solve so primitively and simplistically. This propaganda is entirely based on the following principle: "You do not see God, therefore he does not exist." In other words, it equates faith not with knowledge in general, but with a knowledge that is highly empirical—that is, the lowest and most elementary type.

But if we apply this logic not even to faith, but to knowledge itself, then little remains of it. For how little we actually see, how little we know, how limited and random are the objects that fall within the field of our direct observation! And therefore the difference between men and animals is precisely that man is not limited by gross empirical knowledge, but rises above it. And if we are honest, this higher, speculative realm of our human knowledge should be called *faith*.

After all, we would laugh at a man who said, "I do not love, and therefore there is no love." To this assertion of a single individual we would contrast the whole immensely enormous experience of love within all humanity—the experience that even thousands of years ago was described as being *as strong as death* (Song 8.6), the experience that has sanctified and transformed the lives of countless generations. And isn't the whole of human culture aimed at gradually introducing a child, a teenager, a young man into this experience that exceeds his own, into this common knowledge, this universal treasure?

What impoverished and mediocre beings we would be, in what terrible darkness we would live, if we had only our personal knowledge and nothing else, if our whole life were not an entry into the experience, wisdom, and faith of all mankind! I too, like Thomas, did not see Christ; I too was not among the disciples on the morning of Pascha when he appeared. But across the centuries, love and faith have conveyed to me his image, his words, his teachings, and this amazing story about the Son of Man, in whom everything was light, everything was love, everything was self-sacrifice. Across the ages the joyful faith has reached me that in him, in this impoverished and homeless teacher, divine love has been manifested to humanity. And the light of his image has filled my soul forever.

You read anti-religious propaganda, with all its tedious "evidence," and then you open the Gospel, and all this "evidence" dissipates like smoke. In the former a man, stubborn and blind to everything, babbles about what is beyond him, digs around in the dirt, and refuses to raise his head to see the sky and the sun; but here unique words are spoken, and the heart knows that they are true.

What can be proven here? What arguments can be made against Christ? That he deceived people? That he wanted fame and power? But he died on the cross, abandoned by all. And so for two thousand years people who believe in him have come to him.

Blessed are those who have not seen and yet have believed. Blessed are those who are able to rise into the world of spiritual experience and become real human beings!

Enemies of Spirituality

In the Name of What?

Today I want to touch on some of the arguments of anti-religious propaganda. Once the remarkable Russian thinker and writer Vasily Rozanov wrote: "Do you know that religion is what is most important, what is primary, and what is most necessary? If a person does not know this, there is no point in debates or conversations. One should simply ignore him, passing by in silence."[1] And Rozanov spent considerable time and effort thinking about religion, about Christianity, about the Church; he disputed with them at length, and was indignant at much that he found in them. He was not a person of blind faith; on the contrary, he always doubted, forever trying to understand everything himself, in his own way. He wrote *The Dark Face* and *Near the Church Walls*—books in which he passionately and vehemently argued with historical Christianity. Yet here Rozanov says, "Religion is what is most important, what is primary, what is most necessary."

I remembered these words, reading—for the umpteenth time!—the same old attacks of official propaganda that have been repeated against religion for decades. In these attacks, religion is always represented as a stupid misunderstanding, a thing that ought to collapse at the first touch of logic, the natural sciences, and so on. But Rozanov, who was a very educated man, uttered these amazing words in a moment of total self-concentration! And in the face of this experience, of what possible use can be all the miserable, mundane arguments put forward by the endless procession of atheist brochures? What can they do against the whole religious history of

[1]Vasily Rozanov, *The Solitary*, vol. 2 (Moscow: Pravda, 1990), 243. Vasily Vasilyevich Rozanov (1856–1919): Russian religious thinker, publicist, literary critic.

mankind, against that fire of faith and that spiritual thirst that is embodied in the most famous works of art and literature?

Indeed, Rozanov is right when he says of the preachers of godlessness that they should be "ignored." Sometimes it seems that all this whole struggle against religion, now decades old, is the fruit of some kind of insanity, of some inner blindness and barbarity. And then you realize: no, it's not barbarity, not blindness, but terrible lies and hatred. Only those who hate good, who hate the light, who hate the image of a person who blossoms and becomes radiant in the religious experience of all humanity, can fight against religion as does the state anti-religious propaganda apparatus.

Here is an example of these lies: all anti-religious propaganda is based on the assertion that religion enslaves and humiliates a person, that it is the product of a slavishly low-minded concept of who man is. But here we open the book of a professor of theology, the world-famous philosopher Father Vasily Zenkovsky, and we read: "Man is created to be in the center of all earthly existence, to rule and command—man appears before us as the king of nature, as its master, defining and 'naming' all things, and this attests to the fact that all things are subordinate to man."[2] So writes a Christian scientist. Where is the enslavement, the humiliation? And the images of people in Christian art, these utterly spiritualized, spiritually beautiful faces—do these humiliate a person?

But official propaganda will never admit to all this: it will simply keep repeating its tired slogans. And it is understandable why—because this spiritual beauty, this spiritualization of a person, is precisely what it does not want; because it hates this exalted image of man. But take away this image, and what will remain on earth? Dumb, senseless struggle! And in the name of what?

---

[2]V. V. Zenkovsky, *Fundamentals of Christian Philosophy*, vol. 2 (Moscow: Kanon, 1996), 262 (Russian). Vasily Vasilyevich Zenkovsky (1881–1962): Russian writer, theologian, religious thinker, teacher, and public figure. Since 1920, in the emigration. Since 1942, an Orthodox priest.

A Contraband Ideal

I spoke about the natural religiosity of man in my last conversation. This is evidenced not only by the whole history of mankind, but also by an attentive analysis of the life, motives, and searching of each person.

I said that man lives by essentially relating his life to something absolute—to something that he recognizes as the highest value, as the criterion for assessing his own life and everything related to it. Of course, a person can suppress and crush this desire for the absolute within himself, but such people have always been considered not entirely normal. Therefore, I said, the dispute between believers and unbelievers is not about whether there is a God, but about what they both consider to be God, to what they dedicate themselves. For it is impossible for man (if he is a true man, and not a moral wreck) not to dedicate himself to what he understands to be the highest thing of all. And Vladimir Soloviev wrote well about this: "For there is no consolation for one who has not given himself away."[3] And it cannot even be said that for some God is a transcendental concept, something beyond this world, while for others he is immanent, imprisoned in the limits of this world, since the absolute for both is not within the sphere of empirical, or direct, experience. From the point of view of this experience, to say, "I will live forever" or "Mankind will someday build a perfect, just, and free society" is an act of faith, an act of inner conviction, which is based on nothing but an inner giving of oneself to the absolute. But from where does it arise, whence this thirst in man for the absolute, or what we call "natural religiosity"? This, in essence, is the only real and necessary question. For nothing in nature itself, in the psycho-biological structure of man, explains this thirst or comprises its cause. Biologically, man is only the most highly developed animal, is he not? And what interplay of organic cells could explain his spiritual thirst, his moral demands?

The logical defect of so-called scientific atheism is that it makes every effort to reduce man to the category of animals, denies everything in him except for biologically determined properties, but at the same time

[3]From the poem by V. S. Soloviev, "Why is it that the heart needs . . ." (1892). It goes on to say: ". . . Why is there no joy / For one who has not sacrificed himself . . ."

constantly asserts that such a reduction of man is for some reason a condition of his freedom and self-fulfillment. Here we have an obvious discrepancy. It would seem that one of two things must be true: either man is something radically different from everything else in the world, not reducible to biology, or to economics, or to matter, in which case it is understandable and reasonable that he seek the fulfillment of his humanity in moral values. Or, on the contrary, a person, like everything else in the world, is not free biologically, mentally, or socially, but is entirely determined by external factors; but then there can be no talk of his being freed, of "a leap from the realm of necessity into the realm of freedom."[4] And so we see two possibilities. Either the whole world is a continuous realm of necessity (and indeed, all claims to atheistic materialism are reduced to this and nothing else), and then any "idealism," any spiritual "superstructure" must be discarded. Or else the realm of freedom is a different, spiritual reality, and man belongs to it, or rather, is its medium, its exponent, and at the same time its creator. And then the whole spiritual-moral principle in it is not a "superstructure" imposed on matter, but the defining principle of its unique essence, which cannot be categorized with anything else in the world.

In the first case, the very search for absolute values is an absurdity. And so it is no coincidence that such dissimilar ideologists of consistent materialism and determinism as Marx and Freud agree on one thing: they conduct all these searches not from above, but from below, and they refute all attempts to present these absolute values as an autonomous reality independent of any higher entity. With Freud, this is expressed in reducing not only love, but also all types of human creativity, religion, and everything else in the world to sexual energy; and with Marx, in reducing all the diversity of life to economic relations. Freud, however, has the courage to take all his presuppositions to their logical conclusions. His teaching is deeply pessimistic: all spiritual searches, all absolutes are not only useless, but also harmful. If a person wants to be healthy, he must understand the illusory nature of all his "superstructures" and accept himself as an animal. Marx does not have this courage, and, having reduced a person to an economic level, having deprived him of all spiritual and moral determinations, for no apparent

[4]Expression of Friedrich Engels, in his *Anti-Dühring*.

reason he starts in with his rhetoric about the "leap from the realm of necessity into the realm of freedom." But this "leap" is an obvious absurdity, for as a stone cannot become a column or a building on its own, without the intervention of human creativity, so also an animal organism without an ingrained spiritual and moral principle cannot desire either spiritual or moral freedom. Therefore, that absolute, that religious principle that we find in the intellectual narratives of the atheists, infiltrate them as though smuggled, and having infiltrated them they destroy them from the inside.

This is why all efforts to discredit faith and religion in the name of "liberating" a person appear so ridiculous. Religion allegedly enslaves a person. But is it not clear that religion starts with the assertion that man is by nature free, that he is a spiritual and moral being? The Gospel is entirely based on the affirmation of this freedom: *Seek, and ye shall find* (Mt 7.7). Seeking and thirsting (that is, an expression of freedom) is an a priori premise of that religious worldview in which God is, so to speak, the guarantor and foundation of human freedom. If there is no God, man is nothing more than an animal; if there is a God, this means there exists an immutable, or, as philosophy says, an ontological spiritual and moral freedom.

And so we come to a narrative that is inverse to what is imposed on us as the "authentically scientific" worldview. For this worldview, which deduces freedom from complete determinism, is in essence a farce and a fraud. No, have the courage to say that there is no freedom here and cannot be! And until this becomes obvious to everyone, the greatest farce in the history of mankind will continue.

The Object of Hatred

M an is religious by nature—this is what materialistic dogma is trying to refute by every available means, and this refutation is the ultimate goal of all its efforts. Why?

This question is infinitely important, for in the last analysis everything really depends on it. Everything in the world exists according to its nature, and if religion—that is, belief in immortality, eternity, man's transcendence over this transitory, ephemeral world, recognition that there is an eternal reality that transcends the world—if all this is only a fiction, a deception, or an illusion, then, of course, life's arrangement must be completely different. In this case, for example, everything individual and personal, all that is mine and relates to me, cannot and should not matter, for what kind of meaning can a creature have whose life, consciousness, and labors last for forty or fifty years at most? In this case both good and evil are relative, not absolute, and so on.

I repeat: the question of whether religion is innate to man or, on the contrary, imposed on him by someone as fictitious and false, is a fundamental question. We know that in the past all of human culture, in one way or another, was not simply associated with religion, but it was directly defined by it. And only the religious premise determined man's purpose in the world, and even the purpose of the world itself. Today they tell us that this premise is harmful and false. Let's set aside the so-called scientific aspect of the problem, that is, the attempts to destroy religion with the help of natural science. Any person with a drop of integrity, I think, understands today that these attempts are essentially nonsense. It is high time to recognize that if it is impossible to scientifically prove the existence of God, then it is impossible to "scientifically" refute it. No serious scholar has ever dealt with this issue; such people have always known that this was beyond their competency.

The struggle against religion, therefore, was not born from science, and it did not come from scientists. But then from where? For a long time it could have seemed that it was caused by an alleged organic link between religion and power, violence, exploitation, etc. This accusation is much more serious than the one based on "science," but these days it too is rendered moot. Indeed, organized religions often sinned by acquiescing to unjust societal norms, and were often held captive by those in power. There was even a theory that the very essence of religion (that is, faith in eternity and immortality) arises from the need to find some kind of "compensation" for the weak and exploited, and thereby to divert them from the struggle for their rights and for happiness in this world. But I repeat: no matter what the sins of organized religion in this area, modern experience shows that this theory is false. The era of the privileged position of religion, its links with the state, power, and wealth, have long since passed.

According to anti-religious theory, this state of affairs should have caused religious beliefs to simply die out, but this has not happened. On the contrary, liberated from its former artificial connection with all this, religion acquired a certain aspect that before, perhaps, it never had. Hence, only today, only in our time, the question of the nature of religion, as well as the nature of hatred towards it, can be posited in pure form.

Only now, only in our time, is it possible to ask people seriously, "Why do you believe?" or, "Why do you so passionately disbelieve and try to destroy faith in others?" For the believer no longer derives any external benefits from his faith. It is increasingly difficult for an unbeliever to refer to the connection between religion and "capitalism," "violence," or "exploitation." Since an unbeliever does not believe in God, he cannot hate someone who does not exist. Therefore, his hatred is directed at the believer. This is where one needs to ask: "Why?" And I think that the answer to this question is infinitely important. For the believer, no matter how weak his faith sometimes is, in the final analysis it remains free from final, unconditional subordination to anything on earth—power, ideology, society, etc. All this a believer can obey only insofar as it does not contradict the law that he recognizes as absolute and eternal.

Meanwhile, materialist ideology requires a person to be completely subordinate to its understanding of life, happiness, social order, good and evil. Allowing the slightest doubt here means destroying the entire edifice. After all, only when there is nothing that transcends society can society itself and its particular order be made a god, the ultimate and highest value. Only when there is nothing that transcends the earth can the earth itself, and it alone, be made the measure of all things. Thus, hatred of religion is a hatred for the basis of freedom, for its metaphysical principle.

For millions of people, the question of religion may seem peripheral today. They do not understand its utmost importance; they do not understand that the fate of the human person, of his freedom, depends on his decision one way or the other. Even now this freedom is progressively diminishing on earth. Man has almost been persuaded that he is only a grain of sand, only a cog, that he is completely and hopelessly subordinated to the "laws of science," to the "laws of society," to the "laws of matter." Will he wake up in time and realize that today it depends on a small handful of believers whether he will survive as a person, whether he will retain his freedom, and whether he will return to the world not as a slave, but as a free man, and not as a means, but as an end?

Therefore, the words of the apostolic sermon take on a completely new meaning in our day: *Brethren, ye have been called unto liberty* (Gal 5.13); new meaning is given to the words of Christ: *Ye shall know the truth, and the truth shall make you free* (Jn 8.32); new meaning, finally, is given to all the prophecies, all the warnings of people like Tolstoy or Dostoevsky, who knew, and with all their writings demonstrated, that where God dies, the beast reigns.

An Astonishing Worldview

"C hrist is Risen!"
On the first Sunday after Pascha, the Gospel read in church is about the faith of Thomas. It tells how the risen Lord came to the disciples, but one of the twelve, Thomas, was not there at the time. When the others told Thomas that they had seen Christ, he said, *Except I shall see in his hands the print of the nails . . . and thrust my hand into his side, I will not believe* (Jn 20.25). *And after eight days,* continues the evangelist, *again his disciples were within, and Thomas with them: then came Jesus, the doors being shut, and stood in the midst, and said, "Peace be unto you." Then saith he to Thomas, "Reach hither thy finger, and behold my hands; and reach hither thy hand, and thrust it into my side; and be not faithless, but believing." And Thomas answered and said unto him, "My Lord and my God!" Jesus saith unto him, "Thomas, because thou hast seen me, thou hast believed, blessed are they that have not seen, and yet have believed"* (Jn 20.26–29).

This account—if anyone ever doubted it—is not only about Thomas, but about many people, and first and foremost about modern man, since it was precisely this unbelief of Thomas that our era elevated into a principle, declaring it the only approach to life that is worthy of a person: "If I do not see it, I will not believe it." Are we not being force-fed a worldview that completely rejects everything that cannot be touched, measured, and weighed? Thomas the skeptic became a kind of prototype of modern man, for a similar skepticism brought forth the astonishing teaching of materialism. For what is materialism, if not a reduction of everything in the world to what can be tested by touching, measuring, and weighing?

I say this teaching is astonishing, because it stands in obvious contradiction to the direct experience of man—an experience that is based almost entirely on the opposite—namely, on faith. On faith in what no one can see, on the quest for something that cannot be felt, measured, weighed, or, as they say today, "empirically proven." How, you ask, is it possible to deduce freedom from materialism? Can matter really have freedom? Is it not subordinated to the principle of determinism, which defines all existence, including that of human beings, as entirely predetermined?

In actuality, materialism, which promises humanity "a leap from the kingdom of necessity to the realm of freedom," demands from it a real faith in this leap, and when it comes to power it imprisons those who do not display this faith. Materialism is indeed an astonishing worldview, and the fact that in the twentieth century it pretends to be "the most scientific" and to "liberate from the opium of religion" is even more astonishing. "I do not believe in anything that cannot be proven by experiment, but I live for the sake of a fact that no scientific experiment can prove"—this is how the confirmed materialist of our time might briefly formulate his worldview.

But back to Thomas. Here those closest to him, citing their experience, tell him: *We have seen the Lord* (Jn 20.25). Why did not he believe them? This circumstance, if you think about it, explains a lot in the psychology of modern man. In fact, Thomas had no reason not to believe those whom he knew so well, to whom he was so close—not to believe their joy as eyewitnesses. But both this testimony and this joy Thomas rejects not as an internally free man, but as a slave to his own pride, his egocentricity, his tiny ego. For centuries, millions of people have declared, "We have seen, we have heard, we have experienced God!" But the small, proud, blind man closes his eyes, stops up his ears, and stubbornly repeats: "I have not seen it and therefore I do not acknowledge it." Everyone looks at the heavens, but he stares blankly at the ground and mutters, "There is no heaven, there is only earth." "Look up," they say to him, "and you'll see what we see!" "I will not!" he replies. "Let them prove to me that there is a heaven while I look down at the ground."

This is the dialogue between faith and unbelief that has lasted for centuries. We have just celebrated Pascha, and once again many people have felt with unusual force the presence of the risen Lord among them. "Truly, he is risen!"—this is the joyful confession of this experience. But the unseeing crowd surrounding them, a sort of collective Thomas, still insists: "It's not true! I do not see it, and so I do not believe it!" This Thomas suppresses the world with its stubborn blindness. It presents its own private prison as paradise and freedom, and its own unbelief as the arguments of science.

But Christ did not abandon or despise Thomas, but appeared to him particularly, so that he could turn and exclaim: *My Lord and my God!* And it is never too late for this encounter, this conversion; and therefore not only to believers, but also to unbelievers, to the Thomas present in each of us, the most joyous declaration in the world is addressed: "Christ is Risen!"

The Paradox of the Christian Faith

During these Paschal days one is especially aware of what may be called the fundamental paradox of the Christian faith—the simultaneous presence of sorrow and joy, of the cross and the resurrection. "For through the cross joy has come into all the world." Through the cross—that is, through suffering, torment, and death. The Paschal night, with all of its radiance and light, is preceded by the darkness of Passion Week, the sorrow of Holy Friday, which is penetrated by the cry from the cross: *My God, my God, why hast thou forsaken me?* (Mt 27.46) And all of Christ's teaching is constantly permeated with this double theme: *In the world ye shall have tribulation: but be of good cheer; I have overcome the world* (Jn 16.33).

It is particularly important to be aware of this paradox in our time, in this era of rejection of religion, of attempts to excise it from the life and consciousness of people. I believe I will not be mistaken if I say that, on the deepest level, it is precisely this paradox of the Christian faith that chiefly evokes the hatred of all those who do not desire the cross, that is, the narrow path of self-denial, of perfection, of incessant inner struggle. All or nearly all contemporary ideologies take the struggle to find happiness and to learn the meaning of life and move it outside the human soul, placing the center of gravity of this struggle amid political, economic, and other societal conditions. In simple terms we can say that for all these ideologies the person is never the subject, but rather the object of the historical process. In other words, in these ideologies a person's inner life and its definitive significance for history itself are flatly denied.

We can schematically outline the clash of these ideologies with Christianity in the following way. Christianity tells a person: "Everything depends on you, on that inner decision that only you are capable of making and implementing. In some sense the fate of the whole world depends on you, on your inner freedom, purity, beauty, and perfection." Consequently, everything in this world is thoroughly personal, and therefore it is the person who is the creator of the historical process. Christ did not utter a single word about the social and political problems of his time. His call was wholly directed to the individual, to this or that person, to you yourself. At the same time, it is impossible to deny that historically Christianity brought about the most radical of all revolutions, for its teaching about the person transformed from within the psychology of government and society, to say nothing of all world culture.

Anti-Christian ideology, on the other hand, not only insists that nothing in history depends on the person, but ultimately denies the person himself. For according to this ideology, the person is produced by society, and therefore his whole life depends entirely on the societal environment. Christianity says, in the person of Saint Seraphim of Sarov: "Save yourself, and thousands around you will be saved"; while anti-Christian ideology objects: "You cannot save yourself except by changing the social environment." In Christianity, changing and transfiguring the world depends on the person. But anti-Christian ideology says that society must be transfigured in order for a person to change. Christianity underscores a person's personal freedom and individual responsibility, while anti-Christian ideology entirely subjugates a person to the collective, utterly dissolving him into the party, society, the government, and so forth.

Of course, this conflict is an old one; it is this conflict that led to Christ's death on the cross. But in our day it has surfaced with renewed force.

Technological progress, the so-called "triumphs of science," the necessity of planning and organization, would all seem to support the anti-Christian approach. Indeed, how greatly everything in this world surpasses the abilities of the individual, and how hopelessly it gives him over to the power of the collective! The individual asks, "What can I possibly achieve?" It can seem as though now, more than at any other time, in preaching the primacy of the internal over the external, of the person over the collective, Christianity is nudging its adherents toward egotistically abandoning the world: "What do I care about the world? I'm concerned with my own immortal soul."

But is this indeed the case? Without indulging in the theoretical, simply by looking around us we can be readily convinced of the chaos, the mindlessness, the fear and suffering into which people have been led by ideologies that emphasize the primacy of the external over the internal, subjecting the person always and in everything to the impersonal collective. Is it not time to examine the oft-repeated claim that, by focusing a person's attention entirely on his inner world, the Christian faith thereby compels him to neglect the needs of the world?

Dostoyevsky once said that there is not and cannot be any love for mankind without belief in the immortality of the soul. At first glance this affirmation seems questionable, if not absurd—what does the soul's immortality matter, if elementary freedoms, justice, and basic needs are not being met? Hadn't we better forget about immortality, the better to love mortal men here on this earth? But as Dostoevsky affirms, if one does not believe in immortality, then everything ends in hatred and slavery. If we think about it, the truth of this great writer, and in turn the truth of Christianity, becomes self-evident. For if there is no eternal and imperishable principle in man that raises him above the material, then what is there to love in him? Thus, sooner or later—alas, at the cost of horrible suffering, bloodshed, and tears—the world will return again to these simple words of the Gospel: *The kingdom of God is within you* (Lk 17.21). And every person who has recognized this kingdom, who lives by its beauty, light, and truth, in the final analysis does more for the world and for humanity then all the bearers of abstract programs of future happiness, for which nearly all mankind must first be stripped of its freedom and enslaved.

All of this is brought to mind and witnessed by these Paschal days. For they are filled with lively reminders of him who sought nothing but the triumph of the kingdom of God in the human soul, and who has filled the whole world with his teaching. Assuredly, we have reached the limits of the external world. This is why it is so telling that at this particular moment we hear, more emphatically than ever, the voices of individual people calling us back to the inner, to the internal, to the immortal. Need we cite the names of Pasternak, Solzhenitsyn, and so many others? With their bravery, with their writings they call us from the dead-end of personal ideologies to that one profound reality that alone can free us: to faith.

Blindness and Clarity

E *xcept I shall see in his hands the print of the nails, and put my finger into the print of the nails, and thrust my hand into his side, I will not believe* (Jn 20.25). Thus Thomas, one of the disciples of Christ, answered the other disciples in response to their claim that they had seen their crucified and dead Master resurrected.

Each of responds similarly even to far less incredible affirmations. The "Doubting Thomas" is an image of the most terrible tragedy of mankind—the tragedy of disappointment, of lack of faith, and of skepticism. I am not talking now about our response to this or that religious dogma, but

about the main focus and nature of human consciousness. This consciousness constantly doubts and distrusts; moreover, man has placed the principle
of mistrust and doubt as the cornerstone of earthly wisdom, and hence of
earthly happiness, well-being, and life itself. We live in a strange world
where people believe nothing and no one: one person distrusts the next,
nation distrusts nation, and so on, and we are so used to this fact of life that
we feel it needs neither explanation nor justification. But now one begins
to wonder: is this really the way it should be? For if this is indeed the norm,
the world becomes frightening and dark, and then what kind of happiness
and well-being can there be? If we must always be on the defensive, if we
must always be armed to the teeth, if we are on the alert for lies and trickery
in every word and every look, is life really worth living? I cannot help but
recall a young man who committed suicide in the 1920s, after scrawling on
a scrap of paper: "I do not want to live in a world where everyone cheats."
And yet we live in just such a world with perfect calmness; we drink our
tea and complacently make plans for a "bright future" for mankind. This
is frightening, dark, and endlessly sad!

And when you ponder all this now, when after Pascha, with its light and
joy, the Church recalls Thomas who doubted and his words: "If I don't see
it, I won't believe it," you suddenly realize that this terrible, toxic unbelief
killed Christ himself, and that it was from this that he came to deliver us.
How simple his teaching was: *Thou shalt love the Lord thy God with all thy
heart, and with all thy soul, and with all thy mind* (Mt 22.37); *Love thy neighbor
as thyself* (Mt 22.39); *Love your enemies, bless them that curse you* (Mt 5.44);
Walk as children of light (Eph 5.8). The joy of love cannot be taken away. But
look how the web of mistrust, slander, and hatred began to weave around
Christ from the beginning. His foes did not merely not know what to make
of him; they did not disagree or debate with him. No, they immediately
hated him, for this astonishing mechanism of distrust and suspicion began
its devious work from the outset. And so began the attempts to catch Christ
in his words and deeds, "to expose him." And then they finally trapped
him: "He wants to become a king! He is dangerous, he is an enemy! Crucify
him, crucify him!"

Christ knew all this in advance, and therefore he said, "Even if someone rises from the dead, they will still not believe" (cf. Lk 16.31). That is, they will refuse to believe, they will hold fast to their miserable distrust. And so it remains to this day. Mistrust blankets the earth in a cadaverous stench of decomposition, and from distrust comes fear; and out of fear, malice; and out of malice, suffering and death.

How can we counter this? It is said of Christ that to those who believe in him *gave he power to become the sons of God* (cf. Jn 1.12). And a son of God is one who has overcome his own slavish mistrust. Distrust is blind, but faith sees; distrust tears down, but faith builds up. It is said of faith that it moves mountains, and this is true: Peter believed, and walked on water; he stopped believing—and began to sink. But it is important to understand that what is meant here is faith not simply as trust in something, but as the content and way of life.

Of course, the detractors will object: "How can one believe if every-one around us is deceiving us and we know it?" There is no answer to this besides the fact that at some point someone will have to break this infernal chain: I deceive, knowing that I am being deceived, and I am deceived by those who know that I am deceiving them, and so on ad infinitum. The apostle Paul called this wisdom of this world *foolishness with God* (1 Cor 3.19), but he says that faith is "foolishness for the world," or wisdom in Christ (cf. 1 Cor 1.24–25; 3.19).

But if we accept this "foolishness for the world," something strange happens: our trust turns into a force against lies and deception, weakness becomes power, and defeat becomes victory. And in this lies the meaning of the Gospel. Christ never doubted. Knowing all the anger, all the hatred and treachery of his enemies, he continued his ministry, continued to appeal to what is highest and best in man. Oh, certainly not all people answered his appeal, and it seemed that distrust, anger, and envy had triumphed, for Christ *was numbered with the transgressors* (Mk 15.28). But his faith conquered: *And I, if I be lifted up from the earth, will draw all men unto me* (Jn 12.32). And perhaps it's time for us to wake up from the nightmare of mistrust and lack of faith, time to make our own the cry that we find in the Gospel: *Lord, I believe; help thou mine unbelief* (Mk 9.24).

Pseudo-Science

One of the Chief Accusations

One of the chief accusations against religion made by its official enemies—the accusation of being "unscientific"—is worth revisiting.
Especially since today there is a new onslaught on religion, in which (in
the name of science) even cosmonauts are enlisted. Everyone no doubt
remembers how one of these, after his flight into outer space, declared that
he had not seen God there. But this statement almost literally repeats the
solemn assertion made at the very dawn of Christianity by one of its main
preachers, the apostle Paul, who said that *no man hath seen God at any time*
(1 Jn 1.18; 1 Jn 4.12; cf. 1 Tim 6.16).

And if those who forced the astronaut to make this silly statement had
been true adherents of science, they would certainly have known that one of
the main tenets of Christianity, in the name of which it has fought for centuries against idolatry and superstition in all their forms, is the assertion that
God is invisible and cannot be approached as one of the phenomena of the
visible world. "Unoriginate, invisible, incomprehensible, ineffable"—thus
God is addressed in one of the most solemn prayers of the Church.[1] And
all these and similar words begin with negative prefixes such as *un-* or *in-*:
everyone speaks of him as the One who is beyond the concepts and categories of our everyday experience. Meanwhile, science, by its very nature and
purpose, deals exclusively with what is subject to empirical experience, that
which can be defined in relation to what is visible, that which can be measured and calculated. Therefore, for all its value and enormous potential, it

[1]"Most pure, undefiled, invisible, incomprehensible, unsearchable, inalienable, invincible, inde-
finable, gentle God . . ." (Vespers at Holy Pentecost, the first "kneeling" prayer).

by no means deals with everything, and every authentic scientist is a man of learning precisely because he knows the limits of his art.

For example, no science (I mean laboratory, experimental science) deals with beauty. A scientist, historian, or philosopher can trace what is understood as "beauty" in different eras, and its effects on people. But science cannot determine what beauty is, nor should it. Why do rhyming words become beauty? What is the effect on my soul of this sonata or that symphony? Why, when looking at the sunset, at the starry sky, at the sunlight shining through the foliage, does a person feel with his whole being that to which he cannot give an exact, strictly scientific definition? The scientist responds: "I don't know." And any real scientist, who is not a haughty know-it-all, will never say: "I do not know, and therefore there is no beauty." Uncertainty in science is as valuable as knowledge, and openly acknowledging this is a point of honor for true scientists. And so science cannot say anything about God, except that there have always been, are, and will be people who testify with their whole lives that in their experience God is present as Unoriginate, Unchanging, Invisible, and Boundless, as the One who is behind everything and above all, but in whom nevertheless lies the ultimate meaning and joy, the very essence of all things, the life of life itself. "And I can find happiness on earth, and in the heavens I see God."[2] When Lermontov wrote this, he did not combine the words "happiness" and "God" by accident. For the believer, God is happiness. And what objections can science raise to the experience of happiness, the experience of love, the experience of beauty? And why do faith's detractors so stubbornly insist that science oppose this experience? Is it because in the ideology that they strive to impose on humanity by force, there is ultimately no place for happiness, love, or beauty?

[2]From a poem by Mikhail Lermontov, "When undulates the yellowing cornfield" (1837).

Dogmatized Propaganda

R ecently, a talk was broadcast on a Moscow radio station, entitled: "Marxist atheism and its main features."

There is nothing new or original in it—only an endless repetition of what we have already heard millions of times. Here is an example: "The great victory of Marxism was a materialistic explanation of social life and the expulsion of idealism from this realm of knowledge. Thanks to this discovery, Marxist atheism gave a strictly scientific explanation of the origin and essence of religion as a form of consciousness, showed its social roots and outlined the ways and means of completely freeing the working people from religious delusion." I repeat: we have heard such phrases millions of times, and, as is now obvious, they prove nothing. It is not sufficient to go on endlessly about "strictly scientific" evidence without presenting said evidence. After all, everything that is strictly scientific is proven by facts. The explanation of religion that is passed off as science is now a hundred years old, but this does nothing to stifle the intense prevalence of religion where it is not persecuted by the police and brute force. Nothing strictly scientific ever requires police protection. For example, someone discovers a new medicine: if it cures, it pertains to science; if not, it must be discarded.

Everything really valuable and scientific in Marxism has long been common knowledge; it has been accepted and assimilated as confirmed by facts, and therefore scientifically substantiated. But in the matter of religion, Marx was of course mistaken, for his theory has been disproven by facts for a hundred years running. And it is time to admit it openly.

In the Moscow radio talk there was one phrase worth pondering: "Materialism, in full accord with scientific data, believes that in the material world, nature exists forever, having no beginning or end both in time and in space." This assertion is astounding. What kind of "scientific data," what kind of science in general, says anything about the beginning and the end in such absolute terms? "Neither beginning nor end" sounds like a most genuine confession of faith, like a religious statement; it is, in particular, precisely how Christians speak about God. In the world, however, everything begins and ends, and science is by nature concerned only with what fits into the pattern of "beginning/end." This is why, along with the natural sciences, we also have philosophy and religion, since the field of natural science cannot be unlimited, because the axiom of science is: "Only what is measurable is studied." But without some concept of a beginning and an end, this is no longer science, but faith, and it should be so named.

Let us note right away that if the whole difference between religious faith and a similar atheistic "faith" is reduced to this point, we find that the initial principles of both are not so very incompatible, because the idea of a beginning and an end in religious consciousness is not at all as simple as formulated by the agents of state propaganda. But in that case this becomes a philosophical or even a religious debate, a clash of two faiths, two visions of the world, and not a war between science and religion, as the radio broadcaster is attempting to prove.

Meanwhile, the simplifications and manipulations constantly employed by so-called scientific atheism expose it as narrowly dogmatized propaganda, which only pretends to be science.

A Confusion of Concepts

These days all contemporary talk and debate about religion usually comes down to one topic: religion and science.

By science, of course, they mean exclusively the so-called natural sciences. I have repeatedly argued that such a formulation of the question, which is imposed outright by official anti-religious propaganda, is flawed and hollow from beginning to end. Only concepts and quantities that are commensurate—that is, that belong to the same category—can be compared and, consequently, contrasted. Thus, for example, when an astronaut who has flown around the earth says that he did not find God in heaven, his words may have some meaning, provided that "heaven" means the same thing in the religious understanding of the word as in science—that is, the physical sky. If this is not so, the astronaut's remark is simply ludicrous.

Meanwhile, literally all so-called "scientific" arguments against religion are built precisely on this kind of deliberate confusion of concepts, on the premise that for the believer religion is a kind of science that is dashed to smithereens by contact with "real science." In actuality, the only fruitful topic that can unite the believer and unbeliever in their debate is the world and man in light of their ultimate meaning. A believer is not just one who believes in the existence of an incomprehensible God, but one who, in the world and among people, in the very fabric of life, sees and feels the presence and action of light and love, which he calls divine. For him, the world and life are not a dead end, exhaustively explained with the help of two or three axioms of physics, chemistry, and economics, but a mystery that can only be comprehended by one who has recognized and experienced the height and depths—that is, the spiritual dimensions—of the universe.

Take Pushkin, for example. He was neither a churchgoer nor a scientist in the strict sense of these definitions. He was a creative poet who crafted a beautiful and transparent, exalted and pure world. About this world of Pushkin, one historian of Russian literature said this: "In the hours of longing and despair, doubts about men and humanity, we open up Pushkin, no matter on which page, and . . . we imbibe—what shall we call this drink?—not water, of course, and not wine either, but rather some kind of divine nectar that pours out tranquility, hope, and love for man."[3]

And so we ask ourselves: would Pushkin be satisfied with this obtuse pseudo-scientific "debunking" of religion? Whose side would he be on—that Pushkin who wrote "The Prophet," and who, with all his cheerfulness and openness to everything earthly and human, knew what it meant to "to soar with one's heart into unseen realms"?[4] Would he take the side of those who claim that the world and life can be absolutely explained, exhausted by lifeless formulas, or of those who distinguish the depth and height of any phenomenon, its rootedness in the divine, who discern what cannot be explained by any "scientific" formulas? To pose the question thus means to have answered it already. And to answer it is to acknowledge that, in addition to science, the explanation of man and the world are also

[3]G. P. Fedotov, *On the Humanism of Pushkin* (1949).
[4]From a poem by Alexander Pushkin, "The Desert Fathers and the Undefiled Women" (1836).

aided by poetry, art, and man's indomitable striving upward which they depict—upward towards what the ancient poet called "the fire of things." A religion that is based on chemistry and physics is not religion at all, but a miserable caricature of it. Truly, religion has no response to arguments such as these, just as the artist has no response for children who do not see his painting on the canvas, and are ready to smear it with colored crayons. But the man who wrote:

> There, with a farewell to my cave,
> To mount up to longed-for heights
> There, to my cell above the clouds,
> To hide in secret near my God![5]

—this man knows from experience what he is talking about. Perhaps he has not yet fully come to believe, but neither will he stoop to vulgar opposition to faith.

A "Battle" with Science?

In my talk today I want to return to Kurochkin's article, "Modernization and the Ideology of Contemporary Orthodoxy," recently published in the journal *Political Self-Education*.[6]

I have already said that this article makes a strange impression with its vagueness and lack of substance. In essence, it never explains to us what comprises "modernization" of religion, which is declared baseless at the outset. But today I want to dwell on one dimension of Kurochkin's arguments—namely, on what he says about the relationship between religion and science.

---

[5] From A. S. Pushkin's poem, "Monastery on Kazbek" (1829).

[6] P. K. Kurochkin, "Modernization and the Ideology of Contemporary Orthodoxy," *Political Self-Education* [Politicheskoe samoobrazovanie] 6 (1964): 27–35. P. K. Kurochkin: author of a number of works (1960s – early 1980s) on the Russian Orthodox Church in the twentieth century, which sustained the official Soviet "revelatory" spirit.

As is well-known, the "incompatibility" of religion and science constitutes the main and favorite topic of official anti-religious propaganda. For decades, it has maintained that science "debunks" and "abolishes" religion, and therefore Kurochkin is especially resentful of the assertion by the "new ideologists" of Orthodoxy that such is not actually the case, but rather faith and knowledge constitute a harmonious unity. "Under conditions of enormous scientific and technological progress," he writes, "the advance of the culture of the masses, the Church can no longer openly defame and persecute science as it did before. Its defenders are trying to make the case that Orthodoxy was never an enemy of scientific knowledge. . . . The new situation is forcing the ministers of the cult to increasingly declare that there is no conflict between knowledge and faith."[7] And Kurochkin quotes doctor of theology L. Pariysky, who states that "the data of science, obtained . . . by persistent . . . efforts of the human mind, confirm . . . the close unity of science with faith."[8] He also quotes the priest V. Povetkin: "Separated, science and religion remain barren, like the most beautiful bride and groom in the world. Today I will perform a marriage ceremony for them, and having become husband and wife, religion and science will become the father and mother of truth, which will warm our souls with spring sunshine."[9]

What does Kurochkin answer to all this? Nothing. Or, rather, something so controversial and strange that, upon reading it, one's initial reaction is: did I really understand that correctly? Orthodoxy, he writes, has not given up the fight against science. It now conducts this struggle under the veil of compatibility between knowledge and faith. We ask: how is this possible? One would think it would have to be one or the other—either conflict or compatibility. How can one have conflict "under the veil of compatibility"? But Kurochkin, citing theologians and priests who so clearly affirm not only the possibility, but the unity and mutual necessity of religion and science, argues, doubting nothing, that theology has never agreed nor can it agree

[7]Kurochkin, "Modernization," 31.

[8]Source of quote not established. L. N. Pariysky (†1972): professor of the Leningrad Theological Academy, author of a number of articles in the *Journal of the Moscow Patriarchate*.

[9]Source of quote not established. Priest V. Povetkin—possibly a clergyman of the Simferopol diocese, who died in 1966; see: *Journal of the Moscow Patriarchate* 2 (1966): 35.

with the achievements of scientific thought. Period—end of discussion. No proof, no further conversation.

But the fact of the matter is that there is not and cannot be any "proof," because the main assertion of anti-religious propaganda—that religion opposes science, and science opposes religion—is the chief and grossest lie of all this propaganda, making it a complete perversion from beginning to end. For in actuality, religion has never fought with science, and this can be confirmed by countless facts, starting with the fact that modern science originated in universities established by the Church. And what is styled as their "conflict" was in fact a conflict of different trends—some advanced, others more backward—within science itself. But never, I emphasize, never has a single theologian said that science as such is evil and must be opposed in the name of religion. That is why Kurochkin, who has nothing to say, can only resort to spurious allegations. Therefore, we too speak not at all of the "modernization" of Orthodoxy, but of its response to lies and slander.

Such lies and slander are an embarrassment to our era. And this has long been understood by anyone who is familiar with the allegations of official propaganda, such as those we find in Kurochkin's article.

Captive Knowledge

As the school year launches, one inadvertently recalls an old and well-worn proverb: "Learning is light, and ignorance is darkness."

This saying comes to mind because in our days, sadly, the truth of it ceases to be self-evident—at least, of the first part, since for millions of people learning is not only light, but, alas, also the darkness of propaganda, the darkness of hackneyed theories, which they are commanded to accept unquestioningly. And there is no sadder example of this than what we see directly before us. It seems simply outlandish that the strictly scientific and objective study of religion is now replaced by the most vague and primitive attacks against it. Moreover, both the elementary school child and the college student are obliged to believe that religion is harmful and evil even before they have been told anything about it. And this is the a priori assertion under which all further lessons in "scientific atheism" are framed.

But let us take the example of any field of knowledge and ask: is it possible to seriously, scientifically, and objectively study Russian literature without exposing schoolchildren and college students to its fruits? What will be the value of any course in Pushkin if the teacher holds back the text of *Eugene Onegin* and *The Queen of Spades*? Yet this is precisely how religion is studied. Here we have a brochure on the origin of Christian holidays, published by some kind of institution for the "dissemination of knowledge." In it you can find all sorts of trivia—everything except what would give a true idea of Pascha or Christmas. An even cruder example is the deliberate concealment of the text of the Gospel from students, while at the same time drilling into them that the Gospel is an unscientific, outdated, and harmful book. All these are extreme examples of how the principle of "learning is light" turns into its opposite, and how learning is replaced with memorizing ready-made formulas that neither enlighten nor liberate, but obscure and enslave.

It is no coincidence that the proverb equates learning with "light." Light is needed to see things and phenomena as they are, to learn the truth about everything. In the dark, everything is ambiguous, and takes on strange and sometimes terrible shapes. At twilight an ordinary room can seem to be full of ghosts, but once you light a lamp they scatter. The same is true of learning: from time immemorial the idea has only grown in strength and acceptance that learning is illumination through concourse with truth. Generation after generation learned to fearlessly seek truth, whatever it might be, whatever the cost to achieve it. And in this search there was light, in this lay the pledge of freedom, and everything that hindered it was acknowledged to be darkness. A person has the right to know, and only on the basis of his own free knowledge can he decide for himself what is true and what is false. All liberation movements have sought this freedom of learning. And now, after so many years, or rather so many centuries, we witness a terrible and wretched picture—learning by decree. And if this is the case with the study of religion, are things much better in other areas of knowledge? Human knowledge is an inseparable whole, and if it is enslaved in one area, then it is enslaved everywhere.

We would do well to ponder these things in these first few days of the new academic year.

Objectively and Honestly

We have already talked about the importance of a truly scientific study of religion. Universities in Western countries have long had departments for the comparative study of religions, a science that seeks, on the basis of archaeology, anthropology, psychology, and cultural history, to reconstruct the course of mankind's religious development. And here the whole difference between the scientific and unscientific approach to religion is clearly visible. The unscientific nature of so-called anti-religious propaganda lies in that it views religion without the aid of any historical perspective—as something standing alone and always congruent to itself. How astonished would the hearers of this propaganda have been, had they heard the words of Reinhold Niebuhr,[10] one of the most prominent Christian thinkers of our time: "Nothing in the Bible supports the view that religion, as such, is decidedly something good. On the contrary, the Bible is very suspicious of what many called *religion*." And then the same Niebuhr says: "Religion, as such, very often degenerates into idolatry and strengthens, rather than weakens, the self-deification of people, institutions, and nations. Religion and faith in themselves are not positive at all."

In other words, religion, like absolutely everything in the world, requires study, analysis, and evaluation. This study began long ago, back in the eighteenth century, but reached its zenith, and, most importantly, made its methods fully scientific, at the end of the following century, in the works of scientists such as Uzener, Dietrich, Hackman, and especially

[10]Reinhold Niebuhr (1892–1972): American religious thinker, Protestant theologian.

Chantepie de la Saussaye.[11] These men undertook a comparative study of religion employing the richest data from archeology, anthropology, and psychology. Scientists have established that the origins of religion and its actual evidence date back to primitive times, to the earliest known facts about man. The so-called Neanderthal man, who, in all likelihood, lived one hundred thousand years before Christ, was already burying his dead according to some kind of religious rite. But, as we have said, the fact of religion's antiquity does not imply that it was originally sublime. On the contrary, this primitive religion could have been rooted in fear, in cruelty—anything. Science is interested in its development, and there is no more telling example than the idea of sacrifice, which is characteristic of all religions without exception in any historical era.

At first, the sacrifice was a manifestation of fear, a desire to pacify and "buy" the alliance of a more powerful being. A man offers the deity the best that he has, thinking in return to get health, wealth, or longevity. But, as one historian of religions writes, sacrifice, despite its completely earthly and even egoistical roots, can develop into one of the noblest religious acts, becoming a means of selflessness, gratitude, and, finally, connection with a higher reality. Between the sacrifice of a savage and the Church's teaching about Christ, who sacrifices himself for all people for the renewal and purification of their lives, there is an endless path of development, deepening, and spiritualization of the very concept of sacrifice. When we speak of someone who "sacrificed himself" for his people or for some idea, we mean the best and highest that a man is capable of, and we no longer have in mind the bloody and terrible sacrifices of primitive religion.

Thus, a truly scientific approach to religion takes into account gradual sublimation, that is, the exaltation of those initial feelings from which it is born, on the one hand, and the filling of old forms with new content on the other. And if this method is applied honestly, this will lead to its being objectively understood and evaluated.

---

[11]Herman Uzener (1839–1905); Albrecht Dietrich (1866–1908); Henry Hackman (1864–1935); P. D. Chantepie de la Saussaye (Pierre Daniel) (1848–1920): researchers of mythology and religious beliefs of pagan antiquity.

An Authentic Scientific Approach

The basis of religion is faith. "I believe in God," the believer says. And this means that he claims a certain experience. This experience is an internal experience. It does not lend itself to rational verification, like scientific theory. And yet, in fighting against it, the enemies of religion consciously or unconsciously always make the same logical mistake—they equate the experience of faith, like the confession of faith itself, with a certain scientific theory, and then they demonstrate (rather convincingly, even) that a rational test of this theory is untenable.

But at its core, an error remains in the original premise, for faith is not a rational scientific theory. After all, it does not occur to anyone to verify scientifically, to affirm or deny by chemistry, physics, mathematics, or biology, the experience of human love. "I love," says a person, and if he really loves, we see in him the light, joy, and inspiration of love. And by all this, love is not so much "proven" as shown. Therefore, we say: faith, like love, belongs to the innermost, deepest life of man. And just like love for one who loves, so also faith for one who believes does not require any proof. And if this is so, then no verification and no evidence can refute or destroy them.

But a scientific approach to faith is also possible. A truly scientific approach to it requires, at the very least, an admission that in all eras of human history, in all countries and cultures, we find the experience of faith. But this is not enough. A truly scientific approach also requires that we try to understand this experience from the inside as far as possible. This is what scientists do when in their scientific quest they are free from the obligation to refute faith at all costs. It is these who strive to comprehensively grasp the human experience of faith, and in so doing to describe it. A whole science has long been established—the philosophy and phenomenology of religion. But this science remains completely and willfully unknown to those who force upon millions of people their vacuous theories of the "unscientific" nature of religion—theories that extirpate religion from economics, social conditions, or even the stomach.

Nowadays, when mankind has lost its way on the paths of its destiny, we need to address the question of faith freely, honestly, and completely without bias, to delve into its mystery—its mystery, I say, for everything that happens in the inner world of a person is truly mysterious.

In the following talks I will try to talk about how issues of faith are approached by genuine science that is unconstrained in its investigations.

A Tiresome Obstacle

The essence of religion is a belief in fantastic and non-existent supernatural forces." This phrase is taken from the journal *Science and Religion,* where a certain Belyaev angrily parses Adler's dissertation on the religious philosophy of Lenin.[12]

I quoted this phrase not by chance, for it seems to me to be a key phrase in the kind of debunking of religion quite typically represented in the aforementioned Belyaev, along with all other official ideologues of so-called scientific atheism. Their fundamental premise is approximately this: it is impossible to scientifically prove and defend religion, meaning the existence of God; however, scientifically proving the non-existence of God is possible and necessary. I do not know whether these official ideologues themselves are aware of the paradox of their position. I think that in some sense they are; otherwise their denunciation of religion would not be so passionate and fierce. Real science never employs such language, because its truth is not based on emotions and passions, but on the self-evidence of facts and clarity of evidence. But in this case there can be no self-evidence or clarity for the simple reason that the object of proof, meaning God, is de facto declared non-existent. And since this object is in no way subject to empirical research, all the evidence turns out to be a chain of passionate and far-fetched statements. At their worst, these statements are crude and

---

[12]Article by E. Belyaev, in which the aspiring obscurantist criticizes E. Adler's dissertation on V. I. Lenin, "The Philosophy of Lenin's Religion" (Munich, 1964), in *Nauka i religia* [Science and religion] 10 (1965): 83–84.

ridiculous (like the astronaut Gagarin stating "I didn't see God in the heavens"); at best they are foggy and limited to quoting Lenin and Feuerbach.

It must be said that Adler's thesis which so enrages Belyaev—namely, that the existence of religion essentially proves the existence of God—is methodologically immeasurably more scientific than all the tricks of "scientific atheism." At least it does not contradict the common sense expressed in the well-known saying: "Where there is smoke, there is fire." Indeed, if always and everywhere, in all societies and all cultures, at all stages of development, people have always believed in God, not only in isolation but in vast multitudes, something must serve as the reason for this faith. Scientific atheism says, "Yes, that was exploitation!" But exploitation has ended, and yet people believe in God. "Well then, ignorance!"—but the world is covered with a network of universities, and yet people, even professors, continue to believe in God. "A relic of the past!"—but centuries have passed since the days of Galileo, Descartes, Voltaire, and Feuerbach, and people still believe in God. "Then to profit by it!"—but in the Soviet Union, for example, for the past fifty years it has been highly "unprofitable" to believe in God, and still people believe.

The phenomenon that they wanted to summarily dispense with turns out to be not only more tenacious, but also immeasurably more complex, and this drives official atheism into a rage. "Lenin said . . ." But why should I trust Lenin more than Dostoevsky and Tolstoy, or the academics Pavlov and Teilhard de Chardin?[13] "Feuerbach proved . . ." Yes, but a hundred years later the scientist, geologist, and anthropologist Teilhard de Chardin proved the opposite. "Fantastic faith in the supernatural!"—shouts atheistic propaganda in desperation; but in modern interpretations of religion there is much less of the "supernatural" (in the sense of the mysterious, inexplicable, and magical) than in the absolutely unprovable dogma that communism leads to universal happiness. This dogma is truly neither more nor less than faith, for all its "evidence" concerns a future that is obviously unknown. Religious faith, on the other hand, has a present and a past: there is the truth and beauty of religious art, there is the amazing happiness and joy of

[13]Pierre Teilhard de Chardin (1881–1955): French Jesuit priest, religious thinker, and scholarly researcher in the field of paleontology and anthropology.

the saints, there is the incomparable depth and beauty of the Gospel—such depth and beauty, in fact, that it is forbidden to publish this book.

Religion, in short, has immeasurably more facts, and pointing to them it says: "Look, think!" It does not call people to blind unquestioning faith, but asks: "To what do these facts attest?" But scientific atheism rejects the facts or suppresses them. Indeed, it never even talks about religion in its true essence, but always about some secondary phenomena, about the shortcomings and sins of religion's representatives. But is this a debate? Is this science? Essentially, the most striking thing is the collapse and bankruptcy of this notorious "scientific atheism." In the world there are many unbelievers. But their unbelief is not because someone has proven something "scientifically," but because they have no experience of faith. And there are many believers in the world—not because atheistic propaganda has not yet reached them, but because of their personal experience of faith. But if this experience exists, it is just as pointless to prove it does not as to explain Bach's music or an ancient Russian icon based on Karl Marx's *Das Kapital*.

Isn't it time at least to allow for the possibility that Feuerbach, Marx, and their disciples were simply mistaken about religion? In thrall to their economic analysis, they extended it to everything in the world, but it turned out that a great many phenomena were beyond its control. Phenomena such as art, love for one's motherland, love itself, and, of course, religion. And now the terrifying clenched fist, which, according to their theory, was supposed to irrevocably crush religion, flails in the empty air, because what it crushes has nothing in common with living, experiential faith. And everyone knows that without the constant onslaught of the state, the party, the police, and the whole apparatus of agitators, all this "scientifically atheistic" propaganda will simply burst. This certainly does not mean that everyone will immediately believe in God, but only that "scientific atheism" is a tiresome obstacle on the eternal path of human seeking, for it is organically alien to the ultimate depths in which a person resolves his real concerns.

Philistinism

Science, philosophy, and religion are, first and foremost, an explanation of what exists. Or perhaps it is better to say they seek answers to the one perennial question that man will ask for as long as he truly remains a man. This question is: what is existence? What does it mean to exist, to be, to develop, to live? For man—and in this he is quite alone amid the the immense diversity of all that exists—this question is particularly compounded by his awareness of his own mortality, of the fragility and impermanence of his own existence.

No, it is impossible to conceive of a person who would never contemplate this terrible paradox of death. But the question of death is in fact the question of life, and not only my personal life, the life of my own self, but also the life of the world, the universe, the cosmos. If everything in the universe is subject to death, while the universe itself exists forever, then what for? Some people, perhaps even the majority, upon asking themselves these questions quickly push them away, and begin to live "for today"—that is, in constant forgetfulness. For such people, these questions turn into "forbidden questions" that interfere with life, poisoning the moments of accessible and uncomplicated enjoyment that are to be found in daily living.

Already in antiquity the Epicureans[14] made their slogan the phrase: *Let us eat and drink; for to morrow we shall die* (Is 22.13). Nowadays, the techniques for achieving this forgetfulness, the techniques for distracting people from everything that can somehow touch them at their core, has reached unprecedented dimensions. Modern civilization is, in essence, a hedonistic civilization,[15] from the Greek word *hēdonē*—pleasure. That was the name of the doctrine in antiquity, which stated that since a person cannot answer any of the "forbidden questions" anyway, it is better not even to try, but to seek momentary happiness. But today we have a name for this approach to the theme of life and death: philistinism. The philistine, or uncultured

[14]Epicureans—in the proper sense, followers of the Greek philosopher Epicurus (c. 342–270 BC), whose teaching did not, however, promote thoughtless enjoyment.

[15]Hedonism is a trend in Western European ethics that originated in the Renaissance and, according to tradition, was introduced by the ancient Greek philosopher Socrates' student, Aristippus (c. 435–355 BC).

layman, is first of all one who does not want to be bothered by the breadth or height of life's meaning, who consciously or unconsciously wants only one thing out of life: forgetfulness. And if sometimes a germ of anxiety or fear gnaws at him deep inside (after all, time is running out, and death approaches as the years pass and old age intrudes!), he instinctively seeks to drown it out with the everyday hustle and bustle of life.

It must be frankly admitted that in this pursuit the philistine often turns to religion as well. There is philistine religion, just as there is philistine science and philistine philosophy. After all, if you seriously read the Gospel, it will become obvious that this book offers nothing soothing or comforting—none of what the uncultured layman seeks. On the contrary, everything in it infinitely deepens and intensifies those very "forbidden questions." It deepens and intensifies them, first of all, by making an impossible, unprecedented demand on the individual: *Be ye therefore perfect, even as your Father which is in heaven is perfect* (Mt 5.48). This requirement alone is obviously incompatible with the philistine yearning to be relaxed and carefree, with the philistine ideal of a small, quiet "prosperous life." The Gospel, further, speaks of a narrow path of self-denial, sacrifice, and effort: "He who wants to save his soul will lose it" (cf. Mt 16.25; Mk 8.35; Lk 9.24). It says that the rich and even the seeker of wealth cannot be saved (Mk 10.23–24); it summons men to absolutely breathtaking heights. Philistinism is so entrenched in the world, however, that even this teaching, which upends every kind of complacency, every kind of minimalism—even this the philistine manages to turn to his purpose, citing its impossibility as his excuse for remaining a philistine. And then religion itself becomes philistine in nature.

But the same thing happens with science and philosophy. The philistine very often appeals to science: "Science has proven, science has shown . . ." But every one who has tasted the nectar of science knows that the answers it finds are nothing compared to the bottomless questions that each such answer raises; that the farther science goes, the more clearly it faces the dread mystery of the world, in which everything is so harmonious, so wisely arranged, and where everything is filled with ennui and the senselessness of death that constantly engulfs life. And then all "scientific evidence" becomes useless. And Pascal, looking up in awe from his telescope, exclaims: "I am terrified by the silence of these endless spaces!"[16]

The philistine loves to philosophize, to thrill to poetry and music, but he does not allow himself to acknowledge that philosophy, poetry, and music, all that we call "culture," were born of the same fear, the same trepidation, the same attempt to rise above the world's pointlessness and find eternity in the temporal, to achieve a life which cannot be defined simply and terribly, as in Tolstoy's *The Death of Ivan Ilyich*: "And after a foolish life comes a foolish death."[17]

Mankind has always—and not simply now—been divided into philistines and those who, numbering far fewer, cannot come to terms with this philistinism, knowing that the real and ultimate calling of man is to fearlessly face the "forbidden questions" that confront him with the fact of his very being, and to engage all the abilities of his mind, soul, and heart in trying to answer them. The peculiarity of our time is that, in addition to there being philistines as such, it has also made philistinism an ideology. Previously, society and culture were at least well aware that philistinism is not the highest wisdom of humanity. Now, to our shame, it is philistinism which is declared to be the last word, the ultimate truth.

The best, though not the only, example of this ideology of philistinism is communism, for it consciously, and supposedly "scientifically," reduces all human life to matter. It denies the very existence of "forbidden" issues and it deduces human happiness from the material and economic sphere, which is philistinism in its purest form. Thus, the real struggle today is the struggle with philistinism, both in life and in ideology. And in this effort religion, science, and philosophy must join forces—but genuine religion, and authentic science, and true philosophy.

---

[16]"The eternal silence of these infinite spaces frightens me." Pascal, *Pensées*, §206 (Trotter trans., p. 78).

[17]In the story of Leo Tolstoy's *Death of Ivan Ilyich*, these words (cited with minor variations by Father Alexander in other talks, as well) are absent. He is likely remembering: "But I know that for me a life dedicated to my individual happiness is the greatest stupidity, and that after this foolish life I will certainly have only a foolish death." Leo Tolstoy, *What is My Faith?*

From Above
or from Below?

The Unity of Faith and Reason

There are many theories about the origin of religion, but they all acknowledge religion as a primal phenomenon of human history.

This means that religion appeared along with humanity, arising from the moment man could be considered a creature radically different from other living beings. Whatever the origin of man, from the moment when we know him as a man, we may rightly call him a religious being.

This fact should be kept in mind because modern atheist theorists, gripped by a deep and inexplicable hatred of religion, try to present religion as an incidental, random phenomenon, arising from one cause or another. Objective studies, however, show that religiosity is just as much a primordial and universal property of man as reason.

But the militant atheist consents to reason while rejecting religion. In it he sees something abnormal and hostile, and by no means natural to man. Man needs reason, but religion is superfluous. Why?

In essence, no answer has been given to this question, for surely one cannot take seriously the famous Marxist materialistic thesis that "religion is wholly the product of the exploitation of the have-nots by the haves"—that is, a kind of epiphenomenon[1] of the economy. Indeed, according to Marxism, the mind is also merely a "superstructure" imposed on matter, or rather, on the "material basis." Yet somehow it did not occur to Marx or his followers to deny the prevalence of reason on this basis and declare war

---

[1] An epiphenomenon is an incidental phenomenon.

on it. On the contrary, Marxists struggle with religion from the standpoint of "science," that is, what is rational and reasonable.

Is it not time therefore to openly admit that religiosity, like rationality, has always been a primary property of man? From the very beginning of his conscious, reflective, truly human existence, man has studied the world and himself, and has related to the world in two different yet conjoined ways—by reason and by faith. And over the centuries, reason and faith have not only not been at enmity, but have supplemented and enriched each other.

Their rupture and the onset of the war between them is a relatively recent matter, and if today this situation is declared "natural" and "inevitable," it is only due to the strange aberration of modern reason. For reason—in the view of a relatively small handful of scientists and philosophers who became intoxicated by the newfound possibilities of science—at some point proclaimed itself omnipotent and self-sufficient, able, first, to comprehend and explain everything, and second, to teach man everything necessary for him. But the trouble is that this small handful began to persecute all those who refused to accept the dogma of the omnipotence of reason. And these advocates of reason took great pains to create the illusion that all "advanced" and "truly enlightened" people accept this dogma, with faith supported only by deeply ignorant simpletons with no knowledge of science.

And so it continues to this day, and no one dares exclaim like the child in Andersen's famous fairy tale: "Look, the king is naked!" For all of this is a lie and a deception—one of grandiose proportions! There is no need to look far for examples. Take the best representatives of nineteenth century Russia—those whom history will remember even when the numberless bankrupt ideologies have been forgotten. Take Derzhavin and Pushkin, Baratynsky and Lermontov, Gogol and Tyutchev, Dostoevsky and Tolstoy, and in the twentieth century Pasternak and Akhmatova, Mandelstam and Solzhenitsyn. All these were believers, and quite safe from any accusation of blindness and ignorance. Moreover, for each of them faith, in one way or another, determined their whole worldview and creative work.

But what about those who contrasted reason to faith, discarding faith as a "harmful relic"? How have they enriched the world, and what will remain of them in human memory? Here, before our very eyes, they decided in one country to base all of life on godlessness, on the rejection of faith and the deification of reason. But why in this same country is it still necessary to defend this ideology with prisons and camps, with new persecutions of all dissenters? How in this country has fear increased to such vast proportions?

No, it is apparent that those mindless people made a fatal error when they decided that man needs only one of the two elements that have determined his being since time immemorial: they destroyed man's integrity, so much so that he has completely gone astray and does not know why he exists and where his aimless wanderings will lead.

Is it not time, therefore, to think about how to restore this integrity?

Polar Opposites

Can modern man believe in God? This question, which is often asked by both unbelievers and by believers themselves, has become a feature of the spiritual atmosphere of our time.

Some answer this question in the negative: "No, he cannot and should not." On their side are all those who, for over a century now, have claimed that faith is incompatible with scientific knowledge, that science has effectively (and deservedly!) killed religion. This simplistic conclusion was expressed by the astronaut Gagarin, who had been in space and did not find God there. They dissect a dead body, and find no soul in it; they study nature more and more thoroughly, and find no evidence of divine, supernatural powers, etc.

To this, the defenders of the faith most often answer that the percentage of believers among scientists who study this same nature not only is not decreasing, but is increasing, and this signifies an increasingly indisputable admission that nature has a secret, which science with its empirical methods is powerless to unravel. The same is true in other branches of knowledge, for unbelieving physicists, chemists, psychologists, and sociologists are countered by their many believing colleagues.

The dispute, which began during the Age of Enlightenment and reached its climax in the nineteenth century, has come to a standstill from a certain perspective, because no one ever convinced anyone of anything: the unbelievers did not convince the believers, and the believers did not convince the unbelievers. And it is no accident that in our days religion is attacked not by scientists (because unbelieving scientists get along quite well with their believing colleagues), but exclusively by the state ideological apparatus, which sees it as a source of instability. In other words, the state suppresses faith by brute force, and in extreme cases—by terror.

Of course, one should not conceal the fact that, while not currently, in the past unbelievers have also been subjected to state persecution. But for us, what matters is that in both cases neither true faith nor true science had anything to do with it. Nor, apparently, did modern civilization, whose legacy includes writers, artists, and scientists who openly professed either their faith or their unbelief. Nevertheless, the question of religion has become more acute in our civilization than in any other. What is the matter? Why do we all feel that the question of faith and unbelief is addressed anew to each of us? It seems that in order to answer it, we need to revisit one unprecedented feature of modernity.

Every historian will agree that the civilizations preceding our own (which originated around the time of the Renaissance) looked upward, so to speak. In other words, they applied a certain higher criterion to man and to all aspects of his life. Christianity, which had replaced ancient paganism, was decisively at variance with paganism's higher criterion. Nevertheless, in both cases the basic approach to that criterion was the same: both the one and the other recognized that everything in man comes from above and not from below, and that his life here is connected to some higher purpose, and only in this connection does he become fully human.

So, it was from this "from above," this "higher purpose," that our civilization began to be liberated. Whereas during the Renaissance the slogan advanced was: "Man is the measure of all things,"[2] very soon man himself lost his significance. For if man is not from above, but from below, if the

---

[2]The thesis "Man is the measure of all things" was first formulated by the ancient Greek philosopher Protagoras (fifth century BC), an adherent of so-called ancient sophistry.

individual is just a part of nature, then the true measure of all things is not man, but nature itself. And since impersonal science studies nature, it is up to science to explain nature, and to explain something regarded as merely one of its parts—man.

Indeed, our civilization from the very beginning consciously rejected any explanation of the world and man from above, and in this sense sidelined faith altogether: "Everything is from below, not from above." And this must be remembered if we want to understand the special acuteness of the question of faith for contemporary man. For even when he preserves his faith, he still senses its alienation from the basic attitude of our rationalistic civilization, which strives toward its petty human "happiness."

This conflict between the high and low explanations of man and the world must be discussed in this day and age. To this we will return in our next talk.

The Price of Rejection

In one of my previous talks I spoke about the fact that our modern civilization is in fact the first in the history of mankind to seek the explanation for everything in the world and in man, not from above, but from below. It is the first, in consciously proclaiming such ideas as "progress" and "liberation," to reject what was previously called "metaphysics" (the Greek word made up of *meta*—"after" or "the other side," and *physis*—nature, the root of "physics")—in other words, it refused what lay on the other side of nature and physics, that which is above them, which cannot be explained by physics, the laws of nature, and by empirical science alone.

One must understand that modern civilization is based on a strange paradox: it calls "progress" and "liberation" the reduction of everything in the world to the most elementary, biological processes.

Just recently the famous French biologist, Nobel laureate Jacques Monod,[3] wrote a sensational book, which he called *Chance and Necessity*. Everything in the world, in his opinion, is the result, on the one hand, of pure chance, and on the other, of pure necessity. Some cells accidentally collide, some processes accidentally intersect—this is blind chance, blind necessity, in which there is no revelation, no meaning, no purpose to be discovered or acknowledged. The impression this book leaves is terrible: it turns out that we are living in some kind of frozen wilderness, our life is snuffed out the moment it flares up, and everything in it is an illusion. Personality is an illusion, freedom is an illusion, creativity is an illusion, love is an illusion . . .

All that Jacques Monod expects and demands from man is reconciliation with this pointless existence, and all that he offers is his own peculiar ethic of patience. And since Monod is one of the greatest representatives of modern science, this hopeless book should be recognized as the most significant expression of the spirit of our civilization. Monod is asked: what about religion, spirit, truth, beauty? And he honestly replies: "There is nothing; it is all an illusion, a fiction." Why? Simply because exact science knows nothing of all this, because all this does not follow from an "objective" study of nature. And since man has no way of knowing the world except for the "objective sciences," there is nothing to be said. Thus, the main and end result of our civilization is the renunciation of the higher destiny of man; this destiny is now declared to be an illusion.

It is not only religion that those of one mind with Monod reject. Equally unnecessary, unscientific, and illusory in their eyes are ideologies that have made "progress" their religion, promising humanity freedom, equality, and fraternity, about which, again, no "real" science knows anything. Indeed, what freedom can there be if everything in the world is the product of chance and necessity? What sort of equality is this, and where does this fraternity come from? Fraternity is possible between personalities, but if

[3]Jacques-Lucien Monod (1910–1976): French biochemist and microbiologist, Nobel laureate in physiology and medicine (1965). His book *Chance and Necessity* (*Le Hasard et la Necessité*) was published in Paris in 1970.

the personality itself is the same sort of illusion, the same sort of chance, the same sort of necessity, then does this fraternity come from?

No, only if we look honestly at our civilization, stripping it of all its masks and digging to its very core, will it become clear that at this core lies hopelessness, that it is based on complete darkness, sheer nihilism. True, this hopelessness is hidden from millions of people, because on the surface our civilization looks, on the contrary, extremely optimistic: people have conquered space, they have walked on the moon, they have built an even more powerful and faster plane, they have found another remedy for some kind of disease!

But if you stop to think for a moment and ask what all this speed and power are ultimately aimed at, all this non-stop evolution of knowledge and skills, then the ideologues of our civilization strive in every possible way to evade the question. "That is metaphysics," they protest, "and we are not engaged in metaphysics!" But behind the feigned optimism of modernity, fear is increasingly apparent. For institutions for the mentally ill have never been so crowded, the suicide rate has never been so high, and man has never lived in such terrible bewilderment, in such painful doubt, in such primal confusion.

And maybe it is time to ask of what worth a civilization is that is unable to answer the chief question: what does man live for and what is the meaning of his life? Maybe it is time to question this very rejection of metaphysics, this very deification of science, this whole triumph of bland rationalism, which promised man a paradise on earth and have created either a global home for the insane or else a global prison. And perhaps in this, this rejection of metaphysics and ultimate questions, lies the source of all the terrible entanglements of life in the modern world?

Once a Russian man said with a smile: "Blessed is the believer; he finds warmth in the world!"[4] But in this remark, in this near mockery of faith, is not a profound truth perhaps now revealed? Right now, when life on earth has become so cold, so inhospitable, and so terrifying? Yes, blessed are those who believe, and they find warmth in the world. And isn't it time

[4]The words of Chatsky from the comedy by A. S. Griboedov, "Woe from Wit" (1824), Act 1, Scene 7.

to pose the question: what kind of faith is this that gives one light, joy, and warmth, and has it really been debunked by proverbial "science"? Is it so naïve as we are insistently told by those who have nothing but "chance" and "necessity" to replace this faith with its joyous warmth?

"What Dost Thou Believe?"

In our previous talk I cited an old proverb: "Blessed is the believer; he finds warmth in the world!" This proverb now sounds like a mockery of faith, like the mild pity of the smart man for one who is not so smart, who still believes in "the good Lord," in miracles, and other "nonsense."

But since this smart fellow himself has not been able to create any warmth, has not revealed any light, and has not given anyone any joy, but on the contrary has filled the world with fear and nonsense, I suggested that we listen to this old proverb anew and ask ourselves whether it does not contain that simple and eternal truth without which it is impossible for man to live a full, real life on this earth.

To start with, I offer some simple truths that do not require any evidence.

The first truth: it is in man's nature to strive for happiness, to look for precisely this "bliss" or warmth. Everyone agrees with this—the believer and the unbeliever, the smart man and the ignorant one, and therefore it is precisely happiness that is promised to man by all religions, all philosophies, all ideologies.

The second truth is just as simple: the only happy person on this earth, in this life, is the one who believes. I will instantly add that I mean not religious faith, but faith as an indispensable element of the human worldview: you can believe in God, but you can also believe, for example, in science. It is important to believe and it is important that it is belief, and not something else, that gives us happiness.

And what then is faith? First of all, it is the heart's acceptance of a certain ideal, a love for it, and an experience of it as a source of happiness. And from this point of view, all faith, and not just religious belief in God, is unprovable, precisely because it is faith, and not knowledge. For the lover, happiness is in union with his beloved, but since he has not yet experienced this union, he does not yet know this, but only believes it, and this faith itself is already happiness. When Karl Marx says that the result of the revolutionary process will be a leap from the "kingdom of necessity" to the "kingdom of freedom" and universal happiness, he still does not know anything about this leap, nor about this freedom, nor about this happiness. Consequently, he also believes, and in this faith alone lies the happiness of all who share the same ideology.

Thus, happiness lies in faith, but faith does not require or seek proof, precisely because it is faith: it is the aspiration of the whole person to what he has perceived and experienced as an ideal, as a value—in other words, as something that can offer happiness. But then, truly "blessed is he who believes," and it remains only to ask which faith and which ideal promise and even now bring him the greatest happiness, the greatest bliss, the greatest warmth.

Hence the third truth: essentially, when people debate, they do so only about faith. The real subject of the debate is always not science or religion at all, not socialism or capitalism, not this or that ideology, but what the person has given his heart to, what destiny he believes in, what happiness he seeks for himself and others. In this sense, every person is religious, everyone believes in something, and when he ceases to believe, he ceases to be human, and most importantly, he becomes infinitely miserable. He can stifle this misery with vodka, stop it with a bullet or a noose, but the misery itself always comes from unbelief, from losing the most vital, deepest property of human nature—the need to believe.

And if that is so, then it is not only appropriate, but also necessary to approach each person with the question, "What do you believe?"—that is, what is your ideal, your happiness, your bliss, your warmth?—and then compare this faith with one's own and, if necessary, debate it.

And do not tell us that you do not believe in God because "science has proven" that there is no God. You know better than we that no genuine science has ever dealt with God and could prove neither his existence nor his non-existence. You do not believe in the God in whom we believe, and for this reason you believe in another god! So tell us—which one? You deny our happiness, our warmth, because you want another happiness—tell me, then, which one? Let's debate this honestly and openly. Without citing science, for science knows what one can verify by experience, what one can see, whereas concerning God our faith itself says: *No man hath seen God at any time* (Jn 1.18). Without citing the shortcomings, sins, and crimes of believers of all times, for we all know them, and even our faith itself is a belief in one who was persecuted, crucified, and killed not by unbelievers, but by believers. Nowhere is so much said against the abuse of faith and religion as in the Gospel, and so let us set aside this argument. Only one thing is important, that which is deepest and most essential—what I believe and what you believe.

For, you and I, we both *believe*, and if we did not believe, then we could not live. And so let's start the debate: I will talk about my faith and try to answer questions about it just as if you were answering questions about your own. Only this kind of debate about faith is needed and possible nowadays—a debate without false evidence and recourse to false authorities; a debate about what is happening at the true core of man, in his heart; a debate about that to which a person wants to and ought to surrender himself.

In Search of Common Ground

Afew weeks ago a wonderful book was published in Paris, containing conversations of the young French philosopher Christian Chabanis[5] with twenty prominent representatives of various sciences (physics, philosophy, economics, and others) known for their atheism, that is, their non-affiliation with any religion. He asked them questions about the reasons for

---

[5]Christian Chabanis (1936–1989): French religious philosopher, writer, and journalist; laureate of the Catholic Prize for Literature (1985). *Does God Exist? No! Interviews with P. Anquetil, R. Aron, Ch. Boulle, Denise Calippe, Juliette et A. Darle, P. Debray-Ritzen, J. Du- clos, G. Elgozy, R. Garaudy, A. Grosser, D. Guérin, E. Ionesco, Fr. Jacob, A. Kastler, Cl. Lévi-Strauss, Isabelle Meslin, Edg. Morin, H. Petit, J. Rostand et J. Vilar* [Dieu existe-t-il ? Non, répondent P. Anquetil, et al.] (Paris: Fayard, 1973).

their atheism and its place in their worldview. The conversations yielded striking results, and it seems to us that this book should be of exceptional interest to all who are occupied with the problems of faith and unbelief in the modern world. Chabanis began with Nobel laureate Professor Alfred Kastler,[6] one of the most famous physicists. From the outset, Professor Kastler said that for the modern physicist, the possibility of the accidental origin of the world is excluded: it is too obvious that it has a strange consistency and an inexplicable orientation toward an unknown goal.

"Thus," the compiler of the book asks Kastler, "your scientific findings in no way confirm the usual assertions of atheism? They do not contradict the idea of God?"

"No!" the scientist answers. "I have arrived at the conclusion that today a biologist is in the same position as a physicist in 1900. Then, physicists thought that they already knew everything, that physics was essentially a complete science. But experience has shown that everything needs to be reviewed. Today the same is true with biology, and therefore no synthesis can yet be declared."

"Therefore," Chabanis asks, "although you do not defend the hypothesis of God, you do not deny it, and in any case your unbelief is not based on your scientific knowledge?"

"Precisely so," says Professor Kastler.

"But then on what?" his interlocutor asks.

"I have to say," Kastler responds, "that I'm endlessly worried about my inability to preserve my own childhood faith, and especially the belief in an idea as beautiful as it seems to me to be false, that God is love. If I accepted the existence of an omniscient and omnipotent God, I still could not believe that this God is love. My experience of studying the world forces me to acknowledge that the basis of life at all its levels is death."

"But do you see a contradiction between love and death?"

"Yes," answers Kastler. "If I were the Creator, it seems to me I would find a way to create a world without its progress being based on destruction and suffering."

---

[6] Alfred Kastler (1902–1984): French physicist of German descent, winner of the 1966 Nobel Prize for research in the field of optics.

To this Chabanis observes that it is no coincidence that Christianity has as its cornerstone the victory over death.

"I only know one thing," Kastler says, "and I know this on the basis of many years of research: there is a purpose in the world, but we do not yet see what it consists of."

"And so," his interlocutor concludes, "today science itself brings us to this mystery. As for faith, it remains what it has always been—a leap into this mystery, is it not?"

"Yes, perhaps," replies Kastler.

Here we have an abridged conversation of one of the great, if not the greatest, modern physicists with an honest and open Christian interlocutor. Much of the historical existence of religion troubles Kastler: divisions among believers themselves, the formulas of individual dogmas, etc. And yet how far he is from that stupid enmity, from that cheap omniscience, of which our official atheism smacks with its constant refrain: "Science has proven that there is no God!" But here, listen to Professor Kastler: no, it has proven nothing. And when it remains true to itself, when it is honest, open, and deep, when it acts in accordance with its own principles, science itself ultimately recognizes the existence in the world of a goal, a finality, that surpasses all the possibilities of science and all understanding.

Yes, Professor Kastler has lost his childhood faith. But maybe there is a peculiar dialectic here—the dialectic of faith itself. It is no accident that the Gospel says so much about seeking, about thirst and hunger; it is not by chance that the whole of the Gospel is a fervent call to "knock on the door." And if anything today unites authentic faith with authentic science, then it is a constant willingness to seek, a constant openness to the mystery of being.

The debate between faith and science most often takes place at a disappointingly low level, like the debate between pseudoscience and weak, self-righteous, Pharisaic faith. But when this dispute is at its highest—where the participants are not afraid to look into the eyes of truth and sacrifice everything to achieve it—that lofty conversation begins in which, in essence, the fate of each person and of humanity is decided.

Here is the first conclusion that can be drawn from the wonderful book of Chabanis, dedicated to modern atheism and exposing all its complexity and inconsistency. The fact is, for a long time unbelief and rejection of God were presented as the result of the progressive development of the human intellect. Chabanis' book destroys this myth. Faith appears in it as it has always been, and as it is defined in the Gospel: specifically as a gift. The rejection of God is shown to be not the result of scientific development, but the fruit of stubborn unwillingness to see the light that is present in the world. And it is this light, which Professor Kastler speaks of, that he cannot yet name.

The Need for Something Immeasurably Greater

In our last conversation we talked about a book just published in France, in which the author, the Catholic Chabanis, asks twenty leading academic scientists a question about the reasons for and the nature of their unbelief. I cited several remarks by a Nobel laureate in physics, Alfred Kastler.

Today I want to cite a representative of another science, the renowned sociologist Edgar Morin.[7] Morin is known for his historical, ethnographic, and cultural works, and his sensational book on the development of mankind had just been published.

To the question of what elicited his atheism, Morin replies: "I feel the need to immediately clarify that my disbelief should be called 'neo-atheism.'" To the question of what that is, Morin clarifies: "This is, first of all, the conviction that religion is not restricted to what we usually mean—it is found everywhere and in everything. To speak of Reason with a capital R is in itself a religion, for ideas can take on the role of the Divine, and from this point of view almost all people are religious in one way or another. However—and this is very important—my neo-atheism acknowledges the existence of that which has not yet been explained and is, in essence, inex-

[7]Edgar Morin (b. 1921 as Edgar Nahoum): French philosopher and sociologist, scholar of modern Western civilization.

plicable. When I hear Christian scholars speak of mystical theology, which implies contact with the Inexplicable, I feel that something in me responds to this. In the world, everything is explainable, except for what is ultimate and most important. And therefore, a sense of mystery is inherent in me to the highest degree."

In his youth, Morin was a member of the Communist Party, which he left, by his own admission, precisely because of the lack of depth in communist ideology. For him, communism is a reduction of man to one dimension, yet we are confronted with the incomprehensible mystery of existence. "And in this sense," Morin explains, "I cannot simply identify my neo-atheism as synonymous with unbelief. On the one hand, I cannot join any of the existing religions, and from this point of view I am, perhaps, an unbeliever. But on the other hand, I do not at all think that faith is just an alloy of superstitions, to which the truth of reason stands in opposition; such an attitude to religion is primitive and stupid."

And he adds: "In no way do I make a deity or a fetish of science. I have already said that science by its very nature is very limited. Undoubtedly, there are other ways of thinking and learning—metaphysical and symbolic—and these methods, these ways, are much more profound than scientific methods. Poetry, for example, may say something unusually profound, but when translated into the language of ordinary logic it becomes extremely flat. Poetry, metaphors, symbolism—all these are bearers of truths that science, in my deepest conviction, cannot translate into its own language. I find that there is nothing deeper and more significant than the language of religion when it speaks, for example, of death."

Chabanis asks a question about the relationship between science and faith in the modern world.

"I see no need for a conflict between them," Morin replies. "Pasteur[8] was a scientist and a believer, Teilhard de Chardin—a believer and scientist. One can live on different planes and levels—the natural and the supernatural—at the same time. Personally, I do not believe that the development of science threatens religion in any way. We see with increasing clarity that a person needs the spiritual, poetic dimension, a deep inner life, and that this

[8]Louis Pasteur (1822–1895): French chemist and microbiologist.

need is especially evident where religion is condemned by official ideology. This happens, for example, in the Soviet Union, where official Marxism and Leninism is a worldview so dogmatic, so schematic, so impoverished, that it does not illumine anything whatsoever in any dimension of human life. Science, in essence, exposes and intensifies a person's deep-seated need for something immeasurably greater than itself. And from my point of view, it can only be a question of whether past religions satisfy this need, or whether there will be another religious mutation, a religious metamorphosis—the birth of another religion."

Such are the thoughts about faith and unbelief of the famous French sociologist Edgar Morin. He calls himself a "neo-atheist," but again, as in the case of the physicist Alfred Kastler, we see that this "neo-atheism" is worlds apart from the flat atheism of official propaganda. And one may ask: is this in fact atheism? Is this recognition of mystery and depth in all dimensions of life closer to true religion than cheap godlessness and—alas, no less frequent—cheap faith, of which there is so much in our world? And does this neo-atheism perhaps serve to deepen our own faith, to help us plunge into its ultimate, joyful depth?

Thus, we find that the study of this new atheism, or rather, the atheism of scholars free of all dogmatism, is in some deep sense useful for religion.

Beyond the Bounds of Science

In the two preceding talks I spoke about scholars who consider themselves unbelievers and attempt to explain their unbelief. One of them was the Nobel laureate in physics Alfred Kastler, the other—the famous French sociologist Edgar Morin.

Today we will talk about a representative of a third basic science of our time—economics. The same author, the young French philosopher Christian Chabanis, who recorded the statements about faith and unbelief by Kastler and Morin, turned to one of the world's luminaries in this field—Georges Elgozy.[9] Once again, he did so because Elgozy considers himself to be an unbeliever.

When asked how he understands his unbelief, Elgozi answers as follows: "It seems to me that most people are constantly vacillating, like me, between faith and unbelief. A person always emerges from this persistent internal conflict even more of a human, so to speak: spiritual tension appears in him, and it seems to me that what's important here is not the answer to the question, but the question itself. This is the whole drama of man: there is not a single fundamental problem that, if studied in depth, does not prove even more acute. Hope and love, obviously, are the first stages of faith. But you can stop at them and go no further. As for me, I prefer love without faith to faith without love."

The interlocutor asks him to clarify his last words.

"Love for me," Elgozy answers, "is the most concrete thing that a person can do in life. There is nothing abstract left here—only the sacrifice that a person makes for the sake of another person. He cannot go further than this. And faith without love is a kind of monster of egoism."

"But doesn't faith as such," his interlocutor asks, "signify a belief in love that it is stronger than death and stronger than all that is a denial of love?"

"Yes, of course," Elgozy answers, "for otherwise faith would be nothing more than belief in oneself."

"But then you, in essence, do not distinguish between faith and unbelief?"

"I think," says Elgozy, "that in reality the matter is far more complicated. For the very recognition of man as something completely unique and exclusive, the recognition of him as an entity incomparable to anyone else, this very positing and exaltation of man is a kind of faith, a kind of denial of atheism."

"But then this means," the interlocutor observes, "the recognition of each person as a particle of God."

"Yes," Elgozy answers, "but this does not mean acknowledging the existence of a personal God. For me, honesty means never affirming more

[9]The French economist G. Elgozy (1909–1989) is also known for his writings on political science.

than what you believe. Yes, in man I really see and acknowledge something that is fundamentally different from everything else in the world. This is a self-evident postulate for me, but my scientific formation prevents me from going any further. Oh yes, I admit that besides the material world there is also the non-material—something we cannot deny. Call it 'soul,' call it 'thought,' but to go further and define this intangible is speculation for me, whereas love is concrete, experienced."

"You mentioned," Chabanis notes, "the problem of death."

"Yes," the scientist replies, "this problem has been occupying me more and more recently. Believing in immortality would be faith, but I am still in doubt. And doubt seems to me a basic human property, although in actuality I envy those who believe in the immortality of man."

"In other words, you have doubts about your own doubting?" his interlocutor asks.

"Yes," says Elgozy. "I think that a person's education should have been completely different. Today in our world the main problems of man are simply ignored: they make him forget about what is most important, and therefore people know neither how to live nor how to die."

"Do you think," Chabanis asks, "that religion is a stage in the development of mankind, and that after this stage universal atheism will reign supreme?"

"No, because society never stops in its development, nor is human development completed," Elgozy replies. "With any technological progress, the measurable and defined will always remain an insignificant part of the inexplicable and the mysterious. Therefore, in the future I foresee the same fluctuation between faith and unbelief: a person always doubts when he does not have faith."

The physicist Kastler, the sociologist Morin, and now the economist Elgozy—three scientists who honestly admit that they have no faith—perhaps not yet—but who also admit that the very science they serve is not the conclusive explanation of the world and man; that behind it and beyond it lies the mystery of being, the mystery of love and sacrifice, the mystery of humanity, the mystery of the human soul.

But don't we believers know that in the Gospel faith is called a gift? And are not all these unbelievers nearer this gift than people who have created gods for themselves from small and limited human ideas and ideologies?

We know, we believe that where there is genuine searching, the light is near, the untold joy of faith is close; we know this, and it is not our humanly insignificant arguments that will compel unbelievers to believe.

And therefore the dialogue initiated by Chabanis with unbelievers, who recognize spirit, who recognize mystery, is a dialogue more necessary and more important than any cheap polemics.

Joy or a Satiety?

Christ is Risen!

"Resurrection," "Ascension," "the Descent of the Holy Spirit"— what amazing, what beautiful words, amazing in their very sound, their very orientation! They joyfully echo in the heart before one has time to think about their meaning, their churchly religious significance. With these words we experience all the weeks between Pascha, the feast of feasts, and the day that ends the Paschal period of the church year and which has been known from the earliest times as "the last and great day"—the day of Pentecost. During these fifty days believers do not kneel, and Paschal hymns resound in the churches.[10] This is the brightest, most joyful time in the Church, and one of her hymns says it best: "Today the sweet fragrance of spring abounds, and renewed creation rejoices."[11]

The enemies of religion say that it was engendered by fear, humiliation, and slavery; that it arose from something negative, sad, and gloomy. But how could these words, this stream of joy and light, be born and sound forth from darkness and sorrow? Does not the Gospel begin with words of joy? *I bring you good tidings of great joy,* the angel says to the shepherds on the feast of the

[10]According to the church regulations, Paschal hymns, as well as the troparion "Christ is Risen," are sung in Orthodox churches until the leave-taking of Pascha, celebrated on the eve of the feast of the Ascension of the Lord.

[11]Thomas Sunday, Hymn of Light.

Nativity (Lk 2.10). And does not the Gospel end with the fact that Christ's disciples returned to Jerusalem *with great joy* from the mount of his Ascension (Lk 24.52)? "Yes," answer the enemies of religion, "but this is some sort of a future joy, promised but not yet fulfilled, that pertains to another world and, so to speak, compensates for human suffering, sadness, and humiliation in this life!" Not so: this joy lit up and shone forth in our land, in our lives, and has lain at the heart of Christian life for almost two thousand years. *But I will see you again,* Christ promises the disciples on the night of his betrayal and suffering, *and your heart shall rejoice, and your joy no man taketh from you* (Jn 16.22). *Rejoice!* (Mt 28.9) he says on the morning of the Resurrection to the women who came to weep at his tomb. *Rejoice . . . and again I say, rejoice* (Phil 4.4), writes the Apostle Paul in one of his messages, and defines the whole Christian life as *righteousness, and peace, and joy in the Holy Spirit* (Rom 14.17). And so on throughout the ages. "Fire . . . peace . . . joy, joy, joy," Pascal writes on the night of his conversion;[12] "My joy!"—with these words Saint Seraphim of Sarov greets everyone who comes to him. This joy flows from the icons through which heaven is glimpsed, from the churches, from all the Paschal hymns: "Now all is filled with light . . . let us be illumined by the feast . . . let us embrace each other joyously; let us call brothers even those who hate us and forgive all by the resurrection!"

No, it is time to cast off this unworthy and useless falsehood about religion as something sad, unnatural, full of fear and feelings of guilt. On the contrary, where a person forgets this joy, where he renounces it in the name of earthly, material happiness, sooner or later drabness and boredom will prevail, and despondency seizes the soul. To verify this we need only look around: what do these self-avowed exclusive specialists in happiness promise men in place of Christian joy? Essentially, one thing only: satiety. For they have long proclaimed in their thick treatises that the only

---

[12]From Pascal's *Mémorial*, which records his experience on the "night of fire" (November 23, 1654): "From about half-past ten at night until about half-past midnight, fire. God of Abraham, God of Isaac, God of Jacob. Not of the philosophers and of the learned. Certitude, certitude, feeling, joy, peace. God of Jesus Christ. My God and your God. Your God will be my God. Forgetfulness of the world and of everything except God. He is only found by way of the directions taught in the Gospel. The grandeur of the human soul. *Righteous Father, the world has not known you, but I have known you* [Jn 17.25]. Joy, joy, joy, tears of joy." Translation in Marvin Richard O'Connell, *Blaise Pascal: Reasons of the Heart* (Grand Rapids, MI: W.B. Eerdmans Publishing Company, 1997), 96 (slightly modified).

motivator of all human affairs, of all history, is the struggle for satiety. Satiety, equality thereof, and some sort of fictitious, purely abstract "freedom" from an equally abstract "exploitation"—this is all they have managed to invent and offer man instead. Instead of what? Instead of the Resurrection, the Ascension, the Descent of the Holy Spirit and the joy they offer to all. What a terrible substitution, what a horrific fall of the very ideal, the very meaning of life!

Perhaps, if these apostles and preachers of satiety were themselves joyful, peaceful, and happy, like well-fed animals. But no! Wherever they succeed in imposing their theory, fear and suspicion abound: the land is covered with prisons and labor camps for dissenters, and only brute force can protect this ugly vision of life, which replaces it with a bleak and joyless existence.

One need not fully grasp the full import of the words "Resurrection," "Ascension," "Descent of the Holy Spirit": they can be interpreted differently, as thousands of philosophers and theologians have done for twenty centuries. For each epoch, and perhaps for each person, they sound unique, and cast a special kind of light, and yet everyone senses behind them an exalted, pure, joyful plan for the world, for life, and for man. Everyone experiences here the mysterious source of joy for which he was created, by which alone a man can truly live. And this is why, no matter how much he is compelled to limit himself to satiety, despite all prohibitions and obstacles, a man will go to where these words abide, where their joy shines, where the Holy Spirit blows and the soul is imbued with that peace which is said to pass all understanding (cf. Phil 4.7).

Christ is risen! Truly he is risen!

In a United World

Forty days after Pascha, Christians have always celebrated the feast of the Lord's Ascension. Christ's ascent into heaven is described in the Gospel of Luke. After recounting the appearance of the risen Lord to the disciples, the evangelist Luke writes: *And he led them out as far as to Bethany, and he lifted up his hands, and blessed them. And it came to pass, while he blessed them, he was parted from them, and carried up into heaven. And they worshipped him, and returned to Jerusalem with great joy, and were continually in the temple, praising and blessing God* (Lk 24.50–53).

As you can see, the Gospel account is extremely short and simple. But that is precisely why probably nothing else in Christianity, except the resurrection itself, caused so many doubts, so much ridicule and "debunking," as the fact that Christ, after rising from the dead, ascended into heaven. Long before the heyday of militant atheism and the war on religion in our century, human intelligence was scandalized by the Gospel words concerning the ascension. What kind of heaven is this, and where is Christ now, if he ascended there in his resurrected body? How does faith respond to this, and can it even answer?

But first it is necessary to resolve another crucial question: what is tested against what—faith against reason or reason against faith? The believer has no doubt that it is faith against which we must test our weak, limited intelligence, which is bound by three dimensions and the three laws of logic. But the unbeliever, who only lives by this intelligence, will still not believe it, even if you explain to him how believers understand the word "ascension." And this is because he does not have an internal organ capable of grasping this meaning. One who is born blind can talk about light and colors as much as he wants, but he still does not have, and cannot have, a direct knowledge of the light itself, or of the colors themselves. But does this not mean that faith simply abandons reason, as if to say: "If the mind is not able to understand something, so be it; just believe blindly and do not argue"? No, the fact of the matter is that in the experience of faith the mind itself broadens and deepens, and therefore it is made capable of understanding that which is impossible to understand outside the light of faith. The believer does not live in disconnected worlds of faith and reason, but in a unified world where reason is permeated by faith and where faith is perceived as the highest rationality, as an authentic answer to all the ultimate questions and perplexities of the mind.

"O Christ God, thou hast ascended in glory, granting joy to thy disciples . . ."[13]—these words are sung in the chief hymn of this feast. And in another: "When thou hadst fulfilled the dispensation for our sake, and united earth to heaven: thou didst ascend in glory, O Christ our God, not being parted from those who love thee, but remaining with them and crying: 'I am with you and no one will be against you!' "[14] And so, hearing these words, we immediately feel ourselves at the heart of a joyful mystery: he left, yet remained inseparable from us in the world; he ascended, yet fulfilled the promise: "I will be with you!" And how beautifully we find ourselves spared from that flat logic that states that if he left, then he is no longer with us; if he ascended, then he is no longer on earth. And therefore the whole answer, the whole joy of this faith and this feast, lies in something incomparably deeper, which cannot be expressed in the concepts of our logic. For this is not referring to those "astronomical" heavens which, no matter how high you rise, still remain part of our world, our cosmos. In the language of faith, in the language of the Gospel, the heavens are divine reality itself, that spiritual world with which one can commune only by ascending, by rising spiritually and thereby overcoming the terrible inertia that drags us down and prevents us from experiencing this divine reality.

No, Christ did not leave the world, he did not leave us, but he manifested in the world and in us the light, joy, and power of the ascension, which leads man into that truly heavenly dimension for which he was created and without which he cannot but feel himself a miserable and savage creature. And now in Christ, in this perfect and therefore divine Man, the image of this ascent is given to us; heaven is revealed to us as the triumph of love and truth, goodness and beauty. And everyone who has come to love Christ knows that there is no separation, that he did not go to some unknown heaven in the clouds, but revealed and granted to us heaven on earth. That is why the Gospel says of the disciples that they returned to Jerusalem with great joy. In appearance, everything remained the same: the road on which they were returning to the city, the city itself that they entered, the people they met. Around us also, everything apparently remains the same. But faith

[13] Troparion of the Ascension.
[14] Kontakion of the Ascension.

sees, knows, and joyfully accepts the heavenly light that shines through all this: in everything and everyone faith recognizes the image of Christ. And the mind, illuminated by faith, increasingly comprehends that the sole purpose and goal of each of us is to ascend, to overcome in ourselves all that is base; and that heaven, to which Christ ascended mysteriously, without being separated from us, is the final, all-conquering, and all-defining truth about man.

"Humanism" Exposed

Recently a Moscow radio station broadcast a talk by Professor Vasily Ivanovich Prokofiev, Ph.D.,[15] on the dialogue between humanism and Christianity. The professor began with a simple statement: "Humanism is love and respect for people." And he added: "True humanism in our time can only be socialist, revolutionary humanism. This humanism of the builders of the new world is based on profound faith in the working man, on caring for him and his happiness."

But this affirmation of Professor Prokofiev is only a pretext. The real purpose of his talk is to prove that the aspirations of "modern Christian ideologues" to equate humanism with Christianity are false. In other words, this is yet another attack on religion. "Christian theologians," says Prokofiev, "make every effort to convince people that only evangelical morality is characterized by harmony and humanity. In attempting to attribute humanistic traits to Christian morality, its apologists especially often cite the commandments of love for God and neighbor. Love for people, from their point of view, is unthinkable in itself. A person can be loved only in God and for God."

Christianity does indeed claim that if there is no God, the Source of love, if the essence of human consciousness—mind, conscience, etc.—is just a "superstructure" imposed on impersonal matter and completely

---

[15]Vasily Ivanovich Prokofiev (1909–1987): specialist in the field of "scientific" atheism with a primary focus on a critique of Christian morality.

determined by it, then love for a person is impossible and is inevitably replaced by love for some abstract "humanity." This is what Christianity asserts, and Prokofiev does not answer this basic assertion, since there is no answer to be made. For all non-religious humanism sooner or later leads to the destruction of thousands, even millions, of certain people for the sake of the "happiness" of others. And, of course, it is not easy to prove otherwise to people living in our country who for years have experienced the fruits of "revolutionary" humanism in all its horror. But, I repeat, Professor Prokofiev is not trying to prove anything. The goal of his talk is not to defend non-religious humanism, but to denounce Christian humanism. And here, after starting with a correctly formulated thesis, he proceeds to systematically distort Christian teaching. Why? Because, were he to tell the truth about religion, this truth would be in contradiction with the official, flatly accepted point of view.

Lest this charge be thought groundless, let us cite a few examples. "The love of God, according to Christian doctrine," says Professor Prokofiev, "is the first, main form of love, and love for man is the second, its lowest form." This invites the question: when and where was this ever said, and by whom? The Apostle John the Theologian says the exact opposite. "How can you love God," he asks, "whom you cannot see, if you do not love your brother whom you see?" (cf. 1 Jn 4.20). And Christ himself says that only by their love will people recognize his disciples. Yes, Christ really does say—and Professor Prokofiev quotes—*If any man come to me, and hate not his father, and mother, and wife, and children, and brethren, and sisters, yea, and his own life also, he cannot be my disciple* (Lk 14.26). But if you read the Gospel in its entirety, it turns out that these words are not only *not* directed against love, but, on the contrary, are the most striking example of the Christian understanding of it. For love for "one's own," which is quite often a selfish love, is a manifestation of love not for people, but for oneself. And this selfish, self-contained love is indeed denounced by Christ and Christianity. For true love for others, love purified from egoism, cannot exist without ascribing everything in life to something higher—to that which rises above the level of instinct, above animal attachment only to oneself and one's own. "These words," says Professor Prokofiev, "call upon us to acknowledge nothing and no one in this 'world of sin.'" But about this "world of sin" Christ said: *God so loved the world, that he gave his only begotten Son . . . not . . . to condemn the world, but that the world through him might be saved* (Jn 3.16, 17).

There is more. "Christian morality," Professor Prokofiev says indignantly, "calls us even to love our enemies." Here the whole logic of Professor Prokofiev is unmasked, rendering all his subsequent arguments completely meaningless. For, of course, it is not Christian theologians who contradict themselves, but Prokofiev himself, in his assertion that genuine humanism is on his side. After all, "socialist" or "revolutionary" humanism, as you know, encourages destroying one's enemies. But didn't Prokofiev himself say that humanism is love and respect for man? Not only for the man who agrees with you, not only for the one whose existence is sanctioned by the Party and progressive teaching, but simply for man. Christianity explains that people became enemies of each other because of the triumph of evil and sin. One can and must love one's enemies, it says, because love and brotherhood are primary, while hostility is secondary. Conversely, the ideology of Professor Prokofiev begins by dividing people into two groups—"enemies" and "one's own"—and ends by exalting the mortal hatred of one's enemies as the basic principle of life. And he defines humanism as caring for "one's own," and for them alone. And therefore it is natural that the path of such "humanism" is always the path of violence, bloodshed, and enslavement. What else is left to argue about?

False Antagonism

A Fundamental Difference

According to your faith be it unto you (Mt 9.29)—these words of Christ are often repeated in the Gospel.[1] "Faith moves mountains," says the Russian man. And how important it is to feel the reality and primacy of faith in religion, how important it is to understand that faith is cannot be equated with the philosophical and theological formulas and constructs to which the enemies of religion so often reduce it, against which they then launch polemics in their treatises.

It is possible and necessary to speak of faith as knowledge, but only if we first admit that this knowledge is radically different from what we call "scientific." To agree with the statement that "two plus two equals four," you need nothing more than basic logic. Such knowledge does not depend on the internal state of the one who utters the statement—it is absolute, obvious, and constant everywhere and always. A man at the pinnacle of joy and a man in the depths of despair (for example, one who plans to commit suicide) both know that twice two is four, and this knowledge in no way depends on the joy of the one and the despair of the other, nor is it likely to affect them: it is indisputable, and nothing more. But the assertion that Jesus Christ is God and man or that in the man Jesus God came down to earth to people—this statement cannot become a self-evident truth for all, for outside of faith it makes no sense whatsoever. But for the believer it expresses his inner knowledge, his spiritual experience, with the utmost accuracy.

[1]Cf. Lk 15.28; Mt 9.22; Mk 5.34, 10.52; Lk 7.50, 8.48, 17.19, 18.42

The point, however, is that anti-religious propaganda takes the words and formulas that express faith and uses them as if they were on the "two plus two equals four" plane, in which case it is indeed quite easy to demonstrate the unprovability of these religious statements. God became man—how is this possible? Indeed, from the standpoint of simple logic, this seems impossible, and even if this were theoretically possible, how can we prove conclusively and indisputably that the union of God and man was accomplished specifically in Christ? This whole attack on religion, which for years has been declaring it to be a kind of "science" so as to more easily crush it from the standpoint of real science, only degrades the attackers themselves. For religion begins by distinguishing between faith and knowledge—not setting them at odds, but specifically distinguishing between them. And as love cannot be measured by a thermometer, so faith cannot be reduced to logical and scientific statements.

The real question is whether faith is a special form of knowledge, one that cannot be reduced to knowledge that is wholly and exclusively rational and deductive. Anti-religious propaganda rests on the naïve conviction that everything in man is always and completely rational, and that the proverbial "scientific cognition" in the name of which religion is debunked is the only primary experience and primary human need. In fact, this belief is quite naïve: in human life there are many areas in which the methods used by science are not applicable. Yes, without science, even of the most elementary sort—without "twice two equals four," perhaps—you could not cook a meal, and you certainly could not fly to the moon. But no one has ever loved another person on the basis of scientific calculations. The endless naivety of primitive rationalism—to which anti-religious propaganda wants to reduce all of life inclusively—contradicts the fundamental experience of all people. Quite simply, neither beauty, nor love, nor faith in any way depend on that infinitely valuable, infinitely necessary, but far from comprehensive science that is based on the principle of "two plus two equals four."

And so the very expression "scientific worldview" is in fact absurd. And although science with its conclusions, achievements, and methodology certainly constitutes a part of an integral worldview, the latter no less certainly is not exhausted by science, because it includes, at the very least, the experience of love, and the experience of beauty, and the experience of faith. For all these three experiences in man are primary, just like the need for scientific cognition of the phenomena of nature and life. The more fully a person is human, the fuller his worldview, the more open he is to all the basic manifestations of human nature. The scientist or chemist who is indifferent to beauty is just as incomplete a human as the aesthete who approaches everything in the world exclusively from the vantage of abstract aesthetic criteria.

But this diversity of human experience does not mean that each of its spheres is separated by an impenetrable wall from all others—in other words, that science does not care about love, beauty, and faith, and faith in turn is indifferent to science, etc. If the tragic and, I repeat, naïve mistake of the so-called scientific worldview is that, by reducing everything to proverbial "science," it rejects outright the very existence and independence of other types of human experience, the religious outlook, the genuine Christian outlook, is completely free from such simplification. Christianity, by contrast, argues that each of these experiences enriches the others, that they are all interconnected. The basic religious statement that *faith without works is dead* (Jas 2.20) means precisely that a faith that does not grow into love is not real faith. On the other hand, knowledge that at some point ceases to strive for a holistic mastery of all reality is not real and complete knowledge. And, finally, the experience of beauty that is not transformed into knowledge, love, and faith remains a dead aesthetic.

Ultimately, the Christian notion of man is that of an integral person, in whom everything is reconciled and united, without denying or destroying any face of multi-faceted and infinitely rich human nature. And from this point of view, of course, it is not religion or the experience of faith that narrows, simplifies, and impoverishes a person, but that selfsame "scientific worldview," where there is no place for all that which from time immemorial has comprised the depth and joy of human life.

Only by saying all this, only by establishing all the necessary particularities, can one really pose the question of faith and knowledge.

Unjustified Division

U ntil fairly recently, philosophers considered it their duty to develop evidence for the existence of God. From Aristotle, who lived in the third century before Christ, and up to the famous French philosophers Bergson[2] and Maritain[3] in our own time, philosophy has held one of its main tasks to be proposing to man a symmetrical, harmonious doctrine of the world, impossible without the concept of the Absolute, or God.

Thus, according to Aristotle, it turned out that since the world consists primarily of motion, it is necessary to postulate the presence of a certain Prime Mover that, while remaining outside the world, makes this movement possible.

Thus, in this case the idea of God was deduced from the first elementary principle of physics—the principle of physical causuality. Since, Aristotle continued, people have always believed in gods everywhere, it is obvious that this cause of all causes, the principle of all principles, is God himself.

There was, further, a "teleological proof" of the existence of God, in which the concept of God was derived from the obvious expediency of all things. Everything in the world, from the largest to the smallest, pursues a definite goal and facilitates its accomplishment. Where could this goal come from, this orderliness of universal movement, this mysterious law to which everything is so obviously subordinated? All this, the philosophers answered, is possible only as a work of supreme Wisdom, the name of which is God.

The famous German philosopher Immanuel Kant proposed, for his part, a "moral proof" of the existence of God. A person finds in himself a mysterious law of good and evil that can be deduced from nothing in the world, and these he instinctively recognizes as such. Moreover, he finds in himself what Kant called the "categorical imperative," by virtue of which he not only knows what is good and what is evil, but also in his life strives to follow good and resist evil, without feeling any need to justify this desire. And since nothing in the world contains such a moral criterion, where does

[2]Henri Bergson (1859–1941): French philosopher and intuitionist.
[3]Jacques Maritain (1882–1973): French Catholic philosopher.

it come from in man? And Kant answers: since all the knowledge available to us does not provide an answer to this question, the very existence of a moral law proves immutably that there is a God above the world, a Being in whom this absolute distinction between good and evil is rooted.

Finally, the French philosophers Descartes and Malbranche[4] offer a so-called "mathematical proof" of God's existence,[5] deriving it from the mathematical postulates of the absolute and infinity.

Subsequently, roughly in the mid-eighteenth century, both believers and non-believers alike began to doubt the necessity and the very possibility of this kind of evidence. Believers agreed with the argument that a God who can be "proven" ceases to be an object of faith, and since religion is based on faith, evidence here is not only unnecessary, but harmful. Unbelievers denied the evidence for the existence of God for entirely different reasons, for they contended that empirical science, which began to flourish in the eighteenth century, was in itself a proof against the existence of God.

Thus, with few exceptions, this impasse remains to this day. Believers, considering all science atheistic, lock themselves in the ivory tower of its denial, while unbelievers in their science-worship become increasingly embittered against faith as "unscientific superstition."

And yet, if you analyze this conflict calmly and without bias, you arrive at two very simple and very important conclusions: first, none of these proofs has been refuted by the "scientific worldview," in the name of which philosophical evidence of the existence of God was rejected. And although proverbial "dialectical materialism"—a philosophy that especially claims to be scientific—has simply discarded all questions about God, this does not mean that it has answered them.

And the further one proceeds, the more obvious the poverty and squalor of this philosophy become. Indeed, if no higher meaning, no set goal, can be derived from matter, then why does man have to fight for some sort of

[4]This refers to the "ontological proof" put forward by René Descartes (1596–1650) and the "ontological proof" developed by N. Malbranche (1638–1715), according to which the idea of infinity in the human mind serves as sufficient grounds to conclude that God exists. Anselm developed the first form of the ontological proof in his *Proslogium* (*c.* 1077).

[5]Immanuel Kant (1724–1804) devoted a special section in his essay *Critique of Judgment* (1790) to the moral proof of the existence of God.

future "happiness"? Where does this idea come from? If a person is entirely a product of matter, where does the sense of goodness and justice come from? Or, as Vladimir Soloviev quipped, if we all descended from monkeys, why should we love each other?[6] In other words, it is obvious that science, which deals primarily with matter, does not replace philosophy and cannot answer a number of very real questions, and without those answers a person cannot live.

Thus, the second conclusion is this: if faith arises in man not from proof, not from philosophy and science (as Aristotle pointed out in his day), this does not mean that faith has nothing to do with them. On the contrary, for millions of people, faith turns out to be the light that shines through the all world's complexity and illuminates ultimate and absolute meaning that neither science nor philosophy can discover and see on their own. And this means that the gap between faith, on the one hand, and science, on the other, is unfounded and is harmful to both. A faith that rejects explanations of the world is a sick and defective faith. A science that does not aspire to exceed its own limits is a blind and slavish science. This is food for thought in our times.

Renunciation of True Knowledge

Today let us continue our theme involving the so-called scientific worldview. The fact is—as we have repeatedly pointed out—that in modern disputes between materialism and idealism, atheism and religion, etc., there is much more passion than objectivity. It is as though all the disputants have a painful area, a common sore that is constantly getting bumped, and from the pain and irritation they have lost the ability to listen and understand one another. This is to say nothing of the sometimes patently obvious political control of thought that precludes calm and objective dialogue.

---

[6]"Man came from the monkey, so let us love one another." V. S. Soloviev, "The Idea of Man in August Comte," in *Works*, vol. 2 (Moscow: Mysl, 1988), 579 (Russian).

And yet it is quite clear that in the study of the cosmos, the laws governing its structure, formation, and development, which determine the anatomy and physiology of living organisms, etc.—in all this there remain questions that cannot be answered on the basis of empirical knowledge alone.

Since ancient times these questions have been the subject of what Aristotle called the "first philosophy," and that which afterward began to be called "metaphysics," from the Greek *meta* (after) and *physika* (physics)—that is, that which follows physics as a general and comprehensible conclusion. Only recently, no one would have disputed that this "first philosophy," also known as metaphysics, is also a scientific discipline, and a very important one at that. But nowadays, under the influence of causes to which we will return, a great many people fanatically oppose not only the recognition of metaphysics as a science, but even its very existence. Science, in their understanding, should be only that which is based on experiment and is amenable to experimental verification.

This assertion, which is "philosophical" in its own right, raises the question of whether its proponents are correct. For even if we agree to recognize only reliable or objective knowledge as science, this does not mean a priori that such knowledge is possible only on the basis of empirical experience. If this were so, it would be necessary (for example) to exclude mathematics from the sciences, since it is entirely based not on experience, but on rational inferences. Thus, it remains to be proven that the only foundation of true science is laboratory experiments and that the human mind cannot achieve reliable and objective knowledge without laboratory instruments.

Let us note immediately that, for Aristotle himself, metaphysics was not at all a science with no dependence on what man obtains through empirical experience. On the contrary, he proceeded from the assumption that man is able to generalize and deepen this experience, and on its basis to create mental constructs. Incidentally, the very Greek word "theory" (*theōria*), contrary to its later meaning in other languages, refers specifically to seeing and to comprehending what is seen—in other words, the empirical experience and its organization by reason. The question, therefore, is whether it is possible, based on experience, to achieve true knowledge—that which not only establishes a fact, but also indicates its meaning, as well as the meaning of the totality of the facts. It is this that so many in our day deny, and this is precisely the attitude of proverbial "positivism"[7] or, more simply, of science worship. In actuality, it stands in contradiction not to some other theoretical statement, but to a patently obvious fact. And this fact is that a person always seeks to know the meaning behind the facts. It is not enough for him to know that a thing is so; he needs to know more—to know what it means, and the final conclusions to which it leads.

To deny this fact is as stupid as to deny any other indisputable observation. Why do people deny it? Quite simply, because they have adopted a belief in several unproven premises, which are therefore ideological rather than scientific. By whom and when has it been proven that human reason depends entirely on the senses—that is, on bodily, sensory experience? This is the premise of the so-called empiricists, but it has long been debunked by science itself. For it is impossible to establish even the most "physical" fact without mathematical analysis and statistical computations, which relate to the field of rational investigation, and not of sensory experience.

For example, in 1846 the French scientist Leverrier proved the existence of the planet Neptune by means of mathematical analysis, and only then asked the astronomer Halle to direct the telescope to a certain point in space, after which the planet was indeed discovered. In 1869 Mendeleev, with the help of his periodic system, proved the existence of elements not yet found, and all of them were later discovered. The empirical premise is a kind of superstition, unworthy of science. The method of genuine science is much more complicated than what dogmatic empiricists claim about it. No sensory experience in itself gives or implies knowledge. Millions of people see the moon every evening. But apart from the bare fact of its existence, no other knowledge of it follows from this. All that we know about the moon is the fruit of a kind of "metaphysics," that is, of posing questions and searching for answers and hypotheses, and of their confirmation or refuta-

---

[7]Positivism—in the proper sense, a tendency in Western philosophy in the second half of the nineteenth–early twentieth centuries, which rejected metaphysical problems and recognized as "positive" knowledge only that which is gained in specialized empirical studies. Here it refers collectively to teachings that recognize only the rational-empirical path to knowledge.

tion. Neither direct nor sensory experience will reveal either the Earth's rotation around the sun or its rotation on its own axis.

But if an element of metaphysics is inherent in experimental science itself, then the study of all these individual "metaphysics" as a general field of metaphysics, as the science of the meaning of our knowledge, the meaning of the world and life in general, appears not only possible, but necessary. And then the next question arises: to what metaphysical theory of the cosmos does modern scientific knowledge lead us? We will turn to this question in our next talk.

A Path to Unity

The flight to the Moon, the unique and unforgettable spectacle of man setting foot on mysterious lunar soil—almost a vision, witnessed by millions of awed people—once again presents us with the old and seemingly tired topic of the relationship between religion and science, faith in God and faith in the technical capabilities of man.

This needs to be addressed primarily because at the foundation of this modern civilization—a civilization that produced the lunar leap, and yet has filled the world with the fear of monstrous wars and complete self-destruction—there lies an old and truly tragic misunderstanding.

It is unlikely that anyone except the fanatics of anti-religious propaganda, for whom the end justifies the means, will deny today that the idea of the cosmos not only as diversity of life, but also as a harmonious whole that can be studied, is an idea of religious origin. Were it not for the religious and philosophical insights of the ancient Greeks about world unity and harmony, on the one hand, and the biblical teaching that the world was created by divine intelligence and wisdom, on the other, there would be no scientific knowledge, nor even science itself. But it is also quite impossible to deny that at some point in history the Church retarded scientific progress. It was Christianity that, as it were, renounced the religious source and religious nature of knowledge, and thereby alienated science, for a long time making it a rival and even an enemy of religion.

And so it happened (and herein lies the root of the tragedy) that these two worlds—the world of scientific knowledge with its dizzying successes and possibilities and the world of faith with its focus on the spiritually moral, the internal and not the external—were divided by enmity and misunderstanding, fear and mutual suspicion. And although in the best representatives of faith and science this enmity weakens and even disappears (this change being symbolized in the truly religious inspiration and enthusiasm of the cosmonauts themselves), complete reconciliation and cooperation are still far away. And we should not hide the fact that this enmity is not the fault of scientists alone. Let us recall the persecutions and prohibitions that befell the great thinker Teilhard de Chardin, in whom a Christian priest and a scientist were merged. Even today, after the flight to the moon, there are Christians who saw this flight as something diabolical and wicked, and condemned it as the work of the antichrist.

Meanwhile, it is not merely abstract reasoning that requires us to find a way out of this impasse. For the tragedy of mutual misunderstanding and denial gives rise to the terrible duality of the world today. Yes, the door to infinite space is open, and before our eyes science achieves its greatest victories, but around the world the eruptions of hatred, violence, fear, and cruelty are becoming more and more devastating. And the way out of this impasse lies, apparently, only in uniting moral and scientific principles, the spiritual with the rational. However, for reconciliation to take place not only superficially, but on a deeper level, as a restoration of the organic unity of human consciousness and self-consciousness, it is not sufficient to be merely tolerant, nor to simply delineate "spheres of influence," with religion agreeing to respect science and not interfere in its affairs, while science is obligated to respect religion and refrain from any hostility to it. This is not sufficient, because a person cannot but but strive for a united and integral worldview. If there is a God, he must be the source of everything, and not only that which belongs to a specifically religious sphere; hence, he must also be the source of knowledge. And if there is reason and knowledge, they must have some correlation to faith, and not be disconnected from it. Even the most peaceful "division of spheres" is ultimately unworthy of both faith and knowledge. Therefore, their true reconciliation is possible only by a thorough and sincere acceptance of science by faith, and of faith by science.

Such acceptance requires a profound revision of the age-old and unjustified hatred, mutual fear and suspicion—that is, a restoration of trust. For Christians who are intimidated by science, it's time to remember the apostle Paul's strange, liberating words: *Prove all things; hold fast that which is good* (1 Thess 5.21). After all, in modern language this means: "Study, delve into, comprehend, and in your consciousness, your worldview, let there be a place for all that is true, good, and beautiful!"

But it would also be good for people of science who have a phobia of religion to hear these same words. Let them also understand that true faith lies not in narrow and petty fear, not in encouraging suspicion, hatred, and estrangement, but in joyful and loving freedom, in openness to everything good and genuine. Religion is not only about God, but also about the world. *The heavens declare the glory of God, and the firmament proclaims his handiwork* (Ps 18.1). These words of the psalm are so appropriate to remember today, when the heavens open to human knowledge and contemplation, to love and stewardship! The astronaut, in approaching the Moon, not only transmitted scientific information to Earth, but also exclaimed: "My God, how beautiful it is!" But we also find nearly the same exclamation at the beginning of the Bible: *And God saw that it was good* (Gen 1.10).

In my talks, I would like to show that the mystery of the cosmos is, in its full depth, that very theme that can truly connect the world of faith and the world of knowledge in our day, uniting them in a genuine thirst for common growth.

The Metaphysical "Bias"

In 1955 the Parisian astronomer Paul Couderc wrote: "From now on, it is no longer possible to separate cosmology and cosmogony, because light rays now bring us images of galaxies at the most varied stages of development." We are now witnesses of at least a billion years of evolution. The largest telescopes reach galaxies separated from us by two billion light years. As early as 1960 it was possible to contemplate galaxies located six billion light years away. This means that we can see these galaxies as they were in an era when our Earth was not yet formed.

Indeed, when looking at the celestial bodies, we see them not as they are now, but as they were at the moment when they released the ray of light we are seeing. The further we look, the more ancient the worlds we see. If cosmology is the science of the universe, in our days this cosmology appears before us as cosmogony, that is, the science of the world at the stage of formation and development. For a long time the principle of formation, development, and evolution seemed suspicious to people of faith and religion. I said that in this fear of the expanding horizon of scientific knowledge lay one of the dramas of our civilization, which to this day divides mankind into two camps. It was only relatively recently that the religious consciousness not only ceased to fear the theory of evolution, but actually discovered its religious content. For there is essentially no more religious idea than that of increase and fulfillment.

But the beginning rapprochement of initial positions is perhaps nowhere so obvious as in the field of cosmogony. For nothing has so led science and religion out of the state of narrow dogmatism as the contemplation of the endless and ever expanding universe, our penetration into the mystery of the starry sky, which once so astounded the French philosopher Pascal with its silence.

So, what happens in this amazing and all-revitalizing science? I began with a quote from the astronomer Couderc, and this quote could be confirmed by numerous other testimonies. According to another modern astronomer, "We have ceased to live in the cosmos understood by Aristotle, a cosmos that knows neither origin, nor change, nor aging. For Aristotle, the cosmos is not only uncreated and eternal, but like the essence of Parmenides[8] it is stability itself, eternity itself, and therefore in itself is divine."

[8]The ancient Greek philosopher Parmenides (c. 540–c. 450 BC) taught about the unity, immobility, eternity, and complete unity of the cosmos (he was a monist), the best expression of which is a spherical body (a "sphere of essence").

The rejection of the idea of origin and change was for Aristotelian cosmology the result of a kind of deification of the world. Modern cosmogony, however, "un-deified" the world, having learned to determine its physical and chemical composition, to delineate its history, to measure the age of the stars and to recognize the indications of their age. And in the religious and philosophical interpretation of the world and life, these discoveries in the field of cosmology are exceptionally important. For the first time in the history of science, scientists find themselves facing the problem of the beginning and the end of the universe.

In order to grasp the whole significance of this new problem, we must recall that for centuries mankind held the Aristotelian worldview. In the Middle Ages, the biblical teaching about creation was "grafted onto" this worldview, and according to this teaching God will one day end the existence of the world. Despite this, however, the world of medieval thinkers—Arabs, Jews, Christians, the world of Maimonides, Thomas Aquinas, Descartes—remained a world without any movement, a ready-made world, devoid of development and history. Its beginning and end were seen as external phenomena with relation to it, as a sort of divine "caprice" that does not explain anything in the world itself.

But now this static, extra-historical and extra-evolutionary understanding of the world has finally been relegated to the archives. We now know without a doubt—and no longer on the basis of speculative constructions, but empirically, by experimental testing—that the world is a physical and ongoing process, having its own genesis and its own evolution. The world is constant origin, constant newness. We are at the opposite pole in relation to ancient Greek thought,[9] which denied all genesis, all formation.

Here we arrive at the main result of this profound revolution in the scientific worldview. Its essence is that, for the first time, physics is returning

[9]In relation to one large strand of Greek thought, that is. But it should be noted that the pre-Socratic philosopher Heraclitus of Ephesus (*c.* 540–480 BC) stood in direct opposition to Parmenides of Elea (see n. 8 above). Heraclitus saw becoming, change, and flux as the ultimate reality, hence his famous sayings "All things flow," and "You cannot step into the same river twice." In Plato's dialogues Socrates synthesizes these two views: here in the world that we experience there is becoming and change (as Heraclitus emphasized), but the higher reality of the forms, in which our lower reality dimly participates, is eternal and unchanging (as in Parmenides' philosophy). This privileged the static and unchanging as the higher reality, and came to influence much of later Greek thought.

us to metaphysics—to the problem of the profound meaning of the physical process itself. For if the cosmos is in the process of formation, there quite clearly follows the question of the beginning and the end, the purposeful-ness of this process. While ancient Greek thinking denied every notion of development and formation, the theme of the beginning and the end could be considered only as a religious dogma. Since it did not pertain either to the area of direct experience or to science, it offered no means of understand-ing the world. But today this theme arises from the very heart of scientific problems as such. Everything that we gradually learn about the universe, about stars, etc., persistently puts it forward as a central topic and as a self-evident goal of science itself.

This is the main revolution, which is gradually filling science with completely new content and at the same time placing it in a new position with regard to religious intuitions and religious outlooks. To understand this means to take a huge step forward on the path toward restoring the unity of human consciousness, a unity tragically lost in an era of senseless and fruitless struggle between religion and science.

Converging Points of Reference

As we said in our previous talk, a clear turning point in the develop-ment of modern science is the assertion that cosmology is inseparable from cosmogony and that the world must be perceived as a process of for-mation and growth. As a result of this assertion, science began to study the beginning and end of this process, and thus the problem of the beginning and end of the universe has narrowed the gap between the scientific and the religious agenda.

Let us return now to this topic in more detail. Nowadays, scientists cal-culate the age of the earth, which for the static Aristotelian cosmology of later medieval thought would be not just nonsense, but outright blasphemy. We know that the age of the most ancient minerals is nearly three billion years. The earth's age is about four billion years. We now know the age of the moon, which is known to continually recede from the earth, and the age of the sun and the stars. We know that normal stars are incandescent gas balls.

Since 1938, it has been known that the energy of a star comes from the transformation of hydrogen nuclei into helium—reactions of the so-called Bethe cycle.[10] For example, for a billion years our sun has been converting a mass of hydrogen, equal to about one hundredth of its entire mass, into helium. The sun, as it were, "eats" 800 million tons of hydrogen per second. On the other hand, we know that hydrogen accounts for about fifty percent of the total mass of the Sun. Thus, it becomes possible to calculate the time of the Sun's full utilization of this hydrogen. When all its hydrogen turns into helium, a star dies. Stars vanish at different speeds: while some are dying out, others are born of interstellar gas. Most of the stars in our galaxy originated about six to ten billion years ago. The proportion of oxygen to helium allows us to calculate the age of a star. And finally, we now know that our galaxy covers about one hundred thousand light years and consists of at least a hundred billion stars. Until recently, there was still a question of whether the universe was not limited to our galaxy. But other galaxies were discovered in 1923–1924, so that the universe is now perceived rather as a kind of gas consisting of several billion galaxies.

We know, in addition, that matter itself has a history predicating genesis and evolution. Elements other than hydrogen arise from thermonuclear reactions within the stars themselves. The primary cloud of gas from which galaxies are born does not contain the heavy elements that subsequently appear inside the stars. Thus, the iron or calcium found in the spectrum of a great many stars are a rather late phenomenon. Hence, even Mendeleev's periodic system of elements can be read from a "historical" point of view, taking into account the genesis and growth of matter.

Complex matter of the molecular order is an even later phenomenon. In all probability, the arrangement of matter that precedes the emergence of life spans roughly three billion years. We can draw our first conclusion:

---

[10]Hans Albrecht Bethe (July 2, 1906–March 6, 2005): German-American nuclear physicist who made important contributions to astrophysics, quantum electrodynamics, and solid-state physics; he won the 1967 Nobel Prize in Physics for his work on the theory of stellar nucleosynthesis.

matter has its own age. Roughly a hundred years ago such an assertion
would have seemed absurd. But after the discovery of radioactivity, that
is, the spontaneous decay of unstable atoms, its scientific validity became
self-evident. Each atom has its own lifespan—that is, the time required to
reduce its quantity by half (the lifespan of uranium, for example, is four
and a half billion years). And so it became possible to determine the age of
various atoms.

All this leads to the following question: when in our day scientists talk
about the eternity of matter, what matter are they talking about? Clearly,
it is not living matter—a complex phenomenon that is known to be of
relatively recent origin. But the so-called heavy nuclei are not that old,
either. Therefore, one must go back to the hydrogen atom and even further. But the further back we go, the more obvious the simplification of
matter becomes for us. What happens if we hold that matter's origins can
be traced back infinitely, as do philosophers who insist on the eternity of
matter? Here are the problems and the questions that inevitably arise today
in the minds of scientists.

And since there is no definitive answer to them yet, there are currently
several models of the universe. Let us examine first the theory proposed
by Paul Couderc, astronomer of the Paris Observatory, in his book *The
Expansion of the Universe* (1950). According to this theory, the universe has
a beginning in time and is limited by time and space. On the basis of very
complex mathematical and physical calculations, the author comes to the
conclusion that several billion years ago the universe consisted of a gaseous
mass of relatively limited volume, which at some point began to widen or
expand. Thus, we can posit the zero point of time, its mathematical beginning. "I myself," writes Professor Couderc, "do not attach metaphysical
significance to this theory and do not equate it with the doctrine of the
creation of the world. This theory is primarily scientific and rational, and
so much the worse for those who condemn it a priori, in the name of some
'orthodox' materialism, and also for those who make of it a springboard to
leap into theology."

Here is the point of view of a true scientist. We, too, will not consider this theory as a "springboard to leap into theology." It is important,

however, that the idea of the beginning of the world, which until recently seemed unscientific and absurd, ceases to be such in the opinion of very serious researchers and becomes necessary for understanding the universe and matter itself.

But this theory is not the only one, and before studying it more closely it is necessary, in all fairness, to listen to what other scientists think about cosmogony. This we will do in our next talk.

The Modern Science of the Beginning and the End

In the previous talks I spoke about the turning point in cosmology, or rather cosmogony, that forces modern scientists to completely reconsider the question of matter and its development. Matter has age, matter grows old, matter is reborn. But what then is meant by the eternity of matter and the eternity of the world?

Last time I pointed to one of the answers, citing the words of the French astronomer Couderc about the mathematical beginning of time—that is, the abstract point at which the development of the observable universe began. According to this theory, the universe has a beginning in time and is limited simultaneously by time and space. On the basis of highly complex mathematical and physical calculations, scientists conclude that several billion years ago the universe was confined to a relatively limited gaseous mass, which began to spread or expand. Thus, we can assume a certain zero point in time—its mathematical beginning. "I myself," writes Professor Couderc, "do not attach metaphysical significance to this theory and do not equate it with the doctrine of the creation of the world. This theory is, first of all, scientific and rational, and so much the worse for those who condemn it a priori, in the name of some 'orthodox' materialism, and also for those who make of it a springboard to leap into theology." Couderc anticipated that this theory, at which he had arrived through at purely rational and strictly scientific means, would cause a storm of protest both on the right and on the left: on the left, because he had created a "springboard to leap into theology," that is, into the biblical doctrine of creation; and on the right, because he himself did not use this springboard.

And so it happened. According to one historian of modern science, "There is now a real battle around these problems of cosmology among scientists, the philosophical significance of which is enormous." For example, another French scientist, Prof. Deauville, in the book *Cosmogonical Hypotheses,* writes concerning Cuderc's theory: "This hypothesis is not only not confirmed by experience—it is unacceptable a priori because of its metaphysical nature. It assumes a supernatural creation from nothing, but scientific thought cannot accept this. And even if we are left with nothing but a single principle—the principle of conservation of energy—we at least should not violate it by accepting the idea of the creation, or the beginning, of energy."

In this text the frank admission is striking: a scientific theory should be rejected simply because it opens the way to a religious understanding of the world. Indeed, the truly irrational mutual fear of science and religion is never revealed with such force as in this constant apprehension: "But will my theory help the enemy?" The religious world reacted to the theory of evolution one hundred years ago in the same frightened way. But now many scientists manifest these same symptoms. For them, science a priori cannot have any points of contact with religion, and even if the facts point to the latter, so much the worse for the facts. Such is the case with Deauville. And so, as another researcher writes in response, his own theory is full of contradictions and incongruities, because for science only one thing is important: whether the doctrine of the origin and development is consistent with the current data. The assertion that this theory is unacceptable a priori because of its metaphysical character sounds like nasty joke.

Here we come to the very core of the problem—to the fact that science must inevitably accept this metaphysical dimension one way or another.[11] Indeed, why is it harmful, dangerous metaphysics to say that the world has a beginning, while saying that matter is eternal is science? The concept of eternity is just as metaphysical as the concept of a beginning, for both are

---

[11]The theory of the Big Bang as the beginning of the existence of the universe is now generally accepted in the scientific world without any correlation to the metaphysical dimension.

equally not subject to direct experimental verification. Consequently, the only question is which of the two concepts is most rational—that is, which best corresponds to all that we know about the world and matter.

Any worldview inevitably leads to metaphysical conclusions and generalizations, and to be afraid of them means to deny science. As Couderc observes, "I do not share the opinions of all those who reacted to the theory of origins as something unacceptable for people of science. Some immediately started talking about the creation, while others rejected my theory for its ostensibly bourgeois nature." The only objection to the theory of the irreversible growth of the universe could be an objection based on a cyclical understanding of this growth. According to this, universes succeed each other: they are born, they develop, age, and die, and then they are, so to speak, "resurrected." And some scientists are so panicked about the idea of the beginning and the end, which seems to them to smack of the religion they detest, that they prefer to side with this imaginary cycle. But it is imaginary! For in the field of facts and experimentation, nothing, absolutely nothing, points to it. This is a kind of return to the views of Anaximander, Heraclitus, and the Stoics:[12] the eternal and uncreated universe goes from singular to plural, then from plural it again becomes singular, and so on without end. But Anaximander, Heraclitus, and the Stoics constructed this theory specifically on religious grounds. The eternity and uncreatedness of the world were needed because this world was thought of as divine, or rather as God himself. But then, for many modern materialists matter is a near-religious concept, and every irreverent reference to it is considered blasphemy.

One way or another, we can only repeat that the idea of an eternal and motionless world is not at present confirmed by any scientifically established facts. All that we know about the universe leads us to the notion of irreversible cosmic evolution. If, however, we assert, as do some, that this irreversibility is not absolute, that evolution after a certain period of time begins anew, in a new cycle, then this assertion itself requires scientific proof. The world, as we know it and are constantly getting to know it better, predicates

[12]Anaximander of Miletus (610–*c.* 540 BC) and Heraclitus of Ephesus (see n. xxx above): ancient Greek philosophers of the pre-Socratic age. Stoics: followers of stoicism, a philosophical doctrine originating with Zenon of Kitij (336–264 BC).

a beginning and an end. And on this point there is, therefore, no a priori divergence between the scientific and religious worldviews.

A False Premise

In previous conversations we talked about how the problem of the cosmos is posed and solved in modern science, and about its significance for the philosophical and, ultimately, the religious consciousness. We said that science, whose possibilities have limitlessly expanded over the past decades, based on an extremely precise analysis of the cosmic elements, is more and more obviously moving toward a view of the world as an entity that develops and therefore necessarily requires a beginning and an end. The true meaning, the so-called "metaphysical" possibilities of these discoveries, remains a subject of fierce controversy among scientists. But what is important is that these disputes no longer concern the facts themselves—the facts are no longer disputed—but their interpretations, and that in these disputes there are convictions and premises that go beyond empirical science as such.

But before proceeding to this aspect of the issue, let us review what we have discussed. As one scholar writes, "We do not need hasty generalizations." Nor will our philosophical and religious analysis of scientific discoveries attempt to force itself upon what is still the subject of disputes and inquiries. Thus it is best to use the so-called minimalist method, and this means to rely only on what is no longer controversial and is beyond questioning. Science, in going from theory to theory, establishes a certain irreversible path, the general direction of which should, in our opinion, lie at the basis of our analysis.

For philosophical reflection, there are always two chief dangers. First, the danger of completely identifying with a single scientific theory, so that when this theory is discarded by science itself, its worldview collapses along with it. This danger befell the dialectical materialist, who relied on a kind of materialistic stasis and therefore now finds himself in the rather sad position of a scientific anachronism. Another danger is to philosophize about the world and man in complete isolation from science, and above all from the science of the cosmos and its genesis. This danger lies in wait for many philosophers today. Modern philosophy too often develops outside any connection with physics, chemistry, biology. The philosophers argue as if they were living in the time of Descartes, in a kind of intellectual isolation, where no discoveries and no new facts penetrate. For example, modern physics has done away with the theory of microbodies—the smallest, but, so to speak, "entirely material" particles of matter. It was essentially this fact that put an end to the specific variety of materialism. But most philosophers ultimately know nothing about this consummately scientific, consummately objective fact. As the physicist Bachelard observes, "When you talk about these phenomena—about the destruction and creation of matter—before an audience of philosophers, there is a complete lack of understanding on their faces, a complete lack of interest in what would seem to be of paramount importance to them."

Thus, these two extremes must be avoided. The philosopher must be simultaneously open to the world of scientific inquiry and free from the dogmatic assimilation of one theory alone, one inference alone. He must also rely on what has been established as indisputable. And from this standpoint, the fact that the world (outer space, the universe) is in a formative state can be considered indisputable, universally recognized, and a primary conclusion of modern science. This is the first prerequisite, but a highly important one, for it is immediately followed by a question of paramount importance for both philosophy and human consciousness in general: "Does the formation and evolution of the world presume some absolute beginning?" We already know from previous talks that the fiercest battle rages specifically around this point.

Very well; let's set aside the idea of a "very first," absolute beginning, which to many scientists still seems a shameful surrender of "their positions" to religious consciousness, to faith. But there can be no doubt as to the existence of a "non-absolute" beginning, or, more precisely, a multitude of non-absolute beginnings. That formation, that evolution that we can trace back several billion years, consists entirely of incessant emergence—the emergence of new bodies, new forms of matter, new increasingly complex structures. Galaxies are formed, stars combine, heavy nuclei appear . . . For us, who want not simply to know, but also to philosophically comprehend knowledge and science, this, perhaps, is sufficient. Let us set aside, I repeat, the "very first" beginning. It is enough for us that cosmogenesis, biogenesis, and finally anthropogenesis are, in an objective sense, a history of beginnings—a history contested by no one. And if the scientist of our day is afraid to draw the final conclusion from this and acknowledge the logical necessity of a very first, absolute beginning, let us let him alone—for the time being. What is important is that the idea of matter that is motionless, always congruent, immutable, and eternal contradicts all data, all discoveries, all trends in modern cosmogony. What matters is that, in light of these discoveries, the main problem of philosophy, the problem of being and its ultimate meaning, is posited in a new way—a way in which it has not been posited in all the centuries of senseless, unjustified war between religious and scientific consciousness.

Two Relics

In our previous conversations we hope that we have proven that the modern science of the world (cosmology, cosmogony, biology) raises the increasingly acute question of the world's beginning and end. In other words, scholars are returning, albeit in completely new ways, to the religious questions and insights of the past. But whereas on the religious plane of inquiry these were resolved with the help of mythological language and images, science is approaching them in the context of its own methodology, its scientific terms of reference. And this means that we are on the threshold of a new philosophy—one based on the premises of scientific knowledge and the conclusions drawn from it.

And here scientific knowledge encounters two, one might say, "remnants of the past"—two systems of thought, which increasingly reveal their incompetence and unsuitability: on the one hand, proverbial philosophical idealism, and on the other, Marxist materialism. Let us try to explain as simply as possible, first, the basic attitude of each toward the world, and, secondly, why neither of these philosophies can be of any help to genuine scientific thought.

If we take as our starting point the simple truth that man lives by acquiring knowledge of the world, then the question arises as to how he acquires this knowledge, how the manifold reality of the world is transformed into representations, conclusions, ideas, and so on. In other words, this is a question of the relationship between thought and reality. Well then, the essence of philosophical idealism is that it chiefly emphasizes not reality, but the idea of it that arises in my brain. True reality is not the world itself, but my idea of it. The greatest German idealist philosopher idealist, Immanuel Kant, directly asserted that we cannot know reality itself, which he called "the thing-in-itself," because it is known to us only insofar as it is present in our mind. Thus, knowledge, according to philosophical idealism, is the knowledge not of things, but of our thoughts about things. If we exaggerate somewhat, we could say that for idealism it does not matter whether the world really exists, or, if it does exist, what it actually is. This is impossible to determine—one can only know the images and thoughts of our consciousness.

It was this gap between thought and reality that Marxism opposed. Marxism, in fact, was born as a passionate repudiation of philosophical idealism. In Marxism, the main stress shifts from thought to reality, or, as the Marxists say, to matter. Here we must emphasize—as the opponents of Marxism unfortunately often fail to do—the dual meaning of the concept of "matter" among the Marxists. Its first meaning directly follows from Marxist anti-idealism, signifying first of all the objective existence of the outside world independent of the cognizant human mind. Whereas for the idealist the world is, in the final analysis, his concept of it, for the Marxist the world exists as a primary reality, having existence before man, and independent of human thought. Marxism, then, begins with a kind of faith in the world, in its primacy, in its authentic and full existence. Thought and knowledge, being only derived from this reality, have value insofar as they themselves correspond to it. Hence the innate love of Marxist philosophers for such words as "objectivity" and "concreteness."

Here, I repeat, is belief in the primacy of the world, whereas in idealism there is complete skepticism about it. Let us note, by the way, that from this standpoint the Christian worldview, like the biblical worldview before it, is much closer to this belief in the world than to idealism. In the Bible, in Christian revelation, the world is also always real, and its existence, not the thought of it, is the source of joy and inspiration and praise: *In wisdom hast thou made them all* (Ps 103.24). It was in this sense that Sergey Nikolaevich Bulgakov, a former Marxist who returned to the Church and became a Christian thinker, spoke of the "sacred materialism" of Christianity.[13] In the struggle against skeptical idealism, which dissolves the whole world into some kind of thought and conceptualization, into a kind of subjective illusion, Christianity is much closer to the first meaning of the Marxist concept of "matter" than many Christians think.

But this concept in Marxism has a second meaning of the word "matter." This second meaning no longer emphasizes the objective reality of the world, but its eternity and uncreatedness, its originality and infinity. That the world and its matter are real, and not illusory, is something that the unbelieving scientist and the Christian thinker not only can, but must agree on. Otherwise we are dealing with an illusion, as in Tyutchev's "not smoke, but only a shadow running from the smoke."[14] But why from this correct statement must we conclude that matter and the world have neither a beginning nor an end; that outside of them there is nothing and there cannot be anything? How does belief in the world turn into its deification? And yet this is precisely what the Marxist thought of Marx and Engels maintains as dogma up to the present day.

But here we come to the crux of the matter: it is precisely in this second assertion that Marxist materialism becomes increasingly embroiled in

---

[13]S. N. Bulgakov. The expression "Christian materialism" is encountered, for example, in the preface to his *Philosophy of the Economy* (1912). See his *Collected Works*, 2 vols., (Moscow: Nauka, 1993), 1:51.

[14]From the poem by F. I. Tyutchev, "How the smoky pillar grows lighter in the heights . . ." (*c.* 1849). The lines quoted are: ". . . Not a light smoke shining in the moon, / but a shadow, running from the smoke."

a conflict with science, to which it nevertheless constantly refers, present-ing itself as a "scientific worldview." That science can expect nothing from philosophical idealism has long been apparent. Indeed, the whole of science is based on experience, which in turn assumes the reality of the world. When studying the structure of geological strata or the disintegration of an atom, the scientist does not care about idle questions such as: "Are these strata themselves real, or just my concept of them?" For him, they are real; other-wise it would not be worthwhile to study them. But herein lies the conflict with Marxist materialism. For science itself, the very study of reality, poses the question of the beginning of matter, for example. And Marxism says that this question cannot be raised, because matter must be beginningless. The philosophical collapse of idealism leads to the philosophical collapse of materialism. This is what everyone needs to understand today, and this brings us to the question of the relationship between science and religion.

Where Humility and Wisdom Meet

We came from far away," say the mysterious wise men of the East, who in the Gospel account came to worship the Christ who was born in the cave of Bethlehem. But what brought them "from afar"? How did they know about this Child, about this cave, about this joy, and what does their worship mean? A skeptical person, educated in a spirit of scientific positivism, will merely shrug his shoulders: for him this is a foolish, unim-portant question. For how can one take seriously this long-debunked legend, a fairy tale in which only uncultured people believe? Of course, we might reply that, be that as it may, this "fairy tale" has been part of the lifeblood of mankind for two thousand years, profoundly changed its self-consciousness, and ushered in an unprecedented proliferation of world culture, giving rise to the greatest art of all time. But even supposing we admit that the story of these mysterious sages, who studied the stars and followed them to Christ's cradle—suppose that this story is a myth and we do not know anything his-torically reliable about these people, nor will we ever. It still remains a fact that this "myth" was established by Christianity at the very beginning of its history. Does this not mean that it reveals to us something very important in the faith of Christians themselves, about how they understood and experienced it at the dawn of their historical existence?

We are constantly told that Christianity is a bane of human freedom; that it is pure dogmatism, demanding that a person renounce his intellect and all searching, analysis, and critical verification; that all this is darkness engendered by superstition, fear, and ignorance. But why then, in the very first lines of the Gospel, do we find a story about people who in modern language can only be called scientists? Wise men from the East! We are still studying Babylonian astronomy, and modern researchers know not only its value for its own era, but also that this ancient knowledge has made possible the further development of science. Whatever the science of that time, it was still science, and hence it was research, analysis, critical verification. And whatever the scientists of the time were like, they were people who managed to penetrate the secrets of the universe further than all their contemporaries. Most importantly, what led them to Christ was their readiness to seek—in other words, their science. "We examined the stars," they say; "we searched, and our search led us here." And if the story of the magi, I repeat, is placed at the beginning of the Gospel, does this not mean, first of all, the importance of seeking for Christians?

Seek and ye shall find (Mt 7.7), says Christ. "Seek, and you will find," says science likewise. After all, a scientist very often does not know what he is looking for, but he knows that he is ultimately searching for truth, the whole truth, and nothing but the truth; and if he does not seek, then he is not a scientist. The scientist often does not know where this quest will lead him, but he knows in advance (again, if he is a real scientist!) that he will accept the truth, whatever it is, and will humble himself before it. Humility in the face of truth—is this not the main premise of science, the basis of any scientific view of the world? The whole history of science is filled with all kind of miracles. The seekers were looking for one thing, but they found quite another: they searched for matter, and they found energy; they searched for limits, but found a boundless cosmos; they searched for iron determinism, but they found freedom. Before our very eyes, in our own time, this kind of scientific marvel has been and is being accomplished, and this was made possible only through searching and the humility of scientific reason in the face of the truth.

Today also, in our time, it is not religion, not Christianity that prohibits this searching, but narrow-minded fanaticism and dogmatism—ideologists who have determined in advance what science can and cannot seek and find. Christianity, through the mouth of Christ himself, simply says: "Seek, and you will find." The dogmatism of modern ideology says: "Seek, but do not dare to find spirit and soul, because they do not exist regardless; and most importantly, do not dare to find God!" In other words, when the search leads to what is primary, transcendent, and profound (which Einstein anticipated and wrote about, as did all great scientists), the order is given to halt: "No further," says the modern ideologue; "here is the border, here is the limit, for we have declared on behalf of science that there is no God; there cannot and must not be!" Who then is doing the prohibiting? Who is opposing the search?

This is why the story of the wise men at the very beginning of the Gospel is so precious, so important. Yes, we do not know anything about them except that they were wise men, but we know that they came "from afar," and does not this "from afar" apply to the search of all humanity? We all come "from afar," and infinitely long is the path of human growth, searching, and finding. And so often we do not know where we are going, but only that we must go, that this thirst, this need for truth, must not dry up within us, that we must not be content with superficial, halfhearted, cheap answers! The Christian faith says: "If you go, go to the very end." And so, if we always reconcile ourselves to the truth, if we but think and seek and serve only the truth, if, in other words, we strive to be what genuine science wants a person to be, we will come—how and when, we do not know—to that same light-bearing Christmas night, to the Infant whose coming into the world was marked by the solemn and joyful praise: *Glory to God in the highest, and on earth peace, good will toward men* (Lk 2.14).

There, at the cradle of Christ, some very wise people encountered some very humble people, and there was an encounter between wisdom and humility, science and humanity, truth, love, and endless joy.

PART II

MAN

A Collision of Explanations

The Divine Dimension

In our time no subject is so thought-upon and debated as the destiny of man. Who is he? What is his place in the universe? To what is he called, and what are his abilities?

All these questions seem to be raised anew by the profound spiritual and psychological changes elicited by the scientific and technological revolution that is occurring before our very eyes. On the one hand, it would seem that this revolution has raised humanity to unattainable heights. Indeed, man has conquered nature, has overcome the elements, has reached the moon, and tomorrow he will be able to reach other planets. It would seem that potentially, at least, there is no limit to the scientific comprehension of the world, the penetration of all its mysteries. Even mystery itself seems to have simply evaporated. That which in ignorance was formerly attributed to mysterious forces, about which people could only guess and divine, has now become transparent for sober and rational analysis, has been transformed from a mystery into an equation, which one only has to properly formulate and properly solve. Not a single day goes by without a routine earth-shaking discovery, a routine astounding victory. "I can do everything," says the contemporary man, "and what is impossible today, I will accomplish tomorrow." Such is the first fruit of the scientific and technological revolution. Man has not only learned to take charge of all the elements; he stands at the threshold of active interference in the actions of these elements, absolute mastery of them, and for many the possibilities are breathtaking.

But this is only one side, one aspect. For simultaneously we are witnessing an unprecedented reduction of the individual, his dissolution into an impersonal collective mass. It is no accident that in our day the key terms are "the masses," "the collective," "the people." We hear arguments, concerns, and shouts about these and their destiny, but it is increasingly rare that the word *man* signifies an individual person, a concrete and specific being, and in that concreteness, a unique person. Here there seems to be an inexorable law: the greater the authority and power of humanity, the less room there remains for the human person, for his inner world, for the inner life of the person.

Humanity triumphs, but the human individual is vanquished—thus we might express this indisputable law. To protect these enormous, breathtaking achievements it is essential that there be as little of the personal as possible. It is a nuisance, like a drop of water in an engine that spoils the well-tuned action of a superb mechanism. Indeed, if today we strive to reach the Moon, and tomorrow Mars or Venus, what possible significance can be attributed to the personal experience of this particular poet, the miserable love of that tiny being, the sufferings and joys of individual human grains of sand, these living cogs in the machine? Cogs are not supposed to think; they are only required to fulfill their function. That is why the same forces which attract humanity to scientific victories, to victory over nature, simultaneously draw it towards totalitarianism in the most profound and dreadful meaning of that word. Everything in the contemporary world says: "To achieve anything requires unconditional, absolute submission of all the parts to the whole. And the only truly happy person, the only truly useful person, is the one who submits himself to this whole to the bitter end."

This is why the struggle against the person and against the personal is not a coincidence; it is not just the product of some evil force, of someone's evil will. It is the system itself that demands it: it is inscribed in the inexorable logic of what in today is customarily called progress. And of course, it is still less coincidental that this struggle is directed against everything that defends the personal and the person, which places him as the cornerstone, and this struggle is directed against religion above all else. For religion not only focuses on the person, on personal faith, personal love, and personal perfection, but with all of its essence it confirms and proclaims that a person cannot be reduced to a mass, an element, or a collective. By the paradoxical arithmetic of the Gospel, one person and his destiny are as valuable as the destiny of ninety-nine others. The Gospel is not prepared to sacrifice a single small person for the whole, not even the least, seemingly insignificant, individual destiny. In the words of Ivan in Dostoevsky's *Brothers Karamazov*, if the happiness of humanity is built on the tears of one child, then that happiness is warped and it must be rejected.

And so it seems to me that any person, anyone who is even the least bit capable of giving thought to what is currently going on in the world, cannot and must not simply disregard the decisive and final choice, which each of us faces in our time. What do I want: the absolute, scientifically based victory of humanity at the cost of the extinction of the individual? Or would I prefer the victory of humanity, albeit a partial victory—that is, the recognition of the supreme, absolute value of each individual person, who can never be considered a means rather than a goal?

But we must remember that in this choice the only thing countering totalitarianism is the religious concept of man. No science, no technology has any knowledge of the personal, nor can it. The mystical, divine knowledge of the personal essence of each human being is revealed to a completely different knowledge of him. If this knowledge is disregarded, it will soon become impossible to defend the human individual.

In our next talk we will return to this pivotal theme. It is essential that people finally become aware that the world and society are sliding into an impersonal state. Most importantly, people need to grasp that the religious approach to man or, more broadly, the place of religion in the world, cannot be reduced to a question of the rights of some persecuted minority, but is rather the fundamental question of the meaning and goal of all our earthly actions, of all our hopes and dreams. And I am thoroughly convinced that only now, in this era of scientific, technological, psychological, or any other kind of revolution, is man truly able to comprehend what is happening to him, or more accurately what will happen, if he altogether forgets his divine origin and destiny.

A Saving Mystery

Incredible progress and achievements, on the one hand, and the degradation and enslavement of the individual on the other. That is how in my previous talk I defined the paradoxical situation in which we more and more clearly find ourselves in our great yet tragic twentieth century. Lately I have been thinking of the prophetic verses in Alexander Blok's poem "Retribution":

> The twentieth century . . . still homeless,
> More frightful than the gloom of life
> (Blacker still, and larger
> The shadow of Lucifer's wing).
> Smoky fires of sunset
> (A prophecy about our times),
> The ominous comets with their tails,
> Gloomy omens in the sky,
> The bleak demise of Messina.
> (Powerless before the elemental forces),
> And ceaseless crying of machines
> Forging destruction day and night
> Awareness of the dreadful fraud
> Of all the former tiny thoughts and faiths,
> And the first flight of the airplane
> Into the desert of unknown spheres . . .
>
> . . .
> And black, the blood of earth
> Makes promises, bursting in our veins
> Destroying all the boundaries,
> Unheard of changes
> Unheard of mutinies . . .
> What then, O man?—Beyond the cries of steel,
> In fire, and in the smoke of powder,
> What fiery vistas

Have opened to your gaze?
What does it preach—this ceaseless noise of machines?
Why does the wailing propeller
Cut through the cold and empty fog?

It seems to me that nowhere else is this music of our age expressed so profoundly—a music terminating in this "cold and empty fog." But Blok is not the only one who hears this music and is horrified by it. Today in the West, Albert Camus hears it with the same ennui and horror, and the closer he approaches his untimely death, the more clearly he sees that the cry of machines, this kingdom of machinery and technocracy, this pathos of the collective, of the faceless, and of compulsory happiness, is simultaneously transforming the majority of people into both executioners and victims. I say executioners because everyone is involved in this horrible mechanism of compulsion, and each, willingly or unwillingly, is obliged to put pressure on the other. At the same time I call them victims, because they are subject to the collective whole, with the whole placing pressure on each. This, of course, is the theme of Pasternak's *Doctor Zhivago*, as well as the now-lone voice of Solzhenitsyn.

And I repeat that the problem lies not only in politics or ideology. Already today, their voices calm and steady, geneticists are announcing that they are on the threshold of regulating the formation of human beings, ensuring their biological conformity to the needs of the collective, so to speak. We are already witnessing the gradual elimination from schools and universities of everything that is at all capable of furthering personal self-knowledge, and its replacement with what will more adequately adapt, or rather subject, a person to the needs of the modern world. Even the slightest attempt to protest or simply refuse to participate in this feverish and all-embracing enterprise is already regarded as a crime against the world and society.

The average man, whose mental field of vision is limited to his daily concerns, most likely does not even notice this transformation. Society and the government are cleverly diverting his attention from this ever-increasing pressure. His material situation is improving: an apartment, a little house, a country place, maybe even a nice car . . . what else could he possibly want from life? And again, one remembers Blok:

> Be content with your lives,
> Keeping quieter than water, lying lower than grass!
> Oh, if you only knew, my children,
> The cold and desolation of the coming days![1]

No doubt someone will ask me: "So, according to your reasoning, all of human progress supposedly is an evil, one that must be condemned and rejected? Does this mean that only individualism is good and necessary, the pursuit of personal happiness and personal interests? And where did you get this idea that each person seeks only good, that what he serves is worthwhile? Isn't the primacy of the whole, of the collective, of society over the individual and the isolated actually a victory over the unbridled egoism of the individual? Is not this very individual the source of evil and suffering on earth?"

Here is the impasse at which we find ourselves today; here is the terrible choice that faces us. And it seems to me that only by recognizing the horror of this vicious circle can we understand it, and see that at its center, at the heart of the range of human problems, stands the question of religion. Only a religious approach to man provides a way out of this desperate choice: either humanity or the indivudual man.

And how strange, but also how revealing, is the fact that either choice leads to the persecution of religion. There was a time when religion was decried and rejected in the name of individual rights, as being focused exclusively on the person and not on humanity as a whole. In our day it is exactly the opposite. Religion is persecuted in the name of humanity; it is regarded as the uninvited defender of the individual. For such is indeed the case: only in religion, only in the Christian intuition is there room for both the one and the other, for humanity and for the individual, for humanity in its totality and for the person as an absolute irreducible value. Only in the Gospel did the light appear that shines to this day, which does away with the terrible "either/or" dichotomy: either the darkness of a mechanical

---

[1]From the poem "Golos iz Hora" ("A Voice From the Choir"), 1910–1914.

civilization, its "cold and empty fog," or the darkness of individualism, of the isolated individual who sees only himself as the goal of the universe. Christ always focuses on the world, on everyone, on the whole of humanity, and always on each person, on you and on me, on a given, specific individual. And in this lies the miracle and mystery of the Gospel. In it everyone finds himself, yet in himself he finds all others. In the Gospel everyone discovers everything, and in everything—himself.

Here is the mystery that is increasingly becoming forgotten by the world, which no one wants to consider in the search for solutions to the truly dreadful questions of our time, the mystery that is repelled in the name of happiness, both collective and individual. Today this mystery needs to be shouted from the rooftops, for in it alone can we be saved.

Why and For What Does a Person Exist?

Once a famous German philosopher, the materialist Ludwig Feuerbach, wrote the following famous line: "Man is what he eats." With this formula he had hoped to put an end to all idealistic speculation about human nature. But in actuality he unwittingly expressed a specifically religious idea about humanity. For long before Feuerbach, the same definition of man had been given in the Bible. In the biblical story of creation, man is shown to be first and foremost a hungry creature, with the whole world for his food. Soon after the commandment to multiply and rule over the earth, God calls man to eat of it: *Behold, I have given you every herb beraring seed, which is upon the face of all the earth, and every tree . . . to you it shall be for food* (Gen 1.29). In order to live, man has to eat, that is, to take the world into his own body and to transform it into himself, into his flesh and blood. Yes, indeed, man is what he eats, and the whole world is depicted in the Bible as a kind of banquet prepared for him. And this image of a banquet, a meal, is found throughout the whole Bible as the central symbol of life. It is the symbol of the world and its creation, and the symbol of life at its end, its fulfillment. *That ye may eat and drink at my table in my kingdom*, says Christ (Lk 22.30).

I begin with the theme of food and drink (one generally considered secondary by both believers and unbelievers from a religious standpoint) in view of the central question: what kind of life is referred to in the eternal argument between faith and unbelief, between religion and atheism? Unbelievers accuse believers of indifference to human life and its needs. And it must be admitted that very often believers themselves provide grounds for these accusations. For they all too easily forget what Holy Scripture says concerning the true nature and purport of life, especially as articulated by Christ himself. For a great many Christians, the word *life* always signifies religious life, which in their minds comprises a closed sphere, sealed off tightly from secular or worldly life. In this attitude there is a dominant pathos of "pure spirituality," a pathos of exile, of a putting off of the flesh, of a denial of the world. The temptation to this denial of the world exists and has always existed; for life with all its concerns, misfortunes, suffering, disappointments, and, finally, death has always and everywhere been difficult, often unbearable, for humanity. How great then is the longing to leave everything, to cast off all responsibility, and to plunge into a kind of Nirvana—into the peace of "pure contemplation" and prayer! In this view, everything written in the Bible concerning food is understood to mean spiritual food alone.

But besides this understanding of life and religion there has always existed another approach. According to this approach, the purpose of religion is to improve life, to help the world and people. This view sees Christianity as a political and social program. The adherents of this approach also base their approach on the Bible, since Christ too called his followers to care for the poor, the hungry, this suffering, and the imprisoned.

And so we find ourselves facing a paradox. If Christians call men to spirituality, if they remind people about Christ's words: *Seek ye first the kingdom of God and his righteousness, and all these things will be added unto you* (Mt 6.33), they are accused of indifference to the world and its needs. If, on the other hand, they understand Christianity as a call to fight for a better life, they are accused of interfering in matters that do not concern them, which are outside the sphere of religion. I repeat: Christians themselves are often at odds with each other as to what the Gospel primarily calls them to, as to what comprises the fundamental essence of the Christian life. Indeed, what is more necessary: to withdraw into oneself to pray, or to become involved in the struggle for what all the different worldly ideologies call "a bright future"? What is most important: to spiritualize life or, conversely, to secularize religion, which has become so alienated from the "real needs and issues" of contemporary man? These are the questions that believers and nonbelievers find equally troubling. It is impossible to answer them without penetrating the religious understanding of man. Man is what he eats. But what is it that he eats and why?

This question seemed useless and unimportant both to Feuerbach and to his religious opponents. For him and for them, consumption was understood as an obvious material function, and all that differentiated their views was another question altogether: is there anything in men aside from this function—something above the material, some spiritual superstructure? To this question religion answered: "Yes," while Feuerbach answered: "No." But for us it is important that both the "yes" of religion and the "no" of materialism were understood in the context of that same juxtaposition of the material to the spiritual, the body to the soul. And ironically, from this point of view Feuerbach, the enemy of everything religious, in fact showed himself to be the fruit of many centuries of development of Christian thought, which in part had adopted as its own thesis the opposition between soul and body, the material and the spiritual, the natural and supernatural, the sacred and the profane. Feuerbach concluded that the time had come in the name of the reality of matter, in the name of life "just as it is," to eliminate any kind of structure imposed upon it. In saying that "man is what he eats," he assumed that with this formula he had laid religion to rest. But the tragedy is that all who opposed him from a religious standpoint understood food and consumption, the dependency of man on the world and material, essentially exactly as he did, insisting merely that something spiritual lies beyond the need for food.

But can the dispute be reduced to this contradistinction? We have seen that the Bible also begins with food; that while it understands the formula of Feuerbach, it also essentially rejects the opposition of the material and the spiritual, and speaks about man as a holistic creature. Thus, what does the Bible tell us about the world, about food, and about man's dependence on them? We will try to answer this question in our next talk.

Why and For What Does a Person Exist? (Conclusion)

M an is what he eats." In making this affirmation, the German materialist philosopher Feuerbach was convinced that he was laying to rest and nullifying all idealistic speculation about human nature. In actuality, he unwittingly expressed a deeply religious understanding of man, for long before Feuerbach an identical definition of man was given in the Bible.

In the Biblical account of the creation of man, he is shown first of all to be a creature who is hungry, with the whole world as his food. Soon after the commandment to multiply and to rule the earth, man is given the commandment to eat of the earth: *And God said: Behold, I have given you every herb bearing seed, which is upon the face of the earth, and every tree* (Gen 1.29).

In order to live, man must eat; he must transform the world into himself, into his body and blood. He is indeed what he eats. And the whole world is depicted in the Bible as a kind of banquet prepared for men, and this image of a banquet, a meal, is a constant theme, comprising a major symbol of life. It is an image of life as transformation, but also an image of life in its complete fulfillment: *And I appoint unto you a kingdom*, Christ says to his disciples on the last night of his life, during the mystical supper, *as my Father appointed unto me, that ye may eat and drink at my table in my kingdom* (Lk 22.29).

I begin with this theme of food, one seemingly secondary from a religious point of view, because the question I would like to answer to the best of my ability is the question of what kind of life we are talking about, what kind of life are we preaching, proclaiming, and announcing, when as Christians we affirm that Christ gave himself *for the life of the world* (Jn 6.51). This question has two general answers. Some answer that the life taught by Christianity is a religious life which is self-sufficient and independent of the life of this world. This means that there is a special, closed-off world of "spirituality," and there are many religious persons who live exclusively within that world, indifferent all else, to the world of daily concerns. Lost and crushed amid the noise, amid the rush and frustrations of real life, a person easily gives in to the temptation to seek refuge in the confines of his soul, and to find there another life, another banquet with plentiful spiritual food. And this food helps him to recover his peace of mind, to patiently bear the struggles and frustrations of real life, and even simply to disregard it.

This first general answer to the question posed earlier has many variations—from simple "folk" faith to an almost pathological interest in all sorts of "mystical" teachings. But the results of all these variations is the same: this type of religious life renders real life senseless and barren; the spiritual food deprives the physical food of any meaning, and transforms the whole world into a mere exercise in piety and patience.

But there is a second answer, and for its adherents "for the life of the world" means, first and foremost, for the improvement of life in the world. As a result, we see the supporters of pure spirituality opposed by the supporters of religious activism. The latter are those who hold that Christianity has lost the world because it has almost wholly reduced itself to spirituality, to contemplation, to prayer, to silence and worship, because it has not sufficiently taken seriously the real man, the man who eats and drinks to live. And according to these people Christianity must conquer the world by becoming involved in social, political, and economic concerns, by active participation in "real life." But here too the question remains unanswered. Whereas the first, strictly religious and spiritual answer simply rejects life, the second approach is unclear as to the final purpose of life, the ultimate goal of this life that they are trying to return to religion and Christianity—in other words, they are unclear as to the ultimate goal of all this "religious activism."

Suppose we achieve one of these practical goals, that our activism is crowned with success. What then? Perhaps the answer might seem naïve, but in the final analysis no activism is possible unless people have faith in the ultimate and all-embracing goal of the life for which they are working, struggling, and organizing. We eat and drink, we struggle for freedom and justice, in order to live a full life. But in what does this full life consist? What ultimately makes life "life"? The more deeply we analyze our activity, the more inescapably we come to a dead end, becoming convinced that by themselves these actions are meaningless, because any activity, any effort ought to result in perfect joy. But joy over what? And so we see that not a single answer proves satisfactory. One abandons life for religion, and thereby makes life meaningless; the other, by dissolving religion into life, simply conflates it with external activism, depriving it of its own meaning. And so we must look elsewhere and more deeply for an answer.

And so, "man is what he eats"—but what does he eat and why? This question seemed naïve and silly not only to Feuerbach, but also to his opponents in the religious camp. Both for him and for them, the question of food was reduced to its strictly physical, material function, and the only question remaining was whether man, who is dependent on food, had any kind of spiritual "superstructure" over his physical nature. Feuerbach answered this question in the negative, while his religious opponents answered it affirmatively, but both answers actually proceeded from the same assumption: namely, that the spiritual necessarily opposes the material, and this premise that prioritizes the spiritual over the material, the sacred over the profane, the supernatural over the natural, and finally, religion over life, for centuries remained identical for both believers and nonbelievers.

In a certain sense Feuerbach was a direct successor of medieval Christian idealism. But as we have seen, the Bible also begins with man as a creature that requires food, with man as one who eats and who is that which he eats. Only here the perspective and approach are completely different, for the Bible does not recognize that opposition between the "spiritual" and the "material" that determined the later development of man's self-understanding. We must speak in particular about this religious materialism of the Bible, about this understanding of food, for this is the origin of the Christian dialectic of life, and herein lies the beginning of the answer to life's ultimate meaning. We will continue this discussion in our next talk.

Why and For What Does a Person Exist? (Parallel version)

Man is what he eats." When in my last talk I mentioned the famous phrase of the materialist philosopher Feuerbach, I mentioned that he saw this as a formula that would put an end to all religious discussions about human nature. I mentioned that in actuality this formula can also express the biblical teaching about man, inasmuch as the first book of the Bible shows him to be first and foremost a hungry being, whose life depends on this world for his food. Consequently, the debate is not about food as such, or about how dependent man is upon it, but about the meaning of this food. Finally, I indicated how the biblical teaching about man was to a certain degree perverted by those Christians who too easily accepted the dichotomy between the material and the spiritual, between the earthly and the sacred—a dichotomy foreign to the Bible and the Gospels.

In actuality, nowhere in the Bible do we find this dichotomy. The biblical account shows that the food that man eats, and the world from which he derives his nourishment in order to live, are given to him by God, and are given as a means of communion with God. The world as man's nourishment is not something exclusively material, limited to its material function, and therefore opposed and even antagonistic to the specifically spiritual. According to the Bible, absolutely everything that exists comes from God, and consequently witnesses to God, bringing man to him and into communion with him. If according to the New Testament God is Love (see 1 Jn 4.8), then one can say of the world that it is divine love, given as food, becoming life for us. In the Bible God blesses everything that he creates. In biblical terms, this means that he makes all of creation a sign and a means of his presence and wisdom, love and revelation. *O taste and see that the Lord is good* (Ps 33.8), says the ancient biblical poet, the author of the psalms. Yes, man is a hungry creature, but he is hungry for God. At the root of our whole life of hunger, desire, and aspiration stands God. And in the final analysis, all our desire is the desire to make him our own.

Naturally, man is not the only creature who experiences constant hunger, which is the law of all creation. But only man is capable of responding to God's blessing by blessing God for the gift of life, responding to this with thanksgiving. In the biblical account of man's first days we are struck by how God gave him the responsibility of naming all other creatures. Thus, after creating the animals God brings them to man in order for him to name each of them. But here we must remember that in the biblical understanding a name means immeasurably more than just a means of differentiating one thing from another. In all ancient cultures the name conveys the essence of its bearer. Thus, to name a thing means to expound its meaning and purpose given it by God, to receive with with gratitude as God's gift.

This explains why praise, thanksgiving, and blessing in the Bible are not simply "cult acts," but the very depths, the very primordial form of life. According to the Bible, God blessed the world, blessed man, and blessed the seventh day, or time. This means that he filled all of creation with his love, with his comeliness, and created everything as *very good* (Gen 1.31). And this is why the natural reaction, the natural response of man to this gift of the world and of life is thanksgiving and joy. This means that man sees the world just as God himself created and loves it, and in this act of thanksgiving and praise he recognizes the world, gives it a name, and gains mastery of it. All human abilities—intellectual, spiritual, and volitional—all that distinguish man from the rest of creation, have their root and source in this thanksgiving and blessing, the knowledge of what the object of his hunger and thirst is.

Some scientists have ascribed to man the Latin term *homo faber*, that is, "man the maker," pointing to his ability to cultivate the world; while others refer to him as *homo sapiens*, that is, "man the intellectual," underscoring his ability to think. But prior to any of these categories he must be considered as *homo adorans*—"the man of thanksgiving or praise," that is, one who experiences grateful joy. In his origin and calling, man's role in the universe is that of priest. He is created as the crown of creation, and by his knowledge of God the Creator and the God of love he unites the whole world in himself: he receives the world from God and returns it to God as a sacrifice of praise; filling the world with praise and thanksgiving, he transfigures its life into a ceaseless communion with God. One could say that the whole world was created as the matter or substance of a single all-encompassing cosmic sacrament that man is called to fulfill. And people still understand this—if not intellectually, then with their instincts and feelings. For example, centuries of alienation from religion have failed to transform eating, the consumption of food, into a purely utilitarian, strictly physiological function. Man still treats food with great respect. The meal still remains a ritual, a rite, and one might say that it remains the last "natural sacrament" of the family, of friendship, of communion—of everything in life that is greater and more signficant than simply food and simply drink. We invite friends to visit us and immediately we offer them food. How else could we express our communion, our friendship, and our love?

Thus, even for contemporary man, this technological and utilitarian being, eating and drinking is always more than simply the physiological sustenance of the body. People may have forgotten the source and root of all of this, but they still celebrate food and, in it and through it, the mystery of life. Yes, man is what he eats. But he eats his food so that in living by it he might transform and fill it, that is, his life, with light, with praise, with meaning, with creativity—that is to say, with God. This is the religious understanding of man and his food. But has man remained faithful to this understanding? This question we will now address.

Why and For What Does a Person Exist? (Parallel version, conclusion)

In my last talk I cited the philosopher Feuerbach who said, "Man is what he eats." In the mind of this German materialist philosopher, this declaration put an end to any religious or spiritual understanding of human

nature. But in fact (and this I also discussed previously), a similar definition
was also given in the Bible: it too shows man as a creature that first and
foremost is hungry and thirsty. In the Bible, however, this materialism has
a completely different meaning: the food which man consumes, the world
on which he depends, is given to men by God, and given for communion
with God. The world as food is not something totally material, limited to
its physiological function, and as such opposed to other, specifically spiritual
functions. All that exists is a gift of God, and in all of it and through all of
it God is revealed to man and enters into communion with him. According
to the Bible, the world is divine love that has become food, being transformed into life for men. According to the Bible, God blesses everything
he creates, and in biblical language this means that all of creation is made
by him as a sign and a means of his presence and wisdom, love, and revelation: *O taste and see*, the psalm says, *that the Lord is good* (Ps 33.8). Yes, man
is a hungry creature, a creature of desire, but in the final analysis what he
desires is God.

Indeed, everything in the world, and not only man, lives by nourishment and dependence on food; but man is unique in that he alone knows,
or rather is able to know, for what or for whom he ultimately thirsts; he
is unique in that he alone is able to respond to God's blessing by blessing
God for the food and the life he receives from him. It is significant that in
the biblical account of creation man is entrusted with naming things: when
God brings to Adam animals to help him, he brings them that he might give
them names: *And Adam gave names to all cattle and to the fowl of the air and to
every beast of the field* (Gen 2.20). But in the biblical approach to the world, the
name is something immeasurably more profound than simply a label that
distinguishes one thing from another. The name signifies the very essence
of a thing, or more precisely, the essence of a thing as a gift of God. To call
or to name means to delve into the meaning of a thing, to recognize it as a
gift of God and to recognize also its place in the cosmos created by God. In
other words, to name anything is to bless God, to rejoice in what he gives,
in that which we receive from him. And in the Bible, to bless God is not
some sort of special, specifically religious act, but a primordial and profound
manifestation of life itself. God blessed the world, God blessed man, God

blessed time—this means that he filled everything with his love, and that he made everything, as it is written in the Bible, *very good* (Gen 1.31).

And this is why indeed it is a normal and not supernatural reaction for man, to whom God gave this blessed and sanctified world, to bless God in turn with thanksgiving, to see the world as God sees it, and in this act of blessing and thanksgiving to know the world, to name it, and to have dominion over it. And all the rational, spiritual, and other abilities that distinguish man from the rest of the world are focused and find their fulfillment in this ability of men to bless, to give thanks, and to recognize the ultimate and joyful meaning of that thirst, of that hunger, which constitute his life. *Homo sapiens*, the intelligent man; *homo faber*, the man capable of work—such is the ancient description of men. But the Bible with each of its words adds to this *homo adorans*, the man of thanksgiving. In a certain sense, with his whole life man performs the sacrament of transfiguring the world into communion with God; unites the world in himself; gives it meaning, a goal, and depth; and transforms food itself into communion with a higher life.

And people, even unbelievers who are completely immersed in daily and material concerns, instinctively know and understand this. Thus, for example, nothing, no materialism, no reduction of the person to physiology, has been able to transform nourishment into a simple physiological function. Man continues to treat food with reverence: the meal remains a sacred act and ritual, the last "natural sacrament" of the family, of friendship, of communion—of all that which makes life more than a simple struggle for survival. Eating food and drinking remain something greater and deeper than mere concern for the body. People may be unable to understand what constitutes this "greater" and this profoundness, but they continue to respect them, and they hunger and thirst not merely for food but for the life that this food provides.

And if we are sensitive to this biblical perspective, even if we do not accept it, it becomes understandable why in the Bible, in its system of symbols, the fall and sin of man are also connected with food: man ate the forbidden fruit. Whatever the other meanings of that mysterious tree of the knowledge of good and evil and about the prohibition against eating from it, one thing is certain: the fruit that man ate despite God's prohibition was not given to him, was not blessed, and he ate it for his own purpose, rather than as a means of communion with another, with God. And this is why the meaning of the fall is that, having eaten of this fruit, man cut his life off from God, made it a goal unto itself, and it ceased to be a form of communion, participation, and transformation. From an act of love, life was transformed into an act of egoism, and from an act of thanksgiving into an act of self-preservation and self-affirmation. And in performing this act, man lost paradise—he lost the ability for joyful communion with the world and, through the world, with God. He became a slave of food, and it transformed his whole life into a dull, fearsome, and mortal struggle for existence. Man remained as he was, but he began to eat in a different manner and for a different purpose. Only if we understand this biblical perspective can we proceed further and become sensitive to what the Bible understands the salvation of man to be.

True Greatness

"Man'—it has a proud sound."[2] How often we hear this slogan, and the directly related cry: "Get rid of everything that opposes this greatness of man, especially Christianity with its humility, its patience, and its constant sighs over 'these little ones'!" This, in essence, is the starting point of all anti-religious activity.

Quite recently a young man, a student—pleasant, energetic, and successful—said to me: "Religion is a crutch. And why do I need crutches when I can walk on my own, achieve everything by myself, and answer all questions on my own?" And there are many young people like this, who have no use for religion with its apparent abjection, its cries of, "We have no other help beside thee, we have no other hope,"[3] its entreaties of, "O fervent intercessor!"[4] This perception of religion fills the air we breathe;

[2]The words of Sateen from the play by Maxim Gorky, On the Bottom, Act 4 (1902).
[3]Kontakion from a thanksgiving prayer to the Mother of God.
[4]Troparion of the Kazan icon of the Mother of God.

it is part of our world. And the divide between these two perceptions of what a person is appears to be growing rather than shrinking—the divide between these expressions "'Man'—it has a proud sound!" and "We have no other help." Indeed, how can we disagree with the first proposition? Do we really still need this "crutch"? Yes, it is true that man was so weak, defeated, and helpless, knew so very little, lived in such fear of nature, of people, and even of himself, that in that darkness, abjection, and suffering all he could do was fall on his knees and pray for help and protection. And so we have these numerous churches, this constant prayer for salvation, this longing for another world, "where there is neither sickness, or sorrow, nor sighing."[5]

It is easy to understand the contemporary young person: all of this for him is foreign and beyond comprehension. He does not live in the world of these timorous people. And if religion is only for those "that labor and are heavy-laden," then hasn't the time come to wipe it off the slate of history and start working to make this labor and this burden a thing of pride and freedom? Of course one could easily protest against this, saying that Christianity also teaches about the greatness of the human person; that a person is given glory and honor by God, that he is called to have dominion over the world, that he is the image and likeness of God. But today for some reason these arguments are ineffective. It would seem that the historical experience of religion is rather different. As Rozanov wrote, "It came entirely from the sighs of the people, from these entreaties and this longing for help and protection."[6] And so it would be dishonest to deny this element, which is so important in religion.

No, Christianity does not say: "'Man'—it has a proud sound," but it always repeats the words of the psalm: *A broken and humbled heart God will not despise* (Psalm 50.17). Yes, Christianity assuredly calls men to humility, and not to pride; yes, it truly says that without God and faith man is pitiful, helpless, and also terrible. Christianity does not have that optimism that affirms: "We are going to build a new world of our own!" On the part of Christians

[5]From the Kontakion for the Departed, and the Prayer for the Dead ("O God of spirits . . ."); ultimately derived from Isaiah 51.11 (LXX).

[6]Cf. V. Rozanov's address to the Religious-Philosophical Assembly, in *Proceedings of the Religious Philosophical Assembly*, Collection 18 (Novy Put', 1903), 11:457.

today there are efforts to close this gap that separates Christianity from unbelief, and in so doing to renounce Christianity's compassion, mercy, and humility in the name of the slogan: "'Man'—it has a proud sound." But the whole point is that this gap cannot be closed by this method, for in Christianity what is most important is not man's external success, not his conquest of space, not the speed of his aircraft, and not even the material well-being of society. Christianity rejects none of these achievements, and it recognizes them all as important, but above all else it sets the moral beauty and spiritual perfection of man, or more precisely it denies that man's material achievements are of any value if these achievements hinder his spiritual goals and moral growth. *For what is a man profited, if he shall gain the whole world, and lose his own soul?* (Mt 16.26). This is the only question that the Gospel asks each of us.

The debate between Christianity and materialism is about this alone, and Christianity is anchored in its spiritual, moral approach to everything in the world. And if we consider those elements of Christianity that seem so strange to "modern" man (and that the young man to whom I've already referred called a "crutch") from this point of view, they will appear in quite a different light. "We have no other help, we have no other hope"—no, this prayer is not a call for external help. This is a prayer of a man who sees an image of moral perfection and of the highest spiritual beauty, and knows how far he is from this image, and this is why he calls out for help.

We can fly to the moon, we can beat one more world record. But how can we add even a little bit more love and light to the soul? How can one love a person? How does one conquer evil, jealousy, and pettiness in oneself? How can one avoid being indifferent to even a single tear of a child, as Ivan Karamazov described? People are wrong in thinking that Christianity emerged from sighs of fear and helplessness. Christianity sighs indeed, but it sighs for righteous life, it sighs for a world that shines with truth, compassion, and love; it sighs with longing for true fraternity and unity. "Many of us travel the earth, seeking truth,"[7] says Cassian from Krasivaya

---

[7]"And I'm not the only sinner . . . many other peasants in worn shoes are walking around the world, searching for the truth." From Turgenev's *Cassian with a Beautiful Sword*, in *Complete Collected Works and Letters in 30 vols.* (Moscow: Nauka, 1979), 3:119.

Mecha in the famous story by Turgenev. One listens to this sigh, and suddenly one sees that this majesty, this dignity, this God-likeness of man lies not in technological achievements, not in the conquest of space, but in that very humility in which the enemies of Christianity see its weakness. Take the learned Von Koren in Chekhov's *The Duel.* He is full of the pride and a sense of his own dignity, and from their heights he looks down on the weak, depraved Laevsky. But it is only when he humbles himself, when he begins to understand that love and mercy are higher and greater than his own formal self-righteousness and irreproachability, when he discovers for himself the soul of Laevsky—it is only then that he becomes truly victorious. And Christianity is only in this, only about this! In what lies the majesty, the pride, and the dignity of man? We will return to this question in our next talk.

The Object of the Struggle

Recently, a prominent French communist said that communists have faith just as Christians do. The only difference is that they do not believe in God, but in man. "Faith in God," averred this communist, "is incompatible with faith in man. Here you have an either/or. If there is a God, then man is a slave, his freedom is ephemeral, he's not the master of his own fate and not the creator of his own world. This is why faith in God is not only unscientific, but also harmful and dangerous."

In these words of the French communist we find yet again the most profound basis of anti-religion. Religion must be opposed in the name of man, in the name of his freedom and absolute mastery of the world. Incidentally, Christianity affirms roughly the same: the fullness of man's humanity is only possible with God, and without God man is a slave, a useless grain of sand, who is here today and gone tomorrow, fully and completely subjugated to the laws and forces of impersonal matter. Communism exhorts people to oppose God for the sake of man; Christianity bases the greatness of man on faith in God. And since Christianity asserts that the existence of

God cannot be proven the way one proves any empirical truth, inasmuch as faith is ultimately a gift, it remains to compare these two assertions and to ask oneself: which assertion—that of the atheist who champions man, or that of the Christian, who also champions man—is most convincing?

Our first question for the French communist whom we just cited is this: what does it mean to "believe in man"? What would be the basis of this faith, and what would it comprise? Furthermore, what kind of man are we talking about? Are we talking about some kind of abstract general "Man" with a capital "M," who does not yet exist but will appear in some unknown future? Or are we talking about each concrete, living person?

From a Christian standpoint there is no difficulty here. When Christianity speaks about man, it truly has in mind each individual living person. For his sake alone, the Gospel says, ninety-nine others must be left. He is arrayed in the image and likeness of God, he is called to eternity. This is why his destiny—though he should be the most paltry and insignificant in the eyes of society—is as important as the destiny of a leader, a scholar, or a genius. Even the Christian teaching about perdition and salvation, the teaching that atheist propagandists so love to mock—is based on belief in the individual responsibility of each person and his freedom. If I wish it, I can seek salvation, or if I wish, I can perish; and no one, not even God, can do anything to counter this freedom.

I repeat: when Christianity speaks about faith in man, it is clear. One can refuse to support this teaching, one can argue against it, but it is impossible to deny that at its basis lies the affirmation of the infinite value of each individual—a value that is eternal.

From the communist point of view, this faith in man is decidedly baseless. First of all, according to communist teaching, man, like everything else in the world, is merely a product of the material process, a particle of matter just like any other. In philosophical terms, there is nothing transcendent about him: he appears, then disappears forever. Consequently, man's significance as an eternal value disappears, and with it his significance as a person. Furthermore, as long as a man lives, and as long as, like everything else in the world, he is subject to the absolute laws of matter, he is not free: each action, each thought, each choice of his is determined by causes, which in their turn are determined by other causes, and so on ad infinitum. Where in all of this do we find freedom?

Christianity asserts that man, in contrast to everything else in the world, has a spirit within him. In the Gospel we read: "The Spirit breathes where it will, and we do not know from where it comes or where it is going" (cf. Jn 3.8). Thus, the spirit in man is the medium not merely of some illusory freedom, but rather of a profound one— a freedom that raises him above the laws of matter. But the man of dialectical materialism is deprived of this freedom, because such freedom does not exist in the nature of things.

What then does it mean to believe in man? From this point of view one can only *know*: we can know how a bourgeois or a proletarian will act. But this knowledge has no need of faith. For even the bourgeois or the proletarian will act identically—by virtue of the ironclad and persistent logic of the laws of nature. Consequently, it may be affirmed that communist faith is not in the living, concrete person. But in whom then is this faith? In mankind? But mankind, no matter how you cut it, has always consisted, consists, and will consist of living, concrete persons.

In whom do we believe? People say that the construction of communism will ultimately form the "communist man." But, as far as we can judge, this will be a man who will be fully subject to the collective—that is, a man impersonal, colorless, and bleak. And if it is true that all of history has been leading up to the formation of this man, this man who is indistinguishable from all others, then why is this a good thing, why is this desirable and valuable? Very well; let us suppose that communism has not yet fully formulated its teaching about man (what it likes to call "communist humanism"). Nevertheless, the criteria of this teaching are quite clear: there is no individuality and there is no freedom.

But what then remains? This is a tragic question, and we pose it without any irony. Whole generations are invited to fight for man, but we are offered no teaching about the value of Man, about the object of this struggle. A classless society? But this very definition is negative: it tells us nothing about the positive content of human life— that life in which each person exists, and not "mankind in general." The absence of exploitation? Well then, the *presence* of what? In the final analysis, who really believes in man? Those who deny his eternal value as a person, or those who, following Christ, say that the entire world was created for each individual person, and that in all the world there is nothing more valuable than his soul?

The French communist says that communists also believe, only in man instead of God. But it turns out that without God there is no faith in man, nor can there be. One can have knowledge *about* him—even a great deal of knowledge. One can even have sympathy and love for him, there can be a struggle to provide him with bread and happiness, but there cannot be faith in him as having unique and eternal value. There cannot be that ultimate reality for which one could give up one's life. This is why the struggle against religion, in the final analysis, is always a struggle against the eternal and divine in man.

The Dead End of Materialist Anthropology

The debate about religion, of course, is always and chiefly a debate about man. The affirmation that "God exists" or that "there is no God"—these are not expressions of abstract, metaphysical ideas, but two fundamentally opposed intuitions about man, and it is this that makes the debate so bitter—not a fight for life, but a fight to the death. For ultimately all determinations about the world and about life depend on what man is and what comprises his essence.

Both religion and atheism—at least that atheism that calls itself "scientific" and is grounded in a wholly materialistic worldview—are chiefly concerned with the salvation of man. But why and from what does man need to be saved? What are the deeper motives for this undying attempt to change, to improve, to transfigure human life? This question implies yet another, deeper one: what in fact is man? And we must frankly acknowledge that in the efforts to answer this question there is unbelievable confusion, partly involuntary and partly deliberately contrived. It is essential to eliminate this confusion, for nothing less than the fate of man and of humanity depends on it.

One of the virtues of our endlessly difficult and even tragic era lies in the fact that our search for answers to such pivotal questions forces us to look into the abyss. In addition, it seems that both camps, religious and atheist, are afraid of such questions, and confuse them more and more with secondary and unrelated considerations. And religion, instead of showing its own profound nature, opens itself up to atheism's attacks by providing all sorts of new grounds for its own discrediting. And atheism in turn, by constantly appealing to "science" and "objectivity," employs almost exclusively fraudulent tactics. As a result, instead of a debate, we have something rather pitiful and crass.

The only escape from this situation is to state the fundamental question openly and honestly. To both the religious man and to the atheist we must pose roughly the question: "Both of you seem to be concerned with man, with his life and his destiny; both of you want not only to serve man, but even to save him. Explain then, first of all, what is man, where did he come from, and why, in contrast to the rest of the world, is he in need of this salvation? For, on the one hand, it is obvious that only that which is perishing can and must be saved. But if so, it must be explained in what way man is perishing, and how it all began. On the other hand, it is equally obvious that only something very valuable deserves salvation—something that cannot die, which by its nature is alien to destruction. And so we must ask: what is the nature of man? There is, of course, something sad in nature's autumn demise, but it would never enter anyone's head to feel sorry for a dying leaf, as it slowly wafts down from the sky and lands on the ground. The dying of the leaf is 'engraved' in its nature, and it elicits no questions or astonishment. Here both of you want to serve man, but in the name of what? Why is it necessary and possible to serve him?"

It is only in this way that one can bring any kind of meaning to this debate about religion, to clarify the mindset of both believers and nonbelievers. It is this question that actually began this debate. For the ideology that in our day not only rejects religion, but considers it a sacred duty to release man from the control of religion, begins by accusing religion of demeaning man's destiny. Consistent with the founders of dialectic materialism, Feuerbach, Marx, and Engels, religion is the ultimate, the supreme, and therefore the most dangerous, most terrifying form of "alienation" of man from himself, from his own nature, and therefore it is the most terrifying form of his enslavement. The religious man, according to this ideology, alienates man from his humanity, and thus in a certain sense he is no longer human. Therefore, it is important not only to clarify the reasons for man's religiosity, but also literally to save him from religion.

As we see, all of this contains an idea that is rather lofty in its own way: "to save and to liberate." And yet, in proving its own basic thesis, dialectical materialism skirts around the main idea in silence: who after all is this man who needs to be saved for his own sake, and whose salvation must be accomplished at any cost? One can peruse the entire *Das Kapital* of Marx without finding out what man is, what his life consists of, and, most importantly, what he ultimately lives for. This grand yet monstrous teaching leads to a dead end: to liberate, to save—but whom? We do not know. To liberate—but for what reason? We do not know and we cannot know.

And the more firmly dialectical materialism rams into this terrible dead end, into this nothingness, the more bitterly it hates religion, the more fiercely it wants to destroy it. But here a nagging doubt arises: does it not hate religion and desire to destroy it precisely because the whole purpose of religion, its goal with regard to man, is to answer these "ultimate" questions about man, about who he is and why he exists? In other words, materialism, which in the name of man rejects God, unwillingly and inescapably, despite all of its logic, despite all its passionate rejection of religion, still brings us to the ultimate question: "What is man?"—and, consequently, to the question of God.

To this intuition about the religious man about himself, to the question of how religion understands man's essence, we must now turn. For in discovering who man is for religion, we can then understand the meaning of religion for believers.

The True Plan

At the center of all discussions of religion there should always be the question of its moral side: what plan for man does it proclaim and what goal in life does it propose for man?

One of the principal errors of the critics of religion, voluntary or involuntary, is that they reduce the whole matter to a religious view of the world, that is, to the realm of natural science. Religion, however, regards man from its ethical, moral stance. As a rule, Christians of all eras have shared the views of the natural sciences of their time. But the development of science did not alter the religious and ethical ideal of Christians, which is the true heart of Christianity. Be perfect, love one another, forgive your enemies—these summonses, these commandments did not depend on various scientific outlooks, on various "scientific" worldviews.

Thus, every discussion about religion should come down to an evaluation of its ethical side, its plan for man, and its summons—to whether we accept or deny this plan and this summons. And so for centuries the world has been replete with images of saints who are full of love for the world and for people, calling all men to moral betterment, for man can always improve. Is this image of holiness then good or bad? Should it be accepted or rejected? Thus, in speaking about Christianity, it is essential to underline that everything in it is not only firmly bound up with its moral ideal, with its basic understanding of man, but is wholly subject to it. *Faith without works is dead*, says sacred Scripture (Jas 2.26). And not only without works, but without love and compassion also. For Scripture also says: "If I have all faith, but have not love, then I am nothing" (cf. 1 Cor 13.2), and, *I will have mercy, and not sacrifice* (Mt 12.7).

All of these affirmations witness to one fact: faith and religious teaching have no meaning if they are not rooted in moral law, in moral design, which alone are a sufficient answer to all "unmasking" of religion. But the detractors of religion fully understand that any discussion of this side of the matter would unmask their own lack of solid footing. This is why in order to "unmask" religion it is essential to find diverse ways of perverting it.

And that is what is taking place today.

The Explanation from Above

It would appear that we are all speaking the same language and therefore that we understand one another. But is this really the case?

In these past days I have listened to the words spoken in church during Great Lent, and and I have read them myself. And as I was listening to them I thought: "What do they mean, what can they signify for so-called modern man, what relationship do they have to his language?" Let me cite at random any one of several phrases and expressions: "Let us begin the bright fast shining with the rays of Christ's commandments . . ."[8] And further: "Where shall I begin to weep for the actions of my wretched life? What first-fruit shall I offer, O Christ, in this my lamentation?"[9]

"Oh," they say, "this is in Slavonic, not in Russian, and so not everyone understands it." Very well; let us translate it, and we will still see that these verses are foreign to our mundane language; they still have no place in our normal parlance. "The brightness of love," "the radiance of prayer," "the fortress of manliness"—these are not simply words and concepts, but above all an incarnation, an expression, a record of a certain experience, and it is precisely this experience that is foreign to modern man. He hears these words but he does not understand them; he hears the sounds and he does not absorb them. Of course, it is not his fault. Since childhood he has been told that there is no other possible experience except what is described in specific books, written using specific language—that any other experience cannot and does not exist, that everything else is a falsification, darkness, and nothing more.

Darkness . . . But then why are these words almost entirely about light? Not only do they concern light, but in and of themselves why do they radiate light? And another verse: "Do Thou shine unto me Thy luminous

---

[8] A paraphrase of the Sedalen after the third reading from the Psalter at Matins on the first Monday of Great Lent: "Let us joyfully begin the all-hallowed season of abstinence; and let us shine with the bright radiance of the holy commandments of Christ our God, with the brightness of love and the splendor of prayer, with the purity of holiness and the strength of good courage. . . ." *The Lenten Triodion*, tr. Mother Mary and Archimandrite Kallistos Ware (South Canaan, PA: St Tikhon's Seminary Press, 2002), 190.

[9] The Great Canon of St Andrew of Crete, Ode 1, first troparion; ibid., 199.

lightnings, O my God, Three in Persons and Creator af All: and show me forth as an abode of Thine unapproachable glory, bright and light-bearing and changeless."[10] What kind of darkness is this that is all about light, radiates light, longs for it, and is filled only with it?

Well then, if after all these words, after these services so fully comprised of this "bright sadness" and longing for light, one picks up the usual books and newspapers filled with our day-to-day experiences, one instantly senses an almost palpable impenetrable darkness. And one is astounded: how can people live this way, absorbed in these interests, these questions and concerns? How can they, how could they have believed these hopelessly dull socialist ideas all these years, which reduce the entire life of man to soulless matter and its blind laws?

It is precisely this, this striking contrast between the language of this ideology, this idea of man, and the lenten language of light and longing for light, that raises the chief, final question: how could soulless matter have developed this longing for light, how and why did there arise in it this experience of brightness? "Make me to be a dwelling of your unapproachable glory, bright, light-bearing, and unapproachable . . ." There is no materialism, no economic theory, no struggle for survival that can explain the genesis of these sounds, these words, these concepts, these symbols in human language and human consciousness. How can one fail to see in them this longing for holiness, purity, and perfection; how can one not see in them the special, mystical joy that radiates from those who live by them? One can read and reread the essays of Marx and Engels, Lenin and Stalin, and all their numerous proponents and commentators—and constantly feel the torrent of hatred and darkness. They are all focused on the destruction of various "enemies," and in this alone they see the purpose of human life. And the final, principal, and constant enemy for them is of course the light-bearing human being—the person who is oriented upward, and not downward, the person who at his very core, at the center of his inner experience, has seen the light. He is their enemy because if this light is real,

[10]Sunday Midnight Office, Hymns to the Trinity by St Gregory of Sinai, sixth stanza; *Horologion or Book of the Hours,* Translated with notes by St Tikhon's Monastery (South Canaan, PA: St Tikhon's Seminary Press, 2000), 222.

there is nothing left of the educated but hate-filled and gloom-enshrouded words of all of their leaders and ideologues. For then life cannot be solely reduced to a struggle for "economic liberation," solely to "the expropriation of the expropriators," solely to the problem of satiety. Then one must seek another explanation of man, and this is what most frightens the scholars and dogmaticians of materialism.

In today's world the fight is waged not between conflicting political and economic systems, but between opposing approaches to man, between conflicting intuitions or experiences of man. And experience finds its expression in language, in symbols and explanations. For even the concept of "light" can also be reduced solely to physical and material explanations (for example, to electric light). Religion, too, can be reduced simply to fear, superstition, and habit. But after this there still remains the essential question—"From above or from below?"—and the real debate revolves around this question. Everything can be explained from above or from below, and between them there can be neither compromise nor reconciliation. Materialism has once and for all accepted the explanation from below, and with inexplicable passion desires that everything without exception be attributed to the basest of causes. And for this reason it not only rejects but truly hates the explanation from above, and seeks everywhere and at all times to eradicate it.

Opinions may vary as to who is more successful superficially. But it is sufficient to enter into a church in these bright days of Great Lent, filled with the bright sadness, sufficient to hear the words and symbols of the "unchanging light," in order to fully grasp with the mind and heart that this light is indeed *unapproachable* (1 Tim 6.16), and it can neither be contained, nor dimmed, nor destroyed by any darkness coming from below.

The Spiritual Being

The Principal Thirst

Several years ago I began my first Sunday talk with a quote from Push-kin's "The Prophet": "I am filled with spiritual thirst . . ." However many years, even centuries, may pass, these amazing words remain an epigraph of the fate of humanity on earth.

Civilizations come and go, life forms and even the very face of the earth are altered. Nevertheless, there remains this unslaked spiritual thirst—this precious and at the same time agonizing gift, given to man on earth as the indicator and essence of his very humanity. It is precious, for it draws man upward, not allowing him to find satisfaction in purely animal existence and happiness, imparting to him higher, incomparable joys; and it is ago-nizing, for so often it is disrupted by the base instincts that transform his whole life into struggle, seeking, and frustration.

Almost everything in the world shouts at man: "Renounce this spiritual thirst, and you will be filled, healthy, and happy!" As Alexander Blok wrote in one of his saddest poems: "Be content with your life, which is quieter than water and lies lower than grass." And so we find all sorts of ideologies built on this denial of spiritual thirst, of hatred towards it—ideologies that strive to get a person to stifle the very source of this thirst, to make him admit that it is "an illusion," "self-deception," and join in constructing a life that is thoroughly purged of all thirst, of all seeking.

And if there is anything at the depth and not merely on the surface that differentiates our twentieth century from the previous one, it is specifically the utmost intensification of the conflict between two visions of the life of man and of man himself. According to one, man is man precisely because in him there is this spiritual thirst, this seeking, this higher disturbance of soul. According to the other, man's true destiny begins only when he annihilates this thirst within him. The ongoing conflict between these two visions lies at the very heart of all struggles in the contemporary world, for out of them everything else proceeds—politics, economics, culture—all that people so passionately debate and for which they fight.

And this is why, whether we realize it or not, the main question of our time is the religious question. For religion, by its very nature, is the presence and manifestation in the world of spiritual thirst. Just as the smell of smoke indicates that somewhere there is fire, even if it is not visible, so the very presence of religion in the world, whatever its forms, is a sure witness that in man there still lives a spiritual thirst and a spiritual quest.

Of course, people try to prove to us that, on the contrary, religion is a cheap comfort, a refusal to struggle, man's betrayal of himself; that it is all dead and intractable dogmatism, dissuading man from pressing questions and from searching. Those who think thus, however, inevitably pass over the words which form the very heart of the religious experience: *Blessed are they which do hunger and thirst after righteousness* (Mt 5.6); *Seek and ye shall find* (Mt 7.7); *I came not to send peace but a sword* (Mt 10.34). It is significant that from the beginning the fight against religion has been based on an elementary lie, and that without that lie the fight would not have lasted one day. But today this lie is so obvious that there is hardly any need to discuss it. What we do need to discuss is this spiritual thirst, its object, and its longing, for there is no more important question in all the world. For the world once again finds itself at that crossroads about which the poet writes:

> I languished with soul athirst for grace
> Within a darkening desert land,
> And at a crossing of the ways
> Beheld a six-wing'd Seraph stand.[1]

Today man is confronted as never before by conflicting calls to action: various paths meet and diverge, and unheard of catastrophes and unprecedented cataclysms rage about him more and more terribly and graphically.

[1]Alexander Pushkin, *The Prophet* (1826).

He that hath an ear, let him hear (Rev 2.7). We can no longer escape all this by partial measures, by applying bandages to a disintegrating and rotting materialism. We begin to understand anew why it is specifically salvation that the Gospel proclaims, why it specifically addresses the fallen and the perishing. *I am come to send fire upon the earth*, says Christ, *and how I wish that it were already aflame!* (cf. Lk 12.49). We may not have the courage of the six-winged seraph who met the prophet at the crossroad, but each of us in the measure of his own weak resources is called today to witness concerning what is most essential.

Let our conversations therefore focus on this most essential theme. For religion is truly religion only when it concerns itself with what is essential, when it becomes both a manifestation of spiritual thirst and the answer to it, when it is a consuming fire, but also a purification, a transfiguration by this fire of our weak and so often shameful life. The New Testament ends with words that instill fear and joy at the same time: *He that is unjust, let him be unjust still; and he which is filthy, let him be filthy still; and he that is righteous, let him be righteous still; and he that is holy, let him be holy still. And, behold, I come quickly. . . . And let him that is athirst come. And whosoever will, let him take the water of life freely* (Rev 22.11–12, 17). If only we may be found worthy of these words; if only we may not betray our God-given spiritual thirst! May our eyes and our hearing be open to the flow of light, love, and beauty that is forever poured out upon us!

May God help us all, both those who speak and those who listen, to be faithful and humble, firm and loving. Then the light will not be dimmed, and it will forever shine in the world as the salvation that is given it.

The Root of the Illness

A few weeks ago, in connection with the feast of the Descent of the Holy Spirit, I spoke about spirituality. Today I want to return to this theme—to return because, in my conviction, there is no theme that is more important, more pertinent, more urgently necessary for modern man.

Generally we speak about a person as being smart or foolish, kind or evil. But we have completely forgotten how to see and recognize in him one other characteristic, which exceeds all others in importance: his openness or closed-mindedness to the spiritual world, to the spirit. And we have lost this quality not because it requires some special knowledge that we do not possess, but because the perception of the world that permeates our modern age, and with which we ourselves have unconsciously become permeated, firmly rejects this same spirituality. But this rejection in turn leads to a profound spiritual illness of mankind and lies at the root of a deep pessimism, frustration, and psychological bankruptcy, the examples of which we need not cite, as they are all too obvious.

It's a strange fact: man has rejected the spiritual and spirituality in the name of happiness, for such was the slogan of the proverbial "New Age"— the era that to this day is referred to in textbooks as the "Age of Enlightenment." It has become customary to speak of this era as the antidote to the "Dark Ages," with their emphasis on spirituality and their rejection of simple human happiness in the name of an impossible, otherworldly spiritual happiness. And so began this flood of Voltaires, Diderots, and Jean-Jacques Rousseaus,[2] who said: "Enough of this failed spirituality! Our concern is the earth, and our task is to build upon earth a happy life; nothing else is needed." This inaugurated an era that could be said to be entirely focused on the idea of happiness. In the name of this happiness revolutions were staged, nations were liberated, and grandiose ideologies were established that "scientifically" determined the path to salvation. What is Marxism, for example, if not an effort to "scientifically" construct a final and lasting happiness on earth? In its turn, what is capitalism, if not simply another theory of happiness? I will point out here that although both of these ideologies, Marxist and capitalist, have long been locked in a duel to the death, the fact is that both are rooted in essentially the same conviction: that happiness depends completely on the arrangement of material life, and that it has nothing to do with what used to be called spiritual. And so, for three

[2]François Marie Voltaire (1694–1778); Denis Diderot (1713–1784); Jean Jacques Rousseau (1712–1778)—French philosophers, who in varying degrees paved the way for the triumph of the ideology of the Enlightenment.

hundred years now, we and everyone else in the world have been dominated by this idea of happiness and its pursuit.

But where, one wonders, is this happiness that was so blithely and jubilantly proclaimed by the fathers and prophets of the modern world? Why is it that no other era of world history has ever known so much sadness, disappointment, and tragedy? Why does our age falter, not knowing whom to follow, what to believe, and what to think? Why does half the globe live under totalitarian regimes, born of this same ideology of happiness? Why do philosophers fail to offer anything other than the philosophy of the absurd? Why does art offer nothing but a fragmented and terrifying vision of the world, and poetry nothing but wails of despair? Where, we ask, is this happiness that seemed so near, simple, and attainable? And it turns out that since that time when man limited his horizon to this earth alone and to this small earthly happiness, he lost his ability to understand the earth itself and to find happiness on it.

What if Blessed Augustine was correct when long ago he exclaimed: "You have created us for yourself, O Lord, and our hearts will not find rest until they find their rest in you"? And what if the apostle Paul was correct when he said: *Eye hath not seen, nor ear heard, neither have entered into the heart of man, the things which God has prepared for them that love him* (1 Cor 2.9)? Finally, what if those were right who always affirmed that man is first of all a spiritual being, and that all rejection of the spirit, all renunciation of spirituality, all forgetfulness of one's spiritual essence inevitably and inexorably leads a person to sickness and disintegration? "Man is what he eats," said Feuerbach, and it seemed to him that he had put an end to spirituality once and for all. And in his footsteps Marx builds his entire teaching about future happiness on this paltry theory. However, a hundred years passes, and this teaching has to be defended with terror and censorship; otherwise it would not last a single week. Man is a spiritual entity, and that means he is not simply one who eats or thinks, but one who is destined for possession of spiritual values.

What are these values? In ancient fashion we can list them as follows: truth, goodness, beauty—values which are not at all pragmatic, but which bear within them and reveal true happiness. If it seems to the contemporary man from time to time that this world is overly utilitarian, and that for life and happiness in it a little bit of truth, a little bit of goodness, a little bit of beauty are perhaps even essential, then the spiritual man knows that he lives for the acquisition of truth, goodness, and beauty. He does not ask for happiness, but finds it in the pursuit of these things. And when these things—truth, goodness, and beauty—are joined together into one experience, one happiness, one reality, then man pronounces the word "God." And from that moment on he realizes that whatever may befall him, however hard, sad, or sorrowful his life may be, he knows that his happiness cannot be destroyed. But then, this is precisely what Christ himself describes: *Seek ye first the kingdom of God . . . and all these things shall be added unto you* (Mt 6.33).

Where To Seek Happiness

In my last talk I spoke about the fact that man ceased searching for God because he decided to search for happiness, and he was told that the search for God hinders the search for happiness. However, having left off searching for God, man not only failed to find happiness, but also filled the entire world with disappointment, pessimism, and sadness. When a person seeks God without focusing on happiness, this very seeking will bring him happiness. I know this sounds simplistic and probably in its simplicity seems unconvincing. Nevertheless, this truth is self-evident, born out by thousands of facts.

It is possible that over time, having had his fill of senselessness and horror, modern man will realize that his tragedy began when he took the word "happiness" for his slogan and decided that this happiness comprises the purpose and content of his life. But man forgot to ask himself what the content and purpose of this happiness is. "To be sated!"—the ideologues of "scientifically determined" happiness murmured into his ear. And so he ate his fill, but failed to find happiness. "To be liberated!"—the voices whispered again. And having spilled enormous amounts of blood for his liberation, man found himself in prison. "To be the ruler of the world, to know everything about it, to dominate everything in it, to forever increase this knowledge and domination!" And so man flew to the moon, conquered space, and bridged time, yet he continues to be asphyxiated by hopeless and toxic air, by the dreary monotony of machines, by drab and faceless cities, by the noise and meaninglessness of the technological civilization he has himself created. "To destroy private property, to liberate the worker from exploitation!"—and so they destroyed, they liberated, yet it would seem that never before has the worker been so controlled by the faceless "apparatus" as today.

It appears that this dream of happiness, which the prophets of our time so boldly proclaimed, has degenerated into a pathetic entreaty: "A little bit of rest, a little bit of quiet, a tiny bit of humanity!" Was the proclamation worth it? Indeed, not a single ideology, not a single theory has ever failed so spectacularly as this theory of happiness, for the sake of which man rejected God, truth, goodness, and beauty. Everything in the world became utilitarian, everything lost its innate glory, everything was emptied of joy. That is why what I said at the beginning of this conversation is the truth, simple and bitter. Man followed false prophets and is now paying a terrible price for this mistake. And he must first of all recognize that this was indeed a mistake; he must examine the original positions from which he began the struggle for what he called happiness. Yes, naturally, man is destined for happiness. But this happiness is inseparable from the profound human essence which of old he called spirit or spirituality. Only when he discovers this depth does he also find happiness. And in the neglect and renunciation of this depth lies the inescapable tragedy of contemporary man

As for what happiness is, this is a question for happy people. Any truly happy person will answer that happiness is found not in satiety alone, not in wealth alone, not in freedom alone, not in knowledge alone. "In what then?" you might ask, and probably the happy individual will find it difficult to answer. The answer will probably be partial, fragmented, but roughly as follows: happiness lies within us, in that unattainable sense of clarity and peace that does not depend on external circumstances, and consequently comes not from the outside, but from deep inside. Furthermore, happiness lies in a clear conscience, in inner certitude and integrity; furthermore, it lies in a constant inner focus on what is true, good, and beautiful, in constant inner communion with the joy of truth, the joy of goodness, the joy of beauty. "A thing of beauty is a joy forever,"[3] said the English poet, and so we find its fulfillment in truth, goodness, and beauty. Furthermore, happiness lies in the constant overcoming of busyness and frivolity, envy and fear, self-love and egoism—all of that debris which darkens the soul. Happiness lies in love and in wonderment, happiness lies in gratitude and thanksgiving, happiness lies in orientation upward; happiness, finally, lies in finding the One who is in all of this and who stands behind all of it—in finding God. Over and over we will repeat the words of Blessed Augustine: "You have created us for yourself, O Lord, and our hearts will not rest until they find rest in you"—because there are no better or truer words about happiness.

Inexplicable peace of soul, a pure conscience, the ability to love and to give thanks, to seek and to find, as well as the ability to overcome all ugliness and evil in oneself—all of these components of profound happiness cannot be given to us by anything in this world. And man's spirituality consists in that he finds these things higher than the world, above the world, and in finding them he also finds the world itself. In the end, happiness is revealed in that wholeness when everything together—heaven and earth, soul and body, truth, goodness, and beauty—form a harmonious world, and when all one can do is to repeat these simple words of Gumilev: "All things find their place in the one who loves the world and believes in God."[4]

It is time, high time, to leave all pseudo-happiness and its ennui and to seek the paths to true happiness! It is time to unmask the miserable, cheap prophets, who shout about happiness and have filled the world with fear, hostility, and endless loneliness! It is time to shake off the ageless nightmare and to return to the Spirit, about whom the prayer says so beautifully: ". . . the Comforter, the Spirit of truth, who art everywhere present and fillsest all things"—with himself—"Treasury of blessings, and Giver of life." These words, repeated by the Church every day, every hour, are in fact a true prayer for happiness.

[3]John Keats, "Endymion" (1818)
[4]Nikolay Gumilev, "Fra Beato Angelico" (1912).

That Which Is Deeper And Longer

The man of the new spiritual aspect"—this expression is encountered more and more frequently in the utterances of those in power, and has even found its way onto the pages of the new history of the party.[5]

Only we are not told what this "new spiritual aspect" comprises. Seemingly, this new wording suggests a joyful hope: humanity, renewal, spirituality—this is indeed the desire and the need of our time, perhaps even more than technological success and scientific achievements.

Without a doubt, these new words have become part of the official rhetoric under pressure from the increasing and universal search for humanity and spirituality. Previously they were never heard; they were never part of the official vocabulary. They have suddenly appeared out of another world, out of an alien dimension, out of new and previously unrecognized aspirations. But from which?

The answer to this question is both simple and complicated. Thus, they tell us of the "the man of the new spiritual aspect." But in order for this expression to have any meaning one must first of all recognize the presence of spirituality in man. But spirituality is not simply consciousness, thought, and psychology; otherwise these words themselves would be sufficient. Spirituality implies something deeper, longer, and broader. And it is something alien in relation to everything that man has simply learned, which he has simply been taught, for knowledge is from without; the cultivation of wisdom is from without; ideology, conviction—all of this comes from without. But spirituality comes from within. It is a kind of ray of light, penetrating up through the depths of a person and illuminating his knowledge, his convictions, everything in his life. If there is spirituality in man, if it is inseparably a part of him, then he cannot be regarded as a *tabula rasa*, on which nature, society and history can write whatever they want, thereby fully determining his consciousness and his actions.

---

[5]The cliché of the "spiritual" (more frequently, "moral") aspect of the Soviet man was widely used in the official lexicon of the USSR after the 22nd congress of the KPSS (1961), which announced the path towards the building of a communist society and the education of the "man of the new type."

Several years ago Dudintsev[6] presented the first "negative" determination of this spirituality; he only hinted at it in his novel *Not by Bread Alone*. And this slight suggestion given in the title had the force of a spiritual explosion. For bread is not merely a symbol of the material needs of a person, but it is first and foremost a symbol of that which determines and supports human life from without. It turns out that these externals—bread and knowledge, programs and ideology—are insufficient to make man's life complete. Man also lives by that which comes from within: a flow of love and truth, an aspiration to freedom—everything that transfigures and conquers the external. And so this power, this reality of the inner man, this aspiration to truth, this often stifled but never destroyed longing for some sort of other world—all of this comprises the spirituality in man.

In our understanding the word "spirit" conjures an idea of lightness, transparency, freedom, flight. The spirit is everything that is opposed to heaviness, inertia, ossification of forms, and ideology—everything in man that is open to truth, wherever it might come from. *The spirit bloweth where it listeth* (Jn 3.8), says the Gospel. And this "where it listeth, where it wills" contains the promise and confirmation of that true, spiritual freedom to which man is called. Whatever meaning is intended in the expression "the man of the new spiritual aspect," we know that the root of true renewal and true spirituality lies in freedom, in love, and in truth.

A Reminder of the Forgotten

In the Acts of the Apostles there is a mysterious account of the descent of the Holy Spirit upon the disciples of Christ. Let us hear it:

> *When the day of Pentecost was fully come, they were all with one accord in one place. And suddenly there came a sound from heaven as of a rushing mighty wind, and it filled all the house where they were sitting. And there appeared*

---

[6]Vladimir Dmitrievich Dudintsev (1917–98), Russian writer. His novel, *Not By Bread Alone*, published in the journal *Noviy Mir* in 1956, was severely branded by Soviet critics as "slanderous."

*unto them cloven tongues like as of fire, and it sat upon each of them. And they
were all filled with the Holy Spirit and began to speak with other tongues, as the
Spirit gave them utterance.*

And when those in Jerusalem wondered at this, the apostle Peter cited for
them the words of the ancient Hebrew prophet Joel:

*And it shall come to pass in the last days, saith God, I will pour out of my
Spirit upon all flesh; and your sons and your daughters shall prophesy, and your
young men shall see visions, and your old men shall dream dreams; and on my
servants and on my handmaidens I will pour out in those days of my Spirit, and
they shall prophesy . . . The sun shall be turned into darkness, and the moon
into blood, before that great and notable day of the Lord come. And it shall come
to pass, that whosoever shall call on the name of the Lord shall be saved* (Acts
2.1–4, 17–18, 20–21).

Such is the account, and it does not cease to amaze us. What are we
being told here, and what does all this mean? We cannot answer these questions until we remember a word or concept whose right to exist is denied
by all contemporary ideologues, by all contemporary understandings of the
world and man. This concept is spirituality. In speaking of man we usually
consider him either from the material-physical or from the psychological
standpoint, and only these two poles, only these two realities are acceptable.
For some, even the psychological is deduced from matter and the material,
and all that is above the material they consider mere "superstructure," one
way or another rooted in the material. From their point of view, love comes
from the sexual instinct, creativity comes from the struggle for survival, and
sorrow or happiness in the final analysis depend on the condition of one's
stomach. At the same time there are others who are willing to recognize a
certain autonomy in psychology, to recognize that consciousness, the mind,
the inner feelings in man are not entirely derived from the material. But
in either case there is essentially no place for the spiritual, and I will not
hesitate to affirm that the only essential tragedy and catastrophe of modern
man is precisely in this—this horrible atrophy, this painful rejection of the
reality of the spirit.

And one of the many reasons for this atrophy is that the spirit and spirituality cannot be defined in the language of empirical science, which for contemporary man seems to be the only approach to every question of human life, without exception. The unconscious affirmation of contemporary man is this: if something cannot be determined and explained scientifically, this means it does not and cannot exist. But the Gospel says the following about the spirit and about spirituality: *That which is born of the flesh is flesh, that which is born of the Spirit is spirit. Marvel not that I said unto thee, Ye must be born agin. The Spirit bloweth where it listeth, and thou hearest the sound thereof, but canst not tell whence it cometh, and whither it goeth: so is every one that is born of the Spirit* (Jn 3.6–8). It turns out that the spirit and spirituality cannot be defined: they must first be felt, experienced, and examined. Only then do these words about them become intelligible. But contemporary man seems to have lost the very organ that is able to experience and understand this. His world is one-dimensional, a world of calculation and measures, of rigid rules and determinism. Anything else seems to him almost a sign of mental illness.

All that is left, then, is to point out what everyone knows but tries to forget. Why is it that in all ages, in all circumstances without exception, there are those who do not conform to the one-dimensional world—prophets, holy ones, who proclaim the Spirit and are themselves filled with him, like a soft breeze, and who always call men to another, higher dimension? People are immersed in their petty affairs and concerns, and imagine that this is their "real life." They are prepared to receive as absolute truth that depressing ideology where one only hears about "value added" and "production relations"; they have agreed to live according to the words of the poet: "quieter than water, lying lower than grass." And suddenly there comes from somewhere a spirit-bearer who speaks about God and heaven, about joy and truth, about the fact that in the world there exists such unattainable happiness, such light, that for it one might forsake everything. And suddenly the life and the ideology that a moment before we thought to be self-evident and the only one possible becomes dull, gray, and meaningless. And within us the spirit awakens—that fiery point in the soul and the consciousness that one experiences simultaneously as a terrible longing and as a desire, but also as an encounter, as joy, and as light. The spiritual man is born, and the mysterious birth of the Spirit is accomplished, of which the Gospel says: *If any man thirst, let him come unto me, and drink. He that believeth on me, as the Scripture hath said, out of his belly shall flow rivers of living water* (Jn 7.37–38). And everything in the world becomes new, filled with the new purpose, with new light: *Behold, I make all things new* (Rev 21.5).

All around, life goes on as usual with all its preoccupations, its concerns, its sorrows and joys, but the man who has been born of the Spirit can no longer return to and be swallowed up by it. As the poet said, "And one no longer desires the former joys, having drunk the wine of paradise."[7] This, then, is the essence of the feast of Pentecost: this birth of the Spirit, this reality of spirit and spirituality, the original destiny of man to become spiritual, the impossibility for him to find true joy and happiness in anything else.

The Most Needed Truth

We celebrate the feast of Pentecost and the coming of the Spirit!"[8]— this has been sung in the churches from time immemorial on the fiftieth day after Pascha, the joyous feast of the Trinity. What is this Pentecost, and who is this Holy Spirit, whose coming we celebrate or are called to celebrate?

We ask this question because we are living in an era of almost universal rejection of spirit—an era of materialism. Something has happened to mankind, after which man seems to have forgotten how to hear certain words with his inner ear and heart. More than this—he has decided for some reason to reject them, to reject their meaning, to oppose their very content. Among these words is the word *spirit*. Indeed, how did it happen that suddenly man started to deify matter, and indeed gave the name "materialism" to a whole ideology? How did he begin to reject spirit and everything spiritual?

[7]Alexander Blok, "I Have Planted My Glorious Paradise" (1907).
[8]Vespers of Pentecost, first sticheron at "Lord I have cried."

In posing these questions we come up squarely against the most terrible mystery of our time. For centuries man not only knew, but with his whole being organically felt and experienced that besides matter, there is also spirit. He understood that there is a material existence and there are material laws, but he also knew that existence was not limited to them. He understood that he himself possessed something that cannot be derived from matter, from cells, from nerves, from genes—and he delighted in this possession, this presence, this life of the spirit and the spiritual within him. He knew that there is a time to lower one's eyes to the ground, that is, to matter, and to lovingly cultivate it; but he knew also that there is a time when it is clearly necessary to lift one's gaze to the heights, to measure and to fill one's life with higher purpose. We could put it this way: man understood himself to be a vertical being, standing on the ground, but oriented towards heaven. The body, the spirit, the soul—all of these were real, not needing any proofs, recognizable in the light of love, in prayerful trepidation, and in creative inspiration.

Yet someone decided that this experience, this image, this understanding of man must be destroyed and eliminated. "Only matter! Everything is from below: not only is nothing from above—this 'above' itself simply does not exist!" And so began the destruction, the defamation, the perversion, and all supposedly for men's happiness. But what kind of happiness can there be if there is nothing besides the material, if all insight of the mind and inspiration, of joy and creativity, all a person's aspirations towards the higher, and not the lower, are only an illusion? "Freedom!" they cry—but what kind of freedom can one have from matter and its iron laws? "Creativity!" they say—but where does it come from, if even man's consciousness is nothing but cellular activity? "Happiness!" they say—but whence and in what is this happiness? One recalls the words of the poet: "About the fact that we live. About the fact that we will die. About how everything is so terrible. And so irreparable."[9]

And in the moments when a person is utterly honest with himself, he can tell himself nothing else if he believes that nothing but matter exists in the world. Man rebelled against the spirit, and other prophetic verses began

[9]From G. B. Adamovich, "On an Autumn Night the Two of Us at an Inn" (1928).

to appear—the unforgettable lines of Blok: "Oh children, if only you knew the cold and darkness of the coming days!"

This cold and darkness have arrived. For millions of people the world has become a meaningless anthill, a sort of gigantic structure of this selfsame matter, above and beyond which there is nothing but emptiness.

What answer can be made here? For a person who does not feel or know the Spirit, philosophical arguments are no proof of his existence. Christ said: *The Spirit bloweth where it listeth, and thou hearest the sound thereof, but canst not tell whence it cometh or whither it goeth* (Jn 3.8). If a person has never once felt this presence, this inspiration, this strange and joyful transfiguration of life, how does one begin to tell him about all this? All one can do is affirm that the Spirit exists and that he comes and touches the heart, sets the soul aright, and fills everything with light, joy, and most importantly the experience of another, spiritual reality. "I went with soul athirst for grace"—so begins Pushkin's poem "The Prophet," and few more magnificent testimonials are to be found on earth. "With soul athirst for grace . . ." But how was this thirst born in Pushkin, from what cells and material "processes"? Was this also a deception, an ignorance of dialectic materialism and the economic "revelations" of Marx and Engels?

How absurd such questions appear, yet at the same time it is these questions that must be raised! For it is a question of one or the other: either Pushkin—joyful, transparent Pushkin—had this spiritual thirst within him, in which case all the theories of Marx, Engels, and anyone else, if not totally false, give us only a modicum of the truth; or else all truth is in them, in which case we have no idea, nor any need to know, what Pushkin was talking about—what kind of "thirst," what kind of "spirit." But in this case there remains the incontrovertible fact of the universal and primordial experience of the spirit, as well as another fact—the absolute inability of materialism to explain this experience, to explain beauty, goodness, joy, and especially this unquenchable thirst of man. A person suddenly falls in love, and nothing remains of materialism, for in sadness, in joy, and in creativity all pseudo-scientific reasoning falls apart, and what remains is the person—earthly, but at the same time spiritual, able with his spirit to penetrate the whole earth and to raise it up to the Spirit.

We believers call God a Spirit, and we say that the experience of the otherworldly, the unearthly, and the divine is "spirit-bearing." And on the day of Pentecost we celebrate the coming of the divine and holy Spirit, in whom always and everywhere we recognize with joy and trembling the revelation of the ultimate purpose of our life. After a drought comes the rain; darkness is followed by light; sadness passes, and suddenly everything is filled with joy; there is only matter—and then suddenly through it there shines the radiance of spirit. The earth cannot live without moisture, light overcomes darkness, man is created for the Spirit, and hence for continual victory over that which is only matter. And this is why when at last we greet this "last great day of the feast of Pentecost,"[10] when suddenly the prayer of all prayers descends upon us as though from heaven itself—"O Heavenly King, the Comforter, the Spirit of truth, who art everywhere present and fillest all things, Treasury of blessings and Giver of life, come and abide in us . . ."—we feel and experience that this feast is the most precious, the most necessary truth about the world, about life, about ourselves, and we rejoice, knowing that no one can take from us this joy and this experience.

"We celebrate Pentecost and the coming of the Spirit . . ."—it is for this coming, this presence, and this victory of the Spirit that we pray in the Church. This we await, this we celebrate, and by this we live.

An Unseen History

Two weeks after the celebration of Pentecost, the Church celebrates a special day—the feast of All Saints Who Have Shone forth in the Land of Russia.

This feast was established at the height of the revolution at the All-Russian Church Council, which met in Moscow to the sounds of the gunfire of the October uprising. No sooner did one era of Russian history end in blood and hatred, than another began with that same hatred. The enormous

---

[10]"For on this last and great and saving day of Pentecost the mystery of the feast is shown to us, and the Holy Trinity is revealed." From the third kneeling prayer at the vespers of Pentecost.

edifice of the Russian Empire crumbled, age-old values were cast aside and demolished, and national memory was torn asunder. Again, as had sadly happened before, brother rose up against brother, and the most horrible of wars began—fratricidal civil war. Each participant defined himself by hatred: one towards Imperial Russia, the other toward the revolutionary Russia; one toward the Reds, the other toward the Whites. And what, after all, is a revolution, if not an uprising against the past, a passionate attempt to renounce everything and start over afresh? And so in those horrible days when the national destiny was falling apart, and Russia stood on the brink of an uncertain future, where suffering, grief, and hatred reigned supreme—a few hundred people gathered in Moscow to set church affairs in order, and raised above this chaos of hatred and suffering the standards of Russian holiness—the saints who had been glorified in the Russian land. Not kings, not military leaders, not academics, not writers, and not even laypeople, but simply those who shone forth—specifically shone!—with light, with goodness, and with love. Those who seemingly sought nothing in this life, in this world, who seemed to have exiled themselves from it, but in fact took this life and this world and made them better and brighter, warmer and more loving.

Every people, every land has two histories. One is an external history, woven entirely of wars and battles, of political successes and tragedies, of victories and defeats. Here the keywords are "power," "glory," "national pride," "the welfare of the nation." In this history, permeated with blood and suffering, power, glory, and welfare always occur at the expense of others, and are always a victory of the powerful over the weak, of the proud over the humble. Empires are built, but always on war and subjugation, and for its power and glory to exist someone must always tremble in fear: the Polish land must be drenched in blood, and the Hungarian uprising crushed; proud Soviet tanks must be sent to rumble along the streets of a Prague crushed by fear; there must be iron curtains and millions of soldiers armed to the teeth at all borders; there must be a denial of freedom and the constant noise of self-adulation. At all times and everywhere such is the external history, which is the only one taught in schools and the only history touted as praiseworthy.

But, thanks be to God, each country and nation also has another history. Our nation has one as well. People are trying to quell it, to make it appear nonexistent, but this is impossible, for it always penetrates through the bloody and horrible fabric of external history. And its authors, of course, are the saints—the people who, from the point of view of external history, appear useless, if not harmful: fools and idiots, escaping life into some kind of dream.

But with the passage of time the powerful disappear, and their glory decays. Where are these ancient empires that once terrified the universe—Assyria, Babylon, Persia, Rome? Throughout the world we can see the ruins of Roman columns covered in grass, which so eloquently witness to the poverty and transience of every earthly power, of every earthly glory. But the poor and homeless Teacher, crucified by the all-powerful Roman Empire, reigns to this day in the hearts of millions of people. And as we behold the darkness and poverty of Old Russia, to this day we are immersed in the light of the venerable Sergius of Radonezh and his countless holy disciples. When everything external in the past has rusted over, has rotted and disintegrated, what remains is pure gold, over which the ages and eras are powerless. The great Russian historian Vasily Kluchevsky wrote a book entitled *On the Good People of Old Russia*.[11] In the final analysis, only these good people remain, and Russia is illumined by their light alone. And how many of them there are! Wherever you look, in any countryside, whatever cottage you visit, everywhere the name of a saint is remembered who shone forth there, who filled that particular place with light and with love. From the distant north, Zossima and Savvaty of Solovki shine forth upon us, and from the south—Dmitry of Rostov and Joseph of Belgorod; from the east we have Tikhon of Zadonsk, and from the west, Job of Pochaev. And there are hundreds and thousands of others: bishops, monks, princes, and simply good people, such as the righteous Juliana of Lazarevo, the radiant elder Seraphim of Sarov, the martyred Metropolitan Philip of Moscow, who bravely confronted Ivan the Terrible himself, that personification of terrifying and unjust civil authority, reminding him about truth, love, and justice.

[11]First published as an article: Vladimir Kluchevsky, "The Good People of Old Russia," *Bogoslovsky vestnik* (Sergiev Posad: Jan. 1892); 89–97.

So it is that behind this external history an inner history is revealed in all its changeless beauty and endurance—a history of spirit, faith, and love. If our country is to have a future, if there is any hope, then this future and hope lie not in power and might, but only here—in this spirit, in this faith, and in this love. Only by remembering our inner history, only by returning with love and contrition to all the saints who shone forth in the Russian land, will the Russian land rediscover its soul and find the truth without which strength is powerless and unnecessary, and all might is terrible and useless.

This is what we are reminded of two weeks after Pentecost on this feast of all the saints who have shone forth in the land of Russia.

Witness of the Spirit

Today, let us return to our theme of "spirit and spirituality," of which I spoke in my previous talk. I said then that contemporary man lives in a society, in a worldview and an ideology, that has no knowledge of spirituality and therefore rejects it—in other words, it denies that the individual can attain a higher reality. Moreover, this culture denies man's spiritual calling itself, his essential destiny to become spiritual, to be born of the Spirit as described in the Gospel.

But deep within Russian history there is an event that the official historians naturally conceal, but in which spiritual reality and the spiritual world are clearly manifest. This event occurred not in one of the great cities of that time, but rather in a faraway uncharted forest on a perfectly ordinary cloudy winter day. This event was a conversation between a simple and unremarkable layman, named Nikolai Motovilov, and the old monk Seraphim, who had left the world in his youth for the monastery of Sarov, and was then living alone in a hut in those woods. Seraphim was neither learned nor a leader, but his fame spread, people spoke about him, and many came to see him. And to all their questions he gave the same answer: the goal of human life is to acquire the Holy Spirit, to become spiritual—in other words, to rise towards a higher spiritual reality that is normally obscured to us by our ceaseless activity, concerns, and busyness. But Motovilov was not content with this answer, or perhaps it was unclear to him, just as it is to contemporary man, who demands that everything be scientifically explained and proven. So here, at this secluded meeting, which Motovilov subsequently recorded in his journal, the elder agreed to impart to him what comprises this spiritualization, this acquisition of the Holy Spirit, and how it is expressed.

But let us listen to Motovilov in his own words: "I said to him," he writes, "that I nonetheless fail to understand how I can be certain that I am in God's Spirit. How can I ascertain for myself that this is a genuine experience? The elder replied to me: 'I have already explained to you that it is very easy, and I have shown you in detail how people find themselves within God's Spirit, and how we are to discern his presence in us. What else do you need?' 'I need,' I persisted, 'to grasp this more firmly.' At this point Father Seraphim took me firmly by my shoulders and said to me: 'At this moment both you and I together are in the Spirit of God. Why do you not look at me?' I answered, 'I am unable to look at you, because your face has become brighter than the sun and my eyes hurt from trying.' Father Seraphim reassured me: 'Do not be afraid; at this moment you are as I am, filled with the same light. You too are now fully in the Holy Spirit, for otherwise you would not have been able to see me this way. Give thanks to God for his mercy!' I looked directly at his face after these words, and I was filled with an even greater holy dread. Imagine that right within the very center of the noonday sun, in the very brightness of its most intense rays, you see the face of a man, talking with you. You see the movement of his lips, the changing expression of his eyes, you hear his voice, you feel that someone is grasping your shoulders with his hands; and not only do you not see those hands, but you see neither yourself nor him; you see only the light before you. 'What do you now feel?' Father Seraphim asked me then. I told him that I felt exceptionally peaceful. 'And how would you describe this feeling?' 'I feel such a profound peace and calm within my soul, that I cannot explain it with any words.' 'This is that peace,' explained Seraphim, 'about which Christ said: "My peace I give to you; not as the world gives, do I give it you!" This is that peace which, in the words of the apostle, transcends all understanding. What else do you feel?' 'An unusual sweetness,' I answered, and he continued: 'This is the sweetness about which Scripture says: "You give me drink from the river of pleasure" (cf. Ps 35.9). From this sweetness our hearts melt, and we are both filled with the grace that no words can describe. And what else do you feel?' 'An unusual joy in my whole heart!' And Father Seraphim said, 'The Spirit of God fills with joy all that he touches. It is that same joy about which Christ says: "In the world you will have sadness, but I will see you, and your hearts will rejoice, and no one will take your joy from you" (cf. Jn 16.22, 33). And what else do you feel?' 'An unusual warmth,' I continued. And Father Seraphim again answered, 'It is that same warmth about which the prayers say: "With the warmth of your Spirit bring me warmth." This is how it ought to be, for the grace of God must abide in us, in our hearts, for the Lord said: *The kingdom of God is within you* (Lk 17.21). This Kingdom of God is now within us, and the grace of the Holy Spirit illumines us and warms us and fills our hearts with unspeakable joy.' "

This is merely a small fragment of that remarkable recorded encounter. Of course, we can choose not to believe it, to reject it as something strange and unreal, unrelated to our lives. But it is impossible to claim that all this is a lie and a fantasy. First, Motovilov was not a journalist or a professional writer, and second, something like this is beyond fabrication. This means that it actually happened.[12]

But what is most striking is that this experience is not isolated, and what occurred in the Sarov wilderness occurred similarly in other places and conditions, both recently and long ago, nearby and far away, and it happens even today. We live surrounded by witnesses of the Spirit and witnesses of spirituality, but in our pride, our self-involvement, and our faith in "science" alone we have chosen not to notice them. But if there is anything that our era yearns for, it is precisely for the Spirit and his gifts—for light and joy, peace and quiet, warmth and faith. It is high time that we discovered another reality beyond the vanity and destitution of our lives; it is time to

[12]Motovilov's notes on this encounter were found and published only after his own death, so he had no desire to "sensationalize" the experience.

acknowledge the Spirit and spirituality. Blessed Seraphim is only one of a thousand such witnesses of the Spirit. His words and his experience are backed by the words and experience of countless others. Can we possibly fail to make time to hear them?

An Unrelenting Call

J esus came into Galilee, preaching the gospel of God, and saying, "The time is fulfilled, and the kingdom of God is at hand; repent ye, and believe the gospel" (Mk 1.14–15). This is how the Gospel of Mark describes the beginning of the ministry and preaching of Christ two thousand years ago in Palestine.

By historical standards, Christianity is a very old religion. Yet, as you read these words over and over, listening to them with your inner ear, they do not seem ancient. On the contrary, it seems that someone is speaking them today, preaching this good news to me, to you, to all of us. Most amazing of all is that these words have not ceased to be heard for centuries and yet have not become outdated. How many books written some twenty to thirty years ago are still read today? A few isolated ones. Yesterday's leaders, who filled the world with terror and noise, have been forgotten, and their names are repeated only here and there, and mainly in secret. Once, for example, billions of words were published glorifying Stalin, and who reads them now? But with Christ's words the opposite is true. For over two centuries the mighty Roman Empire persecuted them, but today nothing remains of that empire, while the words of Christ are still very much alive. So many "masters of men's hearts,"[13] politicians, intellectuals, and academics have thought to put a final end to them: their own works have been drowned in oblivion, but the words of Christ resonate with the same power as at the dawn of Christianity.

Let us ask ourselves: why is this so? Before our very eyes, during this twentieth century—a century of the expansion of knowledge, the flourishing and endless achievements of science—for fifty years now, a full half

[13] Alexander Pushkin, "To the Sea."

century, an unprecedented campaign has been conducted against religion, and especially against the teachings of Christ. Everything is mobilized for this task: education, propaganda, the press, and, most evidently, the occasional bloody use of force. Everything that could possibly be said against Christ has been said—said and also done. But is it not time we admitted that even this most terrible, most well organized campaign has failed? Yes, quantifiably, religion has of course waned, squeezed out of the sphere of daily life into the shadows. Without question, unbelievers outnumber believers. But the words of Christ continue to attract a younger generation, and this means that they have not ceased to resonate. It is evident that on the inner spiritual plane, the anti-religious battle has been lost and its horrific assault has proven inadequate. And once again we hear: *"The time is fulfilled, and the kingdom of God is at hand. Repent ye, and believe the gospel."* Wherein lies the power of these words, the power of this unrelenting call? First and foremost, in its profound resonance with the principal aspiration and need of every human being. Anti-religious propaganda is mistaken not only about religion but, more importantly, about the individual, and herein lies its weakness as well as the guarantee of its future downfall. The Gospel says: "Seek, thirst, knock" (cf. Mt 5.6, 6.33, 7.7). In the Gospel, the individual is shown to be a being who is searching, striving for a complete understanding of his life, for continual growth and, finally, for deification. Anti-religious propaganda, however, maintains that there is nothing to search for, because in the mid-nineteenth century one German economist, by some miracle, already found all that is needed. And what did he find? He found that man can be entirely reduced to "relations of production," and that this explains absolutely everything about him. Therefore, when what is incorrect in these "relations of production" disappears or, more accurately, is corrected through terrible violence, the "golden age" will truly ensue. What this "golden age" consists of is unclear, but the individual must nonetheless strive for it alone. And this soulless, deterministic understanding of man is placed in opposition to the Gospel understanding, which they declare to be the fruit of superstition.

We are told: "Religion is nothing but fear and pessimism; it is the preaching of degrading endurance." But compare the Gospel with Marx's

Das Kapital. In the latter, the word "joy" is completely absent, while in the Gospel it is literally on every page. Concerning fear, the Bible says that *perfect love casteth out fear . . . he that feareth is not made perfect in love* (1 Jn 4.18). And, finally, it also says: "Be bold, pursue what is greater, be perfect" (cf. Jn 16.33, 1 Cor 12.31, Mt 5.48). Upon comparison of the image of man that shines in the Gospel with that proposed by an ideology that declares itself to be the last word in science, one does not cease to wonder at the marvelous beauty and freedom of the one and the enslaving bondage of the other. And here we find the explanation for why Christ's words live and will continue to live: they are addressed to what is most important in human nature, and simultaneously to the real, living human being, and not to an abstract invention of scientists and economists.

Christ's words are about life, and therefore they are addressed to anyone, meaning that they are for our time also. "The time has come" means that now, today, one must feel in the world the presence of divine love, divine light, pure joy, without which the world is a suffocating and fearful prison. "Repent" means to take a step back and look at one's life from without, to delve deeper into its hidden meaning, to ask oneself: what do we live for? Where is the ultimate joy and fullness of our existence? And "believe the Gospel" means to believe in the joyful news that there is a spiritual reality, that there is an eternally illumined world of truth, love, and unity, and that this is the Kingdom of God.

How true, how human are Christ's words! But this is precisely why people conceal them, why they replace these words with second-rate slander and pitiful caricature, why they fear these words more than anything in the world. If man had the freedom to at least compare the Gospel of Christ with the pseudo-gospel of the materialistic "paradise," he would turn wholeheartedly toward the One who uttered these eternal words of love and who also said, *Take my yoke upon you . . . for my yoke is easy and my burden is light* (Mt 11.29–30).

The Source
and the Mystery

Cleansed and Uplifted

I have already spoken about the central assertion of Christianity: about faith in Christ as the God-man. "And in one Lord Jesus Christ, the Son of God, the Only-Begotten, begotten of the Father before all ages; Light of Light, true God of true God." I stated that this is precisely what Christ taught about himself, and in this Christians have believed for almost two thousand years. I stated, finally, that this union of God and man in Christ has been viewed by Christians of all eras as the highest manifestation of divine wisdom—the Truth which satisfies all the demands of the human mind and heart.

That which atheist propagandists depict as absurd and ignorant superstition, the best minds and the greatest saints recognized as perfect and radiant truth. In what then did they see this truth?

In order to answer this question we must at least briefly recall the teaching of Christianity concerning man and the concept of God, or rather the intuition or perception of God from which this teaching about man is derived. Christianity has always viewed man as the crown of creation, the greatest and most perfect creation of God. Moreover, it has always seen in man the image and likeness of God, and this means it sees in him the divine foundation, the divine source of human nature. Speaking in philosophical language, Christianity confesses an extreme anthropological maximalism: man is indeed divine, and his intellect, his will, and his creative capabilities are all not only *from* God, but correspond to the divine intellect, will, and creative perfection. Man represents God in the world, so to speak, and through himself, through his capabilities, he carries out God's will for the world and in the world. Man is not God, but he is capable of the divine, resembles God, and is called to be a friend of God. The world and nature are given to him so that he can tend and cultivate them, revealing through them all his talents and gifts. According to Christian teaching, the world is called to become a cosmic temple of God's glory, in which the divine calling of man is revealed in all its fullness. Thus, man in the world lives out a divine ministry and a divine calling.

But this also means that God "resembles" man, so to speak, whom he sealed and adorned with his image and his gifts. God and man share a resemblance: man was created as God's fellow worker, a co-creator, a co-participant with God and a fellow agent in the divine plan for the world. God, for his part, works in the world through man. For Christians, this lofty understanding of man not only leads to the possibility of their union, but makes it the natural result—a unity in which God is manifested in man, and man fully manifests the image of God. This union, according to the Christian faith, is accomplished in Christ. *For in him*, writes the Apostle Paul, *dwelleth all the fullness of the Godhead bodily* (Col 2.9). Indeed, if we believe in God as he is described in the Bible, in God as Love, God who creates and pours out his life on all creation, God as truth, God as goodness—and what other kind of God could one imagine?—then the loftiest and most perfect manifestation of God in the world can be nothing other than his manifestation as Man. It is Christ who is this highest point of contact between God and creation, God and man, the supreme manifestation of the humanity of God and the divinity of man.

Whatever our doubts may be, let us suppose for a moment that, in Christ, God himself appeared in the world, and that he appeared in the most perfect of all people. Then let us ask ourselves: what do we learn by examining and pondering the image of Christ? What do we learn about God and about man? What kind of God appeared in the world? And does not a single word, the all-encompassing, all-inclusive word *love*, persistently suggest itself as the answer? And if Christ is God, then God indeed is love. As the Apostle John the Theologian writes, "He who does not love his brother does not know God, for God is love" (cf. 1 Jn 4.8, 20). We learn from Christ that it was through love and for love that God created the world, that through love God dwells in the world, and that in love he gives himself to the world. *I am come*, he says, *that they might have life, and that they might have it more abundantly* (Jn 10.10)—that is, he came to love, save, restore, and glorify; to leave the ninety-nine for sake of the one; to reveal all truth, all goodness, and all beauty; to resurrect and to give eternal life. God accomplishes all this and more in Christ.

But perhaps even more beautiful and remarkable is what we learn from Christ about man. In what kind of Man did God manifest himself? What is so inescapably beautiful about Christ? Love! Love for God, for man, for the world. Christ lives entirely for others; Christ never violates human freedom, never demands anything from man by force. He is always available to human suffering, he always compassionate, always helps, always heals. And all this he accomplishes with the most unlimited humility!

What religion, what philosophy has achieved a height where God and man are united in love and humility, and where that union of love and humility has revealed the ultimate truth of existence itself? And if someone asks, "What do you believe in?" every follower of Christ will answer, "I believe in a teaching that is loftier and more beautiful, more reasonable and mightier than anything else that exists or has ever existed on earth. In this teaching everything is perfect, and this is how I know it is divine. In it the notion that God is nothing but an absolute Monarch, punishing some and pardoning others, is destroyed, because when Christianity says 'God' it simultaneously says 'God is love.' In this teaching the image of man is purified and elevated to unheard-of heights, radiating a light with which it never shone before. Christ is perfect God and perfect Man, perfect in love, wisdom and power."

The teaching discarded by so many as improbable, in reality opens up tremendous possibilities. In it, human freedom is not diminished in the least, but rather this very freedom leads one to God; in it God is revealed as the breath and the fullness of life. And this is why the saints of all the ages, together with many generations of theologians and philosophers, unanimously maintain that the Christian teaching about God-manhood is the last and most complete revelation of divine wisdom, the foundation of the whole edifice of human culture and all of human history.

"A Wondrous Desire"

The worship services and rites of the Church, so often mocked by anti-religious propaganda, warrant a deeper contemplation of their meaning for man. After all, even those who war against religion have come to the conclusion that church baptisms, weddings, and funerals must be replaced with other rites—not religious ones, but rites all the same. Consequently, there is something in these rites that satisfies some kind of eternal and ineradicable need within man. But a need for what?

The Church terms its principal rites "mysteries." The concept of a "mystery" or "sacrament" is clearly connected with the idea of something mysterious, but the conclusion drawn from this—that focusing on the mysterious is characteristic of a primitive consciousness dominated by fear of magic and superstition—is completely false. We have often stated how it was Christianity that battled against superstition and black magic for centuries, applying more effort in this regard than anyone else. Since the very beginning of its existence Christianity has exposed the pagan deification of the government, nature, and human relations. For this reason, in terming its rites "mysteries" Christianity implied something fundamentally different from the term "mystery" in its everyday usage.

Let us take, for example, the first and fundamental church rite—the rite of baptism. Many centuries have gone by since the time of its establishment. Man's consciousness has changed profoundly, his knowledge has deepened and expanded immeasurably, yet this simple rite—the immersion of a newborn infant in water, of ablution—retains all of its power; it can be neither debunked nor destroyed. What does this rite of baptism tell us about man? It tells us of man's desire for a new life—a life that is pure, cleansed, and renewed, a life in which the principal, inescapable, eternal thirst of man is satisfied: the thirst for completeness. Baptism with water is needed because in it the experience of all nations in all eras finds its symbolic expression. It conveys an amazing premonition that beyond natural everyday life, both within it and simultaneously above it, lies the possibility of a different and better life. In other words, it conveys that evil, suffering, hatred, and discord—all this is not the ultimate truth about man. It is precisely this feeling of inadequacy, this sense of sinfulness, this thirst for cleansing, this striving for completeness, of which the sacramental mysteries speak, pointing to another dimension of life which man has always sensed within himself. This is not magic or superstition, not a holdover from ignorant and blind fears. It is the confirmation, in religious symbolic language, of that which is known to the entire spiritual experience of humanity, about which a poet once spoke in a poem dedicated to the soul: "And long the soul did languish, full of wondrous desire."[1] If you take this wondrous desire away from man, what is left?

In its sacramental mysteries Christianity seems to say to us, "Man is a mystery that you cannot solve with temporal, one-sided explanations. The mystery of love, of freedom and inspiration, the mystery of the 'desire for the wondrous.' However ignorant and cruel man can sometimes be, this desire of his must be preserved."

---

[1] From the poem "The Angel" by Mikhail Lermontov (1831).d

The Soul

The Only Defense

In his semi-autobiographical book *Fallen Leaves*, author Vasily Rozanov writes the following lines: "Always have a focused aspiration, without looking off to the sides. This does not mean that you should be blind to what is going on around you. With your eyes look everywhere: but with your soul look always at one thing, never at several."[1]

How accurately Rozanov has put this, and indeed, how greatly modern man lacks this "focused aspiration"! In other words, modern man lacks depth. All of modern civilization is built on the conscious or unconscious denial of depth, and all of society's debates, pursuits, and dramas ultimately concern things that are unimportant or of secondary importance.

But what Rozanov said was essentially stated long ago in the Gospel: "For what profit is it to a man if he gains the whole world, and loses his own soul?" (Mt 16.26). It is precisely man's depth which the Gospel calls "the soul"—his internal world, which constitutes the value, the uniqueness, the singularity of the human personality.

We see people fighting against religion because, they say, religion is a form of egoism: it exhorts a person to care for his soul and to disregard all of the so-called "problems" of the world, society, etc. A person dare not and has no right, even for a second, to break away from his "duty to society." He is supposed to constantly serve society's goals and be what they call "a useful member of society." This is ingrained in people literally from the cradle. And thus a society is built in which it becomes harder and harder

---

[1] V. V. Rozanov, *Opavshie list'ia: Korob pervyi. Sochineniia v dvukh tomakh* [Fallen leaves: the first box; Collected works in two volumes] (Moscow: Pravda), 2:299.

for a person to be alone with himself, to delve deep into himself, and, as they used to say here in olden times, "to consider his soul."

It seems to me that religion should accept this charge calmly and with a clear conscience, and calmly and firmly respond: "Yes, the soul of the individual, the personality of the individual, is indeed more important, more interesting, and more valuable than all social issues combined. Yes, the world exists and is created for each individual human soul and for it alone."

In this lies the whole argument, the whole struggle in our turbid and, in many ways, terrifying age. Some declare "the world, society, humanity, history" to be what is most important; they subjugate everything to them, and essentially reduce the individual to these four things. Others, who by now are barely audible, declare the chief values to be "man and the soul of man," and they add: "For what profit is it to a man if he gains the whole world, and loses his own soul?" The struggle between these two world orders is not a fight for life, but a fight to the death.

At the center of this struggle, of course, is the question of religion. Religion, after all, is man's "focused aspiration" toward one main thing; religion is, first and foremost, about caring for one's soul. Thus, allowing religion to exist means admitting the existence of something infinitely more important than all "social problems." It means to chip away at the tree that the ideologues of modernity are planting with such pathos; it means to free the individual person from that forced spiritual collectivization which forms the very essence of modern ideology.

It is necessary, very necessary, to understand the full depth and acuteness of this debate. We even have people who feel that the whole thing is merely some kind of misunderstanding and that it is possible to unite ideology and religion in a harmonious union, since in their essence they should not hinder one another. A tragic mistake! Because here we have a clash of two different understandings of man, two different intuitions of his nature—it is one or the other. Society, humanity, and history were deified because at some point people began to deny that a person had a soul, and they reduced man himself to nature, declaring that he is only part of a greater whole and has no worth outside of it.

But if this is the case, then no liberalization will help, nor any political "thaws,"[2] because the danger will always remain that for the sake of the whole the "part" will be coerced, confined, and subjugated. Only when the individual is not a "part," not a product of society, not a cog in some impersonal machine, only when he is a soul and his worth lies in his soul, is man's freedom possible—the same freedom invoked with such eagerness and rhetorical enthusiasm by those who in reality negate it with their whole ideology.

Yes, religion is about the soul. Religion is a call to place the soul and the core of our being at the center of our lives. Religion is caring for the soul, and there is no reason to be ashamed of this, because a person has no value outside of it. If there is no soul there remain only muscles, which are more or less same for everybody; there remains the "objective," impersonal mind; there remains the stomach. But in that case human society and the entire history of humanity is reduced to nothing more than a senseless conflict of muscles.

And that is why there is only one true task both for man and for human society: to protect the soul, to protect the depths of man's personhood by ensuring that the individual, and not impersonal "humankind," becomes the goal and the concern of society itself. Because if a man gains the whole world, but loses his soul, before our very eyes the world will turn—and is already turning—into a prison, a concentration camp, a monstrous anthill, a hell. For this reason one should not be ashamed of the primacy of the soul and the individual in religion, but rather proclaim and confess this primacy as the only defense, the only antidote to inhuman totalitarianism, which destroys all that is precious within a person.

This is what Rozanov had in mind when he wrote, long before the modern catastrophes which have since befallen us, that a focused aspiration toward the one most important thing is the only true task of human life. "With your eyes look everywhere: but with your soul look only at the one

---

[2]Here the author is referring to the "Thaw" in the Soviet Union enacted under Nikita Khrushchev from the mid-1950s until the mid-1960s. It was a time when several prisoners were released from the Gulag and writers and artists were given considerably more freedom.

thing." Only the soul and what is profound and genuine in life are worthy of a person's care and concern.

Don't Lose it!

For what is a man profited, if he shall gain the whole world, and lose his own soul? (Mt 16.26).

In all the Gospel, perhaps even in all religious literature, there are no words that modern man ought to ponder more than these. Indeed, these words could be the epigraph for our entire modern age, with its inherent striving to acquire the world and its remarkable obliviousness toward all things spiritual and internal.

Some thinkers in the West have labeled modern civilization "the consumer society," because in it a person considers himself primarily a consumer—one with an insatiable appetite. Man has left the stage of elemental struggle for existence, and now nothing is enough for him: he always wants more. But in practice this striving proves quite petty and limited.

At one time, the best minds dreamed of an age when man, having been freed from endless and tortuous concern for his own sustenance, from slavery to food, from the natural need for warmth, clothing, and shelter, would be able to fill his life with higher meaning and higher beauty, and would not simply exist, but actually *live*.

But now that humanity's elementary needs are being met, this dream of its best representatives is not only not being realized, but it is actually shrinking in scope and content. Here he is, the well-fed and clothed individual. What does he want? As it turns out, the same as before, only in continually increasing measure: quantity, not quality; the external and not the internal. And so it is with the individual, with whole nations, and with our entire civilization. Some nations, if they are large and strong, literally want "to gain the world"—that is, to conquer the world and subjugate it to their interests and needs. The individual wants to "gain the world" in his own way, snatching up as many of the "good things of the earth" as possible.

How strange and how infinitely depressing! During the times historians have labeled "the Dark Ages," in the era when it appeared man was struggling just for survival, a great culture of the soul was created, and the highest spiritual values were forged. To this day, millions of tourists, day in and day out, gaze in wonder at the monuments left by that culture. They behold and try to understand where these monuments came from, and what prompted those "enslaved" people to dream of such beauty, to develop such a view of the world, to leave us with such concepts, such dreams, and such treasures.

Conversely, the contemporary "liberated" man seems unable to create anything other than ugliness and senselessness. Moreover, whenever it happens that within this consumer society, so exclusively focused on the exterior, by some miracle there appears a person who reminds us of what is internal and directs our attention to our souls, both society and the powers that be immediately silence him and force everyone else to assert that they do not need anything beyond material conveniences, and that they are especially in no need of any kind of soul. But this is quite literally what it means "to lose one's soul." Do we really fail to see that it is precisely our soul that is harmed by our terrible contemporary society with its soulless optimism, its worship of quantity, its triumphant denial of spiritual meaning? Does it really not disturb us to see our own children growing up well-fed and content, but never thinking about the soul?

For ages human beings have said: "When freedom comes, I will no longer tremble over a piece of bread, or die from hunger and cold. I will give my children what I myself never had—I will give them happiness." And now that "happiness" is here: millions and billions of people with damaged souls, with a dying and unnecessary body. They were ordered to desire a consumerist happiness, and they desire it; they were ordered to call this freedom, and they so called it. They were ordered to forget about their souls, and they forgot about them.

But perhaps during these festive days something will stir in their hearts. Perhaps they will sense that deep down inside them there is a strange emptiness, which the whole world cannot fill, even if they were to obtain it. Perhaps they will remember the lines penned so long ago, when the writer was still a boy, concerning heavenly sounds "which could not be replaced by . . . the tiresome songs of the earth." Perhaps they will rediscover their damaged souls, which have dropped off to sleep in a heavy hangover of consumerism, and hear the words, *For what is a man profited, if he shall gain the whole world, and lose his own soul?* (Mt 16.26).

It is precisely about this soul that I would like to remind people today from the very heart of our increasingly soul-negating civilization.

A Loss of Balance

We live in an age where everyone's attention is focused almost exclusively on a person's outward activity—how productive he is at work, how involved he is in social life, in government, and the like. Of course, in and of themselves, all these spheres of life are not only legitimate, but of infinite importance: a person is called to live in society and depends on his social environment. He is a participant in the common life, and he is a social creature. At the same time, there is something deeply unfavorable in this exclusively "social" approach to man. But what is this something?

I believe this unfavorable element is best defined as a loss of balance. In focusing all its attention on the external conditions of human life, society seems to have forgotten about the individual's inner world. And not only does it forget—far worse, it often simply denies its existence or, more accurately, its primacy within the human consciousness. There are teachings that say that the internal is merely a result of the external, a projection of society and of life's outward conditions, and nothing more. And then there have been and remain other teachings that claim the exact opposite, denying everything external, denigrating the role of society and summoning the individual to a kind of internal desert isolation.

It is worth considering the one-sidedness of such views, recognizing the real tragedy within them and the reason human life is becoming something less than human. Here we would do well to recall the Christian teaching concerning man. People often want to present this teaching in a perverted way—as the denial of the external in favor of the internal, as indifference to the social and public life of the individual. But in practice this is not the case. It is precisely here, in the Christian teaching about man, that we find that balance that is so agonizingly lacking in the modern world.

Yes, without a doubt, this teaching puts a person's inner world, which the Gospel calls the soul, in the first place. *For what is a man profited, if he shall gain the whole world, and lose his own soul?* Christ asks (Mt 16.26). But we need to remember that the soul is not just one isolated part of man's makeup, but rather it includes the consciousness, the mind, the heart, the will, and the conscience—that is, that depth at which the individual searches for and finds the meaning of life, the inner unity of his entire existence, that harmony with himself without which he is not a person, but a slave. He is a slave of life's arbitrary circumstances, a slave to another person, a slave to his own passions—in short, a slave of everything external. Only by sanctifying and lending meaning to all that is external from within, by evaluating it in light of his conscience, with all sobriety of mind and the depth of the heart's understanding, can a person become a free participant in external life and even its creator.

Thus, the internal does not negate the external. The Christian teaching about the soul makes no sense without the teaching on love, that force that directs a person's soul in the external world. *Love one another* (Jn 13.34, 15.12), says Christ—love with such a love that one would give one's very soul, if needed, for one's brothers. And so a person's internal world is shown to be a world of love. By retreating into himself, delving deep into his own soul, a person finds within his soul a new miraculous power, enabling him not only to overcome his loneliness, but to build around himself a new and liberated life. *The Kingdom of God is within you* (Lk 17.21), says Christ. But the Kingdom of God is also man's goal and task in this world. At the same time, the Kingdom of God is freedom, love, unity, and happiness of the individual—that is, everything that modern humanity desires and seeks so passionately, not knowing that the road to it lies through the inner world of each individual person—through his or her own soul.

The Conscience

A Particle of God

In Solzhenitsyn's Novel *The First Circle*, just as he is about to depart on a new and interesting assignment in Paris, the rising young diplomat Innokenty Volodin does something very strange. Motivated by a power beyond his own reckoning, he decides to phone an old doctor whom he barely knows, and warns him of an impending scheme against him. The call is suddenly disconnected, and Volodin spends two days in terror anticipating his arrest and wondering what brought him to this move, which will cut short not only his successful career, but possibly also his life. Solzhenitsyn writes:

> In recent years [Innokenty] . . . threw himself into reading. . . . It turned out that you have to know how to read. It is not just a matter of letting your eyes run down the pages. Since Innokenty, from youth on, had been shielded from erroneous or outcast books, and had read only the clearly established classics, he had grown used to believing every word he read, giving himself up completely to the author's will. Now, reading writers whose opinions contradicted one another, he was unable for a while to rebel, but could only submit to one author, then to another, then to a third.
>
> Then he had gone to Paris and worked for UNESCO. While he was there he had read a lot after work. And he had reached a point where he felt less tossed about from one writer's ideas to another's, felt that he himself had his hand on the helm.
>
> He had not discovered very much in those years, but he had discovered something.

Up to then the truth for Innokenty had been: you have only one life. Now he came to sense a new law, in himself and in the world: you also have only one conscience.

And just as you cannot recover a lost life, you cannot recover a wrecked conscience. Innokenty was beginning to realize it when, on that Saturday, several days before his planned trip to Paris, he learned to his misfortune about the trap being prepared for that simpleton Dobroumov. He already knew enough to understand that such an affair would not end with Dobroumov, that it would be the beginning of a long campaign.

. . . For several hours he had paced his office in indecision. . . . He had rocked back and forth, started to tremble, held his head in his hands. Finally he had decided to call, even though he knew that Dobroumov's phone might well be under surveillance. . . . Now, all that seemed ages ago—though it had only been the day before.[1]

This is a brief excerpt from Solzhenitsyn's novel, but in essence the whole of his enormous, wonderful, astonishing book is written specifically about the conscience. The conscience is its hero, its motive force, its inner benchmark. All of its characters, from Stalin to the convict yard-keeper Spiridon, are divided into two groups: those who like Volodin know, or have realized, that our conscience, just like life, is given to us only once, and who realize that "just as you cannot recover a lost life, you cannot recover a wrecked conscience"; and those who do not know this. But what is this conscience, this strange power that is capable of transforming the superficially egoistic and egocentric young Volodin, unremarkable except for his love of life and pleasures, so simply and imperceptibly into a hero and martyr? As if to bid him farewell, in the final chapters of the book Solzhenitsyn shows him to us for the last time on his way to interrogation, and writes: "From those heights of struggle and suffering to which he had ascended, the wisdom of the great philosopher seemed like the babbling of a child. 'Off to interrogation! Hands behind your back!' Volodin put his

---

[1]Alexander Solzhenitsyn, *The First Circle* (New York: Harper & Row, 1968), 344–45.

hands behind him, and with his head held high, like a bird drinking water, he left the 'box.'"[2]

Solzhenitsyn's greatness consists in the fact that in all his writings he poses the main question of our times: the question of conscience. He both poses the question and bears witness: the conscience exists, and it is indestructible.

Thus we must ask ourselves: what is this conscience, what is meant by these simple and at the same time profound and mysterious expressions—"I can do this in good conscience," and "I can't do this in good conscience"? What is this voice that so often and unexpectedly erupts into our destiny and alters it at its core, so that what appeared to be white, habitual, and correct suddenly becomes so obviously black, and that which had been silent suddenly begins to speak? But this is the whole point: conscience is not one of those realities that can be defined, categorized into logical and juridical formulations. One cannot first describe conscience and then live by it. It is within us, yet at the same time it seems to speak to us from outside, from some other depth or height that we do not usually see in ourselves.

The materialistic evaluation of man simply denies that he *has* a conscience. It strives to explain conscience as a social instinct, a hereditary influence, or a collective awareness—that is, once again it reduces the conscience to determinism, to the rejection of freedom in man. From this vantage Volodin's action, being anti-social, a crime against the collective, becomes a harmful and evil act. Christianity, however, quite simply and calmly affirms that the conscience is an innate ability in man, given him at the outset, to discern good and evil—not in their social, relative sense, but rather as a kind of absolute. Conscience is from God, and therefore it is a witness to God. Conscience is the voice of God in the soul of man, and this is why it is heard both from within and simultaneously from without. Conscience is precisely what the Christian religion calls the image and likeness of God in man.

Man has the ability and the freedom to suppress the conscience within himself, and in Solzhenitsyn's novel a striking example of this absolute rejection of conscience is Stalin. He still has a sense of good and evil, but

---

[2]Solzhenitsyn, *The First Circle*, 553 (with alterations by the editor).

he has become his own measure: the good is that which serves him, and the evil is that which opposes him. A person can struggle with his conscience, and in Solzhenitsyn's work there are many conflicted souls who are troubled precisely by this inner strife. Either they are like Volodin, Gerasimovich, and Nerzhin, who ultimately choose to live by conscience, or like Yakonov, their conscience flares up for one agonizing moment, and then they reject it. One way or another, everything in life is connected to the conscience, and everything falls into place around it. Everything comes down to the final question: if the conscience exists, then man exists, freedom exists, rebirth is possible, and happiness can prevail. If there is no conscience, only hell remains, whether at liberty, in the concrete fortress of Stalin's country house, or in jail.

In our tragic decades people debate everything under the sun—cybernetics, economics, the future world order—but these debates will remain fruitless until there dawns upon all people the one sun that illumines and gives life to all things—the conscience, that mystical particle, the power and glory of God within the weak and humble human being.

Last Chance

In my last conversation I spoke about the conscience—that mysterious voice inside a person which Solzhenitsyn described so well in his novel *The First Circle*. He said that besides having one life, man also has only one conscience, and as it is impossible to return a life taken away from a person, so it is impossible to restore a marred conscience.

Today we will continue these reflections on the conscience, mainly because no one seems to be occupied with this in our difficult, complex, unhappy world: neither philosophers who speak of truth, nor political leaders who seem to need no conscience to tell good from evil, nor even theologians who speak and teach about God. Philosophers argue that the truth is provable. But for many centuries no two philosophers have agreed with each other on how to understand the truth. Leaders, politicians, and legislators say, "This is good, and this is evil." But how many times have we heard these same leaders call something good one day and evil the next, and vice versa? How many times have we seen history books rewritten or simply burned on their orders? Apparently, even here the difference between good and evil is not very clear and firm.

Finally, believers talk about God and claim that they know him, and that he himself instructs them in all truth. But once again, for centuries they have been arguing and quarreling about him, and sometimes end up hating each other and shedding each other's blood. Clearly, here too there is something wrong. Hence, proofs of truth, conversations about good and evil, and even faith itself still lack something that would lead people out of the realm of the controversial, the unconvincing, the relative, and give them strength, truth, and light, that would evoke no need or even desire to ask any further questions.

Whatever people tell us about the *sharashka*[3] inmate and engineer Gerasimovich in Solzhenitsyn's work, *The First Circle*, we do not need these explanations. After all, he is offered early release in exchange for doing something that will lead to the arrest of others. Solzhenitsyn writes: "This was the fulfillment of the prayer of Natasha [Gerasimovich's wife]. . . . Her desiccated face with glass-frosted tears seemed to appear before Hilarion. For the first time in many years, the accessibility, closeness, and warmth of returning home embraced his heart. . . . And Natasha was the true friend of his life. This was now the second sentence that Natasha had been waiting for him. . . . She was flickering and about to be snuffed out, and with her Hilarion's life too would be extinguished." And yet he refuses. "Ah," continues Solzhenitsyn, "he could have kept his mouth shut! He could have double-crossed them, as convicts often did—take the assignment, then keep putting it off and never do it. But Gerasimovich got up and looked contemptuously at the pot-bellied, joweled, flat-faced [man] . . . in the sheepskin general's hat: "No! That's not my line of work!" he squeaked shrilly. "Putting people in prison is not my line of work! I'm not a man-trapper. It's enough that they've imprisoned us . . ."

---

[3]Research group composed of prisoners in the gulag.

Thus, in reading or listening to these lines of Solzhenitsyn, we do not need any philosophical, moral, or even religious explanations and arguments. Gerasimovich himself does not think about them; he thinks about his wife and about his life, doomed by this response of his. And even if we began to look at Gerasimovich's deed from different angles, we would know immediately and with absolute certainty that he is right and, most importantly, that this does not require any explanation. What gives us this certainty? What makes all reasoning and proof unnecessary? What is it that unites the sincere philosopher, the believer, and the honest, truthful unbeliever in a unanimous evaluation, without a shadow of doubt? The answer is clear: conscience. Conscience forced Gerasimovich to do what he did, and his conscience resonates with our own conscience, which concurs with it without any words and even without any thoughts. And in this, truth, goodness, and finally faith coincide, for conscience is faith. Faith, no matter how unconscious it may be, knows that there is an absolute eternal truth that does not depend on anything—a law whose transgression and violation is impossible without destroying something most important, sacred, and profound within us—or, more bluntly, our own selves.

Let's take the Gospel. There we find two very important examples for our topic. First we have Pilate, before whom stands Christ, betrayed and condemned. Pilate has the power to hand him over for execution or to release him. The entire political moment, the whole balance of forces in the conquered, occupied, but roiling country, tells Pilate that it is better to yield to the crowd and kill Christ; yet something holds him back. It is conscience. But he concedes and rejects this voice of conscience, remembers the philosophers who argue about the truth, and hurls a truly wise question at Christ: *What is Truth?* (Jn 18.38). How is the truth to be learned? His conscience had already told him everything, but Pilate decided not to obey. His career, in all probability, is saved; everything is all right. But the man Pilate, this unique and inimitable human being, destroys himself in this betrayal, sealed by the shameful washing of his hands.

Several hours pass, and on the cross next to the crucified and suffering Christ hangs a thief. Again, silence; again, no evidence, explanation, or argument. From the breast of the dying thief, who had labored so much for evil, from some inexplicable, incomprehensible depth there thunder the words: "Remember me, Lord, in your Kingdom" (cf. Lk 23.42). Pilate saves himself by betraying his conscience and perishes; while the doomed man enters the mysterious, radiant Kingdom of Goodness, which he had seen and accepted in the last minute of his life.

Two phenomena of conscience, two examples of its mysterious power in man. And since this phenomenon, this absolute law, surpasses all human divisions, since it is a universal law and everyone understands it, since it alone in the whole world is so obviously from above, and not from below, can it perhaps be the path to concord? Perhaps everything can be tested by it? Perhaps it is the last chance for saving man and humanity from the darkness of hatred and destruction into which we are sinking? Let each of us consider this. Let each of us understand that every day, every hour, each one of us always faces a choice that cannot be abolished by philosophical reasoning about good and evil—a choice that ultimately depends on one thing only: whether he will hear that quiet but all-conquering voice of conscience that never ceases in our heart.

Christianity and the Person

The Last Bastion

In our conversations we have spoken often and at length about the Christian understanding of man, and this of course is no accident. For behind the great debate about religion, about God—a debate that at its core is the main theme of our twentieth century—the debate about man becomes increasingly delineated. "Tell me what you think about God, and I'll tell you how you regard man"—this is an extremely precise formula, which essentially can be applied to everyone.

In the world, I repeat, there are two conflicting understandings of man, his nature and his vocation—the atheistic and the religious. And each of us should carefully consider the essence of both, for it is typical for man not merely to live out his life, but to consider life's purpose and try to live in accordance with it.

For decades, the atheistic understanding of man has been inculcated and officially recognized as binding. What does it offer, how does it determine a person, what purpose does it ascribe to life? People are so used to the official rhetoric, and have become so dulled by it, that it often does not occur to them that this atheistic understanding of man is based on an elementary contradiction, all the more terrible in its simplicity: the contradiction between the nature of man and the ultimate goal of mankind. An elementary truth of any science is the truth that the nature of an object always corresponds to its purpose. But in the atheistic doctrine of man this truth is actually denied. On the one hand, it proclaims a supreme, ultimate purpose—universal and absolute happiness, "a leap from the realm of necessity into the realm of freedom." Indeed, it denies religion primarily because religion allegedly hinders the attainment of this goal, taking it beyond the limits of this life and into another life beyond the grave. In order to achieve this goal, atheism calls a person to struggle, to sacrifice, to give one's very life, if necessary. But the atheistic doctrine of man—and here the contradiction begins—is never able to determine in what way this "universal and absolute happiness" will finally come about, why it will be happiness and how it will become so. Here we find complete silence; atheism has absolutely nothing to say. It sounds eloquent only as long as it rattles on about the struggle, its methods and tactics, all the while beckoning with mysterious promises. But why is this "absolute," "universal," and "scientifically substantiated" happiness wholly impossible to describe and define? The answer is very simple: it is because this purpose does not actually exist in man's nature as defined by the atheistic worldview.

For atheism exerted all its power to destroy what it defines as "idealism," that is, all spiritual reality. There is nothing but matter, and therefore man is entirely determined by matter. Matter, in turn, is determined by absolutely impersonal "laws." The concept of "happiness" cannot possibly be deduced from matter, because the concept of "happiness" is of a spiritual, idealistic nature. Matter itself does not strive for anything and has no purpose, except that which is inherent in its nature: the cycle of feeding, growth, and death. Materialism denies and hates the spirit, yet sets for mankind a goal that is in fact spiritual. And then it has to either conceal the content of this goal, or define it "negatively," so to speak, as the absence of exploitation, the absence of hunger, the absence of want, etc.

Very well; all this is an "absence" of this and that, but what then is it a *presence* of? And here we discover not only the philosophical poverty of this ideology, but something much more terrible: the fact that in the atheistic doctrine of the person, the person himself is absent. There is some sort of abstract "humanity," various "masses" and "classes," but there is no human person—yet only the person can be happy. No, there has never been, nor will there be, any "collective happiness," for the collective as such does not exist: the collective is an abstract, ultimately "idealistic" concept. By dissolving man into the masses, atheism thereby denies man's individuality, uniqueness, and inimitability.

And here is the line that separates the atheistic and religious understandings of man. For religion always begins with the individual. Only by establishing the person as an absolute, only by ascribing to him a divine meaning and purpose, does religion apply to humanity. And where atheism says: "The happiness of each lies only in the happiness of all," religion says: "The happiness of all lies in the happiness of each individual." For happiness—that is, a life filled with meaning, light, knowledge, love, and joy—is possible only in each discrete person. And of course, ultimate, eternal happiness is found only in love. And one person loves another person, not "humanity."

This struggle, which is unfolding before our eyes with increasing clarity throughout the world, is a struggle between the personal and the impersonal understanding of life, history, and ultimately the person himself. And then it becomes clear why such hatred is directed at religion, why everything impersonal craves its destruction. For it is religion that is the last bastion of the personal in the world. If there is no person, this absolute and unique value, then how can he have rights, why should he be protected and cared for, why can he not be destroyed for the sake of an abstract "common good"? Where atheism prevails, sooner or later all concern for the person disappears: the kingdom of the impersonal begins, and in the end—deprivation of personal rights, violence, terror, and blood. Many, too many, still do not see this. And they think that it is possible to protect a person, his rights, his dignity, and his very life, while remaining a materialist. Alas, it is impossible! For the very knowledge of the person, or rather the dazzling revelation about him, comes not from below, not from matter, and not even from science. It has come, it always comes, and, we believe, it will never cease to come into the world, over and over again, only from the Divine Light.

Religion and Ideology

We live in an era that celebrates ideologies. Ideology—a terrible word, a word that appeared only recently and which has almost irrevocably destroyed our world and our life.

What is ideology? It is a teaching or theory that not only sets itself up as an absolute and universal truth, but subjects humanity to a specific way of behaving and acting. At its core, ideology is of course an ersatz religion, a falsification of religion. The difference between religion and ideology—an enormous difference—is that religion or faith is always something personal, impossible without a profound personal inner experience, whereas ideology, any ideology, begins with the fact that it negates everything personal and rejects it as unnecessary. Religion, the invitation to faith, is always oriented towards the person. Ideology is always oriented towards the masses, the collective, in the form of a nation, a class, or mankind in general. The purpose of religion is for a person to find God, and thereby to find and become his true self. The purpose of ideology is to subject the person to itself completely, making him its executor and servant. Religion says to us: *For what is a man profited, if he shall gain the whole world, but lose his own soul?* (Mt 16.26). Ideology says: "The whole world must be gained that I might triumph!" Religion calls us to see every man as our neighbor; ideologies are always focused on those far away, on an impersonal and abstract "mankind."

I repeat: we live in the age of the triumph of ideologies and their terrible power over people. In our own era, which is only seventy years old, millions and billions of people have died in their name. And today man faces no more urgent and pressing task then the rejection of this ideological force that tyrannizes humanity. But this task is only possible if we place above all ideologies an idea that supersedes and limits them: the idea of the individual, meaning the living, concrete, unique, and inimitable person.

The decline of religion and the triumph of ideology have resulted in an almost total extinction of the concept of the individual and its attendant experience. This experience is, naturally, a religious one at its foundation.

Only in and from religion is the idea of the individual possible, and this is what contemporary man neither wants nor is able or willing to understand. And so he persists in his desire to be saved by this or that ideology.

I will of course hear the objection that, in the period of its own historical ascendancy, religion itself very often trampled the idea of the individual; that the very principle of individual rights, freedoms, and so forth was born out of the struggle against religion. In part this is true. But we must understand this truth in its full complexity. Yes, of course, Christ was crucified by religious people. But they crucified him precisely because he denounced their religion as false—or, speaking in contemporary terms, he denounced them for transforming religion into ideology. For the whole point of the conflict of Christ with those who crucified him came down to one thing alone: Christ placed the person above everything, making the person and only the person the subject of love, the subject of absolute concern; whereas the enemies of Christ were looking to religion for order, for the deliverance of their homeland, for justification of their self-serving ways, etc., and to this end they demanded blind obedience to impersonal rules.

Christ said not a word about any of these concerns, just as he said not a word about government, about society, about history, about culture—about any of those things that have always concerned all ideologies. His attention was constantly focused on the living persons who surrounded him. But he didn't speak about their rights: rather, he approached them with all his love, all his presence and compassion. It is precisely because he placed the living person above all else in the world that he was condemned, but in this very condemnation—and this is crucial to understand—religion itself was reborn. From being an ideology it became a living force, and for all time the idea of the individual became dominant in the world.

In the centuries that followed we must confess that even Christianity itself all too often became an ideology, demanding blind obedience to itself and serving peripheral goals. But this did not and does not comprise its essence. Its essence lies in the Gospel image of Christ, the image of the Man who is focused on others, who sees them as his neighbor and makes them the goal and purpose of life.

Nowhere else in the history of mankind is there any basis for the individual. He does not exist in the great and profound philosophy of the Greeks; he does not exist in Rome, which created the idea of rights, but did not consider the slave to be a person. And of course this idea of the individual does not exist in any contemporary ideology, which is always concerned with humanity, but which for the sake of humanity destroys millions of people without a qualm.

I repeat: the idea of the individual is a religious one. For it is evident that if it is not rooted in God above, if the person is not "from above," but "from below," if he is only a passing phenomenon, then truly there is no reason to worry about him, and the world is governed solely by the law of large numbers. In this case—and we will come to the subject shortly—we should eliminate all those who are crippled, or sick, or old; in this case we need only be concerned with natural selection. In this case those famous "tears of a child" in Dostoevsky's book become meaningless sentimentality.

It is simplest to put it this way: if there is no God, then in essence there is no person. Then there are only people—impersonal masses, whose biological well-being is relentlessly pursued by ideology at all costs. It is in this horrifying ideological world, the world of masses, of classes, and of collectives, that we now find ourselves.

It is essential that we consider this fact and be horrified by it while it is not too late, while the living person has not yet been replaced by a serial number, while man has not yet become simply a cog in an increasingly complex and enormous machine. The question of religion today is first of all a question of the individual. To this theme, this most important of all contemporary questions, we will return in our subsequent talks.

The Absolute Value of the Individual

In my last broadcast I said that the concept of the person can be grounded only in a religious worldview. I also said that outside this understanding and intuition of the person, all contemporary concerns about humanity are ultimately illusory and doomed to failure.

Moreover, even those who continue to fight for the individual and his rights—whose numbers are sadly diminishing—are unable or unwilling to see that this problem of the person is organically linked with religious teaching about the person. Indeed, they often seek to disassociate themselves from religion altogether.

Until it was forcibly stifled, there was considerable debate in recent times about "socialism with a human face," and these conversations were most likely quite sincere. But without meaning to sound rhetorical or crafty we may ask the following question: why exactly does socialism have to have a human face? And what exactly is hidden behind this seemingly attractive expression?

It seems to me that those who bandy this phrase about are unaware of its inner paradox, for a face is precisely something that is essentially personal, individual. There is no common face; a face is either mine, yours, or his. But socialism in principle, on a scientific basis, always places the common over the private, over the personal, over the individual. Not only has it always affirmed that man lives in a society with other people, which is self-evident, but it specifically reduces the person to the collective, dooming him to total dependence on a class, a nation, a society, and so forth.

I repeat: in any perspective other than the religious one, this reduction is inevitable. For in the framework of the materialistic, atheistic worldview it is completely impossible to demonstrate why the person as such, the individual human being, has any particular value or any innate rights. In the atheistic worldview the person receives these rights from society, which in this worldview is a priori the highest value. In this worldview—need this be proven?—it is not society that lives for the person, but the person for society.

Currently there are certain kindhearted, well-meaning, and (in their own way) heroic individuals who are trying to prove that freedom and a greater respect for the individual are beneficial to society and its goals. They contend that if there is more freedom, production will become more efficient, science will develop with greater speed, and various forms of opposition will diminish. But it is clear that here, too, freedom and personal dignity continue to be thought of exclusively in terms of how they benefit society. And ultimately this approach, however noble the intentions behind it, will yield nothing. Any peasant knows that if you don't feed a horse and give it rest it will stop working.

A utilitarian basis for personal rights is not only insufficient, but simply unworthy of man. For here a person's worth is defined purely in terms of his usefulness to the collective, his productivity: "Give him a little more freedom so that he produces more efficiently; remove some of his fears, and he will be more useful." Everything remains as it was before, in particular that horrendous myth of the "useful member of society," to which millions have fallen victim in corrective labor camps. On the basis of utility, of society, of the collective it is impossible to derive any real human rights, for these rights are only conceivable if one recognizes the absolute value of the person. For the Latin root of the word *absolute* means something that is independent of anything else and cannot be reduced to anything else.

To recognize the absolute value of each person means not only to grant him certain rights that are independent of society, but also—and this is immeasurably more important—to strip everything else in the world of absolute value, especially society itself. This means overturning all our conventional ideas and acknowledging man as a being outside the simple natural order—as a higher being. But only religion says this about man. It is impossible to demonstrate scientifically; one can only believe it.

It is no coincidence that the most virulent hater of Christianity, Nietzsche, exclaimed: "We will replace love for one's neighbor with love for him who is far off!" This far-off person is really no one; he is the person we don't see, a collective, currently nonexistent person. But my neighbor, according to the Gospel, is the person who is near me, always alive, concrete, and unique. It is also no accident that all philosophies, ideologies, and programs that focus on far-off mankind, on the general, on the collective, so strongly oppose religion and by some immutable law always war against it. Their adherents realize, of course, that to abolish religion means to gradually destroy the individual. This is why they fear not those who rally for various freedoms and rights, but rather those who believe in the divine spirit and the immortal soul, which cannot be reduced to any kind of earthly "profit."

What is a man profited, if he shall gain the whole world, and lose his own soul? (Mt 16.26). As long as these words resound on earth, as long as people remember the paradoxical arithmetic of the Gospel according to which one person is always more important and valuable than the ninety-nine, it will be impossible to destroy human individuality, and consequently it will be impossible to construct a fully collectivized humanity, which will call its slavery "freedom," its subjection to impersonal utility "rights," and its prison an "earthly paradise." How horrendous that so many do not yet see that there is only one thing on earth that can oppose totalitarianism in all of its forms: it is faith in God, who created man in his own image and likeness, and called him to freedom and eternity—only this, and nothing else.

The debate of our age is in reality a religious debate. To fail to see this, to fail to see that all the horrendous problems of our time can only be understood at the heart of the religious worldview, is tantamount to hiding our head in the sand, ostrich-fashion. Far-off mankind or our neighbor? Humanity or the person? Where do we begin, and in the name of what do we labor? Such are the questions that, sooner or later, each and every one of us will have to answer.

What is Rejected and Affirmed by Christmas?

In our day the feast of Christ's birth has become acutely significant. This is because at its heart lies an image and an understanding of man that is sharply contested by a directly opposing understanding. And so the feast of Christmas becomes a kind of challenge, one that is at once a rejection and an affirmation.

What is it that Christmas affirms, and what does it reject? First of all, it rejects the image of man that is not only proposed, but alas, forcibly imposed by materialism. However much materialism may speak about the higher destiny of man, in it man does not and cannot have the highest, absolute value, for within it man is entirely of matter and is fully determined by it.

From this point of view, for example, the "defense of the irrevocable rights of man," so much talked of today, is absolute nonsense from the perspective of materialism, and is doomed to complete failure at the outset. For where do these irrevocable rights come from? Do we really have to prove that this very idea, so fundamental to the "Declaration of Human Rights,"[1] is an idea of religious origin, which outside the religious context sooner or later proves to be an absolute absurdity? In the materialist understanding of man, his rights are conferred on him by society, which can also take them away; for society, its development and progress are values of the first order. This is why a person cannot have any "irrevocable rights." He has only one right—to conform to society and to follow the "objective laws" of its development.

All this is rather hackneyed and banal, but this does not prevent people from attempting to mix oil and water—that is, to adopt materialism as a "scientific worldview" while simultaneously advocating for "human rights." The advocates of such attempts still believe that millions of destroyed lives are merely a misunderstanding, a tragic mistake, and cannot suppose that this is an iron law of consequence that flows out of the basic law of materialism. And according to this law, everything that opposes the "objective" course of history must be destroyed.

I am saying all of this in order to emphasize that the whole idea of man, as affirmed by the feast of Christmas, is an absolute rejection of this "fundamental law." If materialism is right, not only would there be no Christmas, but also all that it has been for humanity and world culture turns out to be the greatest delusion ever to appear on earth.

---

[1]The Universal Declaration of Human Rights is a document adopted by the General Assembly of the United Nations in December, 1948. Although of a provisional rather than a binding nature, the UDHR nevertheless became part of the basis for international agreements that laid the foundation of political, civil, economic, and other human rights.

Yes, Christmas rejects, but, in rejecting it affirms. It affirms the one fact that permits us to speak about "human rights": namely, that man is divine by his very nature and destiny, that he is free and therefore can rise above the laws of nature, subjecting them to himself, and that his calling is perfection in freedom and creativity.

It is time we understood that in the context of godless materialism and its worldview, the word *freedom* has no meaning and can have none. This is clearly affirmed by the fact that no society built on this worldview has ever been free. For the only free society is a society that accepts the highest and absolute value of the human person as an axiom. But this is precisely what materialism does not recognize, and cannot recognize, without destroying itself.

Will our fighters for rights and freedoms realize that our defense against the dehumanization of mankind is not declarations and laws, not constitutions and guarantees, but only religion, and therefore no compromise here is possible? There is no such thing as "materialism with a human face," as it is now commonly called, nor will there ever be.

And this is why it is not enough simply to know that Christmas exists; it is not enough to simply celebrate it for old times' sake. In our day we have to gaze into the radiant light emanating from this feast, and to understand that only in this shines the image of profound humanity, that this light is both ultimate and unique, that outside of it all is pitch darkness and the destruction of the individual, regardless of how many exaggerated declarations are made in the world!

And yet how feebly we believers observe this light; how seldom are we immersed in it! But time grows very short . . . Will we fail to see, in this terrible, perhaps even final hour, what lies at the heart of this conflict, and wherein lies the unique power that alone can lead to victory?

The Inner Man

The Most Essential Effort

What contemporary man lacks most is the inner life—the ability, and even simply the desire, to search the depths of his soul for that which is not subject to the vanity and vicissitudes of the external world.

For so long he has been harangued with the message that everything in the world and in his own self is determined by external conditions—or, as they say now, by economic, political, and social "structures"—he is so deafened by information, so beset by the words and ideas of others, and participation in everything external is so relentlessly demanded of him, that he has in fact become deaf to the inner world concealed within him. Our world lives beneath the sign of a truly demonic idea: to transform people into obedient robots, into beings who think identically, who react identically to everything, and who are consequently identically manageable.

And of course, this is why the creators of this society of robots oppose religion: because it is the last force in the world that stands in the way of the progressive depersonalization of man, his transformation into a socialized robot. God addresses each soul, and always in a unique way. In the Gospel there is a prevailing arithmetic, bearing no resemblance to our own, according to which one person is more valuable than ninety-nine, for each of us contains a unique world, and toward each of us a ray of divine love is directed.

Religion is never addressed to the crowd or, as they say today, to the "masses." The Bible knows nothing of "masses" or crowds—it knows only the individual, who is connected to other people not by "common interests," but by love, which orients each person toward the next, engendering the desire to encounter that person not superficially, but deep down inside, and to share in his inner world.

We have a wonderful Russian expression: "The eyes are the mirror of the soul." And indeed, there is something mystically joyful when people meet with their eyes, when if but for a second we are able to see in another not the external, but the internal. And if we love truly a person, then we do not say that we love that person's nose or ears or hands or whatever else—no, we love *that person*, we love the whole self of the person, and the deeper our love, the less we are able to discern why it is that we love that person.

And how characteristic it is, once again, that the ideology that is forced on us says not a word about love, but always only about hatred. It claims that people are divided into "classes" and that each person is determined not by his inimitable inner reality, but by his "class affiliation." What an evil and horrible lie about humanity! It is precisely because we live in this lie, which is gradually conquering millions of people, lulling them to sleep, and absorbing their consciousness, that we must begin the labor of returning to our inner world, to our soul.

"There is an entire world in your soul!"[1] said Tyutchev. And it is only by acquiring this inner world, by acquiring one's own soul, that one can understand the outer world and not become its slave. For only in this inner world does man encounter God—not himself, not what is "his own," but that light that, in the words of the prayer, "illumines every man who comes into the world."[2] God never addresses man in the noise and vanity of the external world—he speaks to him from within, he shines from within his soul, from the depths of his conscience. And so, as another poet has said, "close your eyes, and you will see; close your ears, and you will hear; immerse yourself in the blessed and luminous quiet, and you will find the deepest words"—and you will find that the empty and distorted words filling the air around us are a poor and deplorable caricature of human life.

Oh, if only contemporary man, if only each one of us could make the first and perhaps most difficult effort—to turn our glance and our hearing inward, to place between us and the noise of the world an invisible barrier,

[1]From the poem "Silentium!" (1829).
[2]From the prayer of the First Hour (which in turn refers to John 1.9).

so as not to see everything, not to hear everything, not to give everything access to the precious depths of our soul, so that it might purify itself from the lies that cling to it, and begin to seriously collect itself, to find its true form and orientation, its own harmony.

Love not the world, neither the things that are in the world (1 Jn 2.15)—this is what we read in the New Testament. This by no means suggests that we are called not to love God's world that is given to us by God; rather, we are called not to love that hateful and horrible caricature that we see around us. And by delving into the luminous depths of our soul, we will once more find that light and that joy that men have already ceased to discern in the world.

The effort to live the inner life here and now is what is most essential for men. Christ speaks about this effort in the Gospel when he exhorts each person to enter into the inner sanctum of his soul, and he promises that our Father who sees in secret will reward us openly (cf. Mt 6.18). This exhortation is constantly heard throughout the Gospel. For only a person who finds what is within him will conquer what is without.

Our civilization is oriented against the inner man, and our victory over this civilization must be a victory of the internal—that is, a victory of the spiritual, genuinely free person.

Mortal Combat

In one of my talks I spoke about how hard it is for contemporary man to understand religious institutions such as Great Lent. I said that it was instituted out of the self-evident but forgotten need of man to transform the familiar, busy flow of life, to delve deep into himself, into quiet and contemplation, and thereby to attempt to see his own life from a more profound and spiritual point of view. And, I said, it is because so little of this quiet, this contemplation, this inner reality is left in the contemporary world that we are especially in need of Great Lent, or more precisely of that to which it calls us.

Let us return today once more to our theme of the inner life. How important it is to understand that it is precisely this life that is under attack in our times, it is this life that is targeted for destruction by the world and the system of life that is rising up around us. In the New Testament there is a concept of *the inner man* (2 Cor 4.16). It is this inner man who is being condemned to death by contemporary society, which sees in him the greatest danger to itself. This society demands continual external activism; it demands that each person fully engage himself in this process, without reservation. An engine could not function efficiently if each cog and spring within it were to develop an inner freedom and start thinking independently. And yet in recent years the engine, the impersonally functioning machine, has come to be proclaimed as the ideal metaphor for human society and human life. To be clear: the ideal is not for everyone to function together, but for each to be dissolved in the functioning of an impersonal whole.

Thus, before our very eyes we see two diametrically opposed understandings of man locked in mortal combat. For centuries it was self-evident that anything social, every "togetherness," was inwardly subjected to the individual, that is, to the person, to each participant in this "togetherness." The self-evidence of this was rooted first of all in a religious intuition or understanding of man. In various languages, in various symbols, and at various levels, religion always affirmed one fact: man cannot be wholly reduced to any "whole." Everything on earth is temporary and conditional. Only the human person is eternal and not temporal, and therefore unconditional. Hence, in one way or another, everything in the world exists, every action is performed, so that each person might achieve and accept his calling and thereby become fully human.

People may protest: "How can that be? What about slavery? What about exploitation? What about the poverty and subjugation of millions of people in the past, their inability to obtain even the most elementary goods, the most primitive and basic human happiness?" I will answer: yes, all this certainly happened, but the best people in every place always fought against this. But in opposing these things they fought above all for the recognition of the eternal and absolute value of each person—they fought, in other words, against everything that transformed each person into a thing, rejecting or diminishing his "inner man." And regardless of how terrible and limited this world was, at the very heart of it were always heard these words, which constituted its moral law: "I came to liberate the prisoners into freedom" (cf. Lk 4.18–19). That is, I brought to each person the news of his royal and divine dignity.

This news, this understanding of man, was the measure of his entire life. But a great transformation took place, and I wonder whether we fully understand its full tragic and evil meaning. Someone came along and said, "Man has no royal or divine dignity, there is no eternity, there is nothing that raises him above the blind and impersonal laws of matter. He is merely a bubble, which is born one moment and then immediately disappears on the surface of an endless ocean. And this is why only one thing remains: in merging with the ocean, to find in this the sole purpose of our ephemeral existence." Furthermore: "Man has no purpose," they claimed. "Only humanity has a purpose: to wholly become a homogeneous collective, where no one will ever say 'I,' or look up at the sky, or sigh deeply for another destiny."

And this is why the central purpose of the society being formed around us is to fight against the inner man, and this means to oppose true freedom, and true creativity, but most of all to oppose religion. For every effort must be made to prevent man from encountering the poor and homeless Teacher, who would look into his eyes and say: "Know that you are more valuable than the whole world, that you have an eternal and priceless soul, and even if you gain the whole world but lose your soul, you will not be who you really are." This Teacher must be silenced; he is too dangerous for the engine, for he hinders its functioning, he disrupts the cogs and springs. If this encounter does not occur, then perhaps people will gradually forget about their "inner man," and will silence the voice within, which constantly calls them to the eternal, the profound, and the unutterable.

Let us listen to what we hear sung in the church during Great Lent: "My soul, my soul! Arise, why are you sleeping? The end is drawing near, and you are confounded, but be watchful . . ."[3] This "be watchful" is

---

[3] Kontakion of the Great Canon of St Andrew of Crete.

addressed to each of us. "The end is drawing near"—just a little more, and we will be unable to wake up, having been fully dissolved in the external, decisively transformed into cogs and springs. And what would it profit us if we were to receive this miserable earthly "happiness"—more tasty food, a bigger apartment, a better car, or any other commodity? Is it not about this completely external, completely dehumanized happiness that the poet Alexander Blok said, in one of the saddest of all Russian poems: "Be happy with your lives, quieter than water, lying lower than the grass! Oh, if you knew, dear children, the cold and terror of the coming days!"

This is what Great Lent is about. It looks into my soul and says: *What is a man profited, if he shall gain the whole world, and lose his own soul?* (Mt 16.26).

The Eternal
Childlikeness of God

The Restoration of Wholeness

Whosoever shall not receive the kingdom of God as a little child, he shall not enter therein (Mk 10.15). These extraordinary words we find in the Gospel. In general, the Gospel speaks much and often about children. "Be like children . . . for of such is the kingdom of heaven" (cf. Mt 19.14)—what does this mean?

The world in which we live, the civilization that determines all our opinions, our thoughts and tastes, is now hardly able to hear these words of the Gospel, to believe them, and, I would add, to *delight* in them. For this world and this civilization are decidedly and tragically serious, and proud of their seriousness.

Recently, succumbing to the general worldview, certain Christians in the West have begun to claim that since the world, as they say, has come of age, since man has matured to full adulthood, the old, "childish" religion no longer suits him: it needs to be reinterpreted in an adult manner. And in the mind of these "adult" Christians, this means casting religion in the language of contemporary science. In this way, even religiously-minded people have become ashamed of their childlike faith, and attempt to acclimate it to the "adult," "scientific" worldview of our civilization.

But perhaps we should first ask ourselves: what do these words of the Gospel mean, what is the meaning of this invitation to receive the kingdom of heaven like children? For surely it does not imply an outright rejection of maturity, knowledge, scientific development, and so forth. In that same New Testament we find so many invitations to maturity, to reach full stature in Christ (cf. Eph 4.13)! All of Christianity is one prolonged invitation to grow, develop, and seek the paths to the Perfect One. This is why I emphasize that this invitation of Christ to be like children can in no way be interpreted to mean that Christianity opposes knowledge, or that it desires to keep man in a dark and unenlightened state. And do we need to prove over and over again that that same science in the name of which people now denounce their faith, their religion, and their Christianity, actually began in monasteries? That the first universities were established by the Church? That at the dawn of our civilization practically all knowledge, or "book learning," as it was called, was inspired precisely by religion? Philosophy, physics, medicine—all evolved from this Christian inspiration. The words *doctor, master,* and *candidate* are taken from the Church's lexicon, for initially all academic degrees were awarded by the Church.

Therefore, let us dispense with that extremely superficial, unjust, and calumnious interpretation, according to which "to be like children" means to fundamentally remain at the lowest level of education and development, and consequently to fall victim to deceit and exploitation by self-serving people.

But here Christ says: *Whosoever shall not receive the kingdom of God as a little child, he shall not enter therein* (Mk 10.15). He continues: "Be like children, for of such is the kingdom of heaven." What is the essence of this childlikeness? What is its eternal and irrevocable meaning?

To answer this question correctly, it seems to me, we have to remind ourselves of the universally recognized fact that, for practically all people, childhood is always thought of as a "golden age," a "paradise lost," to which mankind ceaselessly returns in memory with joy and nostalgia, with love and sadness. In other words, in losing his childhood, a person suffers a loss that torments him for the rest of his life: he loses something for which he is perpetually searching, and to which his thoughts continually turn. What exactly is this? We can answer this question with one word—*wholeness.* This mystical quality allows children, and only children, to give themselves up fully to joy and to sadness. Thanks to it, a child becomes entirely wrapped up in whatever occupies him at the moment. For example, he might drop some favorite toy—and oh, the tragedy! He starts to cry, and his whole being is racked with inconsolable sadness. But then someone picks up the toy and returns it to him, and he holds it in his tiny hands, and immediately he becomes filled with joy, and his cheerful face shines with such fullness of life, beaming with such gratitude, that everything around him is illuminated by this light and radiates with this joy.

It is this fullness that we lose as we leave childhood behind. And from this point of view adulthood is a victory within us of duality, fragmentation, of inability to give ourselves fully and without reserve to any endeavor. This profound and all-consuming skepticism, this deep inner mistrust and its consequence—fear—gradually poison our consciousness. Just look around you, and you will see that our world and our civilization are built on skepticism, mutual mistrust, and fear, and that at their heart lies this sad "adult" fragmentation. And all of Christianity is none other than this continual call to look objectively at this joyless world, this adult sadness, in which everything is constantly fragmented and falls apart, poisoned by mistrust, enmity, and listlessness. *Seek ye first the kingdom of God* (Mt 6.33). What is this Kingdom of God, we ask? And we hear the answer: *Peace and joy in the Holy Spirit* (Rom 14.17). What is this joy and peace, which Christ says no one can take from us, if not a return to that childlike ability to live in wholeness?

And all Christian teaching is first and foremost about how to return to this wholeness, how to reestablish it in oneself. *Whosoever shall not receive the Kingdom of God as a little child, he shall not enter therein* (Mt 19.14). One who does not lovingly embrace another way of life at the depths of his own consciousness, with his heart and soul, and who does not consequently begin the slow and arduous return to it, will never understand the ultimate and most profound meaning of Christianity and will not hear its mystical proclamation of good tidings.

Why did Saint Seraphim of Sarov kneel for 1000 days and 1000 nights on a rock deep in the forest, if not to prepare his soul and purify his mind by this prolonged ascetic labor, in order to finally return to this genuine childlikeness, that is, to wholeness; if not in order once more to look upon God's world and to see each person in it as a source of joy? For it is with these words, "My joy!" that the saint greeted every person who came to him.

Yes, the world increases in technical knowledge, in its ability, as we say, to master the forces of nature. And all this will be for nothing, all this will fail to ultimately improve our life on earth, until each of us accepts into our hearts that which one famous poet, Paul Claudel, called "the eternal childlikeness of God."[1]

The Gift of Joy[2]

During these days of Pascha it is fitting to remind oneself and others about joy. It's a strange thing: one can read Marx's entire *Das Kapital*, and not one of its hundreds of pages contains the word *joy* even a single time. One can read Engels, and then Lenin, or any ideologue or promoter of this "comprehensive" and "scientifically-based" ideology, and find not one mention of joy, as if it were a matter so ridiculously childish that even to mention it is shameful. Nothing but "economic bases," "relations of production," "surplus value," "capital," "exploitation," "the masses" . . . As you read this material it suddenly becomes unbearably stifling, and you understand that the chief falsehood of this ideology is not this or that particular statement, but its astounding, profound joylessness. And then you clearly grasp something else: it is precisely due to its joylessness that this ideology cannot fathom or understand any of the gifts or descriptions of joy.

Herein lies the root of its hatred of religion. How typical that official anti-religious propaganda constantly seeks to prove that religion is something dark, joyless, full of fear and some kind of frightening afterlife. But this is a blatant lie! We have Chekhov, who, they always insist, was a non-believer, and for this reason can be trusted; yet Chekhov writes in his short story, *The Steppe*: "The elders, returning from church services, are always filled with radiant light." And every time he touches on the subject of religion, for example in his stories *The Student, In the Ravine, Holy Night*—within

---

[1]An expression of Paul Claudel (1868–1955), French poet, religious writer, dramatist, and diplomat.
[2]A Paschal sermon.

the sadness of his general worldview a small ray of joy begins to shine. Pay attention to the hymnography and prayers of the Church: not only do they speak of joy—they radiate this joy, and they shine with it: *This is the day which the Lord has made, let us rejoice and be glad in it* (Ps 117.24).

And so they write and write about religion, pulling it to pieces, accusing it of lies—and again, not a single word about joy. Is there any talk, for example, of Seraphim of Sarov, who greeted everyone who came to him with the words, "My joy"? Or of St Francis of Assisi, whose whole life was an anthem of rejoicing over the world, over God, and over man? At best, they refer to this joy as "childish naïveté," implying that it is unworthy of a serious, businesslike adult. But Christianity never tires of saying, "Be like children," meaning first and foremost the childlike capacity for sincere and pure joy. For a child, everything is a holiday, everything is joy—each morning, each ray of sunshine, each encounter, each object, each person. And so the question before us is whether this is simply naïveté and silliness, which should pass with adulthood, giving way to a "sober," "scientific" approach to life; or whether, alas, a person gradually loses and destroys in himself something to which he desires to return, but is no longer able.

Christianity affirms the latter. It teaches that the fall has led humanity to a loss of joy, and that salvation and the restoration of man lies in the return of this pure joy. *I bring you good tidings of great joy!* (Lk 2.10)—here is the beginning of the Gospel, the words of the angel to the shepherds on the night of Christmas. "Rejoice!"[3]—here is Christ's commandment to his disciples on the morning of Pascha. "The joy, which no one can take from you" (cf. Jn 16.22)—here is the promise of Christ. Finally, *with great joy* (Lk 24.52)—this is the state in which Christ's disciples returned from the mountain of his Ascension. Thus, joy is placed at the cornerstone of Christianity as its motive power and inspiration. But what is this joy all about, what is its essence?

To answer this question, let us return again to childhood and to children. For a child, joy is not something appended to his world—it is his

---

[3]The literal translation of the Greek and Slavonic word often translated as "Hail," as in the KJV; Fr Alexander here cites Mt 28.9 in the Russian Synodal Translation of the Scriptures, where the Russian in fact says "Rejoice!"

method of learning about the world. The child enters into a relationship with the world and masters it through joy. But then the same principle can be applied to the joy of an adult. As people of a "serious," "technological" era, we believe that we have only one organ of knowledge—namely, our mind. We dissect every object into its parts and we analyze, measure, and weigh it out, believing that in this way we will learn all about it. But this is not the limit of all knowledge. In love, for example we first delight in a person and only then do we begin to know them. One can even say that love itself is joy over a person or a thing, and that in this love the person, the thing, and everything in the world are discovered in ways that reason and scientific analysis can never know. It appears then that both love and joy are not some addendum that did not have to exist, but in their own way are the sole, inimitable route to knowledge and mastery. The Bible informs us that God not only created, but also blessed the world. And this blessing is in fact joy over the world, the joy that permeates all of life. And when we lose this joy, when we betray it in ourselves, the world becomes dark, impenetrable, cold, foreign, and ultimately unknowable. And our knowledge of the world becomes cold and dead. Even if we call it "precise" knowledge—it may indeed be precise, but it is inaccurate. Yes, we can know the weight and the size of the most beautiful painting in the world, we can learn about its colors and all its lines, but this will not open its beauty to us. Yet suddenly we can rejoice in it, and for us it becomes clear and transparent.

And so during these paschal days we must speak about joy. Pascha—this is indeed the entrance into the world of joy, its restoration to us; each time it is a new gift of celebration given to man. It is in this joy that millions of people continue to thrive, and indeed, no one shall take it from them!

Freedom

Pertaining to the Person

Today throughout every corner of the world there is a great deal of talk about liberation. This is probably one of the most popular concepts of our time. There is talk of liberation from oppressive totalitarian regimes, from party control, from ideological dogmatism; liberation from colonial imperialism, social conformism, and moralism; liberation from sexual taboos, and so on and so forth.

Man has suddenly felt himself to be a slave, a toy in the hands of various powers beyond his control, outside his power, and having felt this he has begun to yearn passionately for liberation. The chief danger of this aspiration, to my mind, is that the majority of people think of liberation almost exclusively in its negative sense—as the elimination of this or that obstacle to freedom, as a fight *against* something rather than *for* something. Remove colonialism and suddenly everything good will blossom; destroy the hateful leadership of the party and you'll have freedom; remove the pharisaic sexual taboos and a new age of pure, free love will dawn! Sadly, the majority of people are unaware that the concept of freedom cannot be exhausted exclusively by its negative aspects. In other words, it is not enough to remove or liquidate something in order for freedom to prevail. Karl Marx thought that if only private property were eliminated, and if the production mechanism were socialized, the leap "from the kingdom of determinism to the kingdom of freedom" would happen almost automatically. But by now we know that this is not the case: this illusory freedom has in fact turned out to be unprecedented serfdom and enslavement.

Thus, there is no more pressing issue, no more important theme, than at least a general elucidation not of the negative, but specifically of the positive meaning of this mysterious, elusive concept. After all, for centuries, like one bewitched, man has repeated the word *freedom* as a mantra, yet it remains an unattainable ideal. And this is naturally because man lacks the decisiveness and courage to look down into this abyss, to look straight into the face of freedom. Indeed, Dostoevsky stated unequivocally that man is afraid of this freedom and runs from it, for it is a yoke too heavy for his weak abilities; and hence he always instinctively seeks something to which he can submit, in the name of which he can renounce his freedom. Later, of course, man begins to rebel against that to which he submitted, but rebellion is not freedom. Rebellion is always a negation, never an affirmation.

And so it is time to remind ourselves and others about the source of this elusive concept of freedom. For thousands of years man knew nothing about it; even the great ancient civilizations did not grasp it. Ancient Greece, for example, understood freedom as the political independence of one city from other cities, of one nation from other nations, but had no qualms about the institution of slavery. Ancient Rome established an exemplary system of rights, but as soon as a handful of strange people denied the divinity of the emperor, it threw them to the lions and nailed them to crosses. No, the concept of freedom was not nearly as simple and transparent as the contemporary prophets and ideologues of various kinds of "liberation" claim it was. For this concept is a paradoxical one, and this means that it cannot be derived implicitly from our empirical experience. Do we even need to prove that in nature itself we find no freedom? Nature lies in the grip of an absolute determinism, an iron law of cause and effect, and all of science is dedicated to understanding and defining this law.

But then, if man is only a component of nature, if he himself is a purely natural being, he cannot possibly have any pretensions to freedom. In this case he too, albeit in a more complex way, is subject to the same law of cause and effect—a law that does not tolerate any exceptions—and consequently all his talk of freedom is nothing but empty babbling with no inner principle.

I realize that many will shrug their shoulders when they hear that the only source of genuine freedom is the religious understanding of man—that is to say, that understanding that does not reduce him to nature alone. If we want to move from a negative understanding of freedom to a positive one, we must turn our gaze to that place where for the first time the word *freedom* took on new meeting and was filled with unprecedented power—to the Gospel and to the teaching of Christ.

We hear these mystical words of Christ in the Gospel: *Ye shall know the truth, and the truth shall make you free* (Jn 8.32). And the Apostle Paul, that disciple of Christ who did more than anyone to ensure that the teaching of Christ would be disseminated throughout the world, that it would reach people of different cultures and psychological mindsets—this disciple also reduced the whole teaching of Christ to the preaching of freedom: *Stand fast therefore in the liberty wherewith Christ hath made us free, and be not entangled again with the yoke of bondage* (Gal 5.1).

What can this word *freedom* in the Gospel possibly mean, what is its connection to the truth and to the understanding of man as a creature in need of salvation, which we find throughout all of Holy Scripture? And yet it is specifically in the Gospel that the word *freedom*, formerly understood in strictly national or state terms, was first applied to the individual human person.

It is this source of freedom in our world that we will speak of in our next talk.

The Source and Essence

In our last talk we spoke about freedom, and we came to the conclusion that there really is no freedom in the so-called "natural" order of things. Moreover, if we are able to understand this order, if we are able to gradually erect an edifice of knowledge and science, it is precisely because everything in it is determined by the law of causation, by the dependence of one set of phenomena on another, on the absence of the unexpected—that is, the absence of freedom. This is why we pose the question: where did this undying hope for freedom come from, this freedom that man continues to dream about, and for which he is willing to make every sacrifice?

Furthermore, what comprises this idea of freedom, what is its essence, on what does it thrive? And the only answer we could make to this question was that the concept of freedom and the thirst for freedom have their roots and origin in religion.

I am fully aware that this statement may seem strange and primitive to people who are educated in the certainty that the word *religion* is the chief synonym of slavery—people who are systematically taught that real freedom begins with "liberation" from religion. This is why I am aware of how difficult it is to convince a person of the opposite view—that a tragedy has occurred, a criminal confusion of concepts; that freedom is spoken about and raised as a standard by people who not only do not believe in freedom but in whose worldview there is no place for freedom, nor can there be; and that these regard as slavery that sole source and sole understanding of life, of the world, and of man that gives rise to the eternally brilliant vision of freedom and the thirst to realize that vision.

But however difficult it may be, the attempt must at least be made. Let us therefore begin at the beginning, and emphasize once more that we are speaking here not about religion in general, for this phenomenon is complex and multifaceted and it has had and can have many different roots. Our concern here is the religious worldview and understanding that is already contained in the Bible, but which finds its ultimate realization and expression in Christianity.

I maintain and I will try to prove that at the very heart of this worldview lies the proclamation and promise of freedom. Furthermore, I maintain that outside of this worldview the concept of freedom not only makes no sense, but, strange and tragic as this may sound, it becomes one source of outright slavery.

What is the meaning of the biblical story of man—the symbolic narrative of his creation? Clearly, it is not history, it is not biological or physical facts, but rather a spiritual description of man, a fundamental and decisive revelation about him. And what is this revelation? It is that man is free and called to freedom, and that the realization of this freedom is his purpose and calling in the world, a world thoroughly subject to natural determinism.

Yes, herein lies the whole problem, as clearly shown in the biblical story: freedom cannot arise from *below*, it cannot come from nature, for there is no freedom in nature. Freedom can only come from *above*, and only if there is a free and creative absolute Spirit, only if the world of nature and determinism is governed by a divine freedom that is itself determined by nothing and no one. Herein lies the meaning of the biblical words, *Let us make man in our image, after our likeness* (Gen 1.26): man is from below and from above simultaneously. On the one hand, man is earth, matter, and flesh, thoroughly subject to the law of causation and the law of determinism, as religion is well aware: *For dost thou art and unto dust shalt thou return* (Gen 3.19). And this is precisely the one thing that the materialist sees in him and to which he reduces him, and yet this same materialist promptly gives voice to musings on freedom. But, I repeat, it is impossible for freedom to come from below, for below there is no freedom. This is why, on the other hand, man is from *above*. He is the image and likeness of the free divine Spirit, he is the bearer of freedom in the world of nature. He is not only earthen and earthly; he is also *spirit*.

The biblical Christian religion begins, therefore, by acknowledging that man is a complex being, whereas every anti-religious philosophy seeks to simplify him. Yes, Christianity says that humanity has fallen. But it understands this fall, it derives the very possibility of this fall not from below, but from that which is highest in man—from his freedom. For only what is exalted is capable of falling, and only the fall of something exalted is considered a tragedy. If a clay pot falls to the ground and breaks into pieces, this is no tragedy; but if a priceless vase falls and breaks, this is a tragedy.

Yes, man has always fallen and continues to fall, but for him alone in all the world is this fall a tragedy. For him alone this fall evokes the question of freedom. Here alone a great longing for freedom arises, and all of life becomes a thirst and a search for freedom.

But now we must ask about the content of this freedom. Freedom from what? Freedom in what? We are so accustomed to this word that we have become desensitized to it. I spoke in my previous tallk about the fact that we tend to give the word "freedom" an almost exclusively negative connotation, to think of it in terms of liberation from something, but in the

Christian and religious understanding freedom is not just liberation from someone or something: freedom is the very substance of life, freedom is the filling of a person with something. And this something, a something that bears within itself true and authentic freedom, once again comes to us from the religious, biblical Christian understanding and intuition of man.

We are called to freedom in the name of a host of ideologies, but in fact—and we will return to this later—nearly every ideology ends by enslaving humanity to dead dogma, dead systems, dead premises. The freedom on this earth, in this world, inevitably turns to slavery. This is why it is insufficient to focus on the negative understanding of freedom as liberation *from* something. Liberation in the name *of* something, then? But of what? What is the ultimate truth, the ultimate fullness of freedom? We will attempt to answer these questions in our next talk.

Temporary Liberation or Fundamental Change?

In my previous talks I spoke about the religious or, more precisely, Christian roots and origins of freedom. Despite all the claims of the sworn enemies of religion, there exists no other basis for freedom than the Christian understanding of man and the world.

Today let us listen to and consider this assertion more closely. For I know that it sounds like a paradox not only for the open enemies of religion, but what is far sadder, all too frequently for religious people themselves. Many of them have become so accustomed to reducing religion simply to obedience, to blind faith, to the mindless preservation of obscure traditions and customs, that they no longer understand what obedience means. They do not hear the full depth of the apostolic proclamation: *Stand fast therefore in the liberty wherewith Christ hath made us free, and be not entangled again with the yoke of bondage* (Gal 5.1). It would never occur to them that the very obedience, the very faithfulness and self-sacrifice that lie at the heart of Christianity are inseparable from this proclamation of freedom.

But first, what kind of freedom does Christ proclaim in the Gospel, or rather freedom from what? Here freedom is contrasted to slavery, but this slavery is understood first and foremost as man's enslavement to sin and to death. Again, for us, who understand sin at best as a violation some rule, as some crime against the law, this idea of enslavement to sin is simply incomprehensible. The overwhelming majority of us consider ourselves to be relatively good people—neither better nor worse than others, as we typically say. As for shortcomings, various little sins, moral rationalizations, slip-ups—all of this we consider quite normal, simply in the order of things. After all, who hasn't done all this? We are all human, and like all people we are weak and sinful. But in the end we are really not bad people.

Do we need to demonstrate that in this atmosphere of self-satisfaction and moral minimalism Christianity makes no sense, and if it does, then it is not the sense we find in the Gospels, but that which we ascribe to it ourselves? For Christianity understands sin not as a minor transgression, a shortcoming, or even a fall—no, it understands sin as that inner alienation from God, from his truth and spiritual law, which finds its expression first of all in our self-satisfaction and moral minimalism. The sin is not that we fall and commit certain sins, but that we no longer notice our real falls, we no longer notice the fallenness of our life, that life that we consider normal and natural. And it suffices to compare our petty self-satisfaction and our partial acknowledgment of our individual "shortcomings" with the sense of sin and the wail of repentance and entreaty that pours out from literally every page of the Bible, to be convinced of the incommensurability of the two.

Basically, we do not sense and acknowledge our slavery to sin, our subjection to sin, and therefore we no longer seek freedom from it. As a bird reared in a cage does not fly away to freedom even if the door is left open, so we no longer recognize that our whole life is crippled, poisoned, and perverted by sin, that we are not the kind of persons we can and ought to be.

The same could be said about man's subjection to death. However much we fear death, however we shudder in the face of it, we consider it a fully natural and normal occurrence, one of those self-evident laws of nature, in which we are even taught to see a kind of "wisdom" and to which we are always called to submit. Man is mortal, and that is all, they say. It's unpleasant, but what can you do? Just accept it and come to terms with it, and at the same time concoct some totally irrelevant words about finding rest at last. But how then can we hear the Gospel proclamation: *The last enemy that shall be destroyed is death* (I Cor 15.26), and that Christ came to free us precisely from this terrible enslavement to death? What can be done with slaves who have become so accustomed to their own slavery that they no longer perceive it as slavery, no longer know that they should be and could be free? What can be done with slaves who, having forgotten genuine freedom, play a game that they call "freedom," as if moving from one prison cell to another could be called "liberation"?

But Christianity says that as long as man is subject to sin and to death, as long as he reconciles himself to them and does not sense their awful, inescapable power, all man's discussions about freedom are illusory and empty. It comes down simply to a question of how long our chain is, by which we are all attached to the same post. Thus, only by renouncing this enslavement can one come to an understanding of freedom. For Christianity, this understanding does not presuppose some kind of temporary liberation from this or that dependency, but above all a fundamental inner transformation of human consciousness, and therefore of the whole of human life. For Christianity, this external freedom, or more precisely that which we called "freedom" and which is always temporary and transitory, is unthinkable without the inner liberation of man, without reclaiming his innate capacity for freedom. For it is precisely this capacity for freedom, this thirst for authentic freedom, freedom from sin and death, that has destroyed in him the enslavement of which we have just been speaking. Thus, before applying the Christian understanding of freedom to our mundane concerns and needs, it is essential to fully grasp the Gospel proclamation about the One who reveals this freedom to us.

What Truly Liberates?

Y e shall know the truth, and the truth shall make you free (Jn 8.32), Christ says in the Gospel. What truth must a person discover to be set free, and how can this truth liberate him? These are the questions with which to approach freedom in the Christian understanding, or rather freedom in general. For, as we have tried to show in previous talks, freedom does not have, nor can it have, any source or root besides the Christian perception of the world and man.

There are numerous ideas of freedom, and each one associates itself with one truth or another. For example, Marxism avows that the king-dom of freedom will ensue when men understand the mechanism of eco-nomic realities. And even though endless chapters of Marx's *Das Kapital* are devoted to this mechanism, very little is said about this kingdom of freedom, and then only towards the very end. And so the form and content of this freedom remain unclear.

Another example is the German philosopher Schopenhauer.[1] On the basis of Hindu wisdom he claims that freedom will come only when man understands the mechanism of his own will, and that when he does under-stand it he will simply reject it. The truly free man does not desire anything, for, according to Schopenhauer, the will and its desires are at the root of slavery and suffering.

But now, on the heels of the ponderous theories of the last century, we have contemporary existential philosophers who also affirm freedom. They insist that this freedom will come when man rejects all predetermined, externally imposed truth about himself, when his life becomes a chain of non-predetermined choices and he himself will constantly create his own freedom as if from nothing. No matter how much these existential philosophers write in defense of their theories, it remains unclear how a person can exclude himself from the law of causation by which the world lives, and attempt to create himself. It must be said that the literary works of these existentialists (for example, *Roads to Freedom* of Jean-Paul Sartre) do

---

[1] Arthur Schopenhauer (1788–1860), German irrationalist philosopher.

not actually provide any substantial answer. They show us people cast this way and that, decidedly not knowing what to do with themselves, accepting abstract, contradictory theories and continually entangled in the seaweed of vague concerns, emotions, and desires. The resulting free man turns out to be a slave of an empty and unnecessary freedom.

One could continue this list indefinitely. Each recipe for freedom is founded on some partial truth, but the freedom that comes from it has no substantial basis.

It would seem at first glance that Christianity, with its call to "know the truth and the truth will make you free," adds nothing new to the search for freedom. But that which we propose here is immeasurably far from the abstract doctrine of freedom. For the liberating truth about which Christ speaks is not a new philosophy or ideology, but rather Christ himself, who said of himself: *I am the way, the truth, and the life* (Jn 14.6). Here the truth appears not in words, but in a living and unique Person, a living and unique Hypostasis. Subsequently, freedom here is no longer defined, but revealed. The one who utters these words is himself free. And the entire Gospel is essentially none other then the revelation in the world of a fully free Person, and hence the revelation of perfect freedom.

So how do we understand Christ's freedom? Does it consist of some liberty, in keeping with our perverse concepts of freedom, to constantly change our mind, to live by our own will, to serve ourselves as the center of the universe? Of course not. For Christ's entire earthly life was constant service to people, an absolute giving of himself, a fullness of love. Or does his freedom perhaps consist of seeking our own happiness and security, avoiding suffering in every way? But no, for Christ willingly gives himself up to humiliation, to suffering, and to death. What then does Christ's freedom consist of? First of all, it consists of his perfect inner wholeness, his absolute independence of evil and fear, his being filled with light and with love. The freedom of Christ is not an empty vessel into which we can pour new contents; rather, it is the freedom of a Person who is fully and completely in control of his own life, and who fully and completely gives it over to that which alone is capable of making every life truthful—namely, love. This is why Christ's freedom does not contradict obedience, faith, sacrifice—everything that we normally contrast to freedom and which in the name of freedom we try to evade. For in the final analysis—and this is the Christian proclamation of freedom—only love can liberate! And it liberates because the one who loves offers himself to his beloved not by compulsion, but freely, precisely because he loves. And his obedience is free, and his sacrifice is free, making this the highest action of freedom.

Know the truth, and the truth will make you free. For us Christians this means: know Christ and you will see true freedom. Know Christ, and give yourselves to that to which he gave himself, for only in this giving will you become truly free.

A High and Difficult Ideal

Our contemporary man today is being flattered and deceived; his mind and conscience are being lulled to sleep, and as they are lulled they become enslaved. The fundamental and worst deception lies in the affirmation that man is *already* free, is no longer a slave, and hence he no longer needs to search or strive for some other freedom, some other liberation. The struggle for freedom is a thing of the past, and all that remains is the "scientifically grounded" organization of a free life under the leadership of those who are best equipped with the "most progressive" ideology. And lulled to sleep by this flattery and deceit, man begins to repeat: "I am free, I will live better and better." What a horrible, pitiful picture! For a slave who knows that he is a slave can dream of freedom, can love it as his ultimate desire, as the meaning of life. But the slave who considers himself to be already free because he has been duped by his leaders—this is the epitome of slavery, for it is accepted by one's conscience as the norm. And it is in this deceit that we see the horror of our time, all its immense inhumanity.

Alas, throughout human history there has been much slavery—far too much. But never, it seems, did a slave-driver think it possible to convince his slaves: "Your chains are your freedom; therefore, praise the life that you have, delight in your absolute joy, and go around proclaiming that you are the freest of men!" The lot of all slaves has always been to toil in silence and dream of freedom, but never to sing anthems to slavery. Indeed, from what have we been liberated? From the unbridled power of our leaders, from their directives and orders? No! From being forbidden to think, to speak, to write, and to preach what we wish, what we consider to be the truth? No! From injustice and cruelty? No! From the fear that tomorrow's command will countermand yesterday's, and that the new program will abolish the old truths? No!

So where is the basis of this official happiness, which is forced upon citizens as a duty and a requirement? We see before us a horrible deception—a perversion of words, a gradual and deliberate transformation of their meaning, contrary to what they meant for centuries. This is seen most clearly in the example of the most basic terms. Thus, slavery is now being called "freedom," and freedom, "slavery." When a person accepts without reservation the ideology imposed on him, rejecting in advance his right to criticize its bases and seek another ideology, they do not call this slavery, but "freedom." But when he adheres to the command to search constantly, to test all things, and to hold onto only that which is actually good and just, they do not call this freedom, but "slavery."

This lie is succeeding, and this is the horror of our time. It is succeeding because too many of us have been persuaded that man does not live for freedom, but for other goals; not in order to remain human, but in order to be transformed into a cog in an enormous impersonal machine. The very idea of freedom as the ultimate truth is vanishing. Do we even have the strength to remember it and to desire it once more? I am speaking of the most profound freedom, the freedom to search for truth independently and to live by it in good conscience, freely engendering it in our lives.

And my question continues: does such freedom exist? Is it even needed by mankind? To answer this, it behooves us to approach the question of freedom from a Christian standpoint. It behooves us because nothing has ever been so frequently and so stubbornly identified with blind dogmatism, with unreserved subjection to power and authority, as Christianity. The war on Christianity as the enslavement of man, man's liberation from it as from some kind of slavery—this is the fundamental principle of that ideology that in our day is proclaimed to be "scientifically grounded." But what does Christianity really say about freedom? If we were able to openly study Christian teaching, to acquire the books of Christian teachers and philosophers, it would be easy to see that the teaching about man as a free being is the cornerstone of all Christianity. Christianity is rooted in the teaching of Christ, and the whole Gospel account of Christ proclaims that he desires only the free acceptance of his teaching, and that means that he recognizes man's capacity for freedom. The very image of Christ is the greatest proof that freedom, in the Christian worldview, is an essential property of man.

However, the matter is not limited to the free acceptance of Christ's teachings—that is, the freedom to accept or to reject them. For this freely accepted teaching is, I repeat, the teaching that freedom is the fundamental meaning of all human life. This teaching is not an abstract scientific truth, not a rationalization, but an invitation to a new and free and loving communion of man with everything that exists. If the chief reality and horror of slavery lies in fear, then the essence and joy of freedom lies in love, the most free and liberating of all human feelings. And this is why the Apostle Paul, wishing to express the whole essence of Christianity in one appeal, in one commandment, says: *Stand fast in the liberty wherewith Christ hath made us free* (Gal 5.1).

But though man is created for freedom, this does not mean that he cannot lose it. The whole tragedy of human life, in the Christian understanding, is that that man is capable of freely choosing slavery, of rejecting and not desiring freedom. And it is this rejection of freedom that in Christianity is called *sin*. Sin is subjection to what must not be obeyed; it is love for what does not deserve love. Why does man reject freedom and give himself over to slavery? Christianity answers that it is because freedom is a difficult and high calling; because it destines a person to struggle with himself, to constant effort and searching, making his life a "narrow path"; because it is always easier to subject oneself, to hand one's freedom over to someone else and to live without thinking about anything.

Yes, the Christian understanding of man and freedom is lofty and difficult. This is why this teaching is hated by all those who want humans to be servile and blindly obedient. Desiring to see in human beings only the tools of their own ambitions, they slander Christianity and, most importantly, they conceal the truth about it, substituting for it their own caricature. But truth can never be hidden or enslaved, for truth is always free.

The Law of Brotherhood

"The Best on Earth"

The writer Rozanov has this passage in his book *Fallen Leaves*: "A wonderful person—specifically in the sense of . . . 'kind' or 'generous'—is the best on earth. And assuredly the world was created in order that we might see him."[1]

The moment you consider this phrase, you suddenly understand what is so terribly lacking in our world, in our whole modern civilization, in the very air of our time. What is lacking is precisely this simple kindness, which is expressed in sympathy, compassion, commiseration, and empathy. Our world is saturated with angry debates about principles, programs, and ideologies, and not one of them fails to set as its goal or claim to offer salvation for mankind. One can truly say that there has been no more "principled" era than ours in the history of mankind. And yet we find that in the midst of all these principles, all these claims to hold the key to universal happiness, there simply is no place for human kindness—no place, because none has been left in the name of "principles," in the name of the salvation of humanity and the solution of all the world's problems. Everyone hates everyone else, and the principled attitude of the world has become universal hatred.

In the same essay Rozanov continues: "Of what use is reasoning? Here is an example. The day had passed. Everyone in the house was dog-tired; I was looking through some books near the doorway while Nadia (our thin, pale servant, married with one child) was finishing washing the windows. My wife hobbled over to the window, grabbed Nadia's neck with her right,

[1]Rozanov, *Fallen Leaves*, 328.

good arm, drew her head to her and kissed her as if she were her own child. Frightened, she exclaimed: 'What are you doing, mistress?!' Weeping, my wife replied: 'It is God who sent you to us. And your health is poor, and you have misfortune at home, your husband is sick, he is languishing in the country without work; and your child has a hernia; and you are constantly working and you never leave us.' And she went away, without receiving an answer or any reaction."

Rozanov continues: "There is a form of work and service where there is neither lord nor landowner, neither master nor slave, but rather everyone does his work: they form a harmony, they work simply because it is necessary. Take a crate, some nails, and clothes: the clothes would fall all over the place without the crate, the crate could not be assembled without nails, but even the nails are not what is most important, because it is all for the clothing, while on the other hand the crate contains everything and is greater than everything." Rozanov concludes: "Pushkin understood this, when he did not set himself one iota above 'Captain Mironov' from the Belogorsky fortress: the captain was quite at ease with Pushkin, and Pushkin enjoyed being near the captain. Yet how little this is understood today, when everything is crushed by hatred."

Indeed, Rozanov is indicating or hinting at something that is now entirely incomprehensible to contemporary man. Reading Rozanov's essay, our contemporary man will exclaim with all the authority of his worldly ideologies, laced with worldly principles: "Exploitation, rejection of personal dignity, social inequality, and all under the guise of oily paternalism," and so on in that vein, and will be quite pleased with himself. He has expressed himself as a principled man, he has pinpointed the root of all evil, he has brought everything into the sphere of principle. It would not occur to him that all principles, no matter how justifiable they may be, are of no value without this simple kindness—a kindness that does not differentiate between the important and the unimportant, but rather covers everything with its warmth and its sympathy.

This is why all of Christian teaching is built on the commandment of love for one's neighbor. And here, in this commandment, lies the fundamental difference between Christianity and all the contemporary "principled" ideologies. These same ideologies are in essence built on love for a distant ideal, and therefore reject love for the neighbor who is nearby. The Gospel and Christianity never speak about any far-off goals, or about world problems in universal terms. Christ sees a person and takes pity on him; his friend Lazarus dies, and Christ weeps over him; at a simple wedding the wine runs short, and Christ gets involved. Everything in the Gospels is about this love for neighbor, about this involvement.

"How utterly unpromising!" people will say. "What a lack of broader principles! Don't you know that becoming involved in the sadness of one person does not solve the question of the sadness of all people? Is it possible to devote oneself to private problems, without raising everything to the level of the general and the fundamental above all else?" Very well; the time has come not to be ashamed of answering this question as follows: do you not see that all your ideologies and principles, which are supposed to lead to happiness, have now been filling the world with blood, suffering, and sadness for centuries, and they have not made one person happy? But each time a simple act of kindness is performed on earth, the happiness and joy from this spreads far and wide. And this is why Rozanov is right when he says of the kind individual that the whole world was created that we might see him. Here, and only here, in this personal kindness, is the victory of good over evil; here, and only here, kindness is not some idea or principle, but a living reality, experience, and power. And this is why Christianity does not preach an abstract set of "Christian principles," ideas, and programs, but rather it preaches and reveals Christ—that is, the image of a living Person whose entire life, entire being, and entire vocation comprise this abundant kindness.

"Jesus looked and had compassion . . ." (cf. Mt 9.36; Mk 6.34; Lk 7.13)—these are the words that we constantly encounter in the Gospels. And when they asked him who this neighbor is whom we must pity, love, and include in our lives with empathy and compassion, he pointed to the stranger, a living and concrete person, who at this very moment, here and now, needs our help, participation, and kindness. This is why all our earthly ideologies vanish into nonexistence, delegitimizing themselves one after another, and we are left with the reigning image of that wonderful Person about whom Rozanov said that the whole world was created in order that we might see him.

Brotherhood—Truth and Law

Again a letter of greeting arrives, and again the joyous feeling of connection, the consciousness that regardless of distance and obstacles set up by people, it still exists—that brotherly unity, that common understanding. If we read the newspapers, listen to the radio, and follow politics, we can get the feeling that the world lives in some kind of hopeless lack of understanding, that each of us is surrounded by a thick, impermeable wall. And perhaps what is most important now is to make the effort to return to that simple, bright idea that for almost 2000 years has been tirelessly repeated in the Gospel: that division, mutual hostility, and antagonism among people is not the norm, not the law, but sin, which must be cast off like any other evil.

What does Christ say? "You have only one Father in heaven, and you are all brothers" (cf. Mt 23.8–9). The words *brother* and *brotherhood* are of key importance in the Gospel, and that is why it is such a joy to find in a letter from an anonymous listener the greeting, "Dear brother!" For this is not simply some sentimental expression, but a particular understanding of the world, of life, and of people. Our Russian thinker Nikolai Federovich Federov once wrote that the goal of life is the reestablishment of broken brotherhood, and he wrote that the lack of brotherhood was the chief evil in the world. Long before the faithful acquired the name Christians, they referred to each other as "brothers."

What is this feeling? What gives it its unique, incomparable depth? It is founded on the intuition that people are connected to one another, that they belong to each other not because of common interests or everyday interactions, but irrespective of them, and in fact prior to all this; so that it is not life with its incidental events that connects us in various relationships, but rather life itself is the revelation, the joyful and life-giving realization of a unity that already exists. I do not choose my brother—he is given to me, he is already a part of my life. We certainly find this in family life, and the irreplaceable atmosphere of family life naturally has its roots in this commonality of life, a commonality that is a given and a gift. The warmth of family life, the warmth of brotherly unity warms all of life, and casts its light and its radiance upon everything. My brother may choose a path in life entirely different from mine, but he remains my brother, because that is who he was even before we each chose our life's path.

Christ, however, tells us that brotherhood is not simply within families, but rather it is a law and a truth of human nature, for we are all brothers. This means that each of us is given to the other, and the other is given to me. And suddenly this "other" comes into my life. Life has brought us together, seemingly by chance, and by this same chance it could pull us apart. And it is possible for me not to notice the other, so that he simply remains "someone else," someone far away and indifferent. But Christ teaches us that in fact in each encounter something else takes place. He says, "You have received your brother" (cf. Mt 18.15). This means that in each encounter, in each connection between people, we are given an opportunity to overcome our alienation and lack of understanding, this fragmentation of life, and that this opportunity is the pledge of the miraculous reestablishment of brotherhood and unity. For those who are brought together by life are already brothers, already sojourners on the same path to the same goal. And this goal is the kingdom of love and kindness, which the Gospel calls the Kingdom of God.

Such is my answer to the unexpected greeting of an anonymous listener. We may never meet, but if we look up at the sky, at the world, and at people with the same faith, hope, and love; if we know the mystery of the joy of life, the mystery of love—then we are brothers, however far apart and differently we may live. And this brotherhood of ours is more powerful than all misunderstandings and divisions. And it will conquer the world.

Martin Buber: The Philosophy of Dialogue

Recently the famous Jewish religious mystic and philosopher, Martin Buber, died.[2]

His ideas have had an influence far beyond the confines of the Jewish world. Well-known Christian philosophers and theologians such as Paul Tillich and Reinhold Niebuhr have openly and repeatedly stated that their understanding of Christianity was deepened and renewed by the creative mind of Buber. One of our thinkers, Berdyaev, considered Buber to be one of his own teachers, and he is possibly the only person to ever write about Buber in Russian.

What is the content of Buber's teaching and why has he become so compelling for contemporary man? In 1923 his book *I and Thou* was published with the subtitle: *The Philosophy of Dialogue*. One can say that in this title and subheading we find the whole of Buber's thinking, which he did not cease to develop until his last days, not only theoretically, but in his entire life. He was not afraid to express viewpoints antithetical to those of his contemporaries. Thus, while living out his latter years in Israel, he was not afraid to openly denounce the death sentence of Eichmann.[3]

Buber begins with the contrast of two relational juxtapositions, terming the first "I—thou" and the second "I—it" or "I—that." According to Buber, these are the two fundamental institutions of man's relation to his surrounding reality. Buber teaches that the world is given to man first of all as *it* or *that*. This means that it is something exterior, impersonal, as an undifferentiated mass of phenomena, relationships, and reactions that affect a person, and which a person can in turn affect, but which remain essentially, as we said before, exterior and alien. And the whole purpose of human life—more than that, the only process that enables man to realize himself—lies in the transformation of this external, this alien and impersonal, into the "thou"

[2]Martin Mordecai Buber (1878–1965)—Jewish religious mystic, whose ideas closely resemble early existentialism.

[3]Adolph Eichmann (1906–1962)—SS officer, one of the authors of the plan for destroying the Jewish population of Europe in the years of World War II. In the postwar years he was in hiding in Argentina, but he was captured by Israeli forces and taken to Jerusalem for trial, which ended with his being sentenced to death.

and, consequently, into that with which one can enter into dialogue, into personal communion. Buber says that to the extent that I become more myself, I begin to say "thou." This means that the real life of a human being begins when he enters into a living and personal relationship with the world. As long as the world or another person simply remains "he" or "it," I remain alone. But in my solitude it is impossible for me to become myself. Only in an authentic encounter can a man's fundamental solitude be overcome and destroyed, and he receives life as communion and dialogue, and not merely as some external, mechanical interaction. "Thou" opens to me the door to the profound reality of another, and likewise to him, to that "thou," my own reality is revealed, my inner world, my "I," and it is possible indeed to affirm that he lives in me, and I in him. Thus, this interrelationship of separated individuals and realities, this real and living encounter with one another, is itself the miracle of human life—the miracle in which man becomes truly and ultimately human.

First and foremost, Buber applies this fundamental intuition about life as encounter and communion to religion. For him, God is the eternal "Thou" who can never be understood or encountered in the relationship of "I—it" or "I—that." No science, no abstract speculation can sense God, much less prove anything about him. God is not the "object" of human thought, he is not even that "Absolute" that philosophy sometimes sets as the root source of all that exists. As Buber writes, God is that Being whom I meet directly, but at the same time he is also that One whom I cannot define but only encounter. Man meets God in each of his encounters with reality, to the degree that this encounter occurs in categories of "I—thou." In other words, God is the One who in this world, in this life, makes everything deeply personal, who destroys the darkness of impersonal objective existence and transforms it into personal encounter, into joy, into communion and possession.

Of course, Buber's writings are forbidden by the official ideology, which constantly and loudly proclaims its "scientific approach" and "objectivity." And I am convinced that in some sense not one contemporary thinker so clearly pronounces the death sentence on this ideology as does Buber. For in his every word, and perhaps chiefly by the incredible joyfulness of his thought, he expresses and formulates that which we vaguely and often unconsciously feel but are unable to express. And this, namely, is that the chief and most horrifying and inescapable lie of the official worldview lies in this: in its absolute inability to go beyond the category of "I—it" and to see the "I—thou" experience, to experience it as a breakthrough into genuine life and genuine communion. For science, which the official worldview has allegedly set as the cornerstone of all life and all knowledge, fundamentally belongs to the sphere of "I—it" or I—that." And this means approaching everything as an external and impersonal object; it means a world of horrifying impersonality, and consequently of terrible and almost metaphysical banality. This ideology will never understand or acknowledge that there is no less value than the scientific picture of the world in the encounter that occurs every time one person looks into the eyes of another, that mystical, incomparable, and inexplicable transformation of "it" and "that" into "thou"—a transformation in which we find our true life with its happiness and joy, love and inspiration. All of this remains inaccessible to science—just as science cannot and need not know that each moment of human life is meaningful only to the extent that it is transformed into encounter and communion.

Oh, this does not at all imply that each encounter has to be outwardly significant! It can be merely a sunlit leaf that catches one's eye, or it can be a passing smile, or it can be an encounter with the living God. The important thing is that in each such encounter we break out of our solitude, out of our universal nostalgia, toward the unique and inimitable that is in everything, each fragment of existence, and that alone forms its true reality. And it is the joy of this breakthrough that forms the very foundation of the religious worldview. All Buber's philosophy describes this, and out of this comes the definitive influence of his philosophy on contemporary religious thought.

Labor

Alienation or Transformation?

The theme of labor is a topic on which believers and unbelievers have something to say to each other. Here there are so many passions, mutual misunderstandings, and accusations that one must have the ability and desire to honestly, openly, and freely delve into the heart of the matter, overcoming the many cheap and superficial accusations of the past. This question is the more relevant in that it is always sharply and painfully posed by life itself. In the matter of labor, clearly not all is well: for people to labor conscientiously and increase their productivity is proclaimed as the foundation of the whole grand edifice of the new society, yet in real life this "liberating" labor must always be forced on a person.

But this practical collapse of all lofty theories of labor does not prevent state ideologues from blaming religion for misunderstanding and underestimating the role of labor. "The Christian religion," writes one of them, "evaluates work in a completely different way: according to the Bible, labor is God's punishment for original sin. God has doomed all the generations of men to earn their daily bread by the sweat of their brow, by hard work. The Orthodox Church has always considered service to God to be the most exalted activity. It facilitated the departure of people from socially useful activities, creating thousands of monasteries in which monks devoted their whole lives to fruitless prayers."

Such, according to state ideology, is the Christian approach to work. But is it really? Let's start with the facts. Even if we confine ourselves to Russian history, the falsehood of this accusation is obvious, for even at the dawn of Russian history it would have been difficult to imagine anything more socially useful than the monastery. All historians, believers and unbelievers alike, will agree with this. The monastery was a school, a university, a center of land colonization, a propagator of art, and, finally, an early form of social assistance and organization. The monastery of St Sergius of Radonezh alone produced a whole network of monasteries, which civilized the Russian North. The same can be said about the West: the very word *university*, for example, came from the monastic environment. It was there, in the monasteries of the Christian West, that the discipline of the mind was developed and strengthened, laying the foundations for the present flourishing of science.

But facts aside, let's look at the theory. In calling work a curse and punishment, the official ideology reveals only one side, one dimension of labor. Yes, indeed, labor can be and has been a curse and slavery for centuries. From this, after all, we derive our word "laborious." But does not Karl Marx say the same in his *Das Kapital*?

Labor becomes a curse and slavery when it is divorced from the person, when it does not correspond to human nature and vocation. But the other dimension of labor, based on the Christian approach to it, is that work must be reborn and transformed, like everything else in the world. Created in the image of God, man is himself created as a creator and a worker. *My Father worketh hitherto, and I work* (Jn 5.17), says Christ. And labor is reborn and transformed when it coincides with man's true vocation, with his true nature. Historically, it is the monk who serves as an example here: he works freely and joyfully, because he knows the goal of both the lightest and the most difficult work. He knows that the goal of all labor is not practical benefit, not something external, but the Kingdom of love and light, outside of which there is no goal, either for the individual or for humanity as a whole.

And is it not time to realize that the failure of the theory of labor, forced on us for many years now by official ideology, is that it does not respond to the innate and absolute nature of the human spirit—that there is no inspiration in it for love, light, creativity, and freedom, without which labor was and remains slavery?

A Mystical Unity

It has always seemed to me that the failure of collectivization is deeply rooted in the very nature of man. And I believe that religion has something to tell us here.

On the one hand, everything on which collectivization is based—the denial of personal property, the overcoming of proprietary instincts, the desire to have all things in common—brings it closer, seemingly, to a religious approach to life. On the other hand, however, it is equally obvious (from the religious point of view) that man's attitude toward the earth, the whole sphere of his activity on it, does not fully fit into this abstract notion of property. The same is true of everything related to the sphere of the family, a person's familial relationships. I can say that my wife is "mine," but I can hardly say that she is "my property." For here "my" means not passive belonging, but includes a mysterious and joyful dimension of encounter, communion, and mutual spiritual enrichment.

But the attitude toward the earth of a person who cultivates it is, in a sense, the same. The earth is profoundly different from a machine, and communion with it is quite different than with any property. It is no accident that the whole history of mankind is marked by this deep and joyful love for the earth; it is not by chance that in the poetry of all peoples without exception the earth is so often humanized, lauded as a mother. "Mother Earth," the farmer affectionately calls it, although he tills it in the sweat of his brow.

The official ideology disseminated in communist countries as an all-embracing truth evolved from the impersonal world of cities, from the noise of machines, and therefore it does not grasp man's mysterious and personal connection with the earth. But precisely because this connection is personal, man must have his own land—the very land on which he performs the mystery of the transfiguration of the world year after year and into which he throws the grains, to watch them die and resurrect again as food, as life. And for this reason religion, while denouncing selfishness and possessiveness, not only does not deny this special connection between man and the earth as his own, but sees in it a symbol and expression of life's fullness.

Collectivization, however, destroys this link. But this is just as unnatural as destroying the family, stripping life of those personal ties out of which it is composed and which comprise its depth, all its joy and authenticity. Therefore, we can say with certainty that the collapse of collectivization is inevitable. Because the fabric of life itself, without which it ceases to be life, is impervious to destruction and substitution.

Not a Goal, but a Means

A theists accuse religion, and especially Christianity, of depriving human labor of meaning, of seeing it as a curse. The accusation has been repeated so long that it has become almost habitual. And yet it is the most shameless lie and slander. The atheists, being well aware of this, naturally do not allow believers to openly reply. But we must first of all ask: where did this accusation come from, and what is its basis? Its source is a biased interpretation of the third chapter of Genesis, the first book of the Bible, which recounts the expulsion of man from paradise. According to this account, God told Adam: *Because thou hast hearkened unto the voice of thy wife, and hast eaten of the tree, of which I commanded thee, saying, "Thou shalt not eat of it": cursed is the ground for thy sake; in sorrow shat thou eat of it all the days of thy life . . . In the sweat of thy face shalt thou eat bread* (Gen 3.17–19).

On this the enemies of religion base their theory that work is the result of God's curse and, therefore, from a religious point of view, a pointless evil. But this interpretation is naturally completely false. And the whole history of Christianity testifies to just the contrary—that labor is valued quite highly in the Christian consciousness. But we should consider how exactly it is valued, because it differs significantly from the idolatrous cult of labor that we find in the materialistic ideology of the state. The meaning of the biblical story is not that labor is bad, but that it ceased to be free and creative, and turned into an iron law of necessity. In the above words of the Bible, the emphasis is not on labor as such, but on the "sweat of the face" in which a fallen person is forced to work; or, in other words, on the labor to which man is enslaved. It is no accident that the words "labor" and "laborious" have the same root. Labor has become something laborious, slavish, and compulsory.

This means that the Christian understanding of labor must be interpreted in light of the Christian doctrine of man, set forth in the childishly simple, but therefore eternally young, language of the Bible in the first chapters of Genesis, which describe paradise. The first thing we learn about man is that he is a paradisaical being. But in the Bible the paradisaical state is not an absence of labor and not the opposite of work, but rather a state where man and work are not opposed to each other and labor is a natural and joyful revelation of life's fullness. In the biblical account of paradise it is twice said that man is called to possess the earth and rule over the fish of the sea and over the beasts, and over the birds of the heavens, and over all cattle. Paradise is possession of the world, the royal state of man, the fulfillment of the world itself as a sphere of human creativity and knowledge. And the whole meaning of the Fall is that instead of possessing matter, nature, and the world, man was subjected to them, became their slave, preferred matter and flesh to what raised him above them. He lost his free communion with the world, and his whole life indeed became a labor, a struggle for existence.

A person eats to work, and works to eat, and his whole life is reduced to this vicious cycle. And however they might praise this work to the skies, people naturally and invariably prefer holidays to work—time away from work, free time, full of joy and subject to nothing but freedom. Even on Labor Day no one works, which is the whole point of the holiday. And yet, each of us knows and remembers minutes, hours, and days of inspired labor, which we find neither burdensome nor "laborious," but on the contrary suddenly fill life itself with meaning and joy. And this means that a breakthrough to another perception of labor is possible—a labor not for food, money, and external well-being, but, as they say, for the soul. And the main condition of this labor is that it reveal and fulfill the human vocation, that it correspond to the inner essence of man, and this means that its main condition is the freedom of the individual. The difference between the Christian approach to work and the one imposed on us by the materialistic ideology of the state lies specifically in this—in a certain correlation of labor, freedom, and the person. According to the official ideology, the person is always subordinated to work: labor determines a person and his place in society, and outside this work the human person has no value. A person is determined in relation to some giant and impersonal construction effort, and whoever does not participate in it is stripped, strictly speaking, of all meaning. Thus, the "sweat of the face" mentioned in the Bible, that terrible shackling and sentencing to labor in an impersonal collective, becomes an iron law.

In the Christian perception, both labor and the collective are subordinated to the individual person, who is the highest value, and they exist for man as a means of revealing and fulfilling his gift. And the point of all labor, the point of all technical progress, is for the individual to cease to depend on labor, and for all labor to eventually become a free gift, a vocation and creativity, and even a laudation and a holiday. Ultimately, the materialistic ideology does not know the purpose of labor, because it denies the spirit. According to this ideology, labor does not translate into freedom, for it remains a law of nature. And only by recognizing a person as a spiritual being is it possible to dream of his return to paradise, that is, to free mastery of the world and life.

And only in this do we find the justification and value of labor. Only when a person has a vertical calling—not only forward, but also upwards, to spirit and spiritualization—does his work mysteriously translate into service to God and men, to spiritual victory over the power of matter.

An Ode to Woman

Contempt and Degradation?

I want to say a few words today about the way Christianity treats women, mainly because recently something was written on this subject that requires clarification. In an anti-religious pamphlet published a while ago, I happened to read that "Christianity regarded the woman as a lesser entity, belittled her human dignity, and contributed to the promulgation of a contemptuous attitude towards women."

To respond to this accusation is particularly relevant now, at the end of August, when the Orthodox Church celebrates one of its most beloved holidays—the Dormition of the Mother of God. This holiday has been so popular since the beginning of Christianity in Russia that it has become a truly national holiday, and over time the Dormition Cathedral in Moscow became the most important temple in the country.

The feast of the Dormition is a remembrance of the death of Mary, the Mother of Jesus Christ. This is one of the so-called "theotokian" feasts, in which the individual events of her life are recalled. And, of course, it is in the image of the Mother of God, in this special love for and veneration of her, that we must seek the key not so much to Christianity's understanding of the woman as to its holistic perception of her.

It must be remembered that by the time Christianity began, the woman was universally perceived as being inferior to the man and subordinate to him. The idea of women's equality is of relatively recent origin, and incidentally became widespread only where Christianity was firmly established. But Christianity did not begin with rights. Questions of rights, of equality, of free speech, and so on did not exist in the early Christian era at all, and to impose this subject on it is as absurd as to ask why there were no airplanes at the time! Christianity began by seeing the woman in all the integrity and uniqueness of the human person. "In Christ," said the apostle Paul, "neither male nor female means anything" (cf. Gal 3.28, 6.15).

To say this at that time was completely unheard of, a revolutionary innovation. But Christianity stated this as the most simple and self-evident truth. Of course, this recognition of the fullness of the humanity of woman is the root and the basis for the slow growth of those ideas and ideals that enabled her to take her current place in society.

But by establishing the veneration of the Mother of God, the Church went even further, for in this way she indicated in woman, in her spiritual and moral beauty, in her love, devotion, and patience, the peak of human perfection, the greatest expression of humanity. "More honorable than the Cherubim and more glorious beyond compare than the Seraphim." So can we still talk about the Christian "contempt" for woman, about Christianity "degrading her" to the category of "lesser beings"? Look at the image of the Virgin Mary in the icons, at this striking spiritual beauty, at the image of the Mother and Child, where all that is human, while remaining human, is elevated to such a height, shines with such light, and radiates such all-conquering love! "Rejoice, thou through whom joy will shine forth!" the Church exclaims. Yes, in comparison with this perception of woman, which reveals her miraculous, mystical power in the world, her great calling to be the source of joy and love, all further discussion about "women's rights" and the like becomes flat, petty, and colorless.

The Bearer of the Heart

In connection with so-called International Women's Day,[1] I would like to touch on one manifestation of the war on religion that not only is not weakening, but is constantly intensifying.

[1] March 8; not observed as a holiday in the United States.

Recently it was decreed that a priest does not have the right to baptize a child unless the name of the father is recorded. The purpose of the decree is clear: recording the father's name at the baptism of the child betrays him to the authorities. Previously, women would come alone—mothers, grandmothers, and sisters—to baptize children. They did not involve the child's father in the matter, so that it would not affect his job. And in connection with this I want to point out the very characteristic and significant role of women in preserving religion, in protecting it as the basis of the family.

In this country religion is opposed from an intellectual standpoint, based on reason and "scientific" evidence. Yes, of course, the mind also necessarily participates in the formation of religious faith. In the Middle Ages, theology as a systematic exposition and substantiation of faith was based on the famous principle: *Credo ut intellegam*—"I believe so that I may understand." But the error and one-sidedness of this exclusively intellectual approach lies in the fact that it ignores a deep and living source of faith—the human heart. No science, no philosophy has been able to define what is commonly called the "heart" in popular parlance (for example, when we say that someone "has a good heart" or that he "has no heart"). And yet this mysterious "heart," this innermost depth of a man is, so to speak, his religious organ. And it is disregard for it that has ultimately caused the entire scientific and intellectual fight against religion to fail. In the seventeenth century Blaise Pascal coined the famous phrase: "The heart has its reasons, which reason does not know."[2]

The main bearer of this "heart," which preserves it from destruction in our technological and mechanized era, is woman. We talk a lot about a woman's place in society, about her equality, and we sing her praises, but at the same time we completely forget that woman herself desires not power, not equality, but only her own incomparable place and service. And this service is, first and foremost, the service of the heart—the maintenance of that warmth, that love and light, without which this whole world, with all its achievements and victories, will remain a vast frozen wasteland. Woman has a very special relationship with religion, and let others talk about "superstitious old women" as much as they like—these accusations are not worth

[2] Pascal, *Pensées* §277 (Trotter trans., p. 99).

a dime. From the Gospel there shine forth eternal images of the Mother by the Infant in the manger , for whom no other place was found on earth, and of the Mother at the cross, silently sharing in the suffering of her Son. And when all betrayed Christ, only the love of woman remained true. The women alone were not frightened and came to the tomb to minister to the dead body. And then the risen Christ appeared first to them, and they were the the first to hear the Paschal greeting: "Rejoice!"

And so it is with us: during the forty-seven years of senseless and brutal fighting against religion—a fight that was actually fought against the human heart—it was the woman who safeguarded loyalty to the heart and what religion has to say to this heart. She secretly opened the hearts of children to light, warmth, and love, joined their souls with man's undying longing for God. And that is why she must now be taken out of the picture.

On Women's Day they will make many grandiose speeches. But there will not be one word about what is most important: about woman as the keeper and protector of the heart, of what is deepest, purest, and most divine in man.

An Inherent Vocation

In a very profound sense, Christianity is an anthem to woman and to the female principle in the world. And those who talk about some kind of degradation and enslavement of women understand nothing of Christianity, and are crudely and often maliciously distorting it. But what is the meaning, content, and inspiration of this anthem?

Let's start with the word woman. Its religious meaning is revealed to us at the very beginning of the Bible, in the first chapter of the book of Genesis, which tells about the creation of man, and where the woman is called *life*. Woman is given to man as his life, which in our human language means "as joy and warmth," "as beauty and inspiration." This is how the Christian doctrine of the woman begins. In the life of the world, the woman enters as an object of love and admiration, as one whom the man seeks, without whom he cannot live. Oh, love can be perverted by human freedom, it can turn into something base and beneath human dignity, but this is a distortion of love, the fall of the female principle—but the original essence of woman is high, pure, and all-embracing.

And it is not by chance that in the Bible, which uses the language of poetry to recount the history of the relationship between God and the world, between God and man, these relations are always likened to marriage, to relations between men and women. It is not by chance that the Song of Songs is included in the Bible—an amazing poem about human love, about love for a woman, and this poem is recognized as a symbolic description of God's love for the world, and of the world's love for God: *I am come into my garden, my sister, my spouse . . . I sleep, but my heart waketh. It is the voice of my beloved that knocketh: Open to me, my sister, my love, my dove, my pure one. He brought me to the banqueting house, and his banner over me was love* (Song 5.1–2, 2.4). Anything that a person does, everything that he creates, comes up against love, and finds its reward and its fullness in it: in pure, full, all-encompassing love one finds heaven on earth, the breath and presence of God in man. If this is taken away, the world becomes commonplace, dark, and hateful—such is the eternal experience of all humanity, and such is the religious basis of the Christian attitude towards woman.

But this is not all. Christianity asserts and glorifies in the woman special qualities that are inherent only in her. And perhaps they are best seen in that woman who is always at the heart of Christianity and whom the Church praises as "more honorable than the Cherubim and more glorious beyond compare than the Seraphim." This is Mary, the Mother of Jesus Christ; this is the whole of her image in the Gospel—an image of amazing humility and purity, patience and faithfulness. Here we see her at the very beginning of the Gospel story at the humble manger where her Son lies. There the light of all motherhood shines—the most complete and purest of all possible joys on earth. Then, further on, we see her in the temple, bringing and surrendering her Son to his destiny, purpose, and life. She surrenders him, and in her self-denial she fulfills woman's eternal calling: to give life and to give that life up. To educate, to warm with caresses, to illumine all of life with the light of childhood, but all this not for herself, but for others, and all this is yielded up. Further on, we see the amazingly silent presence of Mary in the life of Christ. She is always there, but in silence. Only once do we hear her voice, and this is in Cana of Galilee at a wedding (cf. Jn 2.3)—there was not enough wine, the people did not know what to do, and their simple human joy was suddenly dimmed. And at this juncture she, a mother and a woman, helps, asks, and arranges. Again, the eternal image of female help: when life is difficult, we run to her. And, finally, the last and most important moment: when all were frightened, ran away, and betrayed Christ, at the cross, in the hour of terrible loneliness and suffering, we again find Mary. This is her hour, her time. There is no heroism here, no struggle, no outrage, but the infinite power of love, pity, and compassion. *A sword shall pierce through thy own soul also, that the thoughts of many hearts may be revealed* (Lk 2.35)—these words were spoken by the elder Simeon to the Mother who brought the Infant Jesus to be consecrated to God.

And here is the reward for patience, for sacrifice, for compassion: the inexhaustible love of generations that glorify her as "more honorable than the Cherubim and more glorious beyond compare than the Seraphim." What marvelous words the people utter in her honor: "Rejoice, thou through whom joy will shine forth; rejoice, though through whom the curse will cease. Rejoice, recall of fallen Adam; rejoice, deliverance of the tears of Eve!"[3]

In our time there is much talk about the "rights" and "public role" of women. But all these are male conversations, so to speak, for the male world translates everything into the field of economics and jurisprudence. But Woman, the Woman whom Christianity came to love so greatly and whom it exalted—this Woman knows her "rights," because no one has ever been able to take them away from her. This right is the vocation to love and to help, to endure and to suffer. This right is the vocation to fill our terrible, evil world with love and affection, to be wherever anyone is suffering, and ultimately to make the world itself that *woman clothed with the sun* spoken of in the book of Revelation (12.1). And those who do not see or feel this—it is they who truly enslave and humiliate women: all those who with their

___

[3]From the Great Akathist in honor of the Theotokos, sung at Matins on the fifth Saturday of Great Lent; cf. *The Lenten Triodion*, 423.

impoverished ideologies reduce everything on earth—love, compassion, sacrifice—to gross materialism, to the struggle of interests and appetites. But all these ideologies ultimately break down when they come up against the Woman and her eternal vocation. For the Woman is given a great gift: to preserve life, to be life, and before this truth, depth, and beauty of life all ideologies are powerless.

An Image of True Humanity

Thinking of Christmas, preparing for it, contemplating its approach in these December days, it is impossible not to let one's inner glance come to rest on the Mother of the Infant—she of whom the Gospel says, *Mary kept all these things, and pondered them in her heart* (Lk 2.19).

How little the evangelists say of her, but how she filled these two Christian millennia of human history with herself, what indestructible light shines from her image, what amazing love surrounds her! "Rejoice, thou through whom joy will shine forth!" "Rejoice, dawning of the mystic day!" Where did these words come from, this impulse of praise and blessing?

But to remember Mary is not just to point once again to some typical detail of Gospel history. It means to ponder, to gaze into the whole vast stratum of the Christian understanding of man. "Tell me in what God you believe, and I will tell you what you think about man"—Christianity could address these words to each of us. We think that we are arguing about God, about whether he exists or not, but in fact we are arguing about man, about his nature, vocation, and ultimate destiny. For disputing about God is ultimately fruitless: the believer will not prove anything to the unbeliever, nor will the latter impose his unbelief on the believer. But when people decide to fight against God and religion and we see them obsessed with some strange hatred of the very idea of God, it becomes clear that it is not God that matters to them—for how can you hate one in whom you do not believe?—but rather man. They do not really hate God, but the person who believes in God, for they hate that he understands and experiences his humanity in a different, completely different way.

Oh, if only the unbeliever would say, "There is no God, and how infinitely sad it is that he does not exist! For faith in him has produced and developed the highest, most beautiful and precious teaching about man; because all that ever was and is best, purest, and most precious on this earth is connected with him and with faith in him; because here we find beauty, goodness, and love!" But no; this is exactly what he hates. Why? Because, of course, he sees man entirely differently.

How exactly? Look around, look at the world, the civilization that is being built before our very eyes by this man who, as he himself says, has renounced all "superstitions" and "deceit," all religious "opium." This is, above all, a civilization without beauty. Today, when beauty is discussed, we are taken to the museum—we are shown the ancient icons (among them, time and again, the Theotokos of Vladimir, with her amazingly sorrowful yet celestially beautiful face), we are taken to see the churches of Suzdal, and we are forced to listen to Bach's music, because contemporary civilization has no beauty of its own. It has none, because there is no source of beauty in a civilization that sees man only as a product of matter and economic relations. One can re-read all of Marx a thousand times, all of Engels, and never once encounter the very word beauty. But then, the logic of this doctrine states that the person must be destroyed, about whom the Church says that he is "the image of an ineffable glory,"[4] a reflection of divine beauty.

Furthermore, this civilization is a civilization of external, technological success, a civilization without depth. In it, man continuously produces and is called only to produce. But what are the "production achievements" of Mary? The Bethlehem cave in the beginning, the silent standing at the Cross at the end—this is all we know about her. And yet this is enough to say that there was no fuller and more beautiful life on earth than hers. But if so, how pitiful all this fuss about "production," this ceaseless laudation of it and the reduction to it of all human life! Again, one must choose, and

[4]From the Evlogetaria for the Dead in the Funeral Service and the Memorial Service (Panikhida).

the person who does not seek, who does not want to know the inner life, its meaning and depth, must necessarily come to hate the very image of the Mother of God. Everything on which our civilization is based—endless struggle, the triumph of physical strength, the intimidation of enemies, the pride of external success—where is all this in the image of Mary? Only humility, only love, only compassion, only a total willingness to give herself up. *Yea, a sword shall pierce through thine own soul also, that the thoughts of many hearts may be revealed* (Lk 2.35). Again and again this choice! But as a result of one choice the world is filled with the knowledge of this beauty, this humility, this goodness, this humanity; while the other choice results in fear, hatred, slavery, and even unbearable boredom and greyness. "We will build our own new world . . ." Well, they built it, all right—and people run from it to this same beauty, to this same icon of the Mother and Child, the eternal image of genuine humanity, of what is most important and ineradicable in man. There is nowhere to escape it, and the feast of the Nativity of Christ is, in fact, the feast of this image, the feast of this intuition, this perception of man.

Once in ancient times pagans celebrated the winter solstice in December as the festival of the sun's rebirth, heralding spring. Then came Christianity and revealed to mankind the image of the Mother and Child, and proclaimed the humble Nativity, the coming into the world of unearthly beauty and goodness. And the ancient pagan holiday became the holiday of the "Sun of Righteousness" (Mal 4.2)—that not merely physical but also spiritual light, on which the destiny of mankind ultimately depends. And now humanity is again at a crossroads and does not know where to go. It was told that it is free and can go anywhere; it was told that machines and science can do everything and that it does not need the image of God, does not need the heavens, does not need beauty—that the unshakable laws of "material production" are sufficient. And now it does not know what to live for; it is in the dark, in fear, in confusion. Do we still not understand what all the best people have already understood—that the Way, the Truth, and the Life is not in this, but in something else, without which a person sooner or later suffocates? It is about this "something else," something essential, necessary, and eternal, that Christmas reminds us, and to this we are called by the image of the Mother and Child, by its heavenly beauty and depth. Oh, if only we too could, like Mary, "keep all this in our hearts" (cf. Lk 2.19), and live it, and from this draw light, joy, and strength!

As Long As She Is In the World

Christ is Risen! The second Sunday after Pascha is dedicated in Orthodox worship to the Myrrh-bearing Women—to those women who, according to the Gospel account, came early in the morning to the tomb of Christ, to prepare his body for burial, and became the first witnesses of the Resurrection. In the Gospel, Christ says first to them: "Rejoice!" (Mt 28.9),[5] and they are sent to announce the Resurrection to the apostles.

In connection with this, it is appropriate that we examine the image of woman as painted in the Gospel, to consider the Christian doctrine concerning woman or, better put, the perception of the woman in Christianity. And this perception is best revealed in the place women hold in the Gospel account of Christ.

When reading the Gospel, one cannot help noticing that a woman appears in it only at the very beginning and at the very end of the earthly life of Christ. In the beginning—the birth in a cave, the bringing of the Infant to the temple for consecration to God—we see his Mother. Then his Mother seems to disappear, or rather, we constantly sense that she is near, close by, but wordlessly, silently, as though against the background of the life and preaching of her Son.

Here we find the unexpected and amazing account of the evangelist John about the wedding feast in Cana of Galilee, when there was not enough wine. This would seem to be a banal detail, a trivial affair . . . but the holiday is spoiled, the joy is clouded, and so a request is made, the intercession of a Mother, and at this request—the first miracle of Christ: the

---

[5]The literal translation of the Greek and Slavonic word often translated as "Hail," as in the KJV; Fr Alexander here cites Mt 28.9 in the Russian Synodal Translation of the Scriptures, where the Russian in fact says "Rejoice!"

transformation of water into wine. Then, again, silence. Christ spends all his time with his disciples, teaching and instructing them. But it turns out that women follow him all the time and, according to the Gospel, minister to him. Finally, we stand at the cross. All have left, all have fled, all have betrayed Jesus, and not only the crowds who followed him in anticipation of miracles, help, and healing, but even those closest to him—his friends and disciples. And now the hour of the women has come. At the cross is his Mother, but she is not alone. As the evangelist Matthew tells us, there also watched from afar many women who followed Jesus from Galilee, ministering to him; among them were Mary Magdalene, and Mary the mother of James and Joses, and the mother of the sons of Zebedee (see Mt 27.55–56). And when death comes, these women help remove the body from the cross and lay it in the sepulcher, then return early in the morning to prepare it for burial. And finally they hear the victorious greeting: "Rejoice!"

Thus, the first thing that the Gospel has forever connected to the image of woman is love. And not just love, but nurturing love, ministerial love, sacrificial love, which requires nothing in return. The disciples of Christ argue about which of them is greater, for whom the best place is prepared; they reason among themselves, they doubt . . . but about the women there are only these two words: that they "followed" and "ministered." This is a love without words and doubts, a love of action; this is the eternal, innate motherhood of women and its eternal domain—to care for, feed, nurture, and give all of oneself, in order to lose everything in the end. For as they grow up and start their own lives, sons and daughters leave their mother. And the Gospel shows us the full beauty of this sacrificial love in joy, sorrow, and death.

The second is loyalty. The disciples fled, the women stayed. In the terrible hour of suffering, loneliness, and death—this silent fidelity, this silent compassion. According to the Gospel, the women did not know Christ's prediction that he would rise on the third day. They could not have had any expectations, any hopes. The One they loved and followed, the One to whom they gave their love, care, and faithfulness, died on the cross. And, humanly speaking, everything collapsed: nothing remained, except for the dead, tortured body. But loyalty remained—fidelity without expectations, loyalty to the end. And how simple, how briefly, and at the same time with what fullness this faithfulness is shown in the Gospel!

Finally, the third is faith and joy. And again, it is a faith that is not discursive, a faith of the heart, a knowledge that only women have. It is no accident that after the resurrection Christ first appeared to Myrrhbearers. Later came Thomas with his attitude of: "If I do not see, I will not believe!" (cf. Jn 20.25). But of the women at the grave it is said: *And behold, Jesus met them, saying, "Rejoice!" And they came and held him by the feet and worshiped him* (Mt 28.9).

All this was a long time ago. But if you examine the long succession of centuries that have passed since that morning, it becomes clear that this image of woman has been preserved, and has filled the world with its simple but heavenly beauty. Human history ran its course, kingdoms were born and fell, bloody wars were waged . . . but always over the troubled and tragic earth there invariably shone the image of woman—the image of silent care, self-giving, love, mercy, and compassion. And without this light, our world, despite all its successes and achievements, would have remained only a terrible world.

And we can say without exaggeration that the humanity in man was saved and is saved by woman. She does not save it by any ideology, but rather she saves man with this silent, caring, loving presence. And if, despite all catastrophes and tragedies, the mystical celebration of life does not end, if in a bare room at a beggar's table it is felt as joyously as in a palace, then the joy and light of it is in her, in woman, in her ceaseless love and loyalty. Perhaps indeed there was not enough wine . . . but while she is here—the mother, the wife, the bride—there is enough wine, enough love, enough light for all.

Falling and Rising

Where is the Real Person?

Let us begin the Fast with brightness, let us purify the soul, let us cleanse the flesh, let us loose every bond of iniquity."[1] With these words the Orthodox Church has summoned us every year since ancient times to enter Great Lent, the seven weeks that precede the feast of Pascha. Let us listen once again to these words: "light," "purification," "soul," "flesh," "the destruction of the coalition of iniquity." Here is the whole man, his whole composition, his whole life. Who or what else in the world calls a person to this purification, saying to him: "It is necessary, and one must begin with oneself"?

Of all his religious knowledge and intuition, in all likelihood there is nothing that the person who has forsaken religion rejects so resolutely as this thirst for purification, this vision of the unrighteousness, sinfulness, and impurity of his life, this passionate desire to reform. To the enemies of Christianity, to the enemies of religion, it seemed that self-condemnation, recognition of one's imperfection, repentance and reconciliation are unworthy of a person and degrade him. "All this is the religion of slaves," they insisted, "but we will free mankind from it, and it will know that the word man has a proud sound!"

And so they liberated him, and they cast off this thirst for purification, reconciliation, and rebirth. But did the life of this new man prove to be proud and perfect? One hardly knows whether to cry or to laugh. Why does humanity, now freed from religious "degradation," need nannies armed

---

[1]Cf. Forgiveness Sunday, Vespers, Lord I have cried, sticheron 3; and First Week, Wednesday, Lord I have cried, sticheron 1; *The Lenten Triodion*, 181, 235.

to the teeth? Why do they spoonfeed this proud man each morning, telling him how he should think, what to obsequiously agree with, what to enthusiastically believe? Why would they quarantine him from the outside world? And why, finally, even many years after all these liberations, are the members of this proud and free humanity kept behind barbed wire, in psychiatric hospitals and detention facilities?

"Man—it has a proud sound!" But then we look at this proud modern man, and we are overcome with pity: how frozen, crushed, and humiliated he is! How drab and hopeless is his life, and what unbelievable and cruel taskmasters reign over him! And how boring, flat, and unconvincing is the ideology for which he was allegedly freed from the path of superstition and mysticism! Long, long ago it was said, *Every tree is known by his own fruit* (cf. Lk 6.44). But if so, what a feeble, dismal tree has grown from the poor soil of this "liberation"!

But there was a time when people told and listened to other stories, when they were inspired by something completely different. How many centuries our people sang the old song about a robber who repented, seeing all the horror and the whole impasse of his life, and found the strength to be reborn: "Kudeyar himself went to a monastery to serve God and men." How many centuries have men listened with bated breath to how the greatly sinful woman prostrated herself before Christ, washing his feet with precious oil mixed with tears, wiping them with her hair, and then hearing the astounding words: "He who loves much will be forgiven much" (cf. Lk 7.47)? They listened also to how another robber was crucified next to Christ, and prayed at his last hour: "Remember me, Lord, in your Kingdom!" (cf. Lk 23.42).

Thus, in all things and from beyond all things there existed, shone forth, and triumphed the true greatness and dignity of man. There was a consciousness that all men could rise, be reborn, and return to the light and joy for which man was created. And so there was genuine faith in man, as well as genuine pity for him. No matter how dark, terrible, and cruel life seemed to be, still this light of humanity burned bright within it. But as soon as they extinguished it, declaring it "unnecessary," life became truly benighted: great fear and great mistrust arose among people, and pity and compassion vanished. Gone was the former faith that all things are possible if only a person can rediscover his conscience, if only he can awaken in himself the thirst for purification and reconciliation with God!

Great Lent, then, is about all of this. And it is indeed great, for it proclaims nothing so much as the true greatness of man, and it does not ask for anything except for man to return to his true dignity. This fast reminds everyone: "You are given the power to purify yourself and be reborn, the power to desire true life, to destroy the coalition of iniquity, woven in the world by lies, hatred, envy, and fear!"

Where then do we find weakness, humiliation, and lack of faith in man, and where do we see real, indestructible faith in his greatness and dignity? Where is the real man and where is the impersonal being bound to cheap egalitarianism? Where is there light and joy and where is there boredom and the mundane? All these questions are elicited by the Great Fast, which is a gradual ascent to the feast of all feasts—Pascha. And everyone must answer all these questions, because in the end they are about whether we can see ourselves in a great and comprehensive light, whether we can measure our lives by the eternal doctrine of the heavenly vocation of man.

Lent is not an antiquated institution for "churchgoers," but something that grows out of the very vision and understanding of man in Christianity. And if we correctly hear and understand his vocation, then we will truly receive this great and beautiful doctrine of man into our souls.

In Light of the Original Idea

Nowhere do we see so obviously and with such depth the difference between the religious and non-religious perception of man as in the approach to guilt and forgiveness. During Lent we believers are constantly called to repentance. "Grant me to see my own transgressions," says the chief lenten prayer. And this call to self-examination, to self-evaluation, to fundamental inner change constitutes the primordial essence and purpose of Great Lent.

What does this mean? It means that, according to the Christian perception of life and man, we are not living properly, not on the proper level, and it also means that we can change our lives if we repent, if we see ourselves in the light of God's true plan for us and for the world.

It would appear that something similar happens with a non-religious approach to a person. For decades we have been hearing about "self-criticism," and everyone still remembers those incredible court cases, where people who held the highest positions in state and society publicly dragged themselves through the mud, accusing themselves of the most heinous and implausible crimes, and all but pleaded with their judges to be sentenced to death. Is this not remorse?

No sooner does one ask this question than one becomes aware of its intolerable hypocrisy. As in all other similar areas, this is not remorse, but a nightmarish caricature of it, something so inhuman that instead of relief you experience an almost supernatural horror. What is the matter? After all, the resemblance is quite strong on the surface: in both instances a person sees his error and finds the courage to acknowledge this error openly, in front of everyone; and in both instances there is self-criticism, the examination of one's life in the light of some law that governs it. But if one only thinks, looks, and listens more closely, the similarity will vanish without a trace, and the aforementioned caricature will reveal its terrible face.

To understand the essence of this terrible caricature it is especially helpful to recall how relatively recently the so-called "rehabilitation" took place, when the prisoners of the so-called correctional labor camps returned after those terrible, ruined years, and it turned out that all their public "self-condemnation" and "repentance" had been a complete farce. And this occurred because—and this is the crux of the matter—no one was looking for any higher law capable of revealing the whole truth. There were only tactical arguments and a bickering over power with the inevitable conclusion: "Woe to the vanquished!" And then they rehabilitated the vanquished and condemned the victors, and then again began to condemn the rehabilitated and to rehabilitate the convicted victors. And so it went without end, in that bloody and stupid nonsense where "self-criticism" and "self-condemnation" are the most pointless and frightening words of all.

For the fundamental difference between the irreligious idea of "repentance," if you will excuse the expression, and religious repentance is that the former demoralizes and humiliates, while the latter liberates and elevates a person. In the first case the judges, as it were, would tell a person: "Admit that you are a scoundrel and a liar," and the convicted man would say: "Yes, you've convinced me; I confess that I'm a scoundrel and a liar." In the case of true, religious repentance, Someone who is infinitely exalted, pure, and loving says to a person: "After all, you are a son of God, you are the image of the ineffable glory of God himself, you are infinitely precious and infinitely loved. Why do you desecrate and ruin your spiritual beauty and dignity, why are you not what you are?" And so the man prostrates himself before this holiness, this purity, this goodness, this beauty, returns to them with all his being, and is reborn. "And there is more joy in heaven over one sinner repenting than of ninety-nine righteous people" (cf. Lk 15.7).

Here, then, everything comes from an infinitely exalted idea of man—of every man, and not of mankind in general. Everything contributes to him finding in himself this dignity, that he would return to it and be filled with joy. In that other conception there is assuredly nothing but dark, ruthless revenge and reprisal, no glimpse of love and compassion. Has a cog in an impersonal machine failed to do its task well? Throw it out and replace it with another, and as a lesson to the other cogs, force it to drag itself through the mud. With the religious approach to a person no such "replacement" is possible, for each person is unique! Religious repentance leads to the realization and the discovery of this indispensability, and therefore it purifies, revives, and gives joy. But elsewhere there is only hatred, only fear, and the road to nonexistence.

And so in these days of Lent it is especially important to understand that at the heart of true repentance lies that lofty plan for man that is rejected and spat upon by the inhuman ideology that reigns in our country. "Grant me to see my own transgressions . . ." Not another's, but my own, and therefore let me see myself in that light, that truth, and that love for which I was created! Thus repentance leads to the restoration of humanity within and among us.

Return and Affirmation

I have already spoken about Great Lent, about the bright sadness permeating this time of year for believers, about that special, unique beauty that is revealed in the Lenten services of the Church and that is so incomprehensible, so alien to people who are accustomed to consign religion to the Procrustean bed of its narrow, flat, prejudiced views.

Let us continue this subject today. Listen to the hymns and prayers of Lent: how much poetry they contain—special, pure, exalted poetry—and how far all this is from what is usually attributed to religion! To better understand them, we shall render these hymns in the vernacular, for even in everyday language they retain their own incomparable tonality.

"Let us radiantly begin the season of the fast!"—with this invitation we begin Great Lent. And further: "Let us purify the soul, let us cleanse the flesh. In fasting, enjoy the fruits of the spirit and, accepting them with love, let us become worthy to see the sufferings of Christ God and in joy to meet the Passover." And here is another hymn: "In the light let us begin the venerable abstinence, shining with the rays of the commandments of Christ, the light of love, the brightness of prayer, the cleansing of purity, the incarnation of courage." But what is fasting? Is it only abstinence from food, gloomy asceticism, and condemnation of the world and the earth? This is answered by the call of the next Lenten hymn: "While fasting bodily, brethren, let us also fast spiritually. Let us destroy every coalition of iniquity, and rebel against all injustice; let us destroy slander and lies, let us give bread to the hungry, and those who do not have shelter and food let us bring into our homes." And again: "Come in faith, and in light let us do the work of God, without hiding anything; let us end all grievances towards our fellow man, in no way tempting him; let us leave the power of the body, let us grow in the gifts of our soul, and let us feed those in need, and so we shall advance to Christ." Again we hear the same words: "light," "love," "joy," "spirit." This is the inner inspiration of fasting, and this is its goal: to restore in oneself that vision of life that is constantly drowned out by life's busyness, and this experience is bright, loving, and joyful, and not a denial of the world.

The whole asceticism of Christianity, all its calls for struggle, for restraint, and for inner effort, proceed from an infinitely lofty idea of man, from faith in his unlimited spiritual possibilities. A long time ago, at the dawn of Christianity, one teacher of the Church, St Athanasius of Alexandria, wrote: God "was incarnate that we might be made god."[2] And this faith in the deification of man, in the possibility of his infinite growth, lies at the heart of the Christian understanding of fasting and repentance. This is not withdrawal, not negation, but a return and an affirmation—a return to our original beauty and integrity, and an affirmation of the divine vocation of man. And in comparison with this ideal, with this concept, all that other philosophies and ideologies say about human life seems petty, defective, and degrading. For they all see it as a derivative of something else—of matter, of biology, of economics—and therefore subordinate to the laws of determinism. As Vladimir Soloviev joked about this, "We all descended from monkeys; let us love one another!" But behind the joke lies a serious meaning. For if man is really only derivative and only from below, such a creature does not and cannot have either real freedom or a vocation that takes him beyond the limits of materialistic determinism. All that he loves and strives for, according to this approach, is merely a "superstructure" imposed on an unreliable material "basis."

Atheist materialists accuse Christianity of denying the person, but in fact it is Christianity that is fighting for the true person and rejecting everything that hinders his fullness, his discovery in himself and in the world of his true image and true vocation. No matter how low a person falls, Christianity tells him: "This fall is contrary to your nature, and therefore you can rise, you can return to your true nature!" And this forms the basis for love, pity, and compassion in Christianity. They are never from the top down, they are never rooted in contemptuous indulgence: "Though you are scum and unworthy of help, so be it; I will help you"—this approach does not and

---

[2]St Athanasius the Great, *On the Incarnation* 54. Translation in St Athanasius, *On the Incarnation*, trans. John Behr, Popular Patristics Series 44A (Yonkers, NY: St Vladimir's Seminary Press, 2011), 167.

cannot exist in Christianity. In every person, it claims, there is an ineradicable image of God, there is that for which God loves him and which defines his infinite dignity. This is how Christian solidarity is built—not the solidarity of slaves who rebel against their masters or blindly obey them, but the solidarity of brothers, bound together by freedom and love. *Henceforth I call you not servants*, says Christ, *for the servant knoweth not what his Lord doeth* (Jn 15.15). "To you," he continues, "everything is open and given, and you can grow infinitely in this fullness of knowledge and gift."

The modern world thinks and teaches that it has freed man from the "dark medieval fears" of religion; that freedom, creativity, and science are impossible where there is religion. It calls on a person to cast off his "religious bonds" and become free. But to this world we can and must apply the words of the Gospel: *Ye shall know them by their fruits* (Mt 7.16). For in practice (and let them prove to us otherwise!), where these "bonds" of religion are cast off, freedom begins to die, and with it—and this is what is most terrible, most tragic—there dies the lofty plan for man, replaced by a plan that is base and joyless.

Yes, religion has often fallen, often betrayed itself, often floundered. But in it there has always been the opportunity to return to one's heart of hearts, and there always prevailed a need for return and repentance. And for this reason religion still has Great Lent, this annual call to rise, to cleanse our inner sight, and to return to what is most important. The world, which considers itself "freed" from religion, has nothing to repent of, nothing to return to; nothing stands behind it, no dream beckons, there is no ultimate thirst. But for this reason it ultimately cannot satisfy a person, and for this reason the thirst for God and for union with him—that is, religion—can never die.

Christianity:
A Religion of Revelation

Two Aspects of Equal Importance

Once, in a bygone era that has often been called "the good old days," with a greater or lesser degree of justification, a religious subject called "The Law of God" was taught in all schools, explaining the essential elements of the Christian faith, its rites, and its worship. Perhaps this course was not always taught sufficiently well; perhaps it was taught in a somewhat formal or routine fashion. Nevertheless, it did leave in one's soul from childhood a certain image or imprint, however superficial, of the Christian faith and way of life, and at least a superficial knowledge of Christianity.

Regrettably, those times are long past. Children are not taught about religion; in fact, they are conditioned against it. Religion is debunked as fraudulent, as a remnant of past ignorance, and as a phenomenon completely foreign to our time, with its ideal of a new society and the like. Yes, there are still churches, and services are held there . . . but believers are forbidden to teach their children the faith, to publish books about it, or to defend their faith in debates with unbelievers. It has become incredibly difficult to learn even the most basic facts about Christianity—what Christians believe, what their rituals mean, and how they encourage believers to live. Only a few people are able to break through all the barriers stacked up around the Church and her life, and even then a great deal of Christianity is still not easy to discern, understand, and accept. The majority, puzzled by the incomprehensibility of everything pertaining to religion, accepts on faith what official propaganda says about Christianity.

Christianity is not a "mysterious religion" with some "ancient and beautiful ceremonies." It is the teaching about which Christ himself said: *What I tell you in darkness, that speak ye in light: and what ye hear in the ear, that preach ye upon the housetops* (Mt 10.27). As for the church services, which actually do have their roots in antiquity, every word, every service has its own meaning, which pertains to our life today just as it pertained to life many centuries ago.

In addition, Holy Scripture tells us to *be ready always to give an answer to every man that asketh you a reason of the hope that is in you* (1 Pet 3.15). These questions are often cunning and malicious. Many Christians, while deeply aware of the truth of their faith, are not always able to provide an answer. This, in turn, gives the enemies of religion an opportunity to call faith the product of deception, ignorance, and wishful thinking. Thus, the method of anti-religious propaganda is very simple: it does not allow people to penetrate to the essence of Christianity, and simultaneously it spreads the crudest of lies about it. A classic example is the stubborn denial of the historical existence of Jesus Christ. From their elementary school days it is impressed on people that "there never was any Jesus Christ; he was invented." But they say nothing of the fact that not a single serious historian in our time, regardless of whether he is a believer or a non-believer, would defend this pitiable and unscientific theory. One can accept or not accept the teachings of Christianity, one can believe or not believe that Jesus Christ is God, but wherever there is basic religious freedom Christ is unanimously recognized as a historical person.

But there is no point in dwelling on the lies, smoke-and-mirrors, and unscientific position of atheistic propaganda. The best way to combat it is to know one's own faith. And so in these talks I would like to explain, simply but without any unjustified over-simplification, what Christians believe and have always believed. I will discuss how the services, rites, and customs of the Church, which are the externals of Christianity, relate to the internal experience that produced them and of which they are an expression. This theme is all the more important since believers and non-believers alike do not understand the connection between the external and the internal, between form and content, in Christianity. As a result, in choosing the "internal" some discard the external as incomprehensible and unnecessary ("Why all these endless services, fasts, feasts, and so on? I have God in my heart; all this external stuff is man's invention"). Others, on the contrary, are more attracted to everything "external," which helps them escape the dull, drab reality of everyday life: the church, the icons, the services . . .

However, just as the first group fails to understand that Christianity assumed external forms of expression from the very beginning, so also the second group doesn't grasp the fact that the church and her services with their inherent beauty were conceived not as a way to escape life, but as weaponry given us to in order to serve Christ on this earth. This is why it is so important to understand that the internal side of Christianity are inevitably embodied in the external, and that its external side is valuable and meaningful only because it manifests the internal, imparting it to us and to every aspect of our lives. Hence, in these talks we will simultaneously discuss both the external and the internal—that is, the content of the Christian faith and how it is externalized.

The Supreme Law of the World

All attempts to understand and explain the essence of Christianity come up against a roadblock at the very outset. This roadblock is the demand for proof, and it is a problem typical of our time. Modern man has been taught (and accepts on faith) that the fundamental question in religion of whether or not there is a God should be resolved like any question regarding the external, material world: by presenting proof. And the only kind of proof acceptable in this case is scientific proof—proof that can be tested by by objective experimentation, independent of our subjective experience.

This is the gist of the main anti-religious argument in its most primitive form: "Since God is invisible, intangible, immeasurable, and consequently his presence is impossible to ascertain, he does not exist." Although a great deal could be said to refute this argument—for example, that it is equally impossible to prove the existence of a person's mind—in this talk we will touch on one question only, and address it not to atheists but to believers.

Here is the key question: on what basis do we claim that there is a God, and are woefully surprised at his rejection by unbelievers, if the Gospel itself tells us that *no man hath seen God at any time* (Jn 1.18)?

Yes, we say that the evidence presented by unbelievers is not applicable to God, and is valid only in relation to the visible, tangible, empirical world; we say that God can be known only by faith. However, how and from where is this faith born within us? The believer, of course, could answer, "I don't need proof; faith is enough for me." This is true, but only true for the believer. If he is asked honestly: "But how did you begin to believe? What led you to faith?"—does he really have to reject the question and withdraw into his proud egoism? If he does, then the question is over and done with. We reject the "proofs" that the godless demand of us, and we laugh at the cosmonaut who says that he was in the heavens and did not find God there. But we cannot brush off the question if we are asked what evidence, in that case, we ourselves have to offer. Here we come to a central concept in Christianity, without which we cannot begin to explain it: the concept of revelation.

Faith is man's answer to God, and it presumes that the initiative for this relationship with God, which we call faith, lies not with man, but with God himself. God reveals himself to man; man receives this revelation and, in responding to it, responds to God. This is why believers do not have any convincing objective evidence for unbelievers. At the same time, for the believer the validity of his faith is self-evident, as is the existence of the God to whom his faith is directed. But when we speak of revelation, we must realize that for the unbeliever such an answer will not appear convincing. "Excellent," he says; "you maintain that God revealed himself to you and that is why you believe. But God has not revealed himself to me, and so my unbelief is justified and we have nothing more to talk about." This is why it is not enough to just refer to revelation.

Here we must ask: is it actually possible to explain to anyone, including an unbeliever, how God reveals himself and what exactly he reveals? We see that the Bible is full of expressions like "and God said to Abraham," "and God said to Moses," and so forth. But what do they mean? To many, they seem like fairy tales precisely because the most important aspect of faith, this self-evident fact of divine revelation, divine initiative, expressed in the simple, childlike phrase "and God said," has not been explained by anyone for a long time.

But if, as Christianity has always claimed, faith begins with a revelation from God, with a call that man hears and answers—if before we address God and find him, he addresses us, finds us, and reveals himself to us—we ought then to say at least something about this revelation. Otherwise, the atheist is right who says, "Well, no God has revealed himself to me, so my unbelief is right and justified." But can we believers accept that millions of people have been forgotten by God, a God who, for some reason, reveals himself to just a few and not to others? Can we, in other words, allow for some kind of injustice in him? If God is love, then he loves everyone and calls everyone to himself, and from all he awaits answering love and faith! But in this case this revelation—the revelation that we have declared to be the principal prerequisite for faith, stating that faith is possible only in response to it—must be recognized to be not some enigmatic miracle, nor a breaching of the laws of nature, but the supreme principle at work in the world. But this principle is hidden from those whose vision is turned in another direction, who, according the Gospel, "looking do not see, listening do not hear and do not understand" (cf. Mk 4.12), and who therefore do not turn their attention to God.

The Church begins each day by triumphantly and joyfully proclaiming that God has appeared to us.[1] What then is this appearance, this revelation of his? We will endeavor to answer this question in our next talk.

---

[1] At the beginning of the Matins service, after the Six Psalms, the psalm verse The Lord is God and has revealed himself [or appeared] unto us (Ps 117.27) is repeatedly sung, while other verses from the same psalm are chanted.

The Invisible in the Visible

God reveals himself to people, and the response to this revelation is faith. This is what I said in my previous talk, and at the end I stated that a feasible explanation of the Christian faith needs to begin by answering the questions of how God reveals himself to people and what it is that he actually reveals.

To begin with, let's remember that the word revelation only fairly recently began to be perceived as a synonym for something supernatural, miraculous, the opposite of "positive" knowledge, and therefore incompatible with science. This took place not as a result of the widening of man's reason and consciousness, but due to their dramatic narrowing and impoverishment. In fact, it was only two and a half centuries ago that this endlessly wretched and tedious worldview that calls itself "positivism" emerged, which gradually stripped man (though thankfully not all men!) of a much deeper and richer conception of the world.

We need to understand that we live amid a tyranny of simplistic worldviews and ideologies. These have declared, once and for all, that everything in the world can only be approached with mathematical equations, and that only this table is able to answer all questions without exception. I would add that genuine scientists are not at fault for this impoverishing of the human consciousness. The fault lies with the ideologues, a strange breed, who not only present their ideas as scientific but impose them by blatant coercion. Where real scientists avoid giving an exact definition of the material, ideologues boldly maintain that all truth is to be found in materialism. And so we live in a world that is ruled by a band of impostors, who hide behind a science they have nothing to do with, and who act only through intimidation. "No kind of revelation is possible—it contradicts science," they self-confidently announce, and millions of people obediently repeat their words.

But if, just for a moment, we can free ourselves from this flat and, more importantly, over-simplified worldview, the most acceptable, convincing, and ultimately self-evident approach turns out to be far different. Then the word revelation no longer appears the spawn of ignorance and benighted-ness, as suggested by positivism, and questions begin to arise of their own accord. What if, in a completely different, profound, and at the same time childishly simple sense, everything in the world is revelation, all is miracu-lous, all is a mystery—one that has nothing whatsoever to do with these idolized mathematical equations?

What if the most profound, yet most apparent experience of every per-son reveals to us not just those things that mathematical equations can see in the world, but something else that no chart can discern, and this shows us the most important and valuable knowledge about the world and life? Science studies the natural world, but isn't it true that poetry, music, and sculpture also study it, each in their own way? Don't they reveal to us a different, perhaps far more necessary truth about nature? "Why do you wail, O wind of the night?" What is this? Nonsense or absurdity with no connection to life whatsoever? Or perhaps the ideologues are lying when they reject the inescapable fact that everything in the world not only con-ceals but actually reveals an unfathomable meaning, that everything in it witnesses to some kind of presence, and promises a different knowledge and understanding?

We could talk about this endlessly. However, I hope that what has been said so far will allow us to understand, even just a little, what Christian-ity has to say about revelation. Christianity sees in revelation not simply something strange and inexplicable, but primarily that which is borne out by the whole experience of humanity. To put it even more simply: our faith perceives the world itself as revelation, as the presence of the invisible in the visible. Remember what the poet wrote: "Dear friend, do you not see that all that we see is just a reflection, just a shadow of the invisible?"

In reality, a person only lives fully by revelations: the revelation of beauty, of goodness, of love—everything about which mathematical equa-tions have nothing to say, and yet has always and everywhere constituted the real meaning and the real content of life. For all this is the very first and most universal revelation, and we know it well: it comes to us from the natural world, from another person, from love, joy, and suffering. It is poured out on us in our childhood, when everything is perceived as a miracle, as revelation. And in the best moments of our life we know that Dostoevsky was right when he called it "a touching of other worlds."

Of course, at this point, in the involuntary experience of this revelation, a person ought to acknowledge that it could have no other source than God. But let us suppose a person does not come to this conclusion, or for some reason he fights it and he doesn't see or hear God revealing himself to him in this world. Let us suppose this, and move on, bearing in mind however that we have experienced a mystery in the world, that we have discredited the flat ideology of mathematical equations, and that we have freed our understanding of revelation and the miraculous from the oversimplified interpretation of the blind slaves of a stillborn ideology. In the next talk we shall speak of what comes next—of how God reveals himself to us.

A Triunity: Revelation, Faith, and Freedom

In the previous talk I said that if not the idea, then the experience of revelation is a person's unquestionable, fundamental encounter with God. Since primeval times man had been aware that he was living and interacting with the world around him on a spiritual as well as a physical level—living, more simply put, not just by reason but by an inner perception. This inner perception is our organ for perceiving all that naked reason is unable to perceive in the world, in nature, and in other people. And there is nothing at all humiliating about religion's acknowledgment that before considering who God is, man felt his presence. Just as genuine and reflective conversation with people allows us to experience their souls—that is, their heart of hearts, which is apparent in their external appearance, their words, and their actions, but is not defined by them—in this same way, a profound look at the world discovers a presence, an action, a revelation in it of something that cannot be reduced to the external alone, which ancient man at some point in his existence called the Divine, or God. This understanding could not emerge outside the reality and the experience of him to whom it pertains, and even the most uncompromising positivist must agree with this.

Since the concept of God is universal, and we find it everywhere throughout history, we are justified in concluding that this manifestation of the internal and invisible in everything external and visible, which we have been calling "revelation," is not accidental, nor does it violate the laws of nature, but is a kind of fundamental law for all mankind, as I have said before. And this law, regardless of claims to the contrary, has not been abolished simply because many people now consider themselves non-believers. These people reject Christian faith and Christian revelation in favor of other values—in favor, neither more nor less, of a different revelation, a different faith. The non-believer claims that religion hinders the establishment of happiness and freedom on earth. But from where has he gleaned these very notions of "happiness" and "freedom"? Obviously, not from physics or mathematics! Thus, in the end people are simply debating about their respective "revelations," and now we see how unshakably true are the words of Christ: *Where your treasure is, there will your heart be also* (Mt 6.21).

But of course this "natural" revelation and man's innate religious feeling does not exhaust the Christian experience of and teaching about revelation. We can go further, or rather, return to the question with which we started our discussion of faith and of revelation as its basis. Remember that the Bible constantly tells us of unique revelations to man: "And God spoke to Abraham: 'Get up and go . . . ' (cf. Gen 12.1, 22.2) or, "The word of the Lord came to me . . ." (Jer 1.4, Ez 13.16). What kind of revelations are these, and how can we connect them to the "general" revelation, so to speak, that we have been speaking of up to this point? After all, the Gospel claims that *no man hath seen God at any time* (Jn 1.18), and every day the Church in its prayers calls God "invisible, incomprehensible, indescribable." Consequently, in these places the Bible cannot be talking about physical manifestations of God. On the other hand, this revelation is so obvious, powerful, and unquestionable that man accepts it and obeys. *Abraham believed God* (Rom 4.3), and he rose up and traveled to an unknown country. Once again, it is clear that here we are talking about a human sense, only this time much stronger and more intense than the senses with which we usually perceive the deepest stratum of existence. Hasn't each one of us experienced similar moments in our own lives, moments exceptionally fateful and intensely experienced, when some inner voice reveals something previously unknown, calling us to a decision that a moment ago would have been unthinkable? Haven't we all experienced flashes of utmost intensity, when our whole life depended on whether we make a certain choice that unavoidably presented itself to our conscience? Regardless of how often we have been told that everything in life is unreservedly subject to some unyielding laws of causation and necessity, nonetheless with our whole being and experience we know that in reality everything, absolutely everything, depends on our choice, on the voice of our conscience, on a mysterious impulse in the innermost depths of our selves.

We will never know precisely what happened on that day when Abraham made his fateful decision: he believed God, left everything, and went to a foreign land, and with this set in motion a whole new series of events which eventually led to the birth of Christ. We will never know exactly what happened when, obeying the same mysterious impulse, Moses climbed Mount Sinai alone and returned bearing commandments for his people—commandments so simple and so eternal that the world hangs on them to this very day. However, we know without a doubt that those events radically changed the spiritual destiny of mankind. We know that at their root lay revelation and faith, a call and a response. We know that, just as there was no compulsion in the divine revelation and the divine call, likewise this faith and its response were not forced upon man but freely accepted by him in the very depths of his spirit. Abraham believed, but he could have not believed. Moses obeyed, but he could have not obeyed. And so this triunity of revelation, faith, and freedom brings us face to face with that which comprises the very heart of Christianity—that is to say, with Christ himself.

The God of Love

his religious revelation, or rather the religious experience of this revelation that we have been discussing in our previous talks, has its focal point and its luminous heart in Christ himself.

Indeed, the meaning of the Christian faith, and a feature exclusive to it, is that in the Man Jesus it sees the revelation of God, his appearing among us in time, and the absolute concreteness of the visible and perceptible world. Christianity and the Church constantly reaffirm the absolute concreteness, the full historical reality, and the complete humanity of Christ. *That which . . . we have heard, which we have seen with our eyes, which we have looked upon, and our hands have handled* (1 Jn 1.1)—this is how the beloved disciple of Christ, the Apostle John the Theologian, begins his epistle, and this is how the Church itself has always invariably identified the source of its teaching.

It is not accidental that the name of Pontius Pilate, the governor of Palestine at the dawn of our current era, is pronounced daily, at every church service and in the prayers of Christians at home, in the brief Creed or Symbol of Faith. By including this name in the Christian confession of faith, the Church connects all the events of the earthly life of Christ with a specific historical era. It confirms that the God-Man Jesus Christ in whom we believe is not a mythical being, like the pagan gods, of whom no one knows when or where they lived. The connection of Divine Revelation with earthly history and life is infinitely important to the Christian faith. And if this revelation took place "under Pontius Pilate," this means it occurred at a specific point in history, in a specific place, and under specific circumstances.

It is true that there have been repeated attempts (which continue even now) to deny the historical reality of the events described in the Gospel, to prove that Christ was an invention, just like all the other "gods." However, it is now clearly obvious that these attempts were made not in the name of science but of ideology. Genuine science, the methods of which are shared by believers and unbelievers alike, recognized Christ as a historical figure long ago, although this naturally does not mean that the whole academic world unanimously agrees with the Christian interpretation of the events recorded in the Gospel. Those who reject the historical foundation of the Gospel do so because their ideology demands it, and for them the chief threat of Christianity lies in its historical reality.

For us, however, what matters is not these outdated and long since discredited attempts, but the question of why, from the very outset, Christianity connected its faith and teaching with the historical reality of specific people and events. History knows only the Man Jesus, but faith alone identifies him as God—this in short is the chief essence of Christianity. This definition reveals something infinitely important for the Christian understanding of God and man. The enemies of faith have always maintained that God was invented out of fear, and that all religion is nothing more than the result of compulsion and coercion. And yet we see neither compulsion nor coercion in the image of the Man Jesus presented to us in the Gospels. Some listened to him, others passed by; some followed him, others did not; some loved him, others hated him. But all those who believed in him accepted him and his teaching as divine revelation.

Does this not mean, then, that the Christian experience of God is the exact opposite of how it is described in atheistic propaganda, which ascribes everything in religion to fear and the abuse of a person's mind and conscience? Doesn't this show us that at the center of this experience is an image of a God who does not abuse human freedom, but who seeks only faith that is embraced freely, and therefore to believe is to be free? "If you love me, you will keep my commandments" (cf. Jn 14.15) says Christ. However, it is impossible to force someone to love: there is not and never can be any compulsion in love. Yes, God reveals himself to people—through the natural world, through history, and ultimately in the life and teachings of the God-Man Christ. But he does this in such a way as to leave the person free to either accept the revelation or not, to experience it as his salvation, as the highest meaning and joy of his life, or to reject what it reveals. And this means that in speaking of a God who seeks a free response to his revelation and his love, Christianity affirms man's freedom, or, more precisely, that man is a free being.

In Christian teaching, God and man are connected not by external constraint, but only by love, the freest of all human characteristics and the very essence of God, whom the Gospel calls "Love." Through love God creates the world, and only through love can we recognize him as Creator. He reveals himself in the world through love, and only through love can we recognize everything in the world as a revelation of divine love. Through love God saves us and only through love can we see in Christ the coming and union with us of the God of Love.

This is the meaning of the assertion that Christianity is a religion of love.

PART III

SOURCES OF CHRISTIANITY

God–Manhood

The Heart of Christianity

The most surprising feature of the state's anti-religious propaganda is the extremely insignificant place it ascribes to Christ himself. In all the many books, the many brochures written against Christianity, what has not been denounced, ridiculed, or debunked? Yet about the main thing, about what indisputably constitutes the living heart of the Christian faith, there is hardly a single word.

From time to time an obsolete, useless argument is put forward that there was no Christ at all, that he was invented, and that having invented him people began to believe in him, to worship and deify him. This argument is obsolete because no serious scholar now doubts the historical existence of Christ, and also because it is quite ludicrous to extirpate the long, complex, and rich history of Christianity from a simple deception. Therefore, it is much easier to denounce the flaws of the clergy and various historical defects of religion than to talk about what actually motivates faith. It is difficult to oppose Christ himself, so it is better to pretend that the center of the Christian faith is not Christ, but something else, some kind of "religion in general." But the center of the Christian faith is not "religion in general," but Christ himself. For this reason the Christian defines himself solely in relation to Christ, and the debate must be specifically about Christ, and not about something else. And if everything that official propaganda says about the harm of religion applies equally to Christ, if it is possible to discredit him with what is contained in the "scientific atheistic" brochures, then their authors are right. If, however, Christ goes unmentioned, it is because they know full well that they would do best to say nothing about him—for if they do otherwise, all this anti-religious propaganda turns out to be a lie.

How do we know anything about Christ? From those who were living witnesses of his life, from those whom he called apostles—that is, messengers. The Christian community, the Church, lived by the testimony of these messengers. Their message was then kept and observed by countless generations of Christians, and was recorded in numerous annals and practices of Church life. The most important historic record of the apostolic witness is the New Testament, a book in which the very first and most important records of the direct disciples of Christ are collected. This book has long been the subject of numerous disputes. It has been studied from all possible points of view, and every phrase and every word has been fought over. The treatises and articles on the New Testament number in the tens of thousands. Many philologists, historians, and archaeologists have labored in this, both believers and non-believers. Although the opinions of these experts differ in many respects, I believe they could be said to agree on the following: the New Testament describes Jesus Christ as he is remembered by the eyewitnesses of his life, such as he was when they came to believe in him. One may not share their faith, but then we are faced with the riddle of the Person who lived as though he were God. For this assertion that Christ is the true God is precisely what the New Testament claims. Again, it is possible not to accept this statement, but it is this affirmation and none other that the New Testament authors defend. And in order to evaluate this statement, one must hear it out. But this is something that official anti-religious propaganda does not want, preferring either to remain silent about Christ, or to evade the issue with general and meaningless phrases.

The Gospel begins with the birth and childhood of Jesus Christ. We learn that he was born in a lowly cave near Bethlehem, a tiny town of insignificant Judea (then a province of the Roman Empire), to a poor family, albeit one of royal lineage. But this poverty—deliberately emphasized by the whole situation of his birth, with the parents of Christ coming from far away and not finding a place in the city—is contrasted in the Gospel with the mysterious cosmic glory that accompanied his birth: the Virgin Mother, the star, the angels singing praise . . . This contrast and this combination of weakness and strength, wretchedness and glory, seems to set the tone for the whole Gospel. God comes to men, but he comes secretly, in weakness and humiliation, not to intimidate and subjugate, but in order to be freely recognized, freely accepted. God is man's freedom, and this is the first statement, the first revelation of the New Testament.

Then we are briefly told about the childhood of Christ. He spent it in the house of a village carpenter and himself became a carpenter. He lived with his Mother, among relatives, and he worked with his hands. He prospered in wisdom, maturity, and love in the eyes of God and men (Lk 2.52)—in other words, he studied and lived righteously and in harmony with all. At around age thirty he left his home and relatives and went forth to preach. Here the event celebrated after Christmas took place, to which the Gospel attaches exceptional importance—the baptism of Jesus by John in the river Jordan.

The Jews of Palestine at that time were avidly awaiting the coming of the Messiah—the Savior sent by God. Some expected that this Messiah would bring them liberation from the Roman yoke; others hoped for a worldwide triumph of monotheism, or belief in a single true God, and the collapse of pagan polytheism; still others awaited the establishment in the world of the Kingdom of God—that is, the fullness of moral perfection and love. This entire period was rife with intense expectation. And shortly before Christ went out to preach in Palestine, a religious teacher named John appeared who proclaimed everywhere that the coming of the Savior was at hand and that all must prepare for it by repentance and purification of life. As a sign of this repentance, crowds of people came to John, confessing their sins and wanting to be cleansed, and he baptized them in the waters of the Jordan. Christ too came to John to be baptized, and the one who baptized him recognized him as the Messiah, the Savior.

The New Testament emphasizes that in this event Christ identified himself with all people, and took on their destiny, or, as the Church says, took upon himself the sins of the world, and it was in this humility, in this love, that he first received recognition, being recognized and confessed as the Savior of the human race. Again the same juxtaposition, coupled with unity; the same idea central to the whole understanding of Christianity: that the path to God is not external, but internal, for it is the way of free recognition, free encounter.

In the Christian perception of God, one cannot understand anything without realizing that God does not force himself upon man, but is the first to humble himself before man. And this is why the humility of God, his most complete and perfect revelation to men, is given in the humble God-Man—in Christ.

The Chief Joy

In these days before Christmas, I want to speak again and again about the chief joy of the Christian faith, about its very core—about what Christian teaching has termed "God-manhood."

At the dawn of Christianity, in the Gospel of Christ's beloved disciple John, these astonishing words were heard: *And the Word was made flesh, and dwelt among us, and we beheld his glory* (Jn 1.14).

God-manhood! God becoming man, in the words of another teacher of Christianity, St Athanasius of Alexandria, "that we might be made god."[1] God coming to the world, to earth, to make the world his kingdom . . . It takes your breath away to think of it, when we recall these oft-forgotten statements of early Christianity. And suddenly we understand why all the prophets and preachers of a wretched and boring materialistic happiness hate Christ and Christianity so much. These preachers only make a pretext of opposing a Christianity that humiliates and enslaves a person, whom they, as representatives of the "scientifically verified" theory of happiness, want to rescue from the opium of religion. In reality, of course, they hate Christ and Christianity for precisely the opposite reasons: because they do not want this deified man, cannot endure this lofty and divine plan for man, and are afraid of his royal freedom—all that the Gospel affirms about man. For while a person remembers and knows all this, he will not be lulled by talk of "production relations." He cannot be forced to believe that the laws of matter and economics hold the key to the mystery of being, or rather, that there is no secret, nor ever was. That the prophets and poets were mistaken.

[1] St Athanasius the Great, *On the Incarnation* 54 (PPS 44A:167).

That neither the blue of the sky nor the joy of love merit gratitude. That the thirst for purity and perfection that consumes his soul is nothing but self-deception, the fruit of superstition and lack of culture. That the answer to all questions, the scientific formula of happiness, lies in the tedious and infinitely cumbersome writings of some obscure "experts," in economic calculations and computations.

So, while there is Christmas in the world, while people celebrate God's coming into the world and firmly remember that in this, in the good news of God-manhood, is the measure of a man and his true vocation, no unyielding theories will succeed, for man's soul is such that "the tedious songs of the earth could not drown out the sounds of heaven."[2] And so this soul with its memory of the heavens must be uprooted, corrupted, and destroyed.

The late Father Sergei Bulgakov, who himself passed through the dark tunnel of this Marxist reduction of man to earth and things earthly and devoted the best years of his life to this deception, put it very aptly:

The insurrection of the kings of the earth and of earthly men against the Lord began long ago. In essence, it arises at the very outset of church history, but not immediately in open rebellion, but by crafty evasions, seeking to belittle, limit, displace, and weaken the coming of God in the flesh, to abolish God-manhood and keep the world in the hands of the prince of this world. Many conscious and only half-aware opponents of God-manhood have employed and continue to employ various pretenses—piety, asceticism, moralism, spiritualism—to abolish the power of the incarnation, seeking to disembody Christ. This is likewise the goal of the jealous doctrine of the deification of man. And all this motley army has succeeded in deafening and intimidating humanity, convincing it that Christ has left the world, and that his kingdom, which is not of this world, will never be accomplished in this world. And the whispered question undulates like a serpent across the earth: to whom does the world belong? To the God-man, or to the man-god? To Christ or the antichrist? All the power of evil and

[2]From M. U. Lermontov's poem, "The Angel" (1831).

heresy and unbelief is now firmly concentrated around this lie: "The world is not Christ's, but your own." But everything is possible to the believer, and faith knows that God-manhood is God's miracle in the world. In Christianity a new sense of life arises: that man need not flee from the world, for Christ comes into the world to the marriage feast of the Lamb, to the feast of the God-man, as King, and therefore as Judge. In their fight for the kingdom of Christ, the faithful turn to Christ who comes, in expectation of him they lift up their hearts, and in the world the forgotten but primordial early Christian prayer is heard—timidly at first, but now definitely present: "O come!" Amid heresies concerning the world, amid unbelief in the royal ministry of Christ, Christians have forgotten this prayer, for it was fear to them; yet love drives out fear. But this prayer remains the anthem of Christ's humanity, for Christ is the King who comes in the name of the Lord. *And the Spirit and the bride say, 'Come.' And let him that heareth say, 'Come'* (Rev 22.17).

So wrote the late Father Sergei Bulgakov toward the end of his life, from the summit of wisdom, love, and faith, having himself passed through a denial of faith, religion, and Christ; having himself believed for a time in the primitivism of materialistic doctrine and the pseudoscientific theories of happiness, and then returned from them to the comprehensive doctrine of God-manhood. And it is good to recall his words in this season of Advent, when we not only recall an event in the distant past, like our own childhood with its purity and integrity, with its faith in the star and the manger, in the angelic doxology, in the mysterious sages who come from afar to the Infant, bringing to him all the treasures of the world; but we also deepen our faith, learning to see it again as the core of Christianity, as the bright and joyful mystery of God-manhood. Let the outside world constantly forget it and deny it, let the din of vain human pursuits raise its clamor. Behind all these external, random, transient, and perishable things, invisibly to men but palpably for faith, the Kingdom of God is waxing strong.

Faith, hope, and love do not die on earth, man does not incline his royally free head before the idol of materialism. And the pledge of this is the feast of Christmas, the feast of God-manhood, the feast of God's call to man not only to ascend to heaven, but also to bring with him the whole world, all creation, all beauty, all creativity—everything that is given to man for the fulfillment of his humanity.

An Incredible "Delusion"

J esus Christ"—everyone, both believers and unbelievers, is so used to the combination of these two names that they forget about its profound meaning. And yet it remains the central affirmation of the Christian faith.

I have already said that this faith begins with the earthly history of the man Jesus, as related in the Gospel. This faith is focused on one event that took place in our own time and space, at a certain historical moment—"under Pontius Pilate," as the Christian Creed says. But the fact that *Christ* is appended to the earthly, human name *Jesus* gives unique and singular meaning to this man and all the events of his life. The Greek word *Christos* is a translation of the Hebrew word *Messiah*, which means "anointed one." From time immemorial, anointing signified a special dedication to and vocation from God, and as such, it indicated that the one anointed received special spiritual gifts, a special mission from God. In the history of the Jewish people, as recorded in the Bible, the word *Messiah* gradually acquired an even more specific meaning. It can be said that their history increasingly came to be regarded by their best representatives, namely the prophets, as a messianic one, focused on the coming of the Messiah. According to the prophets, at the end of time the Anointed One of God would come, who would save people from sin, evil, and suffering, and reveal to them the kingdom of God.

The more time passed, and the more the purely earthly hopes of the Jewish people collapsed, the brighter and stronger grew this expectation of the Messiah, this faith in the ultimate triumph of the Kingdom of God. By the time of the birth of Christianity, the Messianic aspirations had reached their apex. Some were expecting that the Messiah would free them from the hated Roman rule and would restore national freedom; others hoped for the universal triumph of the true religion; still others associated the coming of the Messiah with the end of the world. In one way or another, everyone was living in tense religious expectation.

Shortly before the appearance of Jesus of Nazareth in Galilee, public attention was focused on a strange man named John the Baptist. He came from the desert, preaching that the time of the coming of the Messiah and Savior had come, and calling upon all to repent of their sins, to purify their life, and to enlighten their conscience in order to meet him worthily. As a sign of this repentance and this change, John baptized all those who came to him in the river Jordan, and this baptism, this immersion in water, symbolized the beginning of a new and pure life. And so, according to the Gospel account, like everyone else, Jesus came to John, and John was the first to recognize him as the Messiah! Thus, he confirmed that the entire history of the Jewish people—a history imbued with the expectation of the Kingdom of God—had reached its conclusion. This testimony marks the beginning of Christianity—the dawning of a new era.

It is important for us that Christ accepted John's testimony and proclaimed throughout his earthly ministry that he was the One prophesied by the prophets, for whom the people were waiting—the Messiah, the Savior, the Lord. Moreover, an objective examination of the Gospel shows the following: Christ taught that He is not just the Anointed One of God, but also the Son of God, whom the Father sent into the world to save mankind. And when men recognized him as God who had come to earth, when his disciple Thomas cried out: *My Lord and my God!* (Jn 20.28), he did not deny this, did not forbid Thomas, but, on the contrary, recognized the truth of this faith. And, of course, here, in this faith that Christ is God and Man, lies the heart and the pulse of Christianity. Not just a teacher, a prophet, a righteous man, like many on earth, not just the bearer of a lofty doctrine of love and exalted morality, but God incarnate.

And it is this affirmation, first and foremost, that is targeted by all atheistic criticism and all the hatred of unbelief: "How can you believe this? It's hard enough to believe in God as such, but can you really believe in a God who is born as a child, lives a human life, and shares human destiny?" What answer can be made to this? Yes, of course, at first glance, it is difficult to believe—indeed, it is almost impossible. But if you make an effort to ponder, or rather to really listen to Christianity, then this faith will appear before us in a new light. Most importantly, if we do not believe this, Christianity proves to be a tremendous and truly inexplicable delusion, a delusion that not only has lasted for almost two thousand years, but also gave birth to the greatest culture, the most profound philosophy, the most astonishing art. How, then, can we explain why the greatest minds of countless generations believed this "improbable" teaching? And not only believed, but saw in this doctrine of God-manhood the ultimate expression of wisdom? Can a misunderstanding, a mistake, an illusion endure for centuries and satisfy all the needs of the mind, all the yearning of the heart, all the longing of the soul?

Here comes the self-assured propagandist armed with his little brochure, and says: "Deception, absurdity, nonsense!" But why was it not considered a deception or nonsense by such geniuses as Dante, Pascal, and Dostoevsky, Bach and Beethoven, Pavlov and Pasteur? After all, deception or misunderstanding can produce nothing but a new deception and misunderstanding, yet the doctrine of the God-manhood of Christ has engendered the deepest, most complex, and most beautiful of all cultures. One need only stand beneath the ancient vaults of the church of Hagia Sophia, the Wisdom of God, in the former center of the Christian world that was Constantinople, and see the amazing dome, flooding the interior with light and joy, or but once to feel the joy of the night of Pascha, in order to ask: can all this be a "delusion"? Did St Seraphim of Sarov really rejoice over a "misunderstanding" all his life? Was Rublev's Trinity born of "deception," and is its radiance that of "deceit"? No, it is easier to believe in the truth of Christianity than in this strange and truly inexplicable mountain of "deceptions" and "misunderstandings."

But this is only one argument—a negative one. Through the mouths of many theologians, philosophers, scholars, and saints, Christianity affirms that this teaching about the God and man who is Christ is most profound and indisputable. What is the basis of their affirmation? We will turn to this issue in our subsequent talks.

The Measure of Man

As I said in the previous talk, I do not set myself the task of proving the historicity of Christ—in our time no serious historian calls it into question. It is much more important to consider what Christians mean by faith in Christ.

It is unlikely that anyone, believer or unbeliever, will undertake to deny the exceptional place of Christ in the history of mankind. Christianity has now existed for two thousand years, and for two thousand years successive generations of people have learned about Christ—sometimes in childhood, sometimes in adulthood—from parents, teachers, or preachers, and have been taught to love his image, to place Christ over all their convictions, and to make him the measure of everything in their lives. Of course, throughout our long history people have not always agreed on everything concerning Christ. Christianity itself has long been divided into three main branches, or confessions: first, Orthodoxy, preserved mainly in the eastern half of the Christian world—among Greeks, Russians, Serbs, Romanians, and Bulgarians; then Roman Catholicism; and finally in Protestantism, which broke away from Catholicism in the sixteenth century (what separates these three chief branches of Christianity will be discussed separately at another time). And, of course, the enemies of Christianity always point to this division, using it as an argument against the Christian faith: "If the Christians cannot agree among themselves, how can they demand that unbelievers recognize Christianity to be of special, supernatural, divine origin?"

For the present I will say only that however unfortunate this division, even sinful from the Christian point of view, it does not essentially violate the basic unity of all Christians in their faith in Christ; and, secondly, that this divide is increasingly recognized as wrong and abnormal by Christians of all three confessions in our time. Regarding the so-called "ecumenical movement," that is, the organized and systematic efforts of different churches to restore their lost unity, I will also speak separately. For now, it is important to emphasize that all these divisions do not abolish the most important thing—that exceptional, incomparable place that Christ occupies for believers in the history of the world, in the fate of all mankind and of every single person.

This common faith in Christ that is shared by all Christians, by which the Christian world has lived consciously or unconsciously, to a greater or lesser extent, which permeates our whole culture and inspires the greatest works of art—this is the faith I wish to call to mind in my talks. For in our time some openly declare that Christianity is harmful and dangerous, and make every effort to eradicate it, while others, though they do not fight against Christianity, tend to think it "obsolete," a relic of the past. The truth is that open opposition to Christianity meets with little success, and the unprecedented mobilization of the whole state apparatus against it has not yielded the desired results. The truth is also that literally not a day goes by without more people turning to faith in Christ—the same people who once, under various influences, considered Christianity "obsolete." And yet we would do well to test our faith once again and ask: what lives eternally within it, what gives the heart such joy and such peace, what fills the entire world, and my life and our lives in the world, with light, happiness, and meaning? What remains firm, unquestionable, and unchanged, despite all the evil and the divisions that fill the world?

Of course, faith is always something very personal. But in the faith of every Christian, what is surprising is that, while personal, it encounters the personal faith of millions of other people and is experienced as a common and unified faith. Every Sunday, hundreds of people in the church sing: "I believe in one God, the Father Almighty, Maker of heaven and earth, and of all things visible and invisible; and in one Lord Jesus Christ . . ." Here each confesses his personal faith, but so do all believers, and this "I believe" turns hundreds of people into a living unity, speaking, as the Church says, "with one mouth and one heart."[3]

What do I believe when I say that I believe in one Lord Jesus Christ, the Son of God, when I confess him as Savior and King of the world, when I affirm that the victory of life over death, the fullness of that eternal Kingdom, which Christians call the Kingdom of God, and in which they see the goal of all history, of the whole cosmos—that all this is connected with Christ, depends on him, and in him receives its ultimate and all-encompassing meaning? If we follow the common Christian confession, which every Sunday we solemnly declare "with one mouth and one heart," and which connects millions of Christians, then the main element of this faith is, of course, the unique significance of the man Jesus, who lived in Palestine under the Roman authorities about two thousand years ago and whose image is embodied in the Gospel. In other words, Christians believe that in our human history, in space and time, an event occurred that proved decisive for people of all time. The Man Jesus, born in such conditions that there was no room for him in the inn, who grew up in the poor family of a carpenter, who at the age of thirty began to preach the doctrine of the kingdom of God, who was accused of crimes against the religion of his people and was crucified under the Roman governor Pilate—the Gospel speaks about all this surprisingly simply and truthfully, and this is the beginning of our faith.

We believe in a poor Teacher, who was at times tired and hungry, who suffered and spent his whole life among the poor and destitute, accompanied by twelve fishermen and several loyal friends. But how and why does the Christian see in him the Lord, the King, and the Judge—the focal point of everything that he believes, hopes for, and seeks? How does the human aspect in the Gospel unite with the divine purpose that Christians have always seen as integral to it, since the very beginning? This question leads to another dimension of the Christian faith, to which we will turn in our next talk.

[3]". . . that with one mouth and one heart we may glorify . . ." from the Eucharistic Liturgy (drawing upon Rom 15.6).

The God of Freedom
and
the Problem of Evil

It Depends Entirely on Us

Not only unbelievers but also believers—those of them who give serious thought to questions of faith—often express the following doubt: "If God existed, would he really permit evil to reign in the world for entire millennia?"

This doubt has been expressed from one century to the next, and it cannot merely be brushed off, because everyday experience seems to confirm its validity: indeed, evil too often triumphs in the world, and seems to justify itself by its success. "If God existed, he would not allow this!" people often say in despair.

What can we say to this? Only one thing: the God preached by Christianity and proclaimed by the Old Testament prophets is the God of freedom. Man is by no means a pawn or a toy in God's hands, but the free, responsible creator of his own destiny. And it is this that precludes all discussion of whether God would or would not allow a thing to happen. In his unlimited love for man, God limits himself, so to speak, by man's freedom. He wants man to freely acknowledge him. *Henceforth I call you not servants; for the servant knoweth not what his Lord doeth; but I have called you friends*—so speaks Christ (Jn 15.15).

Let us ask ourselves: what is the difference between a society of free people and a society of slaves? If we disregard random attributes, the difference is that free people are responsible for their lives, for all the good and evil that they do, while for slaves the only law is the will of the master—whether he allows something or not.

History is filled with people constantly fighting for freedom, for only freedom is worthy of man. But are they always aware that the idea of freedom is rooted in the revelation about God? And this revelation, given to us in the Bible and particularly in the Gospel, speaks of him not as a terrible despot that manipulates unaccountable pawns, but as the source of freedom, love, goodness, and moral perfection.

Doubters ask: "But this concept of God allows for the triumph of evil! What is the use of it?" Indeed, if that were so, despair would be justified. But is it? Has good never triumphed in the world and in ourselves? Yes, evil is strong, and the Gospel constantly reminds us of this. Christ speaks of the narrow path of salvation, of difficulties and temptations along this path. In the world there is an unceasing struggle between good and evil. And precisely because a person is free, he always has a choice between the two of them. And any of us who rejects evil, hatred, and slavery, and chooses good, love, and freedom, knows that this choice makes him stronger each time, not weaker. Yes, evil often triumphs. But it is up to us not to hand it the victory. It is up to us to choose the good, to believe in it as did the first Christians, who believed that, through his love, the poor and homeless Teacher who was crucified on the cross showed the world the true victory of good.

The Hardest Question

In the perennial dispute between faith and unbelief, conducted not only in our days and not only among people, but within every human soul, the most difficult question for faith is this: "Why is there so much evil in the world?" How often we hear: "If your God existed, would he allow all this? Would he allow this overwhelming personal and collective suffering, would he allow these misfortunes and diseases, the horror of separation and death, the endless triumph of injustice, hatred, and violence?"

In the novel *The Brothers Karamazov*, Dostoevsky reduces all this to the famous question of the teardrop of a tortured child. Ivan Karamazov asserts that this is intolerable, and that if God allows the slightest evil for the sake of some incomprehensible "future harmony," he for one respectfully declines his "ticket." It is easier for unbelief to answer this excruciating question, because it makes no claim to belief in a kind, loving, all-good God, and therefore it does not ask him how he can permit the endless torment of man whom he created, and in his own image and likeness, at that. Unbelief, as it were, says: "Let's try to diminish and weaken evil and torment. Let's do what we can." But unbelief goes no further than this, for evil in the world is just as natural for it as bad weather, floods, and epidemics. People shelter from the rain with an umbrella, from flooding with dikes, from epidemics with preventive care and medicine. There is no discussion of the origin of evil and who is responsible for it, but only of this or that means of combating it. Therefore, in this dispute disbelief has an advantage over faith. Moreover, unbelief often sees faith as a cowardly flight from evil and from any real effort to combat it.

Indeed, faith sometimes appears to be a kind of moral egoism, on the one hand, and fatalism on the other. Dozens of people die in a disaster, or on the TV screen they show us children dying in Africa from hunger. And from this nightmare of mass destruction, from the terror in these children's eyes, from the intolerability of all human suffering, many believers take refuge in pious excuses: "Well, apparently God so willed it." "Everything is according to God's will." "One cannot argue with God." But what exactly do they mean? Is it God's will that innocent children die in terrible torment? Or for a young body created for life to writhe in pain? Or for mothers to weep in desperate grief for centuries and millennia? And how hypocritical, how false, how self-serving are all the words with which we customarily console the suffering, until this suffering strikes us personally, until a terrible cloud of sickness, suffering, and death overshadows us!

No, faith cannot brush off the most difficult, most agonizing of all human questions: "Where does evil come from? Why does it constantly triumph in the world?" But in order to answer it, one must try to understand that religion and faith differ in their approaches to evil. For there have always been religions whose chief, often unconscious purpose was precisely to help a person to reconcile himself to universal evil and suffering, to ease their impact on his consciousness. As modern medicine helps a person feel no pain while sick and dying, so these "natural" religions helped man to endure evil and, if possible, not even to notice it. And it is this common feature of every "natural" religion that finds its expression in comforting words like, "Everything is according to God's will!"

The modern believer will be surprised, perhaps, by the reminder that Christianity, the Gospel, and Christ himself rebel against this kind of "anesthetizing," fatalistic religion, which they see as a terrible perversion of true faith. Whereas Plato, for example, tries to prove in some of his dialogues that death is the liberation of the soul from the prison of the body, and true wisdom is to desire death, Christianity, in the words of the Apostle Paul, calls death *the last enemy* (1 Cor 15.26). Christ himself, when he came to the tomb of his friend Lazarus, wept at seeing the triumph of death in the world. And during his earthly ministry he never mentions "God's will" at the sight of death, suffering, and evil. Christ raises the widow's son, multiplies bread for the hungry, heals the sick. This is not a religion of reconciliation with evil and suffering, it is not fatalism, it is not empty words of consolation. The whole Gospel speaks of confronting evil face to face.

But it also teaches us to approach evil not with the arguments of reason and the achievements of science, but as an irrational phenomenon, whose origin is unknown to man. In fact, according to Holy Scripture, God did not create death (Wis 1.13), yet here we see it it triumphing in the world; God is love, but in the world hatred reigns; God is light, and there is no darkness in him (1 Jn 1.5), and yet the world is full of darkness. Therefore one of the main issues occupying Christian thinkers has always been the question of so-called theodicy[1]—of how to explain this paradoxical and irrational triumph of evil in the world. To this topic we will turn in our next talk.

---

[1]Theodicy: a vindication of God's justice. This term was introduced in 1710 by the German philosopher G. V. Leibniz (1646–1716) and later became the general designation of all philosophical and theological attempts to reconcile the presence of evil in the world with the doctrine of an all-good God.

The Hardest Question (continued)

I have already said in a previous talk that the human mind has always struggled with the question: "How did evil originate in the world? Why is there so much suffering?" This question has been the focus not merely of abstract thinking, but of all theories and ideologies that promise to rebuild the world, promising man complete and absolute happiness. Our era in particular is marked by an insatiable longing to find at last a remedy for evil and suffering. Some see this remedy in the fundamental restructuring of society, especially the economy, on which the satisfaction of basic human needs depends; while others advocate all sorts of "spiritual" recipes. But all these ideologies concur in asserting that by means of reason mankind is able to destroy evil and achieve happiness, and happiness for all, at that. Therefore, a presentation of the Christian view of evil must begin by exposing the rationalistic approach, which is based on the groundless belief that evil is merely a sort of defect that can be eliminated by accomplishing just one thing: understanding its essence.

This talk and those that follow I have called "On the Mystery of Evil," for the root of the Christian approach to evil is that it is acknowledged as a mystery, something that does not fit into rational categories. Evil is irrational. And this is not just another theory, not an abstract principle, but what a person knows from his immediate, everyday experience. The same is witnessed by all the arts. It is not by chance that one of the main themes of poetry has always been love and the suffering associated with it. What theories, what ideologies can explain the pains of unrequited love, for example—the horror of betrayal, separation, alienation? No matter how rationally society, the economy, the state apparatus and so forth are adjusted, this timeless experience of personal suffering still remains.

I speak of this experience because it best reveals the poverty of all modern theories of future happiness. Let us assume that everyone will ultimately be satisfied and that poverty and hunger will be overcome; let us assume that in the world, as all ideologues of happiness promise, equality, justice, and maximum provision for everyday needs will be achieved; let us assume, finally, that everyone will have the opportunity to freely choose the kind of life, work, and entertainment they desire. However utopian this may seem, rationally speaking, it is at least admissible, as are advances in the medical field, for example, and the subsequent diminishment of physical suffering. But perhaps when in our mind and imagination we have achieved universal happiness, it becomes obvious that true evil runs deeper than all this, and its root is irrational. It is no accident that the biblical account of the origin of evil associates its first manifestation with paradise, and not with deficiencies in the world order. For, according to the book of Genesis, it is precisely in heaven, in the fullness of joy and bliss, that the first human Adam desired . . . oh, not evil as such, of course, but that which led to the fall into sin, in which the Christian faith has always seen a manifestation of the profound essence of evil.

What did the first man Adam want? Simply put, one could say that he desired life for himself and only with himself, unlimited power, and a meaning that he himself had created. Through the mouth of God the Creator the Bible says this: "Adam wanted to be like God" (cf. Gen 3.5, 22). Life was given to man so that its meaning might be outside him—in love, in selflessness, in service, and in the joy derived from them. But it is this meaning that man rejected and continues to reject in theories and ideologies that promise him, as it were, a complete and perfect happiness. For all these theories and ideologies agree that happiness is the complete satisfaction of the external needs and desires of man.

What if this is precisely the truest, deepest source of evil? What if this non-stop self-affirmation of man and mankind is the real cause of the suffering that so patently fills our whole life? What if this reduction of all life to this one desire—not to suffer—is the root of suffering itself? And so we approach the mystery of evil, which, no matter how man may reject it, is invariably present in the life of the world. And in the revelation of this mystery lies the meaning of the Gospel, the meaning of the preaching of Christ, and, most importantly, the purpose of suffering that is left to us as an image of victory, as the path to the only true happiness.

In our next talk we will turn to this Gospel proclamation of the cross, through which, in the words of the church hymn, "joy has come to all the world." We will try to approach the mystery of evil not by reason, not through biology or economics, or through reducing it to some random accident, but as Christianity has always approached it. In other words, we will try to show how the mystery of evil unfolds and how evil itself is vanquished in the life, teaching, suffering, and death of a single Man.

The Hardest Question (conclusion)

In speaking about the mystery of evil and man's perennial attempts to solve it, in our previous talks we came to the conclusion that this cannot be achieved by reason alone, just as evil cannot be destroyed through social restructuring alone. The root and essence of evil is immeasurably deeper, as indicated by man's helplessness before its crude reality and incomprehensible power. It is good to remind ourselves of this in the days and weeks when we are once again approaching Great Lent, the season that since time immemorial in the Church has been a time of repentance, and consequently of deepening of conscience and reassessment of life. "Open to me the doors of repentance, O Life-giver . . ."[2]—with these words, with this deepest of sighs, we begin the approach to Great Lent. And having learned through this sigh the meaning of the whole Lenten period, we can perhaps, at least partly, comprehend the mystery of evil with which our human consciousness struggles.

Today, modern man hardly knows the meaning of remorse or repentance. He does not know it because he has been taught to see the source of everything bad or evil not in himself, but outside himself—in something impersonal, in relation to which he is always but a victim. If life is bad, if there is so much evil and suffering around us, it is because society unfairly distributes material goods—food, clothing, housing. If a person is suffering, it is because science has not yet explained and resolved everything. If he does not feel happy, it is only because he has not sufficiently understood

[2]Hymn at Matins, sung from the Sunday of the Publican and Pharisee until the 5th Week of Great Lent, following Psalm 50.

the laws governing the world and life, and he simply needs these laws hammered into him, to be re-educated so that his consciousness becomes "scientific," completely subordinate to the theory that has explained once and for all what evil is and how to destroy it. Thus, our civilization has no room for that deep sigh that in the Christian experience marks the beginning of all Christ calls us to: *Repent, for the kingdom of heaven is at hand* (Mt 4.17). Without this sigh, without this awakening of conscience, it is impossible to explain for ourselves the mystery of evil; it is impossible to begin to fight against it. Here all theories, philosophies, and reasoning end; here begins the one thing capable of illuminating life with new light, which gives the strength not only to re-imagine it, but also to begin a new life.

Whence is this sigh, and for what? Of course, all conversation and discussion about it are meaningless unless it is recognized as self-evident that a person has within him that inner depth, that mysterious spiritual organ, that from time immemorial has been called the conscience. "To live according to conscience," "my conscience does not permit," "a tortured conscience," "a clean conscience"—man has always used these expressions almost involuntarily, and he continues to do so, no matter how much he is told that evil is "objective," and that both understanding and eliminating it are tasks for "objective" science. Few people can give a "scientific" definition of the conscience, but there is no person who has not felt in himself once in his life, at least for a minute, for a second, a voice that cannot be muffled and that speaks as the voice of supreme truth, of supreme, mercilessly impartial judgment. No, it is not just the "voice of reason," which we so often use to justify every evil in our glib rationalizations. It is not just the "voice of morality," for morality, as we are being constantly told, can be derived from anything: from "class struggle," "interests of the nation," etc. For this is the unique quality of the conscience: its irreducibility to anything else, the fact that it is at the same time something most profound in me—my own self, as it were, in my heart of hearts—and the fact that it is addressed to me as a voice, a call, a command, as if someone else in me were judging, summoning, evaluating, and enlightening me.

One thing is clear: the conscience exists, and it is not an "invention," not a "superstructure" or "a subjective experience." And in the final analysis, consciously or unconsciously, only by the conscience, and by it alone, do we truly evaluate ourselves and others, although we drown it out with all sorts of self-justifications—"To get level with a snake you have to crawl on the ground!"—or with primitive, empty theories; or we flee from it into drunkenness, riotous amusements, and debauchery. This flight is useless, however, for the conscience does exist. And suddenly it heaves this deepest of sighs, striking us like lightning with the awareness of our tremendous guilt, unrighteousness, and inner deformity, but at the same time arousing a passionate desire to be rid of this burden, to be purified, to be reborn. Here repentance begins. It becomes self-evident that the solution to the mystery and essence of evil is revealed not by reason, nor by morality, nor by ideology, but only by the conscience—that mysterious light that burns in the soul, which all the darkness and deformity of fallen life cannot fully extinguish. The conscience is an enigmatic voice: we know not where it comes from and how it becomes audible, but it speaks and we listen, it rebukes us and we accept it. It is a voice that gives us the strength to evaluate ourselves from within and to trust this evaluation.

Thus, it is with the conscience, and therefore with remorse, that we begin our approach to the mystery of evil that we so often discuss.

Victory Over Evil

Christ taught his disciples that it was fitting for him to be betrayed and to suffer and to die—this is the leitmotif of the Gospel.

Christianity has often been defined as the religion of the cross and suffering, and has even been reproached for this. All the indictments against Christianity speak of its "call for passivity," about its "voluntary submission to evil," about its expectation of the triumph of good only in the afterlife. "Christians," the accusers invariably maintain, "have always tolerated evil, injustice, and imperfection, and have always objected to all attempts to improve this world." Is this really so? It is appropriate to ponder this question now, as we are preparing once again to pass through Holy Week, the days of Christ's suffering, as we prepare once again to stand before the cross on which the blood-stained, tortured God-man hangs forever.

Indeed, why is this symbol or, rather, this never-fading memory of the cross and the one crucified on it the very core of the Christian faith? What happened and what was accomplished then that was so unique and inimitable? After all, millions of people have suffered and endured pain and misery throughout the world in every age. The cross certainly did not become our symbol and our faith so that we might tell people: "Brothers, thus it has always been and always will be. Endure it; take an example from Christ, remember that he himself said: *In the world ye shall have tribulation.*" And yet this is the interpretation of the cross of Christ that is often given by Christians themselves. And this interpretation allows the enemies of Christianity to assert that Christianity is a religion of reconciliation with evil, and therefore it is incapable of doing anything to help a person in this world. But why then has the cross always and everywhere been a source of strength and joy, a source of courage for all Christians? Why do they remember not only the initial words of Christ: *In the world ye shall have tribulation,* but also the words that follow: *but be of good cheer; I have overcome the world* (Jn 16.33)? Why, every Saturday evening, on the eve of Sunday, are the same jubilant words heard in all churches: "Behold through the cross joy has come to all the world"? I think that one can understand all this only by pondering more deeply how the cross, the crucifixion, and suffering are connected with evil.

At first glance, the last chapters of the Gospel sound like a tragic validation of the omnipotence of evil. Here the Teacher is betrayed by his closest disciple; whom then can we trust, and on what can we rely? Here thousands of people, whom Christ had done nothing but help and console, showing them all his love—these same people shout: *Crucify him! Crucify him!* (Lk 23.21). And what, then, is man, if not a herd animal, which can be turned into an obedient crowd in the twinkling of an eye, parroting whatever they are told? Pilate says: *I find in him no fault at all* (cf. Jn 18.38), and, having said this, he washes his hands and turns him over to mockery and an agonizing, shameful death. The disciples flee in fear; their Teacher, who is dying in terrible sufferings from thirst, is given vinegar to drink;

educated people mock him as he weakens: *He saved others; himself he cannot save. If he be the King of Israel, let him now come down from the cross, and we will believe him* (Mt 27.42).

And now we remember all this yet again and think: yes, this is the triumph of evil in its purest form. All the illusions about humanity are broken forever, there is nothing left but the terrible plea of a dying man: *My God, my God! Why hast thou forsaken me?* (Mt 27.46). But then, as we ponder this, we suddenly begin to understand another, deeper meaning of this suffering, this cry, this death. For perhaps the chief power of the cross is revealed specifically in this: the fact that it reveals evil in its pure form, showing it specifically to be evil. For evil always hides behind high-sounding and eloquent words. It was hiding even then: Pilate sat importantly upon his seat and thought that he was passing judgment, but we now know for all time that he caved in to fear, and that his judgment was evil. The Roman soldiers who were ordered to crucify Jesus obeyed their authorities, and this obedience is shown to us to be evil. The hours go by, and nothing is left of human excuses and "extenuating circumstances." Everyone obeyed evil, everyone accepted it, but to know evil as evil, to tear off the mask of good that conceals it, to lay it bare in its purest form—this is what it means to fully expose evil. And then we can refer to any traitor as a Judas, and to any unjust judge as a Pilate.

Hour after hour, in silence, bloody torment, and loneliness, it is Christ who triumphs, and not these miserable servants of evil—Judas and the soldiers, Pilate and the crowd of slaves shouting *Crucify him!* He rises above all this. Outwardly they have won, but what kind of victory is this? To persecute and kill, thereby making him whom they persecuted and killed Teacher, Lord, and Leader forever! They condemned him then, but it was they who proved condemned for all eternity; he died then, but this death marked the beginning of a new faith, a new love, a new hope. Thus, the cross is the unmasking of evil, the first and decisive victory over it. Innocent suffering is forever shown to be stronger than all the executioners of the world, silence is forever made louder than all cries, and, most importantly of all—love forever triumphs over hatred. Is this not a victory, is this not a triumph? And look: no sooner had Christ died, no sooner had evil apparently triumphed, than from the very depths of this terrible night comes the Roman centurion—the executioner, the crucifier, the obedient slave of evil—and says: *Truly this was the Son of God* (Mt 27.54). And now he is free. A slow dawning begins, which nothing can stop: "Behold, through the cross, joy has come to all the world."

And here is our answer to the indictment against Christianity. It is not to the toleration of evil, not to reconciliation and compromise with it that the cross calls us. On the contrary, the cross marks the beginning of the denunciation, overcoming, and annihilation of evil, to which the whole Gospel and all of Christianity testifies. This is what must be remembered in these days as we approach the annual remembrance of the Passion of Christ.

Two Self-apparent Proofs

Very often one hears the following question: "How can you believe in God when you see everything that happens in the world? If God existed, would he allow so much suffering, so much injustice? If *God is Love* (1 Jn 4.8, 16), as you claim, how can this constant triumph of evil and mockery of good be explained?"

This question, in essence, is as ancient as the world itself. It has always tormented humanity, and Dostoevsky ingeniously condensed it in *The Brothers Karamazov*. Let us recall Ivan's conversation with Alyosha, when Ivan says that if for the future bliss of paradise one tear of an innocent child is required, then he declines his ticket to heaven. And truly, how are we to answer this question? It is enough to witness even one instance of innocent suffering for all the existing answers, which are numerous, to appear flat and unconvincing. Evil, the triumph of evil, remains for the believer a terrible, inexplicable mystery. And to this mystery faith sees only two answers, or rather not answers, even, but two points of reference, two self-evident proofs. One is the relationship of evil to the mystery of freedom, and the other is the image of the suffering Christ—the experience of the cross, so fundamental to the Christian faith, with the man nailed to it whom we call the God in whom we believe.

Let us briefly discuss each of these proofs and try, as hard as it may seem, to explain them. First, the mystery of freedom. Strangely enough, the same people who deny a God who allows so much evil in the world, condemn religion for allegedly enslaving a person, depriving him of freedom. The revolt against religion, the fight against it is usually conducted in the name of freedom. But what is freedom, if not the freedom of choice, and therefore the freedom to choose between good and evil? If a person cannot choose evil, he is not free. If his freedom is real, and not illusory, he must be able to choose evil. Hence, Christianity has always maintained that God created man absolutely free. And it is this freedom that is the chief source of the evil that so often triumphs in the world. In the biblical account of the creation of man, Adam chooses evil because he is free. But evil breeds evil, itself becoming a source of evil. In other words, if, as is alleged, God permits evil, does not interfere with it, and appears to be powerless before it, it is because by creating a free being—man—he once and for all limited his own omnipotence. If man were not free, he could not freely choose that kindness, that beauty, that perfection to which God freely calls him; he could not be a friend of God. But being free, he can freely choose evil and be entirely responsible for this choice. This is the first proof, the first explanation of the mystery of evil offered by Christianity.

But this explanation would be not only incomplete, but also false, if it were not rooted in the second proof—namely, in the image and experience of the suffering Christ. Why is it the cross, the suffering of Christ, that comprise the heart of the Christian faith? It is naturally because this is the answer of God himself to the triumph of evil, and at the same time the beginning and the source of victory over evil. Simplifying this to the extreme, it can be expressed as follows: if God once and for all limited himself by human freedom and therefore cannot destroy evil from without, for this would mean depriving man of his freedom, then God, who loves man and wishes to save him from evil, has no other option than to take upon himself the sufferings of man, to take upon himself all the evil of the world and destroy it from within by his love. Here is the ultimate mystery of Christianity: *Surely he hath borne our griefs, and carried our sorrows: yet we did esteem him stricken, smitten of God, and afflicted. But he was wounded for our transgressions, he was bruised for our iniquities: the chastisement of our peace was upon him; and with his stripes we are healed* (Is 53.4–5). Being wholly goodness, love, and defenselessness, Christ freely gives himself over to the power of evil, hatred, and anger. On this one Man, of whom Pilate who condemned him says: *I find no fault in this man* (Lk 23.4), all the evil of the world, all its hatred, is concentrated. And that is the whole point of the sufferings of Christ: that not once, not ever, and in no place does he repay evil with evil, violence with violence, hatred with hatred: *Father, forgive them; for they know not what they do* (Lk 23.34).

And here, in this world full of suffering, anger, and hatred, the image of the crucified one lives on indestructibly, and our faith knows that he participates in all suffering, co-suffers with all who suffer, and stands present at every torture. Evil appears to triumph. But to those who ask me: "How can your God stand by silently and allow all this?" I can point to the cross, to the Crucified God, and to the words of the Gospel—how the night before his death Christ *began to be sorrowful and very heavy* (Mt 26.37). No, God did not remain indifferent to our suffering, but entered into and accepted it. And this is why so often it is those who suffer who find God, encounter Christ, and believe in him. And when they find him, they do not ask where God is, for they know: God is near me and in me, giving me the power to bear my cross, and hence the ability to turn suffering itself and even evil into a victory for good. Strange, isn't it? Those who are entirely prosperous, who possess so much, all too often do not perceive God. But the moment a man experiences suffering, and is freed from illusory earthly happiness, his encounter with God begins. For Christ, having taken upon himself all human suffering, has turned it into a path to God, into a total victory over evil.

St Vladimir's
Seminary Press

S t Vladimir's is the largest publisher of Orthodox Christian books in the English language—with a catalogue including over 500 titles.

Our mission is to partner with reputable authors and translators worldwide in order to produce and distribute rich theological texts that preserve the Orthodox faith, tradition, and history, while also fostering a platform for new theological and academic works of excellence.

Our team is committed to building and maintaining a catalog of work covering a variety of topics, not limited to the following: theology, history, ecclesiology, ecumenism, hagiography, iconography, spirituality, scriptural studies, music, pastoral theology, Christian education, philosophy, biographies, and patristics.

SVS Press is one of few seminary presses that makes a profit. 100% of our book sales supports St Vladimir's Orthodox Theological Seminary and its mission to train Orthodox priests and future church leaders.